P R E N T I C E   H A L L

BRIEF REVIEW FOR NEW YORK

The Living Environment

2004 Edition

John Bartsch, Retired
Amsterdam High School
Amsterdam, New York

Mary P. Colvard
Cobleskill–Richmondville High School
Cobleskill, New York

ORDER INFORMATION

Send orders to:
PRENTICE HALL
CUSTOMER SERVICE CENTER
4350 Equity Dr.
P.O. Box 2649
Columbus, OH 43216

or
CALL TOLL-FREE: 1-800-848-9500
(8:00 A.M.–4:30 P.M.)

•Orders processed with your call.
•Your price includes all shipping and handling.

PEARSON
Prentice
Hall

Needham, Massachusetts
Upper Saddle River, New Jersey

Teacher Reviewers

Anthony (Bud) Bertino
Canandaigua Academy
Canandaigua, New York

Patricia L. Nolan
Scotia-Glenville High School
Scotia, New York

Elise Russo, Ed.D.
Administrator for Secondary Curriculum
Amityville Union Free School District
Amityville, New York

Content Reviewer
Jerry Sanders

STAFF CREDITS

The people who made up The Living Environment team—
representing design services, editorial, editorial services, and production
services—are listed below.

Lisa J. Clark, Patricia Cully, Kathleen J. Dempsey, Terence Hegarty,
Kim Schmidt, Jerry Thorne

ISBN 0-13-125577-0
1 2 3 4 5 6 7 8 9 10   08 07 06 05 04

Brief Review in

The Living Environment

About This Book

This book was designed for students who plan to take The Living Environment Regents Examination. Most students using this book will have taken a course that covered basic concepts of biology, scientific inquiry, and laboratory skills. It is important for you to review for this end-of-year Regents Examination, because for nearly all students, passing this test will be a requirement for graduation from high school.

The Regents Examination will be based entirely on the content and understandings specifically addressed by The Living Environment core curriculum. This book is organized to enhance your review of the concepts, skills, and applications that appear in the core curriculum and will be tested on The Living Environment Regents Examination.

- *Review of Content:* The review focuses on the basic content that will be tested on the Regents Examination. For the most part, any material that is NOT addressed in the core curriculum has been eliminated. The book is organized into nine topics, each covering a major area of The Living Environment curriculum. To reinforce the content understandings, many real-world examples are included. You can use these examples—or other examples you choose—to answer questions on the exam. The examples you choose will demonstrate your understanding of the content as well as your ability to apply these understandings to the real world.

- *Review Questions:* Questions appear frequently throughout each topic to help you clarify and reinforce your understanding of the content. The questions are similar to the types of questions that may appear on The Living Environment Regents Examination.

- *Questions for Regents Practice:* At the end of each topic, you will find a variety of questions that are written and organized in the format that is commonly used for actual Regents questions. These practice tests are divided into Part A, Part B, and Part C questions.

- Part A questions are entirely multiple-choice and test your knowledge of The Living Environment core curriculum.

- Part B questions test skills and understandings from the core material and include both multiple-choice and simple constructed-response questions.

- Part C questions require extended constructed responses. For these questions, you will need to provide a more detailed answer, supported with applications or examples, and written in complete sentences. At the end of each Part C question, you will notice a number in brackets. The number indicates how many points this question would typically be "worth" on a Regents Examination. The number of points can give you a clue to the amount of information or number of parts a full-credit answer should have.

- *Required Vocabulary:* The words listed at the beginning of each topic are required vocabulary. You should know the precise meaning of these vocabulary words because they are likely to appear on your Regents Examination. Throughout the text, required vocabulary words are shown in bold type. Each bold word is accompanied by a simple definition in the text. Each is also defined in the glossary at the back of the book.

- *Other Vocabulary:* Words that are underlined in the text will probably not be tested. However, you should be familiar with them. In some instances, these words will help you to understand basic biological concepts; in other cases, they are commonly used in discussions of science concepts. Although you should NOT be tested on the specific definitions of underlined words, they may be used in a Regents question, so you should know what they mean. Underlined words are also defined in the glossary.

- *Memory Jogger* and *Digging Deeper:* These features provide additional content that you do NOT need to memorize. The Memory Jogger is intended to remind you of information that you probably encountered in an earlier topic or in your earlier science education. The Digging Deeper goes beyond what you need to know but is included to help you to better understand the required material.

- *Appendix A:* This appendix at the back of the book provides strategies for answering the various types of questions that will appear on the Living Environment Regents Examination.

- *Appendix B:* Refer to this appendix for more information regarding the skills, content, and types of questions you can expect to find on Part D of the Living Environment Regents Examination.

Similarities and Differences Among Living Organisms

VOCABULARY

active transport	excretion	organic
amino acids	homeostasis	receptor molecule
cell	hormone	respiration
cell membrane	immunity	reproduction
cell respiration	inorganic	ribosome
chloroplast	metabolism	simple sugars
circulation	mitochondria	synthesis
cytoplasm	nucleus	tissue
digestion	organ	vacuole
diffusion	organ system	
enzymes	organelle	

Earth's living environment is made up of millions and millions of diverse organisms, from towering redwood trees, sleek antelope, and mushrooms that grow in huge circles, to microscopic bacteria, microscopic organisms that turn the tides red, and the students in your class. These living organisms are both similar to and different from each other. They also differ from the nonliving parts of the environment. Although that difference may seem obvious, scientists have not been able to agree upon a simple definition of life.

The Characteristics of Life

Although there is no simple definition of life, most scientists agree that living things share certain characteristics that distinguish them from nonliving things.

- Living things are organized structures. All are made of one or more **cells,** which are the basic units of structure and function. They maintain their cellular organization throughout life.

- Living things use energy to maintain life and to grow and develop. These activities require that the cells carry out various chemical reactions. The combination of all the chemical reactions that occur in an organism is called **metabolism**.

- Living things maintain a fairly stable internal environment even when their external environment changes dramatically. The maintenance of this internal stability is known as **homeostasis**. To maintain homeostasis, organisms must respond and adapt to both their internal and external environments.

- Living things pass hereditary information to new organisms of the same type in the process of **reproduction**.

Only living things share the characteristics of life. Nonliving things have no functioning cells and no metabolic activity; they do not maintain homeostasis, nor do they reproduce.

Diversity Among Living Things

Although living things share the characteristics of life, there are differences among the many kinds of organisms. Throughout history, people have tried to bring order to all the varieties of life on Earth by grouping, or <u>classifying</u>, them. Several classification systems have been popular at different times. As we learn more about the similarities among organisms and how they carry out their life processes, classification systems change. Currently, biologists classify organisms into kingdoms, which are large groups of related organisms.

Similarities Among Living Things

Although living things have many differences, they are also alike in important ways. The first similarity is that they share the characteristics of life. They are made of cells, reproduce, maintain homeostasis, and carry out metabolic activities. They also share similar life processes, chemical composition, and organization.

LIFE PROCESSES Living things are similar in that they rely on a variety of specific processes to maintain life. (Organisms differ in the way they carry out these processes, however.) Some of these life processes include

- obtaining <u>nutrients</u> from the environment and breaking them down for transport
- transporting materials throughout the organism
- breaking nutrients into smaller units to release the chemical energy stored in them through the process known as **cell respiration**
- combining simple substances into complex substances during the process known as **synthesis**
- increasing the size or number of cells through the process of <u>growth</u>
- removing waste products from the organism through the process known as excretion
- responding to internal and external stimuli
- reproducing more of their own species

CHEMICAL COMPOSITION All living things are made of four main elements—carbon, hydrogen, oxygen, and nitrogen—as well as many other elements in smaller amounts. The elements combine to form molecules. Organic molecules contain BOTH carbon and hydrogen. Organic molecules include all of the major molecules of life: structural molecules, such as those in cell walls and membranes, as well as biologically active molecules, such as the enzymes that help carry out the chemical reactions of life. DNA, protein, fats, and carbohydrates—such as <u>glucose</u> ($C_6H_{12}O_6$) and starch—are **organic** molecules. **Inorganic** molecules do NOT contain BOTH carbon and hydrogen, but can contain any other combination of elements. Inorganic molecules include salts and minerals, most acids and bases, oxygen (O_2), carbon dioxide (CO_2), and water (H_2O), the most abundant substance in any organism.

ORGANIZATION The shared organization of specialized structures that work together to accomplish a specific task is another similarity of living things. In other words, organisms share a similar "building plan." The basic structural and functional unit of living things is the cell. Simple organisms may consist of just one cell; complex organisms may consist of billions of cells. Most cells contain specialized structures called **organelles,** which have specific life maintenance functions.

This organization of cells into increasingly specialized structures is the basis for much of the complex life on Earth. Complex organisms have several advantages over simpler organisms. For example, many complex organisms can explore their environment or gain energy in ways that simpler organisms cannot. In Figure 1-1, notice that the organizational structure of organisms resembles a pyramid with a base of cells.

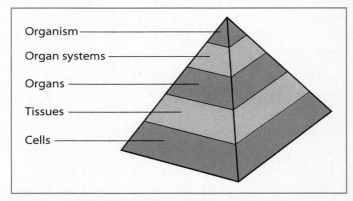

Figure 1-1. The structural organization of organisms

In multicellular organisms, groups of specialized cells may be grouped into **tissues** to expand how they function. For example, a single muscle cell would not be strong enough to move any organism—not even one as light as a hummingbird. Grouped with other muscle cells, however, muscle tissue can move an elephant.

Different kinds of tissues may be combined to form an **organ** that performs one of the life processes; several organs may work together as an **organ system** that also performs one of the life processes. For example, the heart is an organ with the function of pumping blood. The organ may be a simple "arch" like the heart of the earthworm, or it may be a complex four-chambered structure like the heart of a monkey. In either case, the organ's function is to pump blood. Each heart is part of an organ system that transports materials throughout the body.

 Review Questions

1. State two ways in which a single-celled organism, such as an amoeba, and a human body cell are alike.

2. One characteristic of all living organisms is that they (1) make food (2) live on land (3) maintain homeostasis (4) move from place to place

3. A biologist would most likely study all of the chemical activities of an organism to obtain information about the organism's (1) number of mutations (2) reproductive cycle (3) development (4) metabolism

4. Suppose someone brings you a specimen that they claim is a living organism. Explain how you could use a microscope to help determine whether the specimen is a living or nonliving thing.

5. Which of the following statements about cells is NOT true? (1) One or more cells make up all living organisms. (2) Cells carry on the basic life functions of living organisms. (3) Cells contain structures that carry on life functions. (4) Most cells cannot reproduce.

6. Cells are to tissues as organs are to (1) organ systems (2) cells (3) genes (4) organelles

7. The ability of an organism to maintain internal stability is known as (1) metabolism (2) homeostasis (3) circulation (4) excretion

8. Which sequence is listed in order from simplest to most complex?
(1) tissue → cell → organ system → organ
(2) cell → tissue → organ → organ system
(3) cell → tissue → organism → organ
(4) organism → tissue → organ → organ system

9. Living things are made mostly of these four main elements: (1) hydrogen, oxygen, nitrogen, and protein (2) water, protein, carbohydrate, and fat (3) carbon, hydrogen, oxygen, and nitrogen (4) glucose, salt, mineral, and base

10. State two ways living and nonliving things differ.

Cells: The Basic Structure of Life

Many of the world's organisms are made of only one cell, but all organisms—no matter how simple or complex—are made of cells. Each cell contains a jellylike substance surrounded by a thin membrane. Most cells also contain organelles that perform specific tasks for the cell. Despite their seemingly "simple" structure, cells carry out the processes of life and function together in a coordinated manner.

Inside the Cell

The jellylike substance inside the cell is known as the **cytoplasm**. The cytoplasm contains specialized structures, transports materials through the cell, and is the site of many chemical reactions associated with the cell's metabolism.

ORGANELLES Organelles are formed of many different molecules and vary enormously in size, shape, and function. They interact to transport materials, extract energy from nutrients, build proteins, dispose of waste, and store information. Figure 1.2 on the next page shows several vital organelles.

Nucleus The **nucleus** is a large structure that controls the cell's metabolism and stores genetic information (DNA in chromosomes). Many people think of the nucleus as the cell's "control center" because it directs the cell's activities.

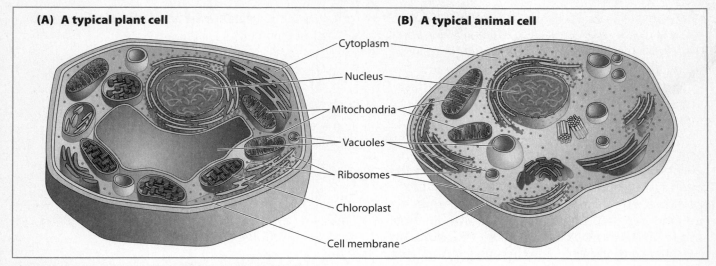

(A) A typical plant cell

(B) A typical animal cell

Cytoplasm

Nucleus

Mitochondria

Vacuoles

Ribosomes

Chloroplast

Cell membrane

Figure 1-2. Some organelles of plant and animal cells

Vacuoles The storage sacs within the cytoplasm are **vacuoles**. They may contain either wastes or useful materials such as water or food. Some vacuoles are specialized to digest food; others pump excess water out of the cell.

Vacuoles in plant cells are usually a lot larger than the vacuoles in animal cells, as shown in Figure 1-2.

Ribosomes The cell contains many tiny structures, called **ribosomes,** that are important to the process of making protein. Some ribosomes are attached to membranes in the cell. Others float in the cytoplasm.

Mitochondria **Mitochondria** are pod-shaped structures that contain special proteins, known as **enzymes**, used to extract energy from nutrients. Mitochondria are sometimes called the cell's powerhouses because they release most of the cell's energy.

Chloroplasts The green structures found in plants and some one-celled organisms are **chloroplasts**. They contain the green pigment chlorophyll and capture light energy, which is then used to produce food for the plant. Animal cells do not contain chloroplasts.

Review Questions

11. Which structure is the boundary between a living cell and its environment? (1) cell membrane (2) cytoplasm (3) vacuole (4) ribosome

12. The structures labeled A, B, C, and D in the following diagram represent (1) organelles (2) organs (3) nuclei (4) mitochondria

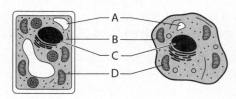

A
B
C
D

13. The cell nucleus functions (1) in obtaining energy for the cell (2) in the storage of digestive enzymes (3) as the center of control for cell metabolism and reproduction (4) in the transport of materials throughout the cell

14. The genetic material of an animal cell is found in the (1) nucleus (2) cytoplasm (3) ribosomes (4) vacuole

15. Structure A is most probably a (1) mitochondrion (2) ribosome (3) vacuole (4) nucleus

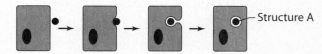

Structure A

16. Current evidence indicates that ribosomes are most closely associated with (1) contraction of the cytoplasm (2) production of DNA (3) synthesis of protein (4) regulation of mitosis

17. Mitochondria are organelles in which (1) digestive enzymes are stored (2) secretory products are packaged and stored (3) the energy needed by the cell is released from nutrients (4) protein manufacture occurs

18. Which cell organelles are most closely associated with energy changes in a plant? (1) mitochondria and chromosomes (2) chloroplasts and mitochondria (3) chromosomes and nucleus (4) chloroplasts and nucleus

19. Which is the most accurate statement concerning protein synthesis in cells? (1) Proteins are synthesized at the mitochondria in all living cells. (2) Proteins are synthesized at the ribosomes in all living cells. (3) Proteins are synthesized at the ribosomes in plant cells only. (4) Proteins are synthesized by nuclei in animal cells only.

The Cell Membrane

The **cell membrane** is a thin structure that surrounds the cell. It is made mainly of fats (lipids), with some proteins embedded throughout. Some of the functions of the cell membrane include

- separating the contents of the cell from the outside environment
- controlling the transport of materials—including waste products—into and out of the cell
- recognizing and responding to chemical signals

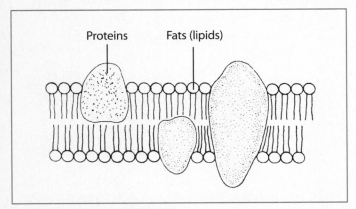

Figure 1-3. The cell membrane

MEMORY JOGGER

Unlike animals, plants and most bacteria and fungi have a cell wall outside the cell membrane. This wall of plant cells is made of nonliving material (a carbohydrate called cellulose) that surrounds the cell and gives it strength and rigidity. If the plant gains too much water, its membranes could burst. The cell wall helps prevent this.

MAINTAINING SEPARATION Cells are organized internally. Without the cell membrane, this organization would be lost.

CONTROLLING TRANSPORT IN AND OUT OF THE CELL If the cell is to survive, the membrane cannot totally separate the cell from its environment. Some materials, such as water, oxygen, and nutrients, must pass through the membrane and into the cell. Other materials, such as waste products, must pass out of the cell. Molecules can enter or leave a cell through either diffusion or active transport.

Diffusion Molecules are constantly in motion. As they jiggle, they bump into one another, then bounce away like bumper cars at an amusement park. In time, the molecules will have bumped and bounced until they are evenly distributed. The result is that the concentration of molecules in any container remains approximately the same everywhere in the container.

However, when the concentration of molecules is greater in one part of a substance, molecules will spread into areas where their concentration is lower. This movement of molecules from areas of high concentration to areas of low concentration is called **diffusion**. Because diffusion results from the normal jiggling of molecules, it requires no outside energy. It is like sledding downhill.

Many molecules diffuse into and out of cells. One of the most important molecules to diffuse into and out of cells is water. The diffusion of water into and out of cells is important to the maintenance of homeostasis. For example, plant cells maintain a stable balance of water and dissolved minerals. This is typically about 98% water and 2% dissolved materials. When salt is spread on roads and walkways, that balance changes. The runoff water from these salted roads may reach concentrations of 5% salt (which means only 95% water). Damage can occur when water in the plant cells diffuses from the higher (98%) concentration to the lower (95%) concentration. Under these conditions, the loss of water places serious stress on the plant. In some cases the plant may die.

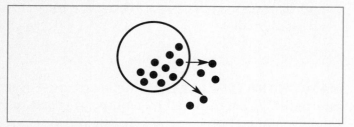

Figure 1-4. **Diffusion:** These molecules are moving from an area of high concentration to an area of low concentration.

Active Transport Moving a molecule from an area of low concentration to an area of high concentration is like pulling a sled uphill. It requires energy. Cells must use energy from ATP to transport molecules from areas of low concentration through the cell membrane to areas of high concentration. The process is called **active transport**. Many desert plants use active transport to bring water (which is at low concentrations in the soil) into root cells where the water concentration is higher. Some pond organisms use active transport to "collect" calcium or other minerals that are in very low concentrations in the pond water.

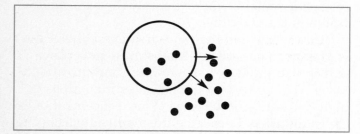

Figure 1-5. **Active transport:** These molecules are moving from an area of low concentration to an area of high concentration.

Molecules in Cells Both organic and inorganic substances are dissolved in cells and are involved in the chemical reactions that maintain life. Some organic molecules, such as proteins and starches, are too large and complex to enter the cell. Large molecules must first be broken down into simpler molecules in the process known as **digestion**. The digestion of proteins results in smaller molecules

of **amino acids;** the digestion of starches results in **simple sugars**. Digestion is vital because only small molecules, such as amino acids and simple sugars, can enter blood vessels or cells.

When some nutrients from our food enter a cell, they become the building blocks of compounds necessary for life. This process, called cell synthesis, is like manufacturing. Simple molecules (such as amino acids and sugars) are assembled or reassembled into more complex molecules of proteins, starches, DNA, or other substances necessary for life.

Not all nutrients are used as building blocks. Some nutrients that enter a cell are broken down even more to release the energy stored in their chemical bonds. This is the process of cell respiration. All of these processes will be reviewed in detail in later topics.

RECOGNIZING SIGNALS Scientists have learned that certain protein molecules in the cell membrane can receive chemical messages from other cells. These molecules are called **receptor molecules**.

When cells are part of a larger organism, receptor molecules play an important role in the interactions between cells. As shown in Figures 1–6 and 1–7, chemicals produced in the endocrine glands—**hormones**—and chemicals produced by nerve cells are primarily responsible for communication between cells. If nerve or hormone signals are blocked, cellular communication is interrupted, and the organism's homeostasis may be affected.

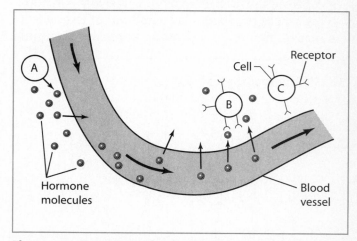

Figure 1-6. **Receptor molecules:** Specific receptor molecules on the membranes of some cells detect hormones that stimulate the cell to respond. In this case, only B (not C) will respond to the hormone from A.

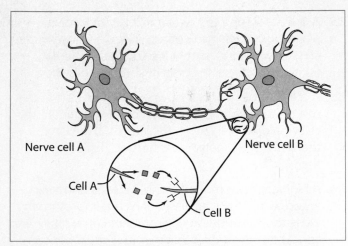

Figure 1-7. **Receptor molecules:** Nerve cells secrete chemicals that signal adjacent nerve, muscle, or gland cells. These secretions are detected by specific receptor molecules on the cell membranes.

 Review Questions

20. Which of the following would be LEAST affected by defective receptor proteins on a cell membrane? (1) homeostasis (2) muscle activity (3) nerve signals (4) diffusion

21. In the following diagram, nerve cell A is communicating with nerve cell B. Write the name of the structures present on the membranes of nerve cell B that enable it to detect a message from nerve cell A.

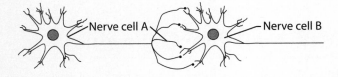

22. Which process accomplishes the movement of gases illustrated by the arrows in the diagram? (1) excretion (2) diffusion (3) active transport (4) chemical digestion

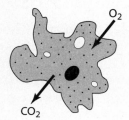

23. In both plant and animal cells, the cell membrane (1) produces enzymes (2) controls reproduction (3) is composed of sugars (4) regulates diffusion

24. Since the relative concentration of water in the pond in which a paramecium (a single-celled organism) lives is greater than the concentration of water in its cytoplasm, water molecules constantly move from the pond into the paramecium. The best long-term solution to the problem of maintaining a stable internal environment is for the paramecium to (1) change the water into carbon dioxide and excrete it (2) store water molecules (3) incorporate water molecules into its structure (4) actively transport water molecules out of its cell

25. A biologist diluted a blood sample with distilled water. While observing the sample with a microscope, she noted that the red blood cells had burst. This bursting is most likely the result of which process? (1) staining (2) diffusion (3) digestion (4) active transport

26. A student using a compound light microscope to study plant cells observed that most of the cells resembled the one shown in the following diagram.

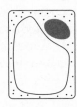

Which diagram best illustrates how the plant cell will appear after being placed in a solution that has a lower water concentration than the cell?

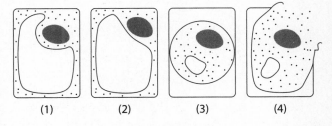

27. Amino acids tend to diffuse from a blood capillary to the adjacent cell because (1) this is the only direction they can move (2) the brain directs the movement into cells (3) the cell needs the amino acids to make protein (4) the concentration of amino acids is lower in the cell

28. In the following diagram of a plant cell, the small circles represent water molecules.

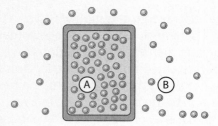

Which statement BEST describes the behavior of most of these water molecules? (1) They move from region A to region B. (2) They move from region B to region A. (3) They do not move in either direction. (4) Their overall movement is equal in both directions.

29. Nutrients that are not used as building blocks for the cell may be broken down to release the energy stored in their chemical bonds. This process, which provides cells with energy, is called (1) chemical synthesis (2) cell respiration (3) digestion (4) homeostasis

30. Cytoplasm in a plant cell will shrink if the cell is (1) placed in a concentrated salt solution (2) kept warm and moist and in medium light (3) placed in distilled water (4) exposed to a different concentration of nitrogen gas

31. The following diagram represents a cell in water. Formulas of molecules that can move freely across the membrane are shown. Some molecules are located inside the cell and others are in the water outside the cell.

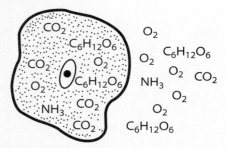

Based on the distribution of molecules, what would most likely happen to these molecules after a few hours? (1) The concentration of $C_6H_{12}O_6$ will increase inside the cell. (2) The concentration of CO_2 will increase outside the cell. (3) The concentration of NH_3 will increase inside the cell. (4) The concentration of O_2 will increase outside the cell.

32. A cell containing 98% water in its cytoplasm is placed in a 2% salt solution. It should (1) lose water (2) gain water (3) neither lose nor gain water (4) gain salt because of the high rate of diffusion

33. A cell is placed in distilled water and then transferred to a 5% salt solution. As a result of this procedure, the cell would be likely to (1) get larger (2) get larger, then smaller (3) get smaller (4) get smaller, then larger

34. A high concentration of calcium salts is normally found within the cytoplasm of a certain protozoan, while the surrounding environment contains a lower concentration of the calcium salts. The higher concentration in the protozoan is most probably the result of (1) diffusion (2) excretion (3) active transport (4) cellular dehydration

35. A student prepared a normal wet mount slide of an *Elodea* leaf and observed it with the compound microscope. He then made drawing A from his observations. His second drawing, B, shows his observations of the same cell after it was mounted in a 5% salt solution. The results are most fully explained by (1) loss of water from the cell (2) entrance of water into the cell (3) shrinkage of the cell wall (4) entrance of salt into the cell

Multicellular Organisms

Multicellular organisms can be highly complex. They require multiple organs and systems to complete their life processes. These systems must interact to maintain the life of the organism.

Human Body Systems

Humans are complex organisms. Their specialized cells must interact to maintain life, and humans require a variety of organs and organ systems to complete the life processes of digestion, respiration, circulation, excretion, movement, coordination, immunity, and reproduction.

DIGESTION The human digestive system, shown in Figure 1-8, is a one-way passage through the body. This passageway includes the mouth, stomach, and intestines as well as other organs.

Food enters the body through the mouth and is moved slowly through the system by muscular contractions. The food never actually enters the body tissue. Instead, it is broken down both mechanically (by chewing) and chemically. This produces molecules that are small enough to pass through cell membranes and that can be transported to wherever nutrients can be used by the body. Undigested food is eliminated from the body as solid waste.

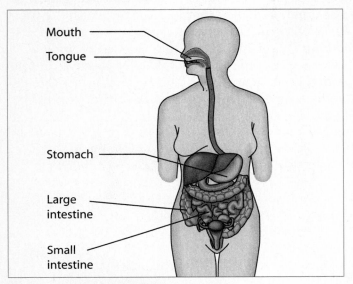

Figure 1-8. **The human digestive system**

RESPIRATION The process of **respiration** uses oxygen to break down food molecules to release energy. The function of the respiratory system is the exchange of gases between the blood of the circulatory system and the environment. The system takes in oxygen for cell respiration and transfers it to the blood. It also removes carbon dioxide—a waste of cell respiration—from the bloodstream and releases it from the body. As shown in Figure 1-9, the lungs and nose are parts of the respiratory system.

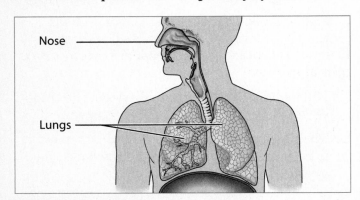

Figure 1-9. **The human respiratory system**

CIRCULATION **Circulation** involves the movement of materials inside the cell as well as the movement between parts of a multicellular organism. The function of the human circulatory system, shown in Figure 1-10, is to transport materials throughout the body. The system carries digested food and oxygen to cells. It also carries wastes from the cells to the lungs, kidneys, and the skin for excretion. The blood vessels of the system also carry chemical messengers (hormones) and the proteins that attack foreign substances to give the body immunity (antibodies). The human circulatory system includes the heart, blood vessels, and blood.

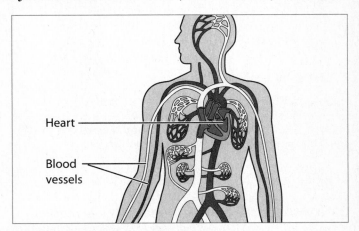

Figure 1-10. **The human circulatory system**

EXCRETION Many people confuse the process of excretion with the removal of the waste products of digestion. **Excretion,** however, is actually the removal of all the waste produced by the cells of the body. The human excretory system includes the lungs and kidneys as well as the sweat glands in the skin.

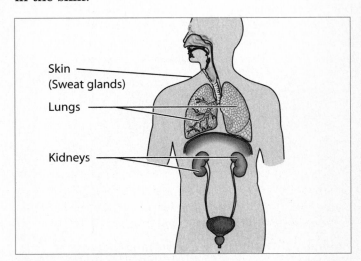

Figure 1-11. **The human excretory system**

MOVEMENT Movement of the body involves the interaction of muscles and bones. The <u>muscular</u> and <u>skeletal</u> systems, shown in Figure 1-12, work together to provide movement and support for the body. These body systems make it possible for the organism to avoid danger and to find food, mates, and shelter.

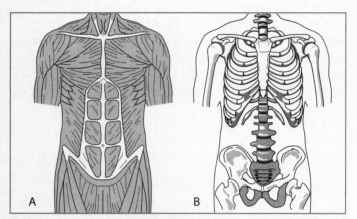

Figure 1-12. The human muscular (A) and skeletal systems (B): The bones provide support; the muscles allow movement.

COORDINATION The nervous system and endocrine system, shown in Figure 1-13, control the coordination of many of the body's activities. Together these systems respond to and send messages to cells throughout the body. The nervous system sends signals along nerves, and the glands of the endocrine system produce chemical messengers (hormones) that travel in the bloodstream. The brain and nerves are part of the nervous system, while the endocrine system includes several glands—such as the pancreas and ovaries or testes.

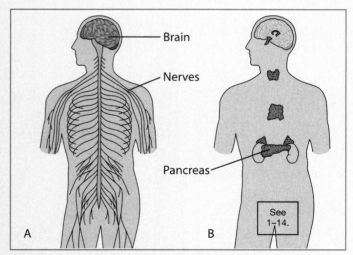

Brain

Nerves

Pancreas

See 1–14.

A   B

Figure 1-13. The human nervous (A) and endocrine (B) systems

IMMUNITY The immune system increases the body's **immunity**—its ability to resist disease. Some white blood cells of the immune system engulf and destroy invading bacteria and viruses by digesting them. Others protect the body against specific foreign invaders.

REPRODUCTION The process by which organisms produce new organisms of the same kind is called **reproduction.** The reproductive system releases sex cells and hormones that are critical to the creation of offspring and the regulation of their development. The human reproductive system allows for sexual rather than asexual reproduction. Sexual reproduction makes it possible for two individuals to produce offspring that are of the same species but not exactly like either parent.

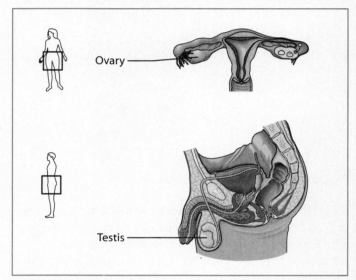

Ovary

Testis

Figure 1-14. The reproductive systems of the human male and female

Interactions for Life Processes and Regulation

Like all organisms, the human body's systems continually interact to perform life processes. Examples of these interactions may involve several systems.

- Nutrients from the digestive system are transported to cells by the circulatory system.

- The functioning of the reproductive system is regulated by hormones from the endocrine system.

- Body systems also continuously interact to maintain a balanced internal environment (homeostasis). To successfully accomplish this, humans and other complex organisms have a variety of control mechanisms that constantly monitor and correct deviations that could throw the body's internal environment off balance. Examples of these control systems include the regulation of body temperature and blood sugar level.

  - When body temperature drops, nerve impulses from the brain signal the muscles to shiver, which generates heat and warms the body.

  - Blood sugar level is constantly monitored, and hormones are released as needed to keep it at acceptable levels.

If any organ or organ system does not function properly, the entire organism may fail to maintain homeostasis. The result may be disease or even death. For example, if the heart fails to beat regularly, the circulation of blood will be affected. This may result in a failure of certain materials (oxygen, for example) to flow throughout the body. Without oxygen, cells may stop functioning and death may result.

Comparing Single-celled and Multicellular Organisms

The organelles of single-celled organisms are far less complex than organ systems of multicellular organisms. However, organelles and organ systems are equally capable of completing metabolic activities. For example, the paramecium in Figure 1-15 has a specialized organelle—the food vacuole—that digests food. The human digestive system is more complex, but it also digests food. The organelle and organ system accomplish the same function: breaking down nutrients so that they can be used by the organism.

Table 1-1 shows examples of life functions that are handled by organelles in single cells and by organ systems in multicellular organisms.

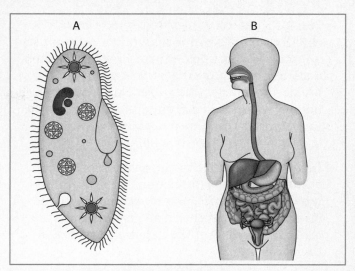

Figure 1-15. Single-celled and multicellular function: The organelles in a one-celled organism (A) are much simpler than the human digestive system (B), but they still digest the organism's food.

Table 1-1. The Function of Organelles in Single Cells and Organ Systems in Multicellular Organisms

Function	Single Cell	Multicellular Organism
Gas exchange	Cell membrane	Respiratory system
Transport of substances	Cytoplasm	Circulatory system
Nutrition	Specialized vacuoles	Digestive system
Excretion	Cell membrane	Excretory system

Comparing Humans and Other Organisms

In most biological respects, humans are like other organisms.

- Humans have much the same chemical composition as other organisms. All organisms—from bacteria to tulips to humans—are made of mainly carbon, hydrogen, oxygen, and nitrogen. These elements combine in different ways and amounts to form carbohydrates, proteins, and other essential organic molecules.

- Humans are made up of different kinds of cells that are similar to those found in other animals. For example, human muscle, nerve, and blood cells are similar in structure and function to the muscles, nerves, and blood cells of other complex animals—from geese to gorillas.

- Humans have organ systems and physical characteristics similar to many other complex animals. For example, worms, frogs, grasshoppers, and pigs have digestive systems that break down large food molecules. They also have systems that circulate blood. Pig hearts, in fact, are so similar to human hearts that they can be used for transplants.

- Humans reproduce in the same way as many other organisms. For example, fish, amphibians, reptiles, birds, and mammals reproduce sexually; the sperm and egg cell combine, each contributing half of the genetic information to the offspring.

- Humans use the same kind of genetic information as other organisms. Like nearly every living organism—from *E. coli* bacteria and fruit flies to roses and dogs—humans use DNA as their genetic material.

 Review Questions

36. Organisms remove metabolic cellular wastes by the process of (1) excretion (2) absorption (3) coordination (4) digestion

37. Finding shelter, avoiding predators, and obtaining food are most closely related to the ability of an animal to (1) use structures adapted for movement (2) increase the rate of mitosis (3) transport carbon dioxide to cells (4) excrete waste products of metabolism

38. Which letter in the following diagram indicates an organelle that functions primarily in the synthesis of protein? (1) A (2) B (3) C (4) D

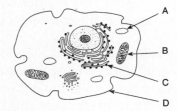

39. A similarity between the nervous system and the hormone-secreting system in humans is that they both (1) are composed of the same type of cells (2) are composed of many glands (3) help to maintain homeostasis (4) secrete chemicals directly into the blood

40. The following diagram shows an air sac surrounded by the thin-walled blood vessels of a human lung.

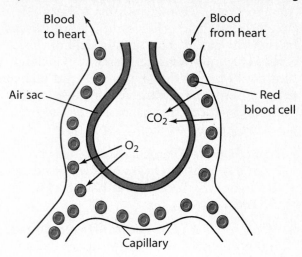

Which two body systems are interacting in the diagram? (1) respiratory and coordination (2) respiratory and circulatory (3) digestive and circulatory (4) reproductive and coordination

41. Inhaling carbon monoxide reduces the ability of red blood cells to carry oxygen. This can lead to brain damage. Which three systems of the body interact in this situation? (1) digestive, respiratory, and circulatory (2) immune, circulatory, and digestive (3) respiratory, circulatory, and nervous (4) excretory, nervous, and respiratory

42. The activity of all human body systems is coordinated by (1) the secretion of hormones and the nervous system (2) the interaction of nerve impulses with the excretory system (3) the movement of digested food by the circulatory system (4) the secretion of hormones and the circulatory system

43. Before it can be used by individual cells, food must be broken down and distributed throughout the human body. Name the two systems that must interact to accomplish this.

44. Your finger brushes against a hot stove and you quickly pull away. Identify which two human body systems work together to respond to this painful stimulus and explain the specific interaction between them.

45. Describe how the chemical composition and genetic information of humans resembles the chemical composition and genetic information of other organisms.

Questions for Regents Practice

Part A

1. A few bacteria are placed in a nutrient solution. After several hours, thousands of bacteria are present. Which life activities are primarily responsible for this?
   (1) digestion and movement
   (2) digestion and reproduction
   (3) circulation and respiration
   (4) excretion and coordination

2. Mitochondria are organelles that
   (1) are necessary for the process of diffusion to take place
   (2) are found in the nucleus of some cells
   (3) initiate cell division in living cells
   (4) contain respiratory enzymes

3. Most of the enzymes found in the mitochondria are involved in the reactions associated with
   (1) extracting energy from nutrients
   (2) storing energy in nutrients
   (3) DNA production
   (4) protein synthesis

4. Which statement best describes a cell membrane?
   (1) It is found only in animal cells.
   (2) It is a nonliving structure.
   (3) It controls reproduction in a cell.
   (4) It controls the passage of materials into the cell.

5. The transfer of specific molecules through cell membranes is an important factor in the process of
   (1) cytoplasmic flow
   (2) mitotic division
   (3) homeostasis
   (4) nuclear transfer

6. After a cookie has been eaten, sugar molecules enter the bloodstream by the process of
   (1) active transport
   (2) diffusion
   (3) excretion
   (4) cellular respiration

7. In the diagram of root cells, in which direction would the net flow of water be the greatest as a result of diffusion?
   (1) A to C
   (2) A to B
   (3) B to C
   (4) C to B

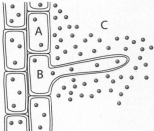

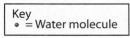

Key
• = Water molecule

8. Diagrams A and B represent two slide preparations of *Elodea* leaves (an aquatic plant).

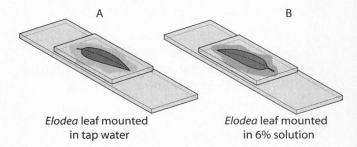

Elodea leaf mounted in tap water

Elodea leaf mounted in 6% solution

The tap water used contained 1 percent salt and 99 percent water, while the salt solution contained 6 percent salt and 94 percent water. *Elodea* cells normally contain 1 percent salt. Ten minutes after the slides were prepared, a microscopic examination of cells in leaves A and B would most likely show evidence that
   (1) water had moved out of the cells of leaf B
   (2) salt had moved out of the cells of leaf B
   (3) water had moved into the cells of leaf A
   (4) salt had moved into the cells of leaf A

9. One reason a fish that lives in the ocean may have trouble living in a freshwater lake is that
   (1) there are more carnivores in freshwater habitats
   (2) salt water holds more dissolved nitrogen than freshwater
   (3) more photosynthesis occurs in fresh water than in salt water
   (4) water concentration in the fish is affected by salt levels in its environment

10. Refer to the following diagram of a beaker with a membrane dividing it into two halves containing two kinds of molecules.

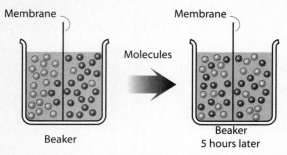

Membrane   Membrane

Molecules

Beaker   Beaker
5 hours later

Which process explains the change in the positions of molecules after five hours?

(1) respiration

(2) photosynthesis

(3) diffusion

(4) excretion

11. The concentration of nitrates is often higher in plant roots than it is in the soil around them. Plants maintain this difference in concentration through

(1) active transport

(2) diffusion

(3) excretion

(4) coordination

12. Most of the reactions by which energy from sugars is released for use by the cell takes place within the

(1) vacuoles

(2) nuclei

(3) ribosomes

(4) mitochondria

13. The diagram shows how an animal is organized.

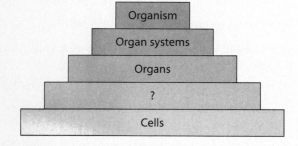

Organism

Organ systems

Organs

?

Cells

Which label is needed to complete the diagram?

(1) atoms   (3) organelles

(2) molecules   (4) tissues

14. Two organs are considered to be a part of the same body system if the organs

(1) are located next to each other

(2) work independently of each other

(3) work together to carry out life functions

(4) are made up of cells with organelles

15. During exercise, the heart beats faster to

(1) carry digestive juices to the small intestine

(2) provide muscles with additional oxygen

(3) lower the blood pressure

(4) digest more food

16. The ability to avoid danger is possible because of the life process of

(1) excretion

(2) reproduction

(3) nutrition

(4) movement

17. The following diagram shows several organs of the human body. All of these organs interact to help carry out the

(1) removal of waste products

(2) digestion of food

(3) production of hormones

(4) coordination of body movements

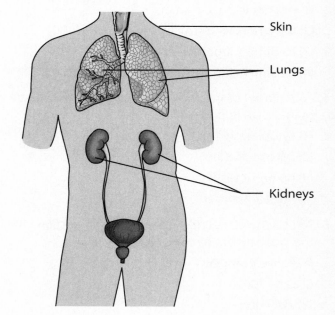

Skin

Lungs

Kidneys

18. The circulatory system helps to maintain homeostasis by interacting with the

(1) nervous system and transporting chemicals produced by nerve cells from one cell to another

(2) respiratory system and producing oxygen for gas exchange

(3) digestive system by removing undigested food from the stomach

(4) excretory system in helping to regulate body temperature through sweating

19. In the diagram of the amoeba (a single-celled organism), the arrows show the direction of movement of various substances.

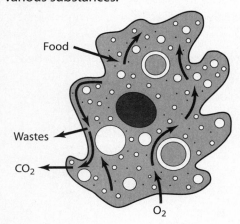

Which of the cell's life activities are represented by the arrows?

(1) digestion, reproduction, and respiration

(2) excretion, transport, and respiration

(3) immunity, digestion, and movement

(4) digestion, coordination, and reproduction

20. All cells are able to continue living because of their ability to

(1) produce food

(2) excrete wastes

(3) produce offspring

(4) produce hormones

21. Which structure in a cell corresponds with the function of the human lungs?

(1) nucleus

(2) vacuole

(3) cell membrane

(4) mitochondria

Part B

22. A scientist wanted to know whether the cells of a particular single-celled green algae could survive without any mitochondria. The scientist removed all of the mitochondria from hundreds of these cells. All of the cells died. Explain the most likely reason the green algae could not survive without mitochondria.

23. Explain the importance of cell-to-cell communication in a multicellular organism, such as a human.

Base your answers to questions 24 through 26 on your knowledge of biology and on the information in the following graph.

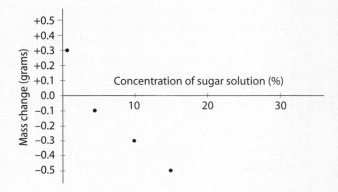

24. Four pieces of apple were cut so that all were the same mass and shape. The pieces were placed in four different concentrations of sugar water. After 24 hours, the pieces were removed and their masses determined. The above graph indicates the change in the mass of each piece. What was the change in mass of the apple piece in the 10 percent sugar solution?

(1) a decrease of 0.45 grams

(2) an increase of 0.30 grams

(3) a decrease of 0.30 grams

(4) an increase of 0.10 grams

25. At approximately what sugar concentration should pieces neither lose nor gain weight?

(1) 6 percent

(2) 10 percent

(3) 3 percent

(4) 20 percent

26. The four points on the graph represent
(1) assumptions
(2) data
(3) hypotheses
(4) conclusions

Part C

27. One of your classmates tells you that diffusion and active transport can both occur in a dead cell. Explain whether your classmate is correct in his thinking. Use an example to support your answer. [3]

28. A scientist placed some skin cells from a pond animal and some skin cells from a land animal in a salt solution with a concentration of 0.85 percent salt. The scientist examined the cells with a microscope and observed that the pond animal's cells had swollen and burst and that the land animal's cells had shrunk. Based on what you know about diffusion, explain these results. [2]

29. People sometimes use large quantities of salt to preserve food. The salt kills bacteria that would otherwise cause the food to spoil. Based on what you know about diffusion, explain how the salt acts as a preservative. [2]

Read the following passage, and then answer questions 30 through 33.

The heart of an older person or of someone recovering from a heart attack may become severely weakened or damaged. This sometimes leads to a serious condition called congestive heart failure in which the heart muscle is too weak to pump enough blood throughout the body. As a result, the heart may become exhausted. Sometimes it completely stops.

In a recent study, 2647 patients were given medication called beta-blockers that lowered their risk of death by 34 percent over 15 months (compared to patients who did not take the drugs). Another study reached a similar conclusion.

Although beta-blockers have long been used for treating heart attacks and other medical problems, doctors thought them too dangerous for patients with congestive heart failure. Their reason was that beta-blockers counteract the body's response to adrenaline, a hormone that prepares the body for emergencies by attaching to receptors on heart muscle cells, stimulating the heart to beat faster. Since beta-blockers attach to these adrenaline receptors too, they keep the adrenaline molecules from making contact. This leads to a slow-

ing of the heart, which would appear to cause a problem for a person whose heart is not pumping blood effectively anyway.

The opposite turns out to be the case. When the heart of a person with congestive heart failure is not pumping enough blood, the body responds by releasing more adrenaline to stimulate the heart. As a result, the heart is overstimulated and works even harder—making it more likely to fail. Since beta-blockers interrupt this destructive cycle, the heart stabilizes.

Doctors hope that once more studies are done, proper use of beta-blockers may eventually save many thousands of lives.

30. Describe how adrenaline is involved in the cell-to-cell communication of a person with congestive heart failure. [1]

31. Label the following on the diagram of the heart muscle cell: [1 point each]
1—beta-blocker molecule
2—adrenaline molecule
3—heart cell receptor

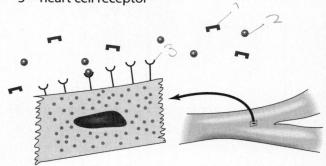

32. Explain how you could tell which objects represent the adrenaline and which represent the beta-blocker in question 31. [2]

33. Many drugs have side effects that make them dangerous to some people. For this reason, individuals who take prescription medicine must watch for any unexpected changes in their health. Based on the information provided in the passage and on your knowledge of biology, describe one possible side effect that might result when people WITHOUT congestive heart failure use beta-blockers. [1]

Homeostasis in Organisms

VOCABULARY

AIDS	dynamic equilibrium	mitochondria
allergy	enzyme	pancreas
antibodies	feedback mechanism	parasite
antigen	fungi	pathogen
ATP	gas exchange	pH
bacteria	glucose	photosynthesis
biochemical processes	guard cells	respiration
catalyst	homeostasis	stimuli
cellular respiration	immune system	synthesis
chloroplast	insulin	vaccine
disease	microbe	virus

All living things—from the simplest single-celled bacteria to the most complex multicellular animals—are organized biological systems. To stay alive, all organisms must keep their biological systems stable even though they live in a changing, and sometimes life-threatening, environment. To maintain this stability, organisms continually monitor and respond to changes in the environment. The internal stability that organisms maintain is known as **homeostasis.**

DIGGING DEEPER

Homeostasis sometimes appears with the words *dynamic equilibrium* or *steady state.* These terms all involve the idea of "a constant balance." To picture this concept, it may help to think of a child learning to balance a bicycle. There may be some wobbling back and forth, but generally the rider remains upright.

Homeostasis is the maintenance of internal conditions within a narrow range that varies only slightly over time. For example, your body temperature must stay within a specific temperature range (approximately 98.6°F, or 37°C) for you to survive. If you become too hot or too cold, the biochemical processes that keep you alive will begin to fail.

Basic Biochemical Processes of Living Organisms

Biochemical processes are the chemical processes that occur in living things. All organisms need both energy and raw materials (atoms and molecules) to carry on the internal biochemical processes that are essential for their survival. Two of these enzyme-controlled biochemical processes are photosynthesis and respiration. **Photosynthesis** is the process by which energy is stored in chemical bonds of organic molecules such as carbohydrates. Plants, algae, and many single-celled organisms carry out photosynthesis. Recall that **respiration** is the process by which chemical energy stored in nutrients is released for use in cells. All living organisms carry out respiration.

Storing Energy: Photosynthesis

The energy for life comes primarily from the sun. In Figure 2-1, notice that photosynthesis is the connection between the energy released by the sun and the energy available to living systems.

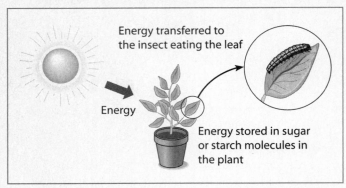

Figure 2-1. Energy transfer: The sun provides energy for most of the life on Earth.

The cells of organisms that carry out photosynthesis contain light-capturing molecules. In plant cells, these molecules are located in the **chloroplasts,** which are green-colored organelles where photosynthesis occurs. In Figure 2-2, the chloroplasts are the oval structures. You may have seen these green structures on microscope slides of cells prepared from plant leaves.

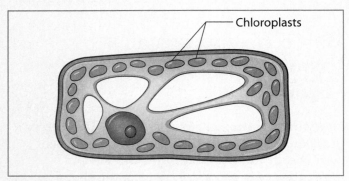

Figure 2-2. Chloroplasts in a typical plant cell: The chloroplasts capture light energy.

All plants, algae, and many one-celled organisms use solar energy to convert inorganic molecules (carbon dioxide and water) into any one of several energy-rich organic compounds. One such organic compound is the sugar **glucose**—a simple carbohydrate. In the chemical reaction shown in Figure 2-3, notice that water and carbon dioxide from the environment are combined to make glucose. Oxygen gas, which is also formed in the process, is released into the environment.

light energy + water + carbon dioxide ⟶ glucose + oxygen

light energy + $6\,H_2O$ + $6\,CO_2$ ⟶ $C_6H_{12}O_6$ + $6\,O_2$

Figure 2-3. Photosynthesis: In the production of glucose, the atoms in water and carbon dioxide are "rearranged" to form sugar (glucose molecules), and oxygen is released. Light energy from the sun powers this process, which takes place in chloroplasts.

WHAT HAPPENS TO THE SUGAR PRODUCED BY PHOTOSYNTHESIS?

Plant cells use the organic compounds (such as glucose) from photosynthesis in two ways. Their primary use is to generate ATP molecules during **cellular respiration,** which is the process of releasing the energy in chemical bonds. Glucose is also used as a raw material for building more complex molecules.

MEMORY JOGGER

Although glucose is the product of photosynthesis that is most frequently used in textbook examples, photosynthesis actually produces a variety of organic compounds.

Using Glucose to Produce ATP Molecules

One way plants (and animals) use glucose is to generate high energy molecules known as **ATP.** This process occurs during cellular respiration. Energy stored in the chemical bonds of ATP molecules is the energy source for almost all life processes from obtaining, transforming, and transporting materials to eliminating wastes. Because cell processes actually "run" on ATP (rather than glucose), the transfer of energy from glucose to ATP is essential to both plants and the organisms that consume them. All organisms—not just plants and animals—use organic food compounds to supply the ATP energy they need to live.

Using Glucose to Build Complex Molecules

Cells also use glucose as the starting point for **synthesis** (chemical combining) that forms complex organic compounds. For example, plants store much of the glucose from photosynthesis as starch. Table 2-1 provides some examples of how organisms use some complex molecules.

Table 2-1. Complex Molecules and Their Functions	
Molecule	**Function**
ATP	Cells run on ATP energy
DNA	Carries hereditary information
Carbohydrates	Food reserve molecule
Lipids (fats and oils)	Food reserve molecule
Protein	Makes up enzymes and many cell parts

When animals eat plants or other animals, they digest the complex molecules into simpler molecules for their own cells to use. Some of these molecules provide energy for the organism. For example, starches from plants and fats from animals can both be digested and used right away for energy. If they are not all needed for energy, the molecules can be stored as fat to provide a food reserve for the animal.

Summary of Photosynthesis	
Energy	The energy comes from sunlight as solar energy and ends up in glucose molecules as chemical bond energy.
Materials used	Carbon dioxide gas and water are used; both molecules come from the environment.
Materials produced	Molecules made from the carbon dioxide and water include molecules of the sugar glucose (a simple carbohydrate) and oxygen gas. Oxygen is actually released as a byproduct of photosynthesis.
Time frame	Photosynthesis occurs in plant cells when light is available, which is generally during the daytime.
Location	Photosynthesis occurs in the chloroplasts of plant cells, algae, and some one-celled organisms when they are exposed to light.
Importance of photosynthesis	Organisms either (1) use glucose to synthesize other molecules they need or (2) break down the glucose to release its stored energy.
Relationship to respiration	The energy originally stored in glucose during photosynthesis is transferred to the chemical bonds of ATP. All cells "run" on the energy released from ATP.

Review Questions

1. In a plant cell, the synthesis of sugar compounds from inorganic raw materials occurs in the (1) cell membrane (2) mitochondria (3) nucleus (4) chloroplasts

2. Which word equation represents the process of photosynthesis? (1) glucose → alcohol + carbon dioxide (2) carbon dioxide + water → glucose + oxygen (3) chlorophyll + water → glucose + alcohol (4) glucose + oxygen → carbon dioxide + water

3. Which activity occurs during the process of photosynthesis? (1) Chemical energy from organic molecules is converted into light energy (2) Organic molecules are absorbed from the environment. (3) Organic molecules are converted into inorganic food molecules. (4) Light energy is stored as chemical energy in organic molecules.

4. The basic raw materials of photosynthesis are (1) sugar and carbon dioxide (2) oxygen and water (3) water and carbon dioxide (4) oxygen and sugar

5. Which compound is formed as a common product of the process of photosynthesis? (1) DNA (2) sugar (3) chlorophyll (4) carbon dioxide

6. In the test tube shown, what is produced by the snail that is used by the plant?
(1) oxygen
(2) carbon dioxide
(3) food
(4) egg cells

Stopper — Sun — Light — Snail — Plant — Water

7. Which factor LEAST influences the rate of photosynthesis? (1) atmospheric concentration of carbon dioxide (2) time of day (3) number of chloroplasts (4) concentration of nitrogen in the air

8. Without chloroplasts and light energy, the process of photosynthesis in plants would not occur. Using one or more complete sentences, name two raw materials that are also necessary and describe why they are important.

Releasing Energy: Cell Respiration

All living things need energy to stay alive. Before the energy in the bonds of complex carbohydrates, such as starch, can be used, the molecules must be broken down (digested) into simpler ones, such as glucose.

Next, the glucose (or other simple molecules) must be broken down further. This process involves a series of chemical reactions controlled by **enzymes,** which are special proteins that affect the rate of chemical reactions.

In the final step, the chemical bonds of the glucose molecule are broken, and their energy is released. This process of releasing the energy in chemical bonds is called cellular respiration.

In many organisms, cellular respiration requires oxygen, which must be brought into the organism from the environment. Obtaining oxygen from the environment and releasing carbon dioxide is called **gas exchange.**

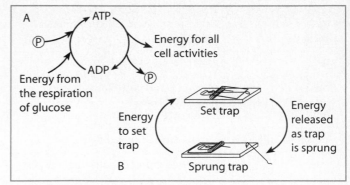

Figure 2-4. Energy storage in ATP molecules: (A) Chemical energy from the breakdown of glucose molecules is used to attach a phosphate (P) to a molecule of ADP. The result is called ATP. When the cell needs energy, the ATP is broken down into ADP. During that process, the phosphate (P), along with the energy that was stored in its chemical bond, is released. (B) A similar form of temporary energy storage occurs when a mousetrap is set. The mechanical energy that is put into the act of setting the trap is stored in the spring. When the trap is sprung, that energy is released.

MEMORY JOGGER

Sometimes people use the term *respiration* when they really mean *breathing. Respiration* is the process that involves oxygen and breaks down food molecules to release energy. *Cellular respiration* refers specifically to the transfer of energy from simple organic molecules like glucose to ATP molecules within cells.

DIGGING DEEPER

The D in ADP is for **Di**phosphate, or two phosphates. The T in ATP is for **Tri**phosphate, or three phosphates. ADP and ATP are converted back and forth as a phosphate is added or removed.

$$\text{ADP} + \text{P} = \text{ATP};\ \text{also, ATP} - \text{P} = \text{ADP}$$

During cellular respiration, cells capture much of the energy that is released from the glucose bonds. The captured energy is then used to form new bonds in high-energy molecules known as ATP. Figure 2-4 shows how ATP temporarily stores energy. Most of the energy that the cell fails to capture to make ATP is lost to the environment as heat.

Cellular respiration in many organisms is completed in organelles called **mitochondria.** (See Figure 2-5.) Mitochondria are common in animal cells; cells that require more energy contain more mitochondria. For example, muscles require more energy to complete their functions than skin cells do, and muscle cells usually contain more mitochondria.

As they generate ATP, mitochondria release carbon dioxide and water molecules that come from fragments of molecules that were involved in the reactions. Most cellular processes use ATP as a direct source of energy. Basically, cells "run" on ATP.

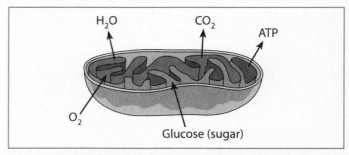

Figure 2-5. Cellular respiration in a mitochondrion: Partially broken down glucose molecules and oxygen (O_2) enter the organelle and are rearranged, with the help of enzymes. Water (H_2O) and carbon dioxide (CO_2) are released as waste products. The energy that was stored in the glucose is transferred to ATP molecules.

Summary of Cellular Respiration	
Energy	Comes from the chemical bond energy of glucose molecules; ends up in ATP bonds where it can be utilized for cell activities
Materials used	Sugar or other energy-rich organic food compounds and oxygen gas from the environment (Food is obtained through photosynthesis in producers and by feeding in consumers. Oxygen is obtained through gas exchange.)
Materials produced	ATP molecules and two waste products—carbon dioxide gas and water. The release of carbon dioxide into the environment is part of the process of gas exchange.
Time frame	Cellular respiration occurs in all cells (including plant cells) 24 hours a day.
Location	Respiration occurs in the cells of all living things. In most organisms, cellular respiration is concluded in mitochondria, in which ATP is produced more efficiently.
Importance of respiration	All cells "run" on the energy released from ATP. Organisms can use the ATP they make as the source of energy to help them obtain raw materials and nutrients, to transform materials in chemical reactions, to transport materials (for example, active transport), and to eliminate wastes. The energy is also used to allow the organism to grow and to move from one place to another.

 Review Questions

9. Energy for use in cells is stored in the form of (1) chemical bond energy (2) physical energy (3) heat energy (4) mechanical energy

10. In which process do organisms transfer the chemical bond energy in organic molecules to ATP molecules? (1) excretion (2) cellular respiration (3) autotrophic nutrition (4) photosynthesis

11. Energy released from the cellular respiration of glucose is (1) first stored within ATP (2) stored in the liver as fat (3) turned into fat (4) used directly for body activity

12. The process during which energy is released from digested foods is called (1) cellular respiration (2) chemical digestion (3) photosynthesis (4) excretion

13. As a direct result of the life process called cellular respiration in humans, (1) liquid wastes are eliminated from the body (2) food is digested and absorbed into the blood (3) energy is released from digested food within the cells (4) nutrients are transported within the cells

14. Which process involves the transfer of energy from carbohydrates to ATP molecules? (1) photosynthesis (2) respiration (3) digestion (4) circulation

15. During respiration, the energy within the bonds of a glucose molecule is released in small amounts in a step-by-step, enzyme-controlled reaction. In this process, the energy released is used to (1) synthesize ATP (2) control the process of diffusion (3) synthesize more glucose (4) produce oxygen molecules

16. Which statement best describes one of the events taking place in the chemical reaction represented below?

$$H_2O + ATP \xrightarrow{\text{enzymes}} ADP + P + energy$$

(1) Energy is being stored as a result of cellular respiration. (2) Energy is being released for metabolic processes. (3) Decomposition is taking place, resulting in the synthesis of ATP. (4) Photosynthesis is taking place, resulting in the storage of energy.

17. Compare photosynthesis and respiration with regard to each of the following:
   • source of energy
   • materials used by each process
   • location of each process in the cell
   • when each process occurs in plants and animals

18. Which statement most accurately describes the process of respiration? (1) It occurs only in plants during the daylight hours and usually involves the exchange of gases. (2) It occurs only in plants during the daylight hours and involves the taking in of preformed organic molecules. (3) It occurs continuously in the cells of all organisms and involves the synthesis of carbohydrate molecules. (4) It occurs continuously in the cells of all organisms and often involves an exchange of gases.

19. Do plants carry out cellular respiration? Explain your answer.

Base your answers to questions 20–22 on the diagram of a mitochondrion and on your knowledge of biology.

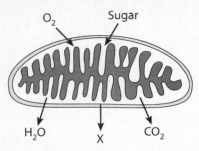

20. The process represented in this diagram is
    (1) respiration (2) coordination
    (3) photosynthesis (4) immunity

21. What term would most appropriately be represented by the "X"? (1) ATP (2) chlorophyll (3) antibodies (4) glucose

22. What is present within the mitochondrion that allows the reaction to occur? (1) enzymes
    (2) chlorophyll (3) bacteria (4) carbon dioxide

Enzymes

A **catalyst** is any substance that can affect the rate of a chemical reaction without itself being changed or used up during the reaction. Because it is neither changed nor used up, the catalyst is capable of carrying out the same function again and again. Protein catalysts known as enzymes affect the chemical reactions in living things.

THE FUNCTION OF ENZYMES Biochemical processes, such as digestion (breakdown), synthesis (building up), cellular respiration (energy release), and photosynthesis (energy capture), are made possible in living things by enzymes.

All living organisms contain enzymes. Enzymes interact with other molecules when they collide. Chemical reactions in living organisms are regulated by many different enzymes that function best at whatever the normal "body" temperature is for the organism.

IMPORTANCE OF MOLECULAR SHAPE
Enzymes and several other molecules, such as hormones, antibodies, and receptor molecules on cell membranes, have specific shapes that influence both how they function and how they interact with other molecules. Many enzymes will interact with some substances, but not others. The enzyme salivary amylase, for example, acts on starches but

not proteins. In Figure 2-6, notice how the shapes of W, X, and Y fit together precisely. If the shape of an enzyme is altered, it will not interact with other molecules the way it must to catalyze a reaction, and its function will be impaired.

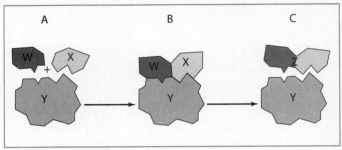

Figure 2-6. Enzymes interact with specific molecules: Enzyme interactions are determined by molecular shape. After the two molecules W and X collide with enzyme Y (A), the enzyme forms a temporary physical connection with them (B) and then separates after a reaction has occurred (C). As a result, the molecules W and X have chemically bonded for the synthesis of the new molecule Z. If the arrows in the illustration were reversed, the reaction would involve splitting molecule Z into two smaller molecules, W and X. This reverse process is digestion.

Enzyme Reaction Rates

Several conditions, such as shape, temperature, and pH, can either quicken or slow the rate of enzyme action.

SHAPE Enzymes are chain-like protein molecules that are folded into precise shapes. Each enzyme must have a specific shape to work correctly, and anything that alters that shape will affect the enzyme's ability to function properly. High temperatures and strong <u>acids</u> or <u>bases</u> can change the enzyme's shape either temporarily or permanently. When this happens, the enzyme cannot function, and the reaction rate will decrease in proportion to the number of enzymes that are altered.

TEMPERATURE Most enzymes have an <u>optimum</u> temperature at which they function most efficiently and produce the highest reaction rate. For human enzymes, this temperature is typically 98.6°F (37°C). As the temperature of a cell or organism reaches its optimum level, enzymes and the molecules they are interacting with will move faster and collide more often, causing the reaction rate to increase. Beyond the optimum temperature, the rate falls rapidly because the fragile enzyme molecules begin to change shape or break apart. Trace the rise and fall of an enzyme reaction rate in Figure 2-7.

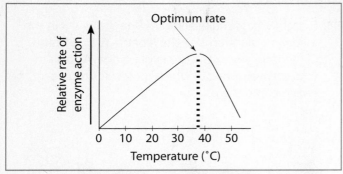

Figure 2-7. **Enzymes and temperature:** Note that the rate of enzyme action is fastest at about 37°C, which is typical of a human enzyme. The reason the rate declines so quickly beyond the optimum is that the higher temperature alters the shape of the enzyme. In this example, by the time the temperature reaches 55°C, all the enzyme molecules have been altered, and as a result, they no longer function.

pH The **pH** of a substance is a measure of whether a substance is acidic, neutral, or basic. Placing enzymes in solutions of varying pH values affects their activity. Many enzymes work best in an optimum pH of about 7, which is neutral. This makes sense, since most body fluids and cells maintain a pH of near 7. However, some parts of organisms have typical pH values that are far from neutral. For example, the human stomach is acidic and has a pH of 2 or 3; the small intestine has a pH around 8. Enzymes in these locations typically have rates that correspond to the pH of their environment, as shown in Figure 2-8.

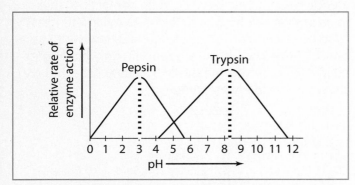

Figure 2-8. **Enzymes and pH:** Pepsin is found in the human stomach and has a pH that matches the acid environment found there. Trypsin is an enzyme located in the small intestine where the pH is close to 8. Notice that each enzyme is less effective if the pH is either raised or lowered from its optimum point.

 Review Questions

23. Only small amounts of enzymes are required for reactions within cells because enzymes are (1) fragile (2) reused (3) small molecules (4) constantly synthesized

24. Which cell organelle indicated in the following diagram controls the synthesis of enzymes?

    (1) A (3) C
    (2) B (4) D

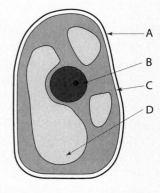

25. In order to survive, all organisms must carry out (1) autotrophic nutrition (2) heterotrophic nutrition (3) enzyme-controlled reactions (4) the process of reproduction

26. Which group of organic compounds includes the enzymes? (1) proteins (2) carbohydrates (3) sugars (4) starches

27. At which point on the following graph can the rate of enzyme activity be increased by increasing the concentration of sugar molecules?

    (1) 1 (2) 2 (3) 3 (4) either 2, 3, or 4

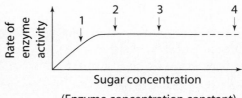

(Enzyme concentration constant)

28. Which statement best describes the relationship between enzyme action and temperature shown in the following graph?

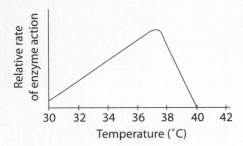

(1) Enzyme synthesis begins at 30°C. (2) Enzyme activity constantly increases with increasing temperature. (3) The pH has a greater effect on this enzyme than temperature does. (4) Enzyme activity increases as the temperature increases from 32°C to 34°C.

29. The enzyme salivary amylase will act on starch but not on protein. This action illustrates that salivary amylase (1) contains starch (2) is chemically specific (3) is not reusable (4) lacks protein

30. A particular human intestinal enzyme is most active at a pH of 8.0 and a temperature of 37°C. The activity of this enzyme would most likely decrease with an increase in the (1) amount of light shining on the reaction (2) amount of enzyme (3) amount of substance being acted on (4) temperature to over 50°C

31. Enzymes influence chemical reactions in living systems by (1) becoming part of the product after the reactions occur (2) combining with atmospheric gases to form waste products (3) affecting the rate at which reactions occur (4) absorbing water during synthesis and digestion

32. The following diagram represents three steps in the digestion of the sugar sucrose. In this diagram, structure X is most likely (1) a molecule of oxygen (2) the end product (3) an enzyme molecule (4) the sugar

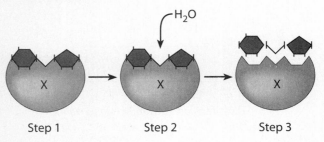

Base your answers to questions 33–36 on the diagram of an enzyme-controlled reaction and on your knowledge of biology.

33. Explain what is happening during Steps 1-3 in the following diagram. Use the labels—A, B, C, D, and E—to help you with your explanation. As part of your answer, indicate which molecules represent the enzyme and the product.

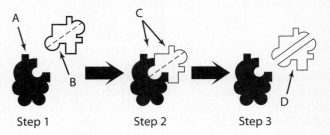

34. Is this reaction an illustration of synthesis or digestion?

35. Why might heating these molecules SLOW the rate at which this reaction occurs?

36. What is another name for a protein catalyst that speeds up chemical reactions during cellular respiration?

___

Base your answers to questions 37–41 on the following diagram and data table and on your knowledge of biology.

A student is studying the effect of temperature on the action of a protein-digesting enzyme that is contained in stomach fluid. An investigation is set up using five identical test tubes. Each test tube contains 40 milliliters of stomach fluid as well as a 20-millimeter glass tube filled with cooked egg white, as shown in the diagram. After 48 hours, the amount of egg white digested in each tube was measured. The data collected are shown in the following table.

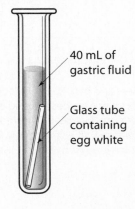

Data Table		
Tube	Temperature (°C)	Amount of Digestion After 48 Hours
1	4	0.0 mm
2	8	2.5 mm
3	21	4.0 mm
4	37	7.5 mm
5	100	0.0 mm

37. Which is the independent variable in this investigation? (1) gastric fluid (2) length of glass tubing (3) temperature (4) time

38. What amount of digestion might be expected after 48 hours in a test tube that is identical to the other five test tubes but at a temperature of 15°C? (1) less than 2.5 mm (2) between 2.5 and 4 mm (3) between 4.0 and 7.5 mm (4) more than 7.5 mm

39. The best graph of the results of this investigation would be made by plotting the data on which set of axes?

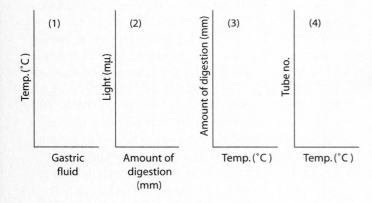

40. The student repeated this same experiment using a glass tube containing potato instead of egg white. After 48 hours, he found no evidence of any digestion. Explain why no digestion occurred.

41. During the winter, many fish eat very little. Some students thought this might be because less oxygen is dissolved in the cold winter water than in the same water during the warm summer months. The students tested the water and found that cold water holds more dissolved oxygen than warm water. They also discovered that the fish have nearly as much food available during the winter as in the summer. Explain why the fish eat very little during the winter.

Feedback and Homeostasis

Because an organism's external and internal environment is constantly changing, its homeostasis is constantly threatened. As a result, living things must monitor and respond to changes in the environment. Stability (homeostasis) results when the organism detects <u>deviations</u> (changes) in the environment and responds with an appropriate corrective action that returns the organism's systems to normal. If an organism's monitoring systems or control mechanisms fail, disease or even death can result.

For example, your body temperature may be readjusted, your heart and breathing rates slightly altered, and your blood flow increased or decreased just to keep you safe and alert as you go about your daily tasks. If your monitoring were to fail, these small adjustments would not be made. Soon, your body's homeostasis would begin to deteriorate. Under extreme conditions, you could become quite ill or even die. However, simple corrective actions usually take care of problems with your homeostasis and life goes on. Some examples of responses organisms have to changes they encounter are shown in Table 2-2.

Table 2–2. Responses to Environmental Change		
Organism	**Change (stimulus)**	**Response**
Species of bacterium	Temperature falls below a certain point.	Bacterium produces a chemical that acts as an antifreeze.
Many plants	Air is hot and dry.	Leaf pores close to conserve water.
Monarch butterflies	Seasons change.	Butterflies migrate.
Human	Person hears a loud noise.	The person becomes alert; heart rate increases in case "flight or fight" is necessary.

Dynamic Equilibrium

Organisms have a variety of mechanisms that maintain the physical and chemical aspects of the internal environment within the narrow limits that are favorable for cell activities. The stability that results from these responses is called homeostasis or a "steady state." To many biologists, the phrase *steady state* suggests an unchanging condition. They prefer to use the term **dynamic equilibrium** to describe the constant small corrections that normally keep the internal environment within the limits needed for survival. In Figure 2-9, notice that these small corrections include a normal range of variations. Certain microorganisms or diseases can interfere with dynamic equilibrium, and therefore with homeostasis. Organisms, including humans, have mechanisms to deal with such interference and restore the normal state. Homeostatic adjustments have their limits. They can operate only within certain set ranges.

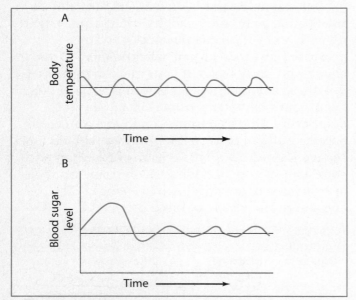

Figure 2-9. Dynamic equilibrium: (A) Temperature: Our body temperature shows a regular pattern of slight changes around a "normal" temperature of about 98.6°F (37°C). The graph represents the slight differences in temperature that are part of a daily cycle. Mechanisms such as shivering and sweating help maintain this range. (B) Blood sugar: Normal blood sugar levels show a rise in blood sugar after a meal, but blood sugar level is quickly restored to equilibrium as the hormone insulin prompts glucose to move from the blood to body cells.

Feedback Mechanisms

A **feedback mechanism** involves a cycle in which the output of a system "feeds back" to either modify or reinforce the action taken by the system. A variety of feedback mechanisms have evolved for helping organisms detect and respond to **stimuli** (changes in the environment). Multi-celled organisms detect and respond to change both at the cellular level and at the organism level. Their systems detect deviations from the normal state and take corrective actions to restore homeostasis.

Feedback responses can be simple or complex. A simple feedback response might involve a hormone that regulates a particular chemical process in a cell. A complex feedback response might be an elaborate learned behavior.

POSITIVE FEEDBACK Feedback mechanisms can also be either positive or negative. In positive feedback systems, a change prompts a response, which leads to a greater change and a greater response. An early stage of childbirth is a positive feedback system. The first contractions push the baby's head against the base of the uterus, which causes stronger contractions in the muscles surrounding the uterus, which increases the pressure of the baby's head against the base of the uterus, which causes stronger contractions and so on. Eventually the baby is born, and the feedback cycle ends.

NEGATIVE FEEDBACK Negative feedback systems are the most common. In this case, a change in the environment can prompt system 1 to send a message (often a hormone) to system 2, which responds by attempting to restore homeostasis. When system 1 detects that system 2 has acted, it stops signaling for further action.

A typical house heating system is an example of negative feedback. The furnace has a thermostat that is set to a specific temperature called the set point. When the room cools below the set point, the thermostat sends a message to turn on the furnace. When the room temperature rises above the set point, the thermostat stops sending the message, and the furnace shuts down. (See Figure 2-10.)

Regulating human body temperature uses a similar system. A structure in the brain detects that the temperature of the blood is too low. This brain structure then sends a signal to muscles, causing them to contract and relax in rapid cycles. The result is shivering, which generates body heat. When shivering has sufficiently warmed the body and blood, <u>sensors</u> in the brain detect the change, and the shiver signal stops.

Negative Feedback and Cell/Organ System Interaction

Maintaining dynamic equilibrium often involves interactions between cells and body organs or systems. For example, certain cells in the body monitor the level of glucose in the blood. When the glucose level is above normal limits, an endocrine organ called the **pancreas** secretes insulin. **Insulin** is a

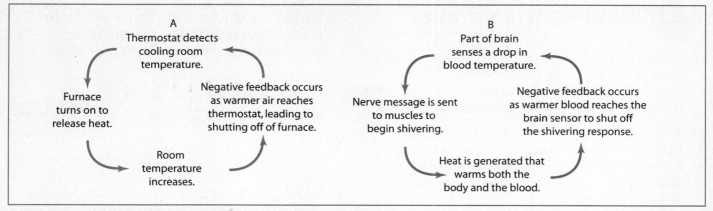

Figure 2-10. Negative feedback systems: (A) The furnace and thermostat in most houses are part of a negative feedback system. (B) Like the household heating system, the regulation of body temperature is a negative feedback system.

hormone that prompts glucose to move from the blood into body cells, resulting in a lower glucose level in the blood. Another hormone secreted by the pancreas works in the opposite way. When the glucose level in the blood is too low, this hormone prompts the release of glucose stored in the liver. The negative feedback process is shown in Figure 2-11.

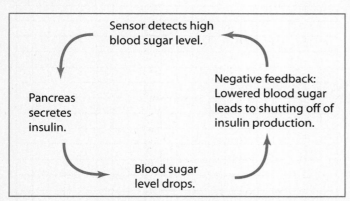

Figure 2-11. Negative feedback involving blood sugar level

Other examples of cell/organ feedback interactions include:

- Increased muscle activity is often accompanied by an increase in heart rate and breathing rate. If this did not occur, the muscles would not receive the increase in blood flow and oxygen they need to continue working.

- When leaves detect a water shortage (either due to a drought or just a very hot, dry day), **guard cells**—specialized cells that surround pores on the surface of the leaf—change shape to close the pores and reduce evaporation. The process is shown in Figure 2-12.

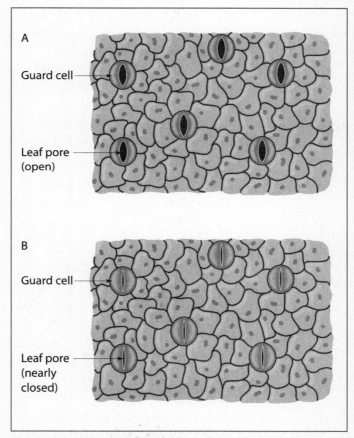

Figure 2-12. Guard cell activity on the surface of a leaf: (A) The guard cells have opened the pores in the leaf, allowing gas exchange between the leaf and the environment. Water can exit from the leaf, and CO_2 can enter. This situation commonly exists when the sun is shining, the air is warm, and water is available in the soil. (B) The guard cells have nearly closed the pores in the leaf, thus protecting the leaf from drying out. Under these conditions, gas exchange is limited, and photosynthesis slows down because little CO_2 is available. This situation commonly exists when the sun is shining, the air is hot and dry, and little water is available from the soil.

42. Some plants respond to light with a sudden enlargement of their leaf pores. This response is important because it enables the plant to increase its intake of (1) carbon dioxide (2) water (3) oxygen (4) nitrogen

43. An increase in the blood's level of a thyroid gland hormone decreases the release of thyroid-stimulating hormone. This mechanism illustrates (1) negative feedback (2) enzyme action (3) immune response (4) positive feedback

44. Maintenance of the pH of human blood within a certain range is an example of (1) chemical digestion (2) synthesis (3) respiration (4) dynamic equilibrium

45. Homeostasis is illustrated in the human body by the effects of insulin on the amount of (1) proteins digested (2) amino acids absorbed into the blood (3) oxygen transport to the lungs (4) glucose in the blood

46. The following chart shows the amount of oxygen and carbon dioxide exchanged through the skin and lungs of a frog for a period of one year.

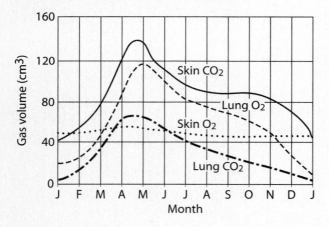

The lowest rate of gas exchange is most likely the result of (1) increased mating activity (2) elevated body temperature (3) environmental conditions (4) competition with other species

47. A student is frightened by a loud noise, which results in a hormone being released into the blood. The hormone causes the student's heart to beat rapidly. The two systems that work together to cause this reaction are the endocrine system that secretes the hormone and the (1) nervous system (2) reproductive system (3) excretory system (4) digestive system

48. Which important human process is represented in the following diagram? (1) coordination (2) digestion (3) excretion (4) cell respiration

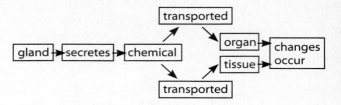

49. What normally happens to a person's blood sugar level soon after he or she eats a meal that contains carbohydrates?

50. How does insulin affect blood sugar levels?

51. Using the following graph grid, draw a line representing the relative blood sugar levels for two individuals (Person A and Person B) over a 5-hour period after a meal. Both people ate the same foods. Person A produces a normal amount of insulin, and Person B does not. Explain any differences in the lines representing Persons A and B.

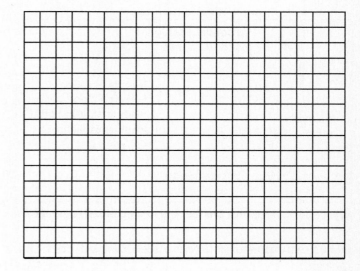

52. During hot weather and vigorous exercise, people sweat. As the water on their skin evaporates, the water molecules absorb heat energy. Why is this process important to the individual?

53. Many different feedback mechanisms have evolved over time. These mechanisms allow an organism to respond to changes in both its internal and external environment. Select an organism from those you have learned about and, using one or more complete sentences, describe how a specific feedback process works within that organism. Include how the feedback specifically helps the organism maintain homeostasis.

Disease as a Failure of Homeostasis

Disease is any condition that prevents the body from working as it should. As a result, the body may fail to maintain homeostasis. Diseases in humans may result from foreign invader organisms, called **pathogens,** or from abnormal cells in the body that lead to cancer. Disease may also result from <u>toxic</u> substances, poor nutrition, organ malfunction, an inherited disorder, or risky personal behavior. All can lead to a disruption of the body's ability to function normally—that is, to maintain homeostasis. Sometimes the onset of a disease becomes apparent right away, as in the case of some birth defects or poisoning. Sometimes, however, the disease may not show up for many years, as is the case with lung cancer caused by exposure to tobacco smoke. Some examples of these kinds of diseases are noted in Table 2-3.

PATHOGENS There are many potentially dangerous disease-causing organisms in the air, water, and food we take in every day. A variety of pathogens—viruses, bacteria, fungi, and other parasites—can interfere with our normal functioning and make us seriously ill. Plants and other animals can also be infected by these and similar organisms. Some examples of pathogens and the diseases they cause are shown in Table 2-4.

CANCER Certain genetic mutations in a cell can result in uncontrolled cell division called cancer. Exposing cells to certain chemicals and radiation increases mutations and thus increases the chance of cancer. In this disease, genes that control and coordinate a cell's normal cycle of growth and division are altered by mutation. As a result, the cell begins to divide abnormally and uncontrollably. The result is a mass of abnormal cells referred to as a <u>tumor</u>.

Once they are identified, often by abnormal proteins on their surfaces, cancer cells may be attacked by the immune system and destroyed. If the immune system is unable to destroy the cancer cells, the disease may become life-threatening.

Table 2-3. Causes of Disease

Cause of Disease	Examples
Inherited disorders	Down syndrome, cystic fibrosis, sickle cell disease
Exposure to toxins	Lead poisoning, radiation poisoning
Poor nutrition	Scurvy (vitamin C deficiency), goiter (iodine deficiency)
Organ malfunction	Heart attack, diabetes
High-risk behaviors	Lung cancer, drug addiction, skin cancer

Table 2-4. Pathogens and Disease

Pathogen	Description of Pathogen	Examples of Disease
Virus	**Viruses** are particles composed of nucleic acid and protein. They reproduce when they invade living cells.	Viral diseases can spread quickly. Examples include the common cold, influenza, AIDS , and chicken pox.
Bacterium	**Bacteria** are one-celled organisms.	Bacterial illnesses include poisoning (from the toxins given off by some bacteria), strep throat, syphilis, and food poisoning. Antibiotics, such as penicillin, are used to treat many bacterial diseases.
Fungus	**Fungi** are organisms made of either one or many cells. They include yeasts and molds. They eat by absorbing organic substances.	Examples include athlete's foot and ringworm. Fungicides and antibiotics are used to fight fungal diseases.
Parasites	Some animals and one-celled organisms are **parasites** that survive by living and feeding on other organisms.	Parasites include leeches and tapeworms. Malaria (a disease caused by a one-celled organism and transmitted to humans by mosquitoes) and heartworm (a parasitic worm that lives in dogs and cats) are diseases caused by parasites.

The Immune System

Humans have many ways of protecting themselves from danger and disease. For example:

- Our eyes, ears, and sense of smell help us detect danger.

- We release hormones that stimulate emergency responses to danger.

- Our muscles allow us to fight off some threats and to flee from others.

- Our skin—when unbroken—keeps out many foreign organisms that could be harmful.

- Our tears, saliva, and other body secretions trap and/or destroy invaders that come into contact with them.

- Our nervous system provides rapid coordination of many of our responses to danger.

Once invaded, however, the body needs an effective way to combat invaders or body cells that malfunction. The **immune system** is the body's primary defense against disease-causing pathogens.

Pathogens, foreign substances, or cancer cells that threaten our homeostasis can usually be identified by molecules on their outer surfaces or membranes. These molecules, called **antigens,** trigger a response from the immune system. Toxins, the poisonous wastes of certain pathogens, can also act as antigens.

All cells have potential antigens on their surfaces, but the immune system can usually tell the difference between the molecules of "self" cells, which belong to the body, and "non-self" (foreign) cells, which come from outside the body. When cells of our immune system recognize foreign antigens, specialized white blood cells and antibodies attack them and the cells that display them.

WHITE BLOOD CELLS AND ANTIBODIES Some white blood cells are specialized to surround and engulf invading pathogens that are recognized as a threat. Others produce **antibodies**—proteins that either attack the invaders or mark them for killing. The marked invaders may then be killed by other white blood cells. In Figure 2-13, notice the Y-shaped antibodies that match the shape of antigens.

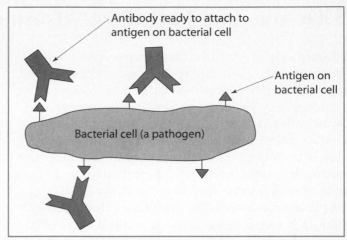

Figure 2-13. Certain white blood cells produce Y-shaped antibodies: The antibodies match the shape of certain antigens on pathogens or abnormal proteins on cancer cells. Note that the antibodies and antigens are not drawn to scale. They would be MUCH smaller than the pathogen cell.

Most of the antibodies and white blood cells that attack an invader break down soon after they have defended the body. However, some specialized white blood cells will remain. These cells are capable of quickly dividing and producing more antibodies of the same kind to fight off later invasions of the same **microbes** (microscopic organisms). Antibodies are effective even against microbes that appear years later.

MEMORY JOGGER

Remember germs? At one time *germ* was the word of choice for people who were talking about the tiny living things that cause disease. *Germ,* however, had two meanings in science, so the term *microbe* became the more accurate word choice. You still need to know that a microbe is any microscopic organism, but scientists now usually use the term *pathogen.* The reason is that the meaning of pathogen also includes viruses, those tiny "almost-organisms" that don't quite fit the description of a living thing.

VACCINATIONS Scientists have discovered that weakened microbes (pathogens) or even parts of microbes can stimulate the immune system to react. The antigens found on the live pathogens are usually present on the weakened or killed ones, too. As shown in Figure 2-14, **vaccines** are made using these weakened, killed, or parts of microbes (pathogens). When vaccines are injected into the body, the immune system responds just as if it had been invaded by a live pathogen. It produces antibodies. These antibodies can attack and destroy any of that pathogen that is still present in the body. After a vaccination, the immune system "remembers" specific pathogens by leaving behind white blood cells that protect the body for years. The vaccinated body reacts as if it has already defeated the specific pathogen and responds faster in the future than it did when attacked the first time. The second response is so rapid that in most cases the disease will not even have time to develop before the immune system wipes it out.

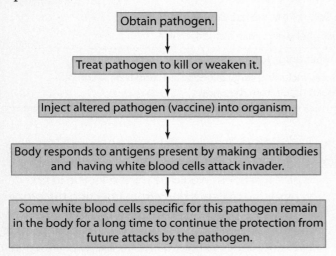

Figure 2-14. Preparation and use of a vaccine

DAMAGE TO THE IMMUNE SYSTEM A person's immune system may weaken with age or other factors. Stress and fatigue, for example, can lower our resistance and make us more vulnerable to disease. Some viral diseases, such as **AIDS,** result from an attack on the immune system. Damage from the disease may leave the person with AIDS unable to deal with infections and cancerous cells. Their weakened immune system is one reason people with AIDS often die of infections that a healthy immune system would easily destroy.

Problems Associated With the Immune Response Although our immune system is essential for our survival, it creates problems for some people. These people have an **allergy**—a rapid immune system reaction to environmental substances that are normally harmless. Examples of such substances include certain foods, pollen, and chemicals from insect bites. In people with

allergies, the immune system reacts by releasing histamines. This leads to anything from a runny nose and sneezing to a rash and swelling. It is the swelling that makes some allergies dangerous: Occasionally, the throat swells, interfering with the victim's ability to breathe. People with allergies often use antihistamines to reduce the effects of the histamines and the symptoms they cause.

Sometimes the immune system fails to recognize the "self" molecules and attacks the body's own cells. For example, in some cases, the immune system attacks and destroys the pancreas cells that produce insulin. The result is one type of diabetes.

Since transplanted organs come from another person, they have foreign antigens on their cells. As a result, the immune system recognizes transplants as "invaders" and attacks them. To avoid "rejection" of their new organ, transplant patients receive injections of special drugs to reduce the effectiveness of their immune system. Of course, because the immune system's ability to protect the transplant patient from normal pathogens is reduced, the patient may become ill from a pathogen that normally would be no threat.

RESEARCH AND PROGRESS AGAINST DISEASE
Biological research of diseases and their causes has generated a vast amount of knowledge that is used to find ways of diagnosing, preventing, controlling, or curing diseases of plants and animals. Some examples of how medical knowledge has developed are shown in Table 2-5 on page 32.

Table 2-5. Biological Research of Diseases

Category of Research	Methods Developed
Diagnosing disease	• Culturing (growing) bacteria from the infected person to determine what specific pathogen is responsible for the illness • Using X-rays, CAT scans, ultrasound, blood pressure monitoring devices, and other methods to determine the cause or extent of the illness • Detecting genetic abnormalities that may be present in cells
Preventing and controlling disease	• Promoting improved sanitation measures, including frequent hand washing, safe garbage disposal, and sewage treatment • Sterilizing surgical instruments and treating wounds with antiseptics and other chemicals • Controlling populations of rats, flies, mosquitoes, and other disease-carrying organisms with pesticides or sanitation measures • Treating water, milk, and other foods to reduce the presence of pathogens • Vaccinating to promote the body's immune response to pathogens • Identifying the dangers of risky behaviors such as tobacco use
Treating and curing disease	• Developing antibiotics and other drugs to kill pathogens • Developing medical procedures, including surgical operations and laser techniques, to remove damaged or diseased tissue from the body

 Review Questions

54. When a person is suffering from an infection, such as strep throat or chicken pox, his blood usually shows a significant increase in the number of (1) enzymes (2) antibodies (3) hormones (4) sugars

55. When microscope slides are stained to show blood cells, the small red blood cells that appear on the slides are much more numerous than the large white blood cells. This supports the concept that (1) the body's need for white blood cells is less than its need for red blood cells (2) red cells are more numerous because they are smaller than white blood cells (3) the nuclei of the white blood cells help them work more efficiently than the red blood cells, which lack nuclei (4) each kind of cell is present in the numbers best suited to meet the needs of the body

56. Which response usually occurs after an individual receives a vaccination for the influenza virus? (1) Hormones in the blood stop reproduction of the virus. (2) Pathogens from the vaccine deactivate the virus. (3) Enzymes released from platelets digest the virus. (4) Antibodies against the virus are found in the blood.

57. A patient has just received an organ transplant. Which treatment would be most effective in preventing the patient's body from rejecting the organ? (1) Treat the patient with medications that decrease the immune system's response. (2) Treat the patient with antibiotics to fight off a possible viral infection. (3) Restrict the patient's salt intake. (4) Give the patient blood transfusions.

58. The body makes chemicals that can help to destroy harmful viruses and bacteria. These chemicals are called (1) antibodies (2) vaccines (3) hormones (4) antibiotics

59. A vaccine can protect you against a disease because it (1) destroys toxic substances from bacteria before they can make you sick (2) stimulates your immune system against the pathogen (3) kills any pathogenic bacteria in your body (4) changes pathogenic bacteria into harmless bacteria

60. The body is protected against harmful flu viruses by (1) red blood cells and hormones (2) white blood cells and antibodies (3) white blood cells and enzymes (4) red blood cells and antibodies

61. A scientist wishes to determine how effective a vaccine is in protecting rats against a contagious disease. Which experimental procedure should the scientist use to determine the vaccine's effectiveness? (1) Expose 100 rats to the disease and then vaccinate them all. (2) Give vaccinations to 50 of the 100 rats and then expose all 100 to the disease. (3) Give vaccinations to 100 of the rats and expose them all to the disease. (4) Vaccinate 50 of the 100 rats and then expose only the 50 vaccinated rats to the disease.

62. Parasitic strains of *E. coli* may produce poisonous chemicals that attack living tissue and cause disease in humans. These chemicals are called (1) antibodies (2) toxins (3) viruses (4) antibiotics

63. Uncontrolled cell division is known as (1) meiosis (2) cancer (3) antibody production (4) sexual reproduction

64. The resistance of the body to a pathogen is called (1) immunity (2) antigen (3) cancer (4) infection

65. Diseases can be caused by inherited disorders, exposure to toxic substances, organ malfunction and certain personal behaviors. Choose TWO of the above causes and FOR EACH ONE give a specific example of an associated disease.

66. Our immune system normally helps us resist infection and disease. Sometimes, however, it may actually work against us by attacking certain tissues or organs in the body. Give an example of such a situation and tell how we try to counteract the problem.

67. Describe the steps you would follow to prepare a vaccine to immunize people against a newly discovered virus.

68. Biological research has generated much knowledge about diagnosing and preventing disease. Give one specific example of how research has helped us DIAGNOSE a disease and one specific example of how research has helped us PREVENT a disease.

69. Various types of pathogens, such as viruses, bacteria, fungi, and other parasites, can make us ill and interfere with normal body functioning. Choose ONE OF EACH of the above pathogen types, and for each type, name a specific organism (or its associated disease) that can make us ill or negatively affect body functioning.

 ## Questions for Regents Practice

Part A

1. Most of the oxygen in our atmosphere comes from processes carried out
   (1) in the soil
   (2) by animals
   (3) in factories
   (4) by plants

2. Which organism releases oxygen into the atmosphere?
   (1) mold
   (2) bird
   (3) fish
   (4) tree

3. Plants provide food for animals through the process of
   (1) respiration
   (2) digestion
   (3) photosynthesis
   (4) excretion

4. Which word equation represents the process of photosynthesis?
   (1) starch → many glucose molecules
   (2) glucose + oxygen → carbon dioxide + water + energy
   (3) carbon dioxide + water → glucose + oxygen
   (4) fats → sugar molecules

5. Which statement correctly relates the two organisms in the illustration at the right?

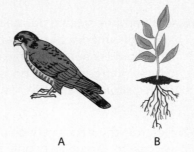

A   B

(1) A carries out cell division, but B does not.
(2) B transports needed organic materials, but A does not.
(3) Both A and B carry out cellular respiration to release energy from organic molecules.
(4) Neither A nor B is able to use energy to combine carbon dioxide and water to make organic compounds.

6. A plant cell that lacks chloroplasts will not
(1) give off oxygen
(2) take in food
(3) give off carbon dioxide
(4) take in water

7. Which process removes carbon dioxide from the atmosphere rather than adding it?
(1) cellular respiration
(2) combustion of gasoline
(3) photosynthesis
(4) deforestation

8. Which process in plants produces carbon dioxide?
(1) respiration
(2) photosynthesis
(3) coordination
(4) digestion

9. The size of the openings in a leaf through which gases move in and out is controlled by the
(1) root cells
(2) chloroplasts
(3) chromosomes
(4) guard cells

10. What process does the following word equation represent?

enzymes

glucose + oxygen $\longrightarrow$ carbon dioxide + water +energy

(1) photosynthesis
(2) breathing
(3) transport
(4) respiration

11. The major source of weight gain in a growing plant is
(1) sunlight
(2) carbon dioxide
(3) oxygen
(4) soil

12. Green plants do not release large amounts of CO_2 all the time because they use CO_2 in the process of
(1) photosynthesis
(2) respiration
(3) reproduction
(4) evolution

13. The following diagram represents some events that take place in a plant cell. With which organelle would these events be most closely associated?

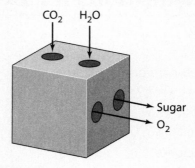

(1) mitochondrion
(2) chloroplast
(3) ribosome
(4) vacuole

14. An enzyme that digests starch will not act upon the sugar sucrose. This fact is an indication that enzymes are
(1) specific
(2) synthetic
(3) starches
(4) generalized

15. Which statement best describes the enzyme represented in the following graphs?

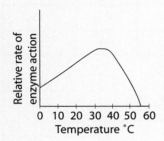 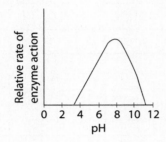

(1) This enzyme works best at a temperature of 37°C and a pH of 8.
(2) This enzyme works best at a temperature of 55°C and a pH of 12.
(3) Temperature and pH have no effect on the action of this enzyme.
(4) This enzyme works best at a temperature near freezing and a pH above 4.

16. The body usually responds to foreign material by forming
(1) hormones
(2) antibodies
(3) vaccines
(4) antigens

17. A sudden increase in the number of white blood cells in a human may be an indication of
(1) growth
(2) color blindness
(3) mental retardation
(4) an infection

Part B

Base your answers to questions 18 and 19 on the following equation and on your knowledge of biology.

$$C_6H_{12}O_6 + 6 O_2 \longrightarrow H_2O + 6 CO_2 + 36 ATP$$

(glucose) + (oxygen) $\longrightarrow$ (water) + (carbon dioxide) + ATP

18. The equation represents the process of
(1) excretion
(2) photosynthesis
(3) respiration
(4) coordination

19. Explain the energy connection between the glucose and the formation of ATP in this process.

_____

Base your answers to questions 20 through 24 on the following selection from the work of an early scientist and on your knowledge of biology.

A sprig (stem with leaves) of a nettle plant was put in a jar full of air fouled by breathing so as to extinguish a candle; it was placed in a room and left overnight; the next morning the air was found to be as bad as before. At 9 o'clock in the morning, the jar was put in the sunshine and, in the space of two hours, the air was so much corrected that it was found to be nearly as good as common air.

20. The "jar full of air fouled by breathing" probably contained an excess of what gas?

21. The fact that "the air was found to be as bad as before" was due to a process taking place in the plant. Name that process.

22. What process did the plant perform to produce air nearly as good as "common air"?

23. Name the gas produced by the plant in the process that improved the air in the jar.

24. Name the gas that was produced by the plant in the dark.

_____

Base your answers to questions 25–29 on the following information and data table and on your knowledge of biology.

An investigation was designed to determine the effect of temperature on respiration in germinating seeds. Two sets of test tubes were prepared. In each set of two test tubes, one tube contained a number of germinating peas, and the other tube contained an equal number of glass beads. An equal amount of chemical was placed in each tube to absorb the carbon dioxide produced so that the volume of oxygen consumed could be measured. One set of tubes was placed in a controlled-temperature water bath at 10°C. The other set of test tubes was placed in a controlled-temperature water bath at 26°C. Total oxygen consumption was measured every 5 minutes for a period of 20 minutes. The data are summarized in the data table.

Use the information in the data table at the right and follow the directions in questions 25–27 to construct a line graph on the grid provided.

25. Label each axis and mark an appropriate scale on each axis.

26. Plot the data for oxygen consumption by peas at 10°C on the grid. Surround each point with a small circle and connect the points.

    Example: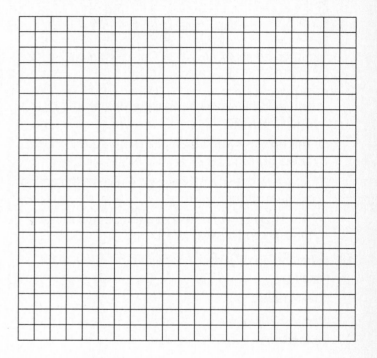

27. Plot the data for oxygen consumption by peas at 26°C on the grid. Surround each point with a small triangle and connect the points.

    Example:

28. State one conclusion that relates the rate of respiration in germinating peas to temperature.

29. State one reason for including the tube containing the glass beads in each set.

Data Table

Time (in minutes)	Total Oxygen Consumption (mL)			
	10°C		26°C	
	Beads	Peas	Beads	Peas
0 (Start)	0	0.0	0	0.0
5	0	0.3	0	0.5
10	0	0.6	0	1.0
15	0	0.9	0	1.5
20	0	1.2	0	2.0

30. The greenhouse effect leads to global warming by trapping heat in our atmosphere. Carbon dioxide produced through the burning of coal and oil for industrial processes, power generation, and transportation is one of the main atmospheric gases that contributes to the problem. Some people have suggested that planting many long-lived trees along the interstate highways in New York and other states could help counteract the greenhouse effect. Explain how this could help.

Base your answers to questions 31 through 34 on the following reading passage and on your knowledge of biology.

Lyme Disease

Since 1980, the number of reported cases of Lyme disease in New York State has been increasing. The vector (carrier) of Lyme disease is the black-legged tick, *Ixodes scaphlaris*. The disease is spread from infected animals to ticks that bite these animals. Humans bitten by these ticks may then become infected.

The symptoms of Lyme disease do not always occur immediately after a tick bite. An individual may develop a skin rash several days to weeks after being bitten by a tick. Flu-like symptoms, such as headaches, muscle aches, joint pain, and fever, may also develop. Generally, these symptoms clear up even if the individual does not seek medical help. Also, in some cases, there may be no symptoms other than a sudden onset of arthritis. However, in a small number of cases, if the infection is not treated, it may lead to chronic arthritis, disorders of the heart and nervous system, or in a few cases, death. A blood test can help to confirm a diagnosis, and antibiotics are effective in treating the infection.

People may take preventive action by frequently checking themselves and their pets for ticks, tucking their pant legs into socks when walking through woods or high grass, wearing light-colored clothing to aid in spotting a tick, and using insect repellent.

31. Describe how Lyme disease is transmitted.

32. State one way people might protect themselves from Lyme disease.

33. State two symptoms that may occur if a person has Lyme disease.

34. State one danger of ignoring any symptoms that may develop after a tick bite.

Use the information provided below to answer questions 35 through 37.

Twenty-five geranium plants were placed in each of four closed containers and then exposed to the light conditions shown in the data table. All other environmental conditions were held constant for a period of two days. At the beginning of the investigation, the quantity of carbon dioxide (CO_2) present in each container was 250 cm³ (cubic centimeters). The data table shows the amount of CO_2 remaining in each container at the end of two days.

Data Table			
Container	Color of Light	CO_2 (cm³) at Start	CO_2 (cm³) After 2 Days
1	blue	250	50
2	red	250	75
3	green	250	200
4	orange	250	150

35. The variable in this investigation was the
(1) type of plant
(2) color of light
(3) amount of CO_2 in each container at the beginning of the investigation
(4) number of days needed to complete the investigation

36. State the problem being investigated in this experiment.

37. Identify the source of the carbon used in photosynthesis.

Part C

Base your answers to questions 38 through 41 on the following information and on your knowledge of biology.

A student was working on an investigation to measure the relative activity of an enzyme at various pH values. He collected the following data:

pH 2, enzyme activity 10; pH 8, enzyme activity 50; pH 12, enzyme activity 10; pH 4, enzyme activity 20; pH 6, enzyme activity 40; pH 10, enzyme activity 40

38. Organize the student's data by completing the data table provided. Follow these directions when completing your data table:

- Fill in an appropriate title for the data table. [1]
- Label the top box of each column with an appropriate heading. [2]
- Complete the two columns in the data table so that the pH values are increasing. [2]

Title: _____

39. Using the information in the data table, use the grid at the right to construct a graph as follows:

- Label and make an appropriate scale on each axis.
- Plot the data and connect the points. Surround each data point with a small circle. [1]

40. According to the data, this enzyme would probably work best at what pH values? [1]
(1) 7 and 8
(2) 2 and 12
(3) 6 and 7
(4) 4 and 10

41. Enzymes are also influenced by temperature. Summarize the effect of temperature on enzymes. In your answer be sure to explain:

- why heating enzymes usually produces a faster rate of reaction [1]
- why heating enzymes to temperatures higher than their optimum rate usually causes the rate of reaction to decrease [1]

42. You have been asked to demonstrate the effects of different amounts of light on the growth rate of bean plants. State an appropriate hypothesis and then describe the design of an experiment you would conduct to test your hypothesis. You may describe your design by listing the procedures. [4]

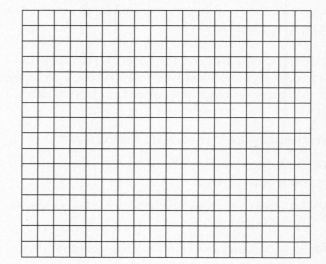

Genetic Continuity

VOCABULARY

asexual reproduction	expressed	selective breeding
biotechnology	genes	sexual reproduction
bond	genetic engineering	sperm
chromosome	genetic recombination	subunit
clone	heredity	template
DNA	mutation	traits
egg	replicate	

When two organisms reproduce, their offspring receive genetic instructions, called **genes,** from each parent. The genes determine which **traits**—or characteristics—each offspring will have. All organisms—whether they are animals, plants, or members of one of the other kingdoms—pass their genetic characteristics along in this manner. Because of this transfer of genetic information, offspring tend to resemble their parents.

Heredity and Genes

Heredity is the passing of genetic information from one generation to the next through reproduction. The hereditary information (**DNA**) is organized in the form of genes located in the **chromosomes** of each cell. Recall that chromosomes, which are found in the cell nuclei, contain the DNA molecules. (See Figure 3-1.) It is the DNA molecules that carry the genetic information of the cell.

A human cell contains many thousands of genes in its nucleus, and each gene carries a separate piece of coded information. The traits inherited by an individual can be determined by one pair of genes or by several pairs of genes. It is also true that a single gene pair can sometimes influence more than one trait. Table 3-1 shows several examples of these variations.

Some traits that an organism inherits are readily observable. These include traits such as hair color, leaf shape, flower scent, and wing struc-

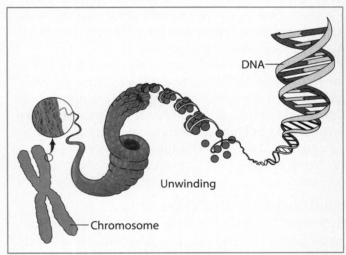

Figure 3-1. Chromosomes contain DNA: Notice that the chromosome contains one very long double strand of DNA.

Table 3-1. Human Traits Inherited with Different Numbers of Genes

Trait	Number of Gene Pairs Needed to Affect Trait
Cystic fibrosis	Single gene pair
Skin color	Multiple gene pairs
Sickle cell disease	Single gene pair affecting multiple traits

ture. The overall structure of the body is also an observable trait that is inherited from the parents. Some children, for example, inherit long, slender toes or large ear lobes.

Other traits are not so obvious. Less obvious traits may involve a defective heart, a single kidney, or how some of the body's chemicals function. Examples include the ability to produce insulin, the types of receptors present on a cell membrane, and whether an individual can make a particular respiratory enzyme.

Methods of Reproduction

There are two common methods of reproduction: asexual and sexual. The major difference between these two methods is whether one or two parents are involved in producing the offspring. **Asexual reproduction** involves one parent or individual (often a single-celled organism); **sexual reproduction** involves two parents.

ASEXUAL REPRODUCTION In organisms that reproduce asexually, all the genetic instructions (genes) come from one individual or parent. Since the genes are all from one parent, offspring are usually identical to the parent.

Because the coded instructions in their cells are the same as the instructions in their parent's cells, asexually produced offspring are genetically identical to their parents. Identical genetic copies are known as **clones.** Because they are asexually produced, entire populations of bacteria—perhaps millions of cells—may be genetically identical clones.

SEXUAL REPRODUCTION In organisms that reproduce sexually, two parents are required to produce offspring. Each parent produces sex cells. **Sperm** are the sex cells produced by the male; the **egg** is the sex cell produced by the female. Recall that genes in body cells occur in pairs, but each sex cell contains only one gene from each pair. The offspring that results from sexual reproduction therefore receives half of its genetic information from the female parent (via the egg) and half from the male parent (via the sperm).

Genetic Recombination When a sperm and egg combine to form a new cell with a complete set of genetic instructions, a unique combination of genes results. The term for this is **genetic recombination.** This unique combination of thousands of genes produces an offspring that may resemble either or both parents in many ways but will not be identical to either of them.

 ## Review Questions

1. Which is primarily composed of DNA? (1) proteins (2) genes (3) nerve secretions (4) fluid in vacuoles

2. A cell is represented in the following diagram.

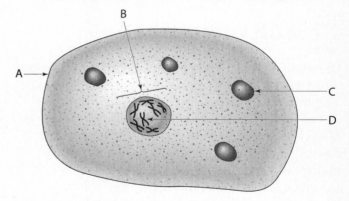

Which statement about the cell is correct?
(1) Structure A synthesizes and secretes cellular products. (2) Structure B contains chromosomes involved in transmitting genetic information. (3) Structure C utilizes DNA in the process of photosynthesis. (4) Structure D is the site of protein synthesis.

3. Which cell structure includes all of the others?
(1) nucleus (2) gene (3) DNA (4) chromosome

4. In an animal cell, DNA is found in the greatest concentration in the (1) vacuole (2) ribosome
(3) nucleus (4) cytoplasm

5. Cystic fibrosis is a genetic disease. Examine the following illustration.

Father with cystic fibrosis
Father has two abnormal genes for the trait

Mother who does not have cystic fibrosis
Mother has ???

Child with cystic fibrosis
Child has two abnormal genes for the trait

The mother's cells most likely contained
(1) a disease-causing virus (2) one normal gene and one abnormal gene (3) two normal genes
(4) an abnormal number of chromosomes

6. The following diagram represents the gene map of a fruit-fly chromosome.

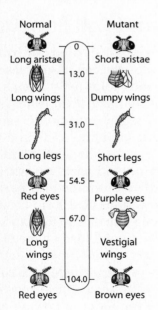

A valid observation based on this gene map is that
(1) more than one gene may affect a single trait such as eye color (2) each trait is influenced by genes that are identical (3) each trait is influenced by only one pair of genes (4) genes for traits such as eye color are always next to each other

7. Bacteria in culture A produce slime capsules around their cell walls. A biologist removed the DNA from some of the bacteria in culture A. He then injected it into bacteria in culture B, which normally do not produce slime capsules. After the injection, bacteria with slime capsules began to appear in culture B. What conclusion could best be drawn from this investigation? (1) The bacteria in culture A are mutations.
(2) Bacteria reproduce faster when they have slime capsules. (3) The slime capsules of bacteria in culture B contain DNA. (4) DNA is most likely involved in the production of slime capsules.

The Genetic Code

The inherited instructions (genes) that are passed from parent to offspring exist in the form of a chemical code. This genetic code, as the chemical code is called, is contained in the DNA molecules of all organisms. DNA molecules resemble a flexible, twisted ladder formed from many smaller repeating units, as shown in Figure 3-2.

DNA Structure

Like other large molecules of life, the DNA molecule is made of thousands of smaller sections called **subunits.** Each subunit has three chemical parts: a sugar, a phosphate, and a base. The subunits vary from one another according to the kind of bases they contain. The bases are represented by the letters A, G, C, and T. The four subunits of DNA molecules are arranged in pairs, each subunit forming one side and half of one rung of the "twisted ladder." Base A of one subunit always pairs with the base T of another subunit. In a similar way, base G always pairs with base C. Figure 3-3 shows the details of the structure in an untwisted molecule.

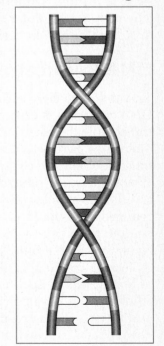

Figure 3-2. Model of a section of a DNA molecule: Notice the twisted-ladder shape.

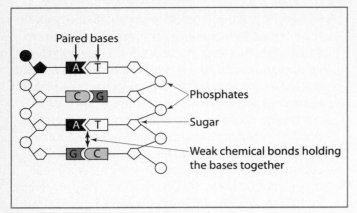

Figure 3-3. **Portion of a DNA molecule:** A single subunit is shown in black. The bases of the DNA molecule are arranged in pairs, represented here by letters. The base pairs form the rungs of the twisted DNA ladder. The sugar and phosphate of each subunit form the sides of the ladder and are connected by strong chemical bonds. The two sides are held together by weak chemical bonds between the paired bases. (**Bonds** are the links between atoms that hold molecules together.)

Once the chemical and structural properties of DNA were discovered by scientists, it became clear how this molecule could contain a kind of message that functions as a code. Notice in Figure 3-3 that the sequence of bases on this molecule's left strand, reading from top to bottom, is ACAG. A different molecule might have a sequence in the same position reading GCAG or AACG. The specific sequence of bases in a DNA molecule forms a coded message. The message of a single gene is often a sequence of hundreds of bases. The code for an entire human is estimated to be around 3 billion bases!

DNA Replication

The ability to copy the coded instructions in the DNA molecule is critical to its function. Knowing the chemical makeup and structure of DNA molecules gave scientists an immediate clue to how the molecule could be copied, or **replicated.** When scientists realized that the bases used weak chemical bonds to pair with each other, they also realized that the DNA could separate at that weak bond to form two single strands. Each single strand became a **template,** or pattern, for a new molecule. The new molecule was built by attaching new subunits to each template strand, always following the base pairing rules of linking A with T and C with G. The result is the formation of two new molecules whose base pair sequences are exactly alike. See Figure 3-4.

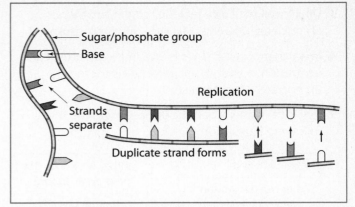

Figure 3-4. **The replication of a DNA molecule:** This is how cells copy their genetic information to be passed on to two off-spring cells when cell division occurs. Both strands are replicated at the same time.

When the structure of DNA was determined, scientists finally understood how cells could copy and transfer information to new cells each time they divide and to new offspring during reproduction. Replication produces two identical copies of the cell's genetic information, each ready to be passed from the parent cell to two offspring cells during cell division. Offspring cells are commonly called daughter cells.

Proteins and Cell Functioning

The work of the cell is carried out by the many types of molecules the cell assembles (synthesizes). Many of these molecules are proteins. Protein molecules are long chains formed from 20 kinds of amino acids arranged in a specific sequence.

The sequence of amino acids in a particular protein influences the shape of the molecule, since some of the amino acid parts are attracted to (and may bond with) other amino-acid parts of the chain. The connections that form between different parts of the chain cause it to fold and bend in a specific way. The final folded shape of the protein enables it to carry out its function in the cell. For example, many proteins made by a cell become enzymes that regulate chemical reactions. Refer to Figure 2-6 for a reminder of how an enzyme can interact with a specific molecule because their shapes correspond.

Some of the proteins made in cells become parts of organelles, such as the cell membrane. Other proteins include the hormone insulin or the many antibodies that bind to antigen molecules on pathogens. The color of your eyes and skin are also the result of proteins synthesized by your body.

The DNA-Protein Connection

Cells store vast amounts of coded information in their genes. Much of this coded information is used to make the thousands of proteins that each cell requires for its functions and the structures it contains. The proteins for these structures and functions are made at the ribosomes according to the directions stored in the cell's DNA code.

Because offspring inherit genetic information from their parents, their cells make many of the same proteins. This is what causes the resemblance between some children and their parents. Making many of the same proteins causes both parent and offspring to form similar structures that give them similar features. One example of a protein-dependent trait includes hair texture (curly, straight, or kinky).

If a parent's DNA carries a code for a protein that does not function correctly, the children may also make that defective protein. For example, an albino does not produce the usual amount of eye, hair, or skin color pigment. The condition is caused by a defect in the gene that codes for the protein that produces color pigment. If albino parents pass this gene to their offspring, they, too, may not produce the normal color pigment.

PROTEIN SYNTHESIS The process of synthesizing a protein from DNA begins in the nucleus. There, the DNA code of a particular gene is "read" by a special enzyme and used to produce a "messenger" molecule. This messenger molecule then travels to the ribosomes in the cell's cytoplasm. With the aid of specialized transfer molecules, amino acids are moved to the ribosomes for assembly into protein. They are bonded in the order specified by the messenger molecule. In this way, the sequence of amino acids of any protein, and therefore its overall structure, is determined by the gene's DNA sequence in the nucleus. The process is shown in Figure 3-5.

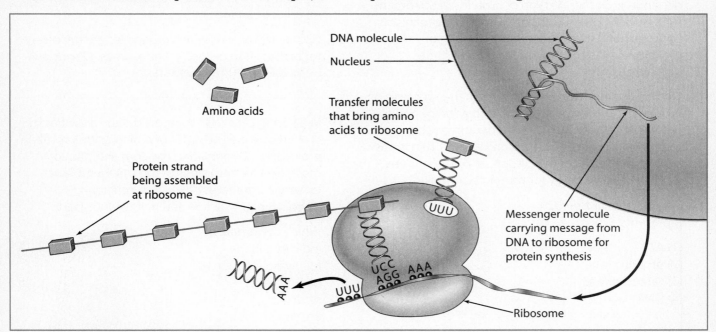

Figure 3-5. Protein synthesis: Notice that the DNA in the nucleus supplies the instructions for how to assemble the protein to the messenger molecule. The transfer molecules help assemble amino acids. The whole assembly occurs at a ribosome.

 Review Questions

8. In a DNA molecule, the letters A, T, C, and G represent (1) bases (2) sugars (3) starches (4) proteins

9. The individuality of an organism is determined by the organism's (1) amino acids (2) nitrogen bases (3) DNA base sequence (4) order of ribosomes

10. What would be most likely to happen if the ribosomes in a cell were not functioning? (1) The cell would undergo uncontrolled mitotic cell division. (2) The synthesis of enzymes would stop. (3) The cell would produce antibodies. (4) The rate of glucose transport in the cytoplasm would increase.

11. The following diagram represents a portion of a DNA molecule.

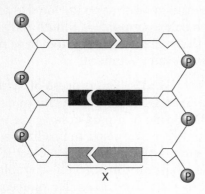

The letter X represents two bases that are (1) identical and joined by weak bonds (2) identical and joined by strong bonds (3) a part of the genetic code of the organism (4) amino acids used to build folded protein molecules

12. The kinds of genes an organism possesses are dependent on the (1) type of proteins in the organism's nuclei (2) sequence of bases in the organism's DNA (3) number of ribosomes in the organism's cytoplasm (4) size of the mitochondria in the organism's cells

13. What is the role of DNA molecules in the synthesis of proteins? (1) They catalyze the formation of bonds between amino acids. (2) They determine the sequence of amino acids in a protein. (3) They transfer amino acids from the cytoplasm to the nucleus. (4) They supply energy for protein synthesis.

14. The diagram at the right represents a molecule of

(1) ATP
(2) protein
(3) carbohydrate
(4) DNA

15. During replication, the strands of a double-stranded DNA molecule separate when the bonds are broken between their paired bases. In terms of the genetic code, why is it important that the molecule separate between the bases and not at some other point?

Base your answers to questions 16–17 on the following diagram and on your knowledge of biology.

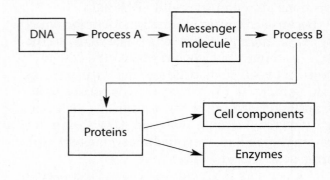

16. Within which organelle does process A occur? (1) ribosome (2) nucleus (3) vacuole (4) cell membrane

17. Within a living cell, which organelles are necessary for process B to occur? (1) ribosomes (2) nucleus (3) vacuoles (4) cell membranes

18. In all living cells, DNA controls cellular activities by (1) determining the order of amino acids in protein molecules (2) regulating the concentration of molecules on both sides of the cell membrane (3) varying the rates of starch synthesis (4) coordinating active and passive transport

19. Which cell organelle indicated in the following diagram controls the synthesis of enzymes?

(1) A (2) B (3) C (4) D

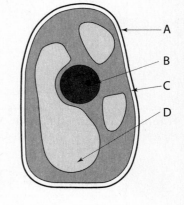

20. The sequence of amino acids that makes up a protein molecule is determined by the sequence of (1) bases in DNA (2) glucose in DNA (3) ribosomes in the cytoplasm (4) chloroplasts in the vacuoles

21. In DNA, the base represented by an A always pairs with the base represented by (1) A (2) T (3) C (4) G

22. The presence of DNA is important for cellular metabolic activities because DNA (1) directs the production of enzymes (2) is a structural component of cell membranes (3) directly increases the solubility of nutrients (4) is a major component of the cytoplasm

Mutations

Genes are actually segments of DNA molecules. Any alteration of the DNA sequence is a **mutation,** which changes the normal message carried by the gene. Many mutations involve the substitution of one base for another. This often causes a different amino acid to be placed in a particular position in the growing protein chain. Some mutations involve the insertion of an additional base into an existing DNA sequence. This affects all of the code past the change, just as skipping a blank on the answer sheet for a test can cause all of the remaining answers to be shifted to the next blank, making almost all of them wrong. The deletion of a base from the normal gene sequence would also alter all the code past the change. Some mutations occur when the bases within a gene are accidentally rearranged. This, too, alters the genetic code. Figure 3-6 shows several ways that DNA can mutate.

All of these alterations are totally random and can occur anywhere along the molecule, making the result of the change almost impossible to predict. However, when a DNA sequence is changed, it is quite likely that the protein it codes for may be assembled incorrectly. If some amino acids are replaced by others, or if their sequence is different, the folding of the protein may be different. Incorrect folding means that the protein's shape would not be normal. This could cause the protein to malfunction. One mutation caused by a substitution is sickle cell disease. (See Figure 3-7.)

Mutations can cause such serious changes that the cell may die. However, if a mutated cell does survive and can replicate its DNA, its changed instructions will be copied and passed on to every cell that develops from it. In sexually reproducing organisms, only mutations found in sex cells can be inherited by the offspring.

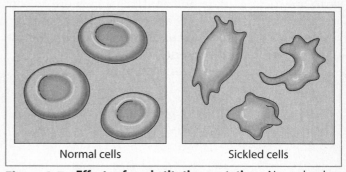

Normal cells   Sickled cells

Figure 3-7. Effects of a substitution mutation: Normal red blood cells are round. The abnormal cell shapes are due to a substitution mutation that forms a defective protein which changes the cell's shape.

DNA AND INDIVIDUALITY Although an individual's body cells all originally come from a single cell, the body is made up of many types of cells. Each body cell's nucleus—whether it is a nerve cell, skin cell, or bone cell—has a complete set of identical genetic instructions for that individual.

For years, scientists wondered how cells with identical genetic instructions could be so different. The answer is that each kind of cell uses only some of the genetic information it contains. It uses only the instructions it needs to operate its own kind of cell. For instance, information for building all of a person's enzymes is coded in the chromosomes of each cell, but a muscle cell uses only the specific enzymes that are needed by a muscle cell.

Both the internal and external environment of the cell can influence which genes are activated in that cell. Some of this influence may occur during development, leading to the many different types of cells that an organism needs.

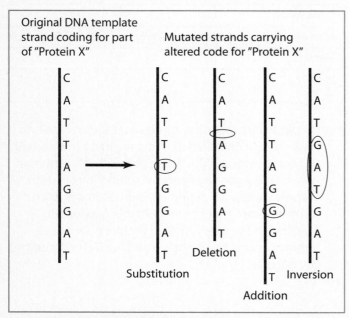

Figure 3-6. Mutation of DNA: The DNA on the left is part of the original template strand that codes for protein X. The four strands on the right show the DNA that would result from several types of mutations.

The selective activation of genes in a cell may continue as conditions change throughout life. For instance, chemical signals from within the cell or from other cells may activate a particular gene. Hormones are one kind of molecule that can activate parts of a cell's DNA code, leading to the production of a particular protein.

Although genes are inherited, an organism's environment can affect the way some genes are revealed, or **expressed,** in the organism. For example, in some animals, such as the Himalayan rabbit, the outside temperature can cause the activation or inactivation of the genes for fur color. When the rabbit's body area is cold, black fur grows. If the same body area becomes warm, white fur grows instead. (See Figure 3-8.) The environment can also influence human genes. Studies of identical twins (those with identical genetic information) who were raised in different environments show that they have differences that can only be explained by the influence of the environment on gene expression.

Figure 3-8. Body temperature and fur color in the Himalayan rabbit: From what you know about the activation and inactivation of the genes for fur color in this animal, why do you think the ears, feet, nose, and tail are black?

 Review Questions

23. A dog breeder can determine that the sudden appearance of hairlessness in one of the puppies is a mutation if the dog (1) is still hairless after 5 years (2) shows no change in the hairless condition after its diet is changed (3) develops other conspicuous differences from the parent (4) is bred and the trait is capable of being inherited

24. Which mutation could be passed on to future generations? (1) a gene change in a liver cell (2) cancer caused by excessive exposure to the sun (3) a chromosomal alteration during gamete formation (4) random breakage of a chromosome in a leaf cell of a maple tree

25. Mutations can be transmitted to the next generation if they are present in (1) brain cells (2) sex cells (3) body cells (4) muscle cells

26. Overexposure of animals to X-rays is dangerous because X-rays are known to damage DNA. A direct result of this damage is cells with (1) unusually thick cell walls (2) no organelles located in the cytoplasm (3) abnormally large chloroplasts (4) changes in chromosome structure

27. The diagram at the right shows a portion of a DNA molecule.

The base sequence of the unlabeled strand shown in the diagram is MOST likely (1) G-A-G-T (2) C-U-C-A (3) T-C-T-G (4) G-A-G-U

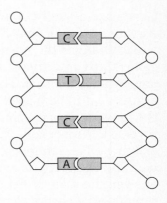

28. The individuality of an organism is determined by the (1) sequence of bases in DNA (2) number of amino acids in a cell (3) position of ribosomes in the cytoplasm (4) number of bases in the mitochondria

29. In which situation could a mutation be passed on to the offspring of one of the organisms listed in the following table?

Data Table	
Name of Organism	**Number of Chromosomes in a Body Cell**
Human	46
Fruit fly	8

(1) Ultraviolet radiation causes fruit-fly wing cells to undergo uncontrolled division, resulting in cells with 9 chromosomes. (2) A cell in the wall of the human uterus undergoes a change, resulting in cells with 47 chromosomes. (3) A primary sex cell in a human forms a sperm that contains 23 chromosomes. (4) A cell in the ovary of the fruit fly undergoes a chromosomal change that results in 5 chromosomes per egg cell.

30. A change in the sequence of bases in a DNA molecule is most accurately referred to as (1) an insertion, deletion, or substitution (2) a chromosomal replication (3) carbohydrate molecule synthesis (4) selective breeding

31. How could a change in the sequence of nitrogen bases in a DNA molecule result in a gene mutation?

Genetic Engineering

Genetic engineering is a new technology that humans use to alter the genetic instructions in organisms. The idea of altering organisms to have more desirable traits, however, is not new. In fact, **biotechnology**—the application of technology to biological science—has been producing useful products for thousands of years. Cheese and bread are just two examples of "biotech" products made with the use of microbes.

Throughout recorded history, humans have also used **selective breeding**—a process that produces domestic animals and new varieties of plants with traits that are particularly desirable. Many meat products, for example, come from animals that have been bred to contain less fat. In addition, many of the fruits and vegetables we consume have been selectively bred to be larger, sweeter, hardier, or even juicier. To breed a better plant, farmers might select a bean plant that produces many pods and then crossbreed it with a bean plant that resists fungus infections. The farmers would expect to get seeds that would grow into bean plants with both features.

Gene Manipulation

In recent years, plants and animals have been genetically engineered by manipulating their DNA instructions. The result of this genetic manipulation is new characteristics and new varieties of organisms. Consequently, we have been able to produce plants with many beneficial traits. In one instance, plants can now contain genes with the instructions for making chemicals that kill the insects that feed on them. Scientists have also engineered bacteria that can be used to clean up oil spills or that produce human growth hormone.

The basic method that alters genes in organisms uses special enzymes. These enzymes cut DNA segments in a way that allows the segments to be spliced, or moved and attached, to the DNA of a new organism. Once in the new organism, the transferred genes direct the new organism's cells to make the same protein product as the original organism. For example, when we move a human insulin-producing gene into a bacterial cell, the bacterium—and all its offspring—will produce human insulin. This provides a way to produce large quantities of a hormone at low cost. Genes for other human proteins have also been inserted into bacterial cells, as illustrated in Figure 3-9.

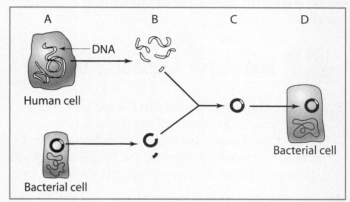

Figure 3-9. Genetic engineering using bacteria: (A) A special enzyme is used to cut a segment of DNA from a human cell and a circular piece of DNA from a bacterial cell. (B) When the piece of human DNA is mixed with the open loop of bacterial DNA, they join in a closed loop. (C) That loop is then inserted into another bacterial cell, (D), where it will produce its protein product and be duplicated every time the cell divides.

Other enzymes have been found that can be used to make many copies of segments of DNA. These can be used to increase the amount of DNA available from a tiny sample. This procedure is helpful even when only a drop of blood or saliva is found at a crime scene. By copying and re-copying the DNA in the sample, criminal investigators can produce a sample that is large enough to test. The test results may identify or clear suspects.

Applications of Biotechnology

The health care field has much to gain through our increasing knowledge of genetics and biotechnology. New methods enable us to locate and decode genes that cause diseases. Once we have a better understanding of the gene's specific defect, we may be able to develop ways to treat victims of the disease. In some cases, we may be able to alter the DNA in affected cells and cure the person.

Due to mutations in their genes, people with genetic diseases are sometimes unable to produce certain hormones, enzymes, or other body chemicals. At times, we can extract these chemicals from animals, such as sheep and cattle. These extractions, however, can be expensive, and the chemicals may contain contaminants that cause side effects. If scientists can produce the chemicals using genetically engineered organisms, we may be able to economically provide the missing chemicals in a pure enough form to avoid the side effects associated with chemicals obtained from animal sources.

 # Review Questions

32. Genetic engineering is used in the biotechnology industry to (1) eliminate all infections in livestock (2) synthesize hormones such as insulin and human growth hormone (3) increase the frequency of fertilization (4) eliminate asexual reproduction

33. Describe two examples of how an understanding of genetics is making new fields of health care (treatment or diagnosis) possible.

34. The insertion of a human DNA fragment into a bacterial cell might make it possible for (1) the bacterial cell to produce a human protein (2) the cloning of the human that donated that DNA fragment (3) humans to become immune to an infection by this type of bacteria (4) the cloning of this type of bacteria

Base your answers to questions 35–39 on the following passage and on your knowledge of biology.

Advances with Cells and Genes

Recent advances in cell technology and gene transplanting have allowed scientists to perform some interesting experiments, including splicing human DNA into the chromosomes of bacteria. The altered bacteria express the added genes.

Bacteria reproduce rapidly under certain conditions. This means that bacteria with the gene for human insulin could multiply rapidly, resulting in a huge bacterial population capable of producing large quantities of human insulin.

The traditional source of insulin has been the pancreases of slaughtered animals. Continued use of this insulin can trigger allergic reactions in some humans. The new bacteria-produced insulin is actually human insulin. As a result, it does not produce many side effects.

The bacteria used for these experiments are *E. coli*, bacteria common to the digestive system of many humans. Some scientists question these experiments and are concerned that the altered *E. coli* may accidentally get into water supplies.

For each of the following statements, write the number 1 if the statement is true according to the passage, the number 2 if the statement is false according to the passage, or the number 3 if not enough information is given in the passage.

35. Transplanting genetic material into bacteria is a simple task.

36. Under certain conditions, bacteria reproduce at a rapid rate.

37. The continued use of insulin from animals may cause harmful side effects in some people.

38. The bacteria used in these experiments are normally found only in the nerve tissue of humans.

39. Bacteria other than *E. coli* are unable to produce insulin.

---

40. In recent research, the DNA that codes for a different key enzyme was removed from each of three different species of soil bacteria. A new bacterium, containing DNA for all three key enzymes, could be produced by (1) selective breeding (2) screening for mutations (3) genetic engineering (4) random alteration

41. Assume that a section of double-stranded DNA contains 100 base pairs. If 40 of the pairs contain base C, how many of the pairs would contain base A?

42. Explain the following: An individual has a nutrient deficiency due to a poor diet and is missing a specific amino acid. How would this affect the ability of

• the individual's DNA code to replicate itself?

• the cell to synthesize particular proteins?

Questions for Regents Practice

Part A

1. Hereditary information for most traits is generally located in
   (1) genes found on chromosomes
   (2) chromosomes found on genes
   (3) the ribosomes of sperm cells
   (4) the mitochondria in the cytoplasm

2. An analysis of chromosomes in a culture containing mutated cells may show the loss of one or more bases making up the chromosome. This type of chromosomal change is known as
   (1) an addition
   (2) an insertion
   (3) a deletion
   (4) a substitution

3. What is the technique of genetic engineering in which DNA is transferred from the cells of one organism to the cells of another organism?
   (1) gene splicing
   (2) chromatography
   (3) electrophoresis
   (4) selective deleting

4. A change that alters the base sequence in an organism's DNA is a
   (1) mutation
   (2) replication
   (3) clone
   (4) zygote

5. The technique illustrated in the diagram is known as
   (1) genetic engineering
   (2) protein synthesis
   (3) internal fertilization
   (4) external fertilization

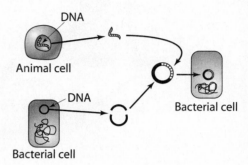

6. The diagram represents a portion of DNA.

Which DNA strand could correctly pair with the one illustrated?

(1)	(2)	(3)	(4)
G	T	A	C
C	A	T	A
A	G	G	T
T	C	C	G
C	A	T	A
G	T	A	C

7. The diagram illustrates what happens to the fur color of a Himalayan rabbit after prolonged exposure to a low temperature.

The change in fur color is most likely due to

(1) the effect of heredity on gene expression

(2) the arrangement of genes on chromosomes

(3) environmental influences on gene action

(4) mutations resulting from a change in the environment

Part B

Base your answers to questions 8 and 9 on the following diagram, which represents a part of a double-stranded DNA molecule, and on your knowledge of biology.

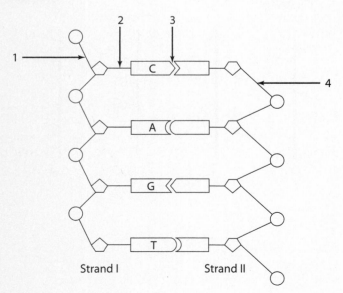

8. The base sequence of Strand II is most likely

(1) C–G–G–A

(2) G–A–G–T

(3) G–T–C–A

(4) T–G–A–C

9. Which event must occur if a nucleus containing this molecule is to undergo mitotic cell division?

(1) The bonds at point 3 break, and the molecule replicates.

(2) The molecule separates at point 2, and new bases attach.

(3) The bonds at point 3 break, and the molecule deletes bases.

(4) The bonds at points 1, 2, and 4 break, and new sequences of bases form.

Base your answers to questions 10 and 11 on the following information and on your knowledge of biology.

Some geneticists are suggesting the possibility of transferring some of the genes that influence photosynthesis from an efficient variety of crop plant to a less efficient crop plant. The goal is to produce a new variety with improved productivity.

10. To produce this new variety, the project would most likely involve

(1) genetic engineering

(2) a gene mutation

(3) chromatography

(4) vaccinations

11. Which technique would most likely be used to produce large numbers of genetically identical offspring from this new variety of plant?

(1) cloning

(2) sexual reproduction

(3) electrophoresis

(4) selective breeding

12. The technology of genetic engineering has allowed humans to alter the genetic makeup of organisms. Describe one example of such an alteration.

Part C

Base your answers to questions 13 through 17 on the following reading passage and on your knowledge of biology.

Genetic Engineering

Genetic engineering is a technique used by scientists to combine or splice genetic material from different organisms. Gene splicing involves changing the normal base sequences of DNA by removing a section of DNA and introducing another gene. The technique may involve the use of the bacterium *E. coli*. The bacterium has one large chromosome and several small plasmids, which are ring-shaped pieces of DNA found in the cytoplasm.

Genetic engineers have been able to extract plasmids from *E. coli*. Restriction enzymes are used to cut the DNA of the plasmid at designated places in the base sequence. The same enzymes are used to cut a section of human DNA. This section of human DNA is then placed into the space in the cut DNA of the bacterial plasmid. The human DNA codes for the synthesis of a product such as human growth hormone. The spliced bacterial DNA, which now contains a piece of human DNA, is referred to as a hybrid. This hybridized plasmid is then transplanted into *E. coli*. When the bacterium reproduces, the hybrid DNA will replicate. The offspring will possess the ability to synthesize the human growth hormone.

13. What is a bacterial plasmid? [1]

14. What is a hybrid plasmid? [1]

15. Explain how genetic engineers remove sections from human DNA for splicing into bacterial DNA. [1]

16. State one benefit of gene splicing. [1]

17. Explain why it is not necessary to continue splicing the gene for human growth hormone into *E. coli* once cultures of the bacteria with the spliced gene are established. [1]

Base your answers to questions 18 through 20 on the reading passage below and on your knowledge of biology.

The Plight of the Monarch

Along with producing most of the corn consumed by humans and livestock, the U.S. Corn Belt also produces about half of the monarch butterflies that migrate between Canada and Mexico. During migration, the butterflies mate and lay their eggs. The caterpillars that hatch from these eggs immediately begin to feed on milkweed leaves. This is what monarch butterflies have done successfully for decades. Now it seems that this behavior could be the cause of their extinction.

Cornell University scientists have discovered that the increased use of genetically engineered corn is the problem. Caterpillars feeding on milkweed dusted with pollen from this corn die. The new strain of corn has had the bacterial gene that codes for the production of a toxin referred to as Bt inserted. Bt functions as a natural pesticide and kills European corn borer caterpillars, which are responsible for the destruction of millions of ears of corn every year. The use of Bt corn saves crop growers from having to purchase and apply toxic chemical pesticides.

Originally everyone thought that Bt corn was the answer to many financial, environmental, and health issues associated with pesticide use. However, nearly half of the monarch butterfly caterpillars fed milkweed dusted with Bt corn pollen died within four days during the Cornell University study. None of the caterpillars in the control group died.

18. Corn plants that contain the Bt gene in their cells make the toxin that kills corn borer caterpillars. Explain how the gene enables the plants to make the toxin. [2]

19. Explain the benefit to farmers of using Bt engineered corn. [1]

20. Pollen is the male sex cell. It performs the same role in plants as sperm does in animals. Explain why it is reasonable to expect pollen produced by the genetically engineered corn plants to carry the Bt gene. [1]

Base your answers to questions 21 through 24 on the following information and data table and on your knowledge of biology.

Certain chemicals cause mutations in cells by breaking chromosomes into pieces. Cells containing such broken chromosomes are known as mutated cells. Certain nutrients, such as beta carotene (a form of vitamin A), have the ability to prevent chromosome breakage by such mutagenic chemicals.

   The results of an investigation of the effect of beta carotene in preventing chromosome damage are presented in the following data table. In the investigation, varying amounts of beta carotene per kilogram of body weight were added to the diets of hamsters. A mutagenic chemical at a constant dose rate was also added to the diets of the hamsters.

The Effect of Beta Carotene Added to Hamster Diet on Cell Mutation	
Amount of Beta Carotene per Kilogram of Hamster's Body Weight	Percentage of Mutated Cells
0 mg	11.5
20 mg	11.0
30 mg	8.0
40 mg	7.0
50 mg	4.5
75 mg	3.5
100 mg	2.0
150 mg	1.2

Using the information in the data table, construct a line graph on the grid provided. Follow the directions given.

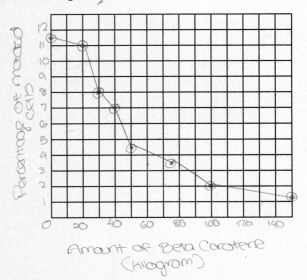

21. Mark an appropriate scale on each of the axes. Label the axes. [2]

22. Plot the data from the table. Surround each point with a small circle and connect the points. Example:

23. State an appropriate conclusion for the above experiment regarding the use of beta carotene for the prevention of chromosome damage. Use experimental data to support your conclusion. [2]

24. Vitamins A and E are essential vitamins that can dissolve in oil. A student, knowing this and seeing the above results with beta carotene, suggested that vitamin E will increase the percentage of mutations in the cells of hamsters. State whether or not this is a valid conclusion. Support your statement with an explanation. [2]

Reproduction and Development

VOCABULARY

asexual reproduction	gamete	sexual reproduction
cloning	gene expression	species
differentiation	meiosis	sperm
egg	mitosis	testes
embryo	ovaries	testosterone
estrogen	placenta	uterus
expressed	progesterone	zygote
fertilization	recombination	
fetus	sex cell	

A **species** is a group of closely related organisms that share certain characteristics and can produce new individuals through reproduction. For any species to survive past a single generation, reproduction is essential. All individuals eventually die, but the species continues because individuals reproduce. When individuals reproduce, their offspring begin a period of development that ends in adulthood. Once an individual reaches adulthood, it is usually able to reproduce and continue the species for another generation.

Types of Reproduction

As discussed in Topic 3, there are two methods of reproduction associated with living organisms: asexual and sexual. **Asexual reproduction** involves just one parent and results in one or more offspring that are genetically identical to that parent. **Sexual reproduction** involves two parents and results in offspring that have some genetic material (DNA) from each parent. The result is an organism that may be similar to one or both parents, but is not identical to either.

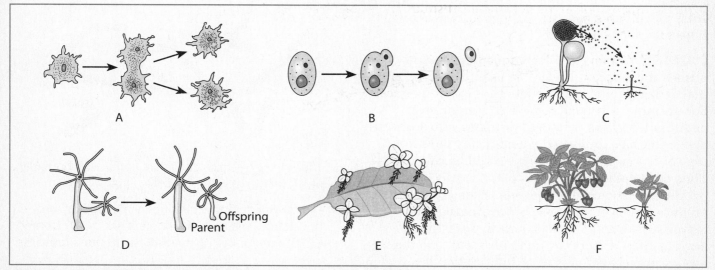

Figure 4-1. Examples of asexual reproduction: (A) An ameba divides to form two new amebas. (B) A yeast cell divides into two cells that are different sizes but genetically alike. (C) Mold spore cells reproduce the mold. (D, E, and F) Some offspring develop attached to the parent, but later separate to become independent individuals.

ASEXUAL REPRODUCTION Organisms that reproduce asexually produce their offspring in a variety of ways. In some cases they merely divide in two, producing two new individuals. (The parent in this case *becomes* the offspring!) Other organisms produce special cells that have a complete set of genetic information, and these individual cells can develop into new members of the species. Still others produce an outgrowth of the body that later detaches to become a separate individual. Many plants can develop from parts that are either broken off intentionally by humans or separated naturally from the parent plant. In every case, organisms produced by asexual reproduction have only one parent, and they have the same genetic information (in the form of DNA) as the parent. Figure 4-1 on the previous page shows some examples of asexual reproduction.

SEXUAL REPRODUCTION In sexual reproduction, offspring receive half of their genes from one parent and half from the other. The genes are carried on chromosomes in **sex cells** (also known as **gametes** or egg or sperm cells), which join in **fertilization.** Each parent supplies half of the genetic information needed to form a complete individual. The **sperm,** which is the sex cell from the father, provides half of the information; the **egg,** which is the sex cell from the mother, provides the other half. Offspring produced by sexual reproduction, therefore, combine genes inherited from each parent's gametes. Since an offspring gets only half of its DNA from each parent, it will not be identical to either of its parents. Also, since each offspring gets a unique combination of genes from its parents, it will differ from its <u>siblings</u> (brothers and sisters).

CLONING **Cloning** is a technique that accomplishes the same end result as asexual reproduction. It is a way of making identical genetic copies. For example, if you cut a piece of stem from a plant and it grows roots and develops into a new plant, you have produced a genetically identical copy of the original plant. This could be called a clone of the plant.

Recently, however, it has also been possible to produce clones of animals that ordinarily only reproduce sexually. This is done by inserting a nucleus from a "parent" organism's cell (one that has a complete set of genetic information from that individual) into an egg cell from which the

nucleus has been removed. The result is an egg that now contains not 50%, but 100% of the genetic information from a single parent. If this new egg cell with all of its genes can be made to develop normally, the resulting offspring is a clone of the individual that donated the original cell nucleus. (In mammals, the egg would be implanted and develop inside the body of the female.) Cloning has been accomplished with animals as complex as sheep and pigs.

 Review Questions

1. Which statement best describes the process of asexual reproduction? (1) It involves two parents. (2) It requires the combination of sperm and egg. (3) It results in variation in the offspring. (4) It involves the production of genetic copies.

2. Which statement concerning an organism produced by cloning is correct? (1) The clone is genetically identical to the parent. (2) The clone has the combined genes of both of its parents. (3) The genetic makeup of the clone will be somewhat different from that of its parent. (4) The appearance of the clone will be entirely different from that of its parents.

3. A student using a compound light microscope to observe a cell saw a number of threadlike nuclear structures resembling those shown below.

These threadlike structures are composed primarily of (1) fat (2) glucose (3) DNA (4) ATP

4. Plants with desirable qualities can be rapidly produced from the cells of a single plant by (1) cloning (2) gamete fusion (3) meiosis (4) immune response

5. Asexual reproduction differs from sexual reproduction in that, in asexual reproduction (1) new organisms are usually genetically identical to the parent (2) the reproductive cycle involves the production of gametes (3) nuclei of sex cells fuse to form a zygote (4) offspring show much genetic variation

6. Orchid plants reproduce slowly and take many years to produce flowers when grown from seeds. One technique that can be used in genetic research to reproduce rare orchid plants more rapidly is (1) sexual reproduction (2) fertilization (3) selective breeding (4) cloning

7. Some bacteria produce an enzyme known as penicillinase, which prevents their destruction by penicillin. Since these same organisms reproduce asexually, they normally produce offspring that (1) can be killed by penicillin (2) have an abnormally high rate of mutation (3) have variable numbers of chromosomes (4) are resistant to penicillin

8. In plants, one way sexual reproduction differs from asexual reproduction is that in sexual reproduction (1) more offspring are produced (2) more genetic variation is seen in the offspring (3) the offspring and the parents are identical (4) more offspring survive to maturity

9. A man cuts some stems from several plants that are growing in his garden. He places the stems in wet sand until they grow roots, and then he transplants them to new pots. This method of reproducing plants is most like (1) sexual reproduction (2) cloning (3) natural selection (4) fertilization

10. Compared to the offspring of sexual reproduction in animals, the offspring of asexual reproduction will (1) show greater variety (2) be more resistant to disease (3) be genetically identical to the parent (4) grow larger

Cell Division

Cell division is the orderly separation of one cell into two. Before a cell divides, the genetic information in the DNA of the cells is duplicated exactly. During cell division, one copy of this information is distributed to each new cell. As a result, each new cell has all the information it needs to function properly. One-celled organisms make use of cell division for asexual reproduction. Multicellular organisms mainly use cell division for growth and for cell replacement and repair. This process, by which a cell's genetic material divides, creating two complete sets of the cell's genetic material, is known as **mitosis.** Mitosis produces two cells that each have a full set of identical genes and chromosomes (unless a mutation occurs somewhere along the way).

A second type of cell division is **meiosis.** This process divides the genetic material in a way that results in the production of the sex cells required by organisms that reproduce sexually. Each sex cell has only half the genetic material needed for a cell to function properly.

MEMORY JOGGER:

Recall that DNA replication makes an identical copy of all the genetic information in the molecule. The replica carries the instructions for the same proteins as in the original strand. When the DNA replicates, it is actually turning a single-stranded chromosome into a double-stranded one. The double-stranded chromosome then has a duplicate set of instructions to pass on to each of two cells, as shown in Figure 4-2.

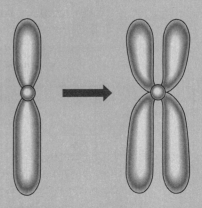

Figure 4-2. Chromosome duplication resulting from DNA replication: As a result of DNA replication, chromosomes become double-stranded.

Mitotic Division

During the process of mitotic cell division, the double-stranded chromosomes that are visible during mitosis split into two identical single strands and move apart to opposite ends of the cell. This process is shown in Figure 4-3.

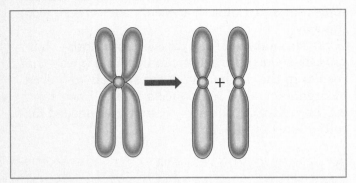

Figure 4-3. **Chromosome during mitosis:** When cells divide, each double-stranded chromosome separates into two identical single strands.

The process concludes when the cytoplasm divides, resulting in two smaller, but genetically identical, cells. Mitotic cell division in plants is illustrated in Figure 4-4.

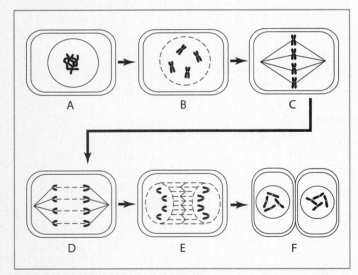

Figure 4-4. **Mitotic cell division:** The chromosomes in cell A have replicated, forming the double-stranded chromosomes that are finally visible in the cell at stage B. The four chromosomes line up single-file (C). Then the strands separate and move apart (D and E). The final result is two cells (F), each with four single strands of chromosomes containing identical genetic information in their nuclei.

Meiotic Division

The gametes (sperm and eggs) formed during meiotic cell division each have only one half of the organism's genetic information—only one chromosome of each pair that is present in the body cells of that organism. However, a full set of genetic information is needed to produce a complete individual. When sperm and egg combine during **fertilization,** all of the newly paired chromosomes and all of the required genetic information are present in the fertilized egg.

Meiotic division begins with a body cell that has the full number of chromosomes typical of the species. Depending on the species, the cell contains one or more pairs of chromosomes, carrying paired genes that determine the traits of the organism. Figure 4-5 shows an example.

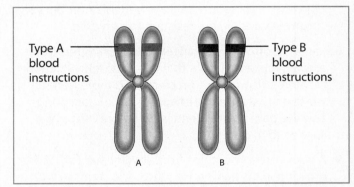

Figure 4-5. **Two chromosomes with different information:** The two chromosomes of each pair differ in the specific information they carry. For example, chromosome A may have coded gene instructions for type A blood, while the coded gene information on chromosome B may be for type B blood. Information for many other traits coded in the genes of these two chromosomes will be different, too.

During the first phase of meiotic division, the double-stranded chromosomes line up in pairs in the center of the cell. The two chromosomes of each pair (still double-stranded) then separate, moving to opposite ends of the cell. Following this separation, the cell divides physically to form two cells. The second phase involves the division of each of these two new cells. This time, however, the chromosomes line up in single file in the center of each cell. Each chromosome still consists of two strands. The strands soon separate and move to opposite ends of each of the dividing cells. When the process is complete, four cells have been formed, each having half the number of chromosomes of the organism's body cells. Each contains only one member of each original chromosome pair. Meiotic cell division is illustrated in Figures 4-6 and 4-7.

Figure 4-6. Meiotic cell division in the testes of males: Note the FOUR double-stranded chromosomes (two pairs) present in the original cell. The pairs separate from each other during the first division—resulting in TWO chromosomes in each of two cells. In the next division, the double-stranded chromosomes separate, leaving each final cell with TWO single-stranded chromosomes. These four cells can develop further into sperm cells in the testes of male individuals.

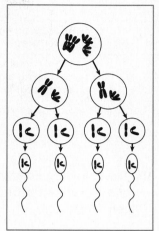

Notice that the formation of cells during meiotic division, in which each cell has half the usual number of chromosomes, is very different from the duplication and distribution of a full set of chromosomes that occurs in mitotic division.

Meiotic division in females involves the same number of divisions and chromosome changes as in males, except for the division of the cytoplasm. The cytoplasm in a cell destined to become an egg cell divides unequally, resulting in one large egg cell and three small nonfunctioning cells. Meiotic division in females is shown in Figure 4-7.

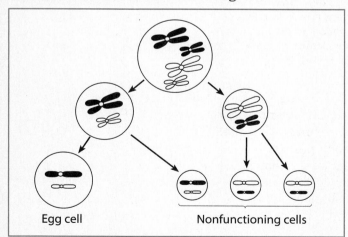

Figure 4-7. Meiotic cell division in the ovaries of females: This process is different from sperm cell formation because the cytoplasm divides unequally in each division, resulting in one large egg cell and three smaller cells that do not function. The egg cell is the one with the most cytoplasm.

MEIOSIS AS A SOURCE OF VARIATION The events that occur during meiosis do more than simply divide chromosomes into smaller sets and form smaller cells. Meiosis is responsible for much of the genetic variation among the sex cells of each individual. For example, the two members of each pair of chromosomes carry different ways of expressing many of the organism's traits, so the way the different pairs randomly line up *in relation to other pairs* leads to many possible combinations in the sex cells that result. Two combinations are shown in Figure 4-8.

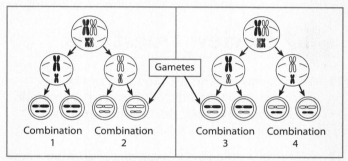

Figure 4-8. Two equally likely combinations of chromosomes lined up for meiotic division: A pair of chromosomes can be arranged in two ways when they pair up at the start of meiosis. This helps increase genetic variation. How many combinations do you see in the gametes? How would more pairs of chromosomes affect the number of possible arrangements?

Another way variation can arise is by the exchange of parts of chromosomes, which occurs as they pair up during the first division. The process is sometimes called crossing-over. The result is shown in Figure 4-9. After separation, each set is unique. This means that there are no two sperm or egg cells, even from the same parent, that are alike. Each time a sperm and egg combine, a unique combination of genetic information results.

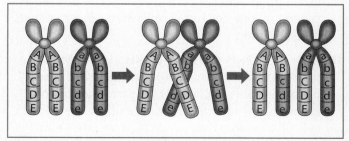

Figure 4-9. Result of exchanging parts between chromosomes: When chromosomes line up in pairs during meiosis, their strands may connect or cross over (A) and then separate in a way that parts are exchanged. All four strands now carry different combinations of information (B).

Summary of Mitotic and Meiotic Cell Division		
Points of Comparison	**Mitotic Division**	**Meiotic Division**
Number of cell divisions	One	Two
Exchange of genetic material between chromosomes	No	Yes
Number of functioning cells produced from original	Two	Four sperm (in males) or one egg (in females)
Genetic makeup of final cells produced	Same as original	Highly variable gametes produced, each containing half of the genetic information of the original
Function of cells produced in multicellular organisms	Growth or replacement of body cells	Combine to form the zygote for reproduction

 # Review Questions

11. When complex plants are produced by cloning, which process is most directly involved? (1) mitotic cell division (2) meiotic cell division (3) gamete production (4) sperm cell fertilization

12. If a lobster loses a claw, it is capable of growing a new one. What process makes this possible? (1) meiosis (2) fertilization (3) sexual reproduction (4) mitosis

13. Organisms that reproduce asexually usually do so by a form of cell division called (1) meiosis (2) mitosis (3) gamete formation (4) sperm formation

14. A normal body cell of a fruit fly contains eight chromosomes. Each normal gamete of this organism contains (1) four chromosomes as a result of meiosis (2) four chromosomes as a result of mitosis (3) eight chromosomes as a result of meiosis (4) eight chromosomes as a result of mitosis

15. The process of mitotic cell division normally results in the production of (1) four cells with half the number of chromosomes as the parent (2) two cells with the same number of chromosomes as the parent (3) two cells with only one chromosome from each parent (4) one cell with a replicated set of matched chromosomes

16. Each of the two daughter (or offspring) cells that result from the normal mitotic division of the original parent cell contains (1) the same number of chromosomes but different genes than the parent cell (2) the same number of chromosomes and genes identical to those of the parent cell (3) one half of the number of chromosomes but different genes than those of the parent cell (4) one half of the number of chromosomes and genes identical to those of the parent cell

17. The following diagrams represent the sequence of events in a cell undergoing normal meiotic cell division.

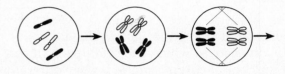

• How many cells will finally be produced?

• How many chromosomes will be in each cell?

• Sketch one of the final cells, showing its chromosomes.

18. The species chromosome number of orangutans is 48. Which diagram represents normal fertilization in orangutans?

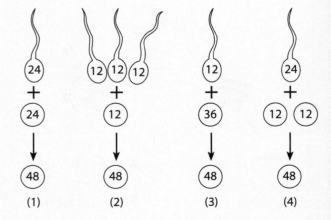

19. Which process is represented in the following photographs?

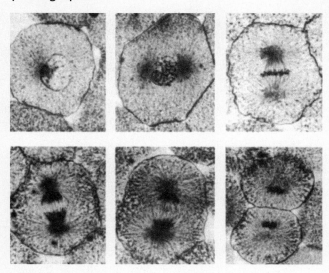

(1) mitotic cell division (2) zygote formation
(3) fertilization (4) recombination

20. All types of asexual reproduction involve the process known as (1) mitosis (2) fertilization (3) meiotic division (4) aging

21. If the sperm cells of a fish have 12 chromosomes, how many chromosomes would be found in the cells forming the scales of the fish?

(1) 6 (2) 12 (3) 24 (4) 48

ZYGOTE FORMATION During fertilization, the gametes unite to form a **zygote**—a cell that contains all of the genetic information needed by the offspring. This process is known as **recombination,** since the genes from both parents recombine when fertilization occurs. Since a sex cell contains a unique combination of genetic material, the result of the random combination of any sperm and egg explains the variation found in offspring produced by sexual reproduction. This variation plays a key role in evolutionary change and species survival.

The zygote contains all the information necessary for growth, development, and eventual reproduction of the organism. The zygote divides by mitosis to form a multicellular organism. Fertilization, zygote formation, and some early mitotic divisions that occur in development are shown in Figure 4-10.

EARLY DEVELOPMENT During the early stages of development, the cells that are formed by mitotic division begin to undergo **differentiation,** which simply means that they become different from one another. This leads to the formation of specialized cells, which form the tissues, and then the organs, of multicellular organisms. In an **embryo,** an organism in an early stage of development, all the genetic information in each cell starts out the same. However, different genes are activated or deactivated in certain cells, causing them to make only some of the many proteins they are capable of synthesizing. As a result, these cells become different from others, and may develop into skin cells, muscle cells, or any of the other specialized cells of the organism. The activation or inactivation of genes can be due to environmental influences from within the cell, from surrounding cells, or from outside the organism.

When a gene is actively producing its protein, scientists say that the gene is **expressed.** There is much evidence that **gene expression,** which is the result of activated genes, can be modified through interaction with the environment. For example, fruit flies that have genes to develop curly wings will develop straight wings instead, if they are raised in a cooler than normal environment. Another example of an environmentally produced gene modification is a plant grown without light. Such a plant is white instead of green, because sunlight is needed to stimulate the gene that produces chlorophyll.

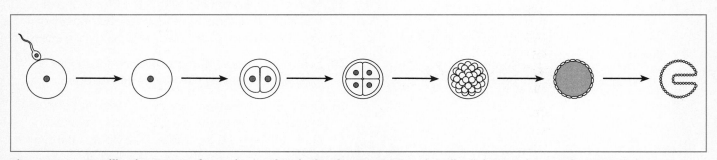

Figure 4-10. Fertilization, zygote formation, and early development: Note that all cell divisions here are by MITOTIC division.

Review Questions

22. An exact duplication of the complete set of chromosomes of a cell, followed by the separation of these duplicate sets into two new cells, is known as (1) mitotic cell division (2) zygote formation (3) meiotic cell division (4) fertilization

23. The following data table summarizes the results of an experiment using primrose plants grown under different temperature conditions. Which conclusion can be drawn from this data table? (1) Color in primroses is determined only by gene action. (2) Many traits are not inherited. (3) Gene exchanges only occur when the plants are grown at lower temperatures. (4) There is an interaction between environment and heredity.

Data Table: Primrose Color Under Two Growing Conditions				
Flower Color	**Temperature of 20°C**		**Temperature of 31°C**	
Color coded in DNA	Red	White	Red	White
Actual color expressed	Red	White	White	White

Base your answers to questions 24–27 on the following diagrams and on your knowledge of biology.

Diagram A represents the chromosomes in the nucleus of the body cell of a worm. Diagrams B through G represent chromosomal arrangements that may occur in other cells produced by this worm.

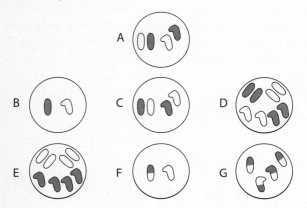

24. If meiosis failed to occur in both male and female worms, the zygote nucleus would resemble diagram (1) E (2) G (3) C (4) D

25. If genes were exchanged between a single pair of chromosomes during gamete formation, the gamete nucleus would most closely resemble diagram (1) F (2) B (3) C (4) G

26. The nucleus of a normal zygote formed when fertilization occurs in this species would most likely resemble diagram (1) E (2) F (3) C (4) D

27. The nucleus of a mature gamete from a female worm would most likely resemble diagram (1) E (2) B (3) C (4) D

---

28. When organisms reproduce sexually, the species number of chromosomes is maintained. This can be demonstrated with a diagram like the one below. Complete the diagram by filling in the blanks with the appropriate information.

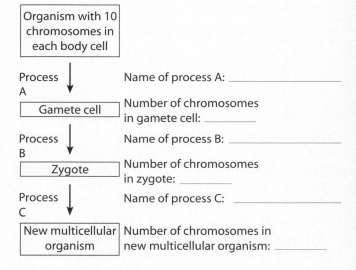

29. New cells are produced within the uterus as a direct result of (1) gamete formation (2) meiotic cell division (3) mitotic cell division (4) ecological succession

30. In human females, gametes are produced in the (1) uterus (2) testes (3) ovaries (4) estrogen

31. Complex organisms produce sex cells that unite during fertilization forming a single cell known as (1) an embryo (2) a gamete (3) a clone (4) a zygote

Human Reproduction and Development

Human reproduction and development are carried out by specialized organs. The function of these organs is regulated by hormones from the endocrine system. In humans, as in nearly all mammals, fertilization and development occur internally—within the mother's body. Reproductive organs in other mammals are similar in appearance and function.

FEMALE REPRODUCTIVE SYSTEM The human female reproductive system is organized to produce gametes, to support internal fertilization and development, to exchange materials through the placenta, and to provide milk to the offspring.

In human females, the **ovaries** produce egg cells (female gametes) and the hormones **estrogen** and **progesterone,** which are associated with sexual development and the reproductive process. The ovaries are located near the open ends of tubes called <u>oviducts</u> (egg ducts). The egg cell can be fertilized in the oviduct if sperm are present. The oviducts lead to the **uterus,** where the embryo develops into the fetus. The main parts of the female reproductive system are illustrated in Figure 4-11.

Table 4-1. The Functions of the Parts of the Human Female Reproductive System	
Structure	**Function**
Ovary	Produces egg cells; releases the hormones estrogen and progesterone
Oviduct	Site of fertilization; carries egg to uterus
Uterus	Site where embryo and fetus develop in association with placenta
Birth canal (vagina)	Site where sperm enter and swim to egg in oviduct; passageway for the birth of baby

After the fertilized egg sinks into the thickened wall of the uterus, a placenta begins to form. The **placenta** is the organ responsible for the passage (by diffusion) of nutrients and oxygen from the mother's blood to the fetus. Wastes from the fetus also diffuse to the mother's blood through the placenta. During birth, the muscular uterus undergoes a series of contractions that eventually push the baby out of the mother's body. The early events of pregnancy are shown in Figure 4-12.

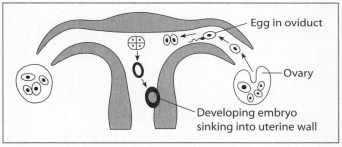

Figure 4-12. Early events of pregnancy: The egg released by the ovary travels down the oviduct where fertilization occurs. Mitotic divisions of the zygote begin as it continues to the uterus, where the developing embryo sinks into the uterine wall, and the placenta forms. The placenta will supply essential materials and remove wastes throughout the rest of the pregnancy.

MALE REPRODUCTIVE SYSTEM The **testes** of the male reproductive system are the organs that produce sperm cells. The testes also produce the hormone **testosterone,** which is associated with male sexual development and reproduction. Other structures associated with the male reproductive system produce the fluids and nutrients that are needed for the proper function and delivery of the male gametes to the female reproductive system. The essential parts of the human male reproductive system are shown in Figure 4-13.

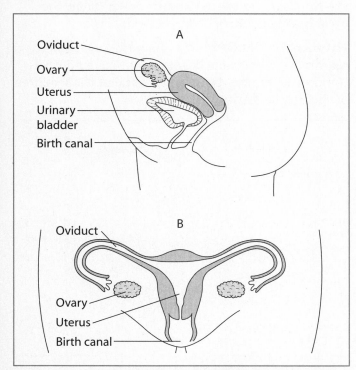

Figure 4-11. Two views of essential parts of the human female reproductive system and other structures: View A is from the side; View B is from the front.

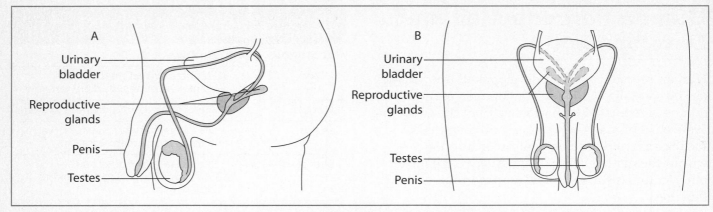

Figure 4-13. Two views of the essential parts of the human male reproductive system and other structures: View A is from the side; View B is from the front.

HORMONAL REGULATION The male reproductive system and other male characteristics, such as facial hair and a deep voice, that develop as sexual maturity is reached are influenced by several hormones, including testosterone from the testes. The development of the female reproductive system and female features, such as breast development and widening of the hips, also involves several important hormones, such as estrogen and progesterone.

Once sexual maturity is reached, females begin a regular cycle of about 28 days, during which an egg is released at about day 14. The timing of the events of this cycle is regulated by two hormones from the ovaries, along with several others from an endocrine gland in the brain. Figure 4-14 illustrates the changes in the level of several hormones associated with regulating this monthly cycle. The cycle varies slightly from individual to individual.

Although the interactions of the hormones are quite complex, estrogen and progesterone play important roles in the female reproductive cycle. Estrogen from the ovaries influences the sexual development of females. Together, estrogen and progesterone influence the preparation of the lining of the uterus so that a fertilized egg that embeds itself there can develop normally. Progesterone also maintains the uterine lining throughout pregnancy. For this reason, progesterone is often called the hormone of pregnancy. At the end of the cycle, if an egg is not fertilized, the levels of estrogen and progesterone decrease, and the lining of the uterus breaks down. Then the cycle begins again.

HUMAN DEVELOPMENT As with most other mammals, embryonic development continues in the uterus. Figure 4-15 shows some of the features of the uterus during pregnancy.

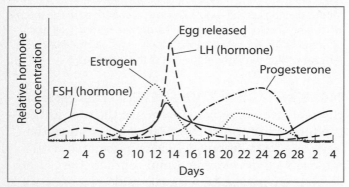

Figure 4-14. Hormones and events associated with the monthly reproductive cycle in human females: Notice the rise and fall in hormone levels at various times. These changes influence such events as the release of the egg from the ovary, the preparation of the uterus for a possible pregnancy, and the breakdown of the uterine lining if no pregnancy occurs. Remember that the timing of this cycle is NOT the same for everyone.

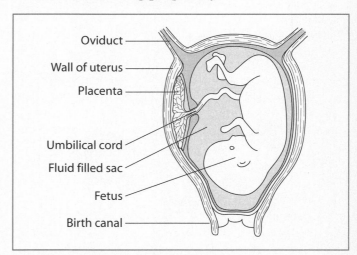

Figure 4-15. The uterus during pregnancy

During the first part of pregnancy, cells continue to divide by mitotic division and begin to differentiate, forming tissues and organs. The placenta and a fluid-filled sac that cushions and protects the developing embryo both form at this time, too. After about two months, when all the major organs have begun to form, the embryo is called a **fetus.**

During the first few months, when essential organs are forming in the embryo, things can go wrong. Problems associated with either the embryo's inherited genes or the mother's exposure to various harmful environmental factors can affect the embryo. Harmful environmental factors that a woman should avoid at any time during pregnancy include alcohol, drugs, and tobacco. Use of these can lead to the birth of a baby with brain damage, drug addiction, and/or low birth weight and the problems associated with it. An embryo or fetus may also be harmed if the mother has a poor diet, is exposed to certain toxic substances, or gets certain infections, such as German measles or AIDS.

After birth, cell differentiation and body growth continue until adulthood. During adulthood, the structures of the body slowly begin to age. Eventually, the organism weakens and dies. This process of birth, growth, development, aging, and death is a predictable pattern that applies not just to humans, but to all organisms.

Applications of Reproductive Technology

Recent discoveries by scientists have greatly changed the way we can deal with many problems involving the reproduction of humans as well as plants and other organisms. The knowledge we have gained has a variety of agricultural, ecological, and medical applications.

In the field of agriculture, scientists have produced plants that are resistant to insects, weed killers, and even frost. Such altered plants can then be cloned to produce thousands of genetically identical offspring. Using artificial insemination, scientists can generate hundreds of offspring from one farm animal. They can also freeze the sperm or fertilized eggs of an animal and transport them to animals thousands of miles away, at far less cost than transporting the animals themselves.

In the field of ecology, reproductive technology is being used to help build up populations of endangered species. Embryos from the endangered species have been transplanted into related species, who later give birth to offspring that are no different than they would be if they developed in the bodies of the endangered animals themselves. Also, hormones of insects that regulate their reproduction and development have been studied in an attempt to find ways to control insects without using poisonous chemicals.

In the field of medicine, recent scientific discoveries have led to new ways of dealing with reproductive problems in humans, other animals, and plants. Some women cannot become pregnant because of problems with their hormones, ovaries, or other parts of their reproductive systems. Reproductive technologies have enabled doctors to help infertile women become pregnant by using hormone therapy to adjust their hormones to normal levels. Sometimes doctors can extract several eggs from a woman's ovaries and fertilize them with sperm in a laboratory dish. When these fertilized eggs are implanted in the woman's uterus, a successful pregnancy may result.

Ultrasound and miniature video cameras allow doctors to view ovaries, oviducts, and other reproductive structures, or even a developing fetus, to determine if or where problems exist. Methods have also been developed to retrieve fetal cells that are present in the fluids around the developing fetus. (See Figure 4-16.) Doctors can then analyze the cells for chromosome abnormalities and the fluids for biochemical deficiencies that may threaten the health or development of the fetus.

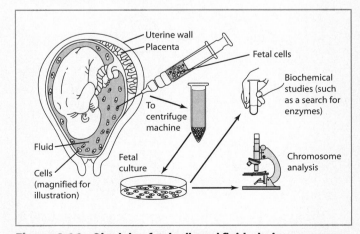

Figure 4-16. Obtaining fetal cells and fluids during pregnancy: Biochemical studies and chromosome analysis of the fetus can be done with cells and fluids removed during pregnancy.

32. What substances are involved in controlling the production of sperm and eggs in humans? (1) vitamins (2) hormones (3) starches (4) minerals

33. Which practice is essential to good prenatal care? (1) increased egg production (2) frequent dieting (3) avoidance of drugs (4) intake of antibiotics

34. Which part of the human male reproductive system produces hormones that influence the development of male sex characteristics? (1) penis (2) testes (3) gametes (4) ovaries

35. The diagram below represents a series of events that takes place in the life cycle of humans.

Egg and Sperm Formation

↓

X

↓

Many Rapid Cell Divisions

↓

New Organism

Which term best describes the event taking place in the box labeled X? (1) fertilization (2) immune response (3) meiosis (4) protein synthesis

36. The following diagram represents a sequence of events in a human ovary.

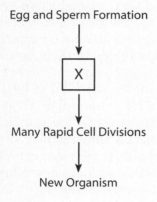

The process that occurs between stage A and stage B is known as (1) egg formation (2) sperm formation (3) mitotic cell division (4) cell recombination

Base your answers to questions 37–41 on the following diagram and on your knowledge of biology.

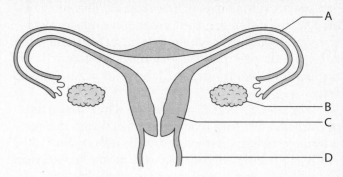

37. Fertilization usually occurs within structure (1) A (2) B (3) C (4) D

38. A placenta normally develops in this structure. (1) A (2) B (3) C (4) D

39. The structure that produces estrogen and progesterone is (1) A (2) B (3) C (4) D

40. The structure that produces egg cells is (1) A (2) B (3) C (4) D

41. Shortly after implantation, tissue from the embryo normally grows into the wall of (1) A (2) B (3) C (4) D

Base your answers to questions 42–44 on the following diagrams and on your knowledge of biology.

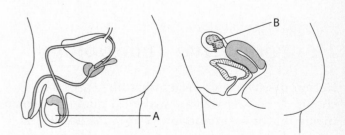

42. Gametes are produced in (1) A, only (2) B, only (3) both A and B (4) neither A nor B

43. Estrogen and progesterone are produced in (1) A, only (2) B, only (3) both A and B (4) neither A nor B

44. A substance is produced that influences both the reproductive cycle and the development of sex characteristics in (1) A, only (2) B, only (3) both A and B (4) neither A nor B

45. In humans and other mammals, nutrients are transferred from the mother's bloodstream to the embryo's bloodstream across the (1) placenta (2) uterus (3) ovary (4) intestine

46. Which substance is a waste that would normally diffuse across the placenta from the embryo to the mother? (1) glucose (2) oxygen (3) amino acid (4) carbon dioxide

47. The egg of a mammal is smaller than that of a bird because the embryo of the mammal obtains its nutrients from the (1) placenta through the process of diffusion (2) mammary glands of the mother (3) blood of the mother when it mixes with the blood of the embryo (4) yolk stored in the uterus of the mother

---

Base your answers to questions 48–49 on the diagram at the bottom of the page, which represents an experiment, and on your knowledge of biology.

48. An inference that can be made from this experiment is that (1) adult frog B will have the same genetic traits as the tadpole (2) adult frog A can develop only from an egg and a sperm (3) fertilization must occur in order for frog eggs to develop into adult frogs (4) the nucleus of a body cell fails to function when transferred to other cell types

49. Other scientists substituted a nucleus from a frog sperm cell and no adult frog developed. Explain why a sperm cell nucleus would not work in this procedure.

Base your answers to questions 50–52 on the following information and on your knowledge of biology.

Some women have a blockage in that portion of their reproductive tract where fertilization of the egg cell would normally occur. *In vitro* fertilization is a technique that has been developed to make it possible for such women to bear their own children. This technique involves fertilizing an egg in a sterile petri dish and then implanting the developing embryo into the mother.

50. To ensure that the mother will have mature egg cells available for *in vitro* fertilization, she must be treated with chemicals that regulate her reproductive cycle. What are these chemicals that regulate both the female and male reproductive cycles called?

51. Egg cells for *in vitro* fertilization must be surgically removed from the mother. What structure in the mother's body is the source for these egg cells?

52. An embryo that developed from *in vitro* fertilization would be implanted in the mother's (1) ovary (2) stomach (3) uterus (4) placenta

---

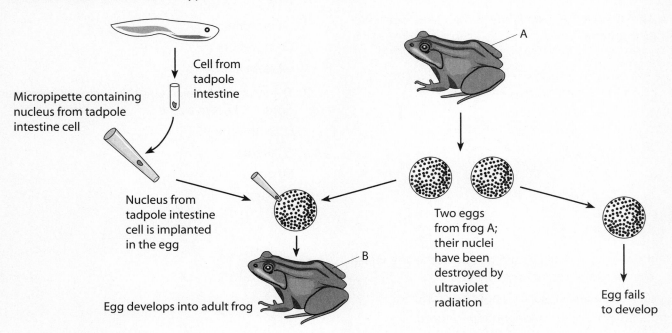

Cell from tadpole intestine

Micropipette containing nucleus from tadpole intestine cell

Nucleus from tadpole intestine cell is implanted in the egg

Egg develops into adult frog

B

A

Two eggs from frog A; their nuclei have been destroyed by ultraviolet radiation

Egg fails to develop

Part A

1. Compared to the number of chromosomes in a normal human body cell, the number of chromosomes in a normal sperm cell is
   (1) the same
   (2) twice as great
   (3) half as great
   (4) four times as great

2. Children born to the same parents are usually very different from each other. These differences result primarily from the process of
   (1) mitotic division
   (2) meiosis
   (3) asexual reproduction
   (4) cloning

3. Human growth and sexual development are controlled by
   (1) nerves
   (2) hormones
   (3) the digestive system
   (4) the excretory system

4. The diagram represents the human male reproductive system.

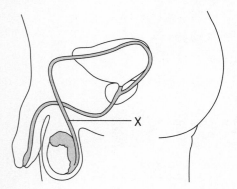

If structure X were cut and tied off at the line, which change would occur immediately?
   (1) Hormones would no longer be produced.
   (2) Sperm would no longer be produced.
   (3) Sperm would be produced but no longer released from the body.
   (4) Urine would be produced but no longer released from the bladder

Base your answers to question 5 through 7 on the following diagram, which represents a stage in human development.

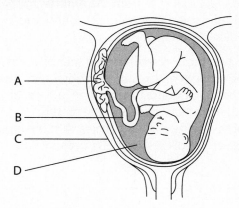

5. The exchange of oxygen, food, and wastes between mother and fetus occurs at
   (1) A
   (2) B
   (3) C
   (4) D

6. What is the function of the fluid labeled D?
   (1) nourishment
   (2) protection
   (3) excretion
   (4) respiration

7. The structure labeled C, within which development occurs, is known as the
   (1) birth canal
   (2) uterus
   (3) ovary
   (4) placenta

8. Which is arranged in the correct sequence?

   (1) fertilization → embryo development → meiosis → birth

   (2) embryo development → meiosis → fertilization → birth

   (3) meiosis → fertilization → embryo development → birth

   (4) fertilization → meiosis → embryo development → birth

9. The diagram at the right represents a cell that will undergo mitosis.

   Which of the diagrams best illustrates the daughter cells that result from a normal mitotic cell division of the parent cell shown?

Part B

Base your answers to questions 10 through 14 on the following diagram of some events in the human female reproductive cycle and on your knowledge of biology.

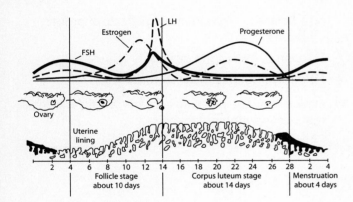

10. During which part of this cycle does the breakdown of the thickened uterine lining occur?

    (1) ovulation

    (2) corpus luteum stage

    (3) menstruation

    (4) follicle stage

11. On or about which day is the egg released from the ovary?

    (1) day 8

    (2) day 14

    (3) day 20

    (4) day 28

12. The hormone FSH stimulates the development of a follicle in the ovary of a human female. As the follicle develops, it secretes estrogen. A high level of estrogen decreases the secretion of FSH. This mechanism is an example of

    (1) gamete development

    (2) cell differentiation

    (3) positive feedback

    (4) negative feedback

13. Which hormones are secreted by the ovaries?

    (1) progesterone and estrogen

    (2) FSH and progesterone

    (3) FSH and LH

    (4) LH and estrogen

14. What is the average length of this reproductive cycle?

    (1) 32 days

    (2) 28 days

    (3) 14 days

    (4) 4 days

15. Compare the number of chromosomes present in the offspring with the number of chromosomes present in the parent organism in the process of cloning.

Base your answers to questions 16 through 19 on the following passage and on your knowledge of biology.

Some researchers state that the level of a particular hormone present in the bloodstream of a pregnant woman may be used to predict whether birth will occur prematurely, on time, or late. During a study involving 485 pregnant women, the level of corticotropin-releasing hormone (CRH) was measured during weeks 16 through 20 of the usual 40-week gestation (development) period. A comparison of these hormone levels to times of birth indicated that women who delivered prematurely (less than 37 weeks) had an average of 3.6 times more CRH than those who gave birth on time.

CRH, a hormone produced by a hormone-secreting section of the brain called the hypothalamus, aids in regulating the secretion of hormones produced by the adrenal glands. CRH is also secreted by the placenta. Secretion of CRH by the placenta usually begins early in the second trimester of pregnancy. The level continues to increase dramatically as the delivery date approaches. For most of the pregnancy, another protein molecule binds to CRH, blocking its action. Researchers suggest that when CRH levels rise high enough to counteract the blocking protein, labor begins.

The placenta has a regulatory role over activities in the body of the mother during pregnancy. Secretions of placental estrogen and progesterone begin after the first few weeks. From the third to the ninth month, the placenta supplies these hormones at levels necessary to maintain pregnancy. Progesterone inhibits the uterine contractions necessary for delivery. It has been suggested that cortisol, an adrenal hormone released by the fetus, overcomes the inhibiting effects of progesterone as the level of progesterone drops toward the end of gestation. Also, at this time, oxytocin, a hormone synthesized by the hypothalamus of the mother, is released, stimulating uterine contractions and the onset of labor.

Although it is still not known whether CRH determines the length of pregnancy, researchers expect that experiments to lower CRH levels to prevent premature labor are not far off.

16. According to the passage, which structures play a role in initiating the birth process at the end of the gestation period?
    (1) adrenal glands and ovaries
    (2) uterus and ovaries
    (3) hypothalamus and placenta
    (4) placenta and zygote

17. In humans, the length of the period of gestation is usually
    (1) 120 days
    (2) 140 days
    (3) 250 days
    (4) 280 days

18. According to the passage, the release of cortisol by the adrenal gland of the fetus causes
    (1) a decrease in CRH levels in the blood of the mother
    (2) a decrease in the inhibiting effects of progesterone
    (3) contractions of the ovaries
    (4) the secretion of progesterone

19. Explain how the placenta controls certain activities that occur during pregnancy.

Part C

20. Early in the 1960s, many pregnant women took the drug thalidomide. Women who took thalidomide during their first three months of pregnancy gave birth to babies with severe birth defects. The babies typically had deformities of their arms and legs. Women who took thalidomide later in their pregnancies gave birth to normal babies. Explain why the babies born to mothers taking thalidomide during their first few months of pregnancy suffered from birth defects while the others did not. [1]

21. Describe how the human fetus obtains food and oxygen during its development. In your explanation be sure to include

- a description of how the food and oxygen move from the mother to the fetus [1]

- an explanation of the role of the placenta in this process [1]

22. The production of a normal baby involes protecting the developing embryo from harmful environmental factors. State three ways in which the pregnant woman could avoid exposing the developing embryo to environmental risks. [3]

23. The following diagram shows some steps involved in preparing tissue cultures in plants.

Transfer to soil

Remove leaves, roots, and top third of plant

Wash, break, and sterilize stem pieces

Insert cork borer to remove pith

Place pith disks on growth medium

Cut pith transversely in sterile petri dish

Transfer to root initiation media

Compare the genetic makeup of the offspring plants that are transferred to the soil to that of the parent plant that provided the stem pieces.

24. The process of meiosis followed by fertilization is necessary to maintain the species chromosome number of a sexually reproducing species. For instance, a species with 24 chromosomes in each body cell normally has offspring that also have 24 chromosomes in their body cells. Explain the specific way that meiotic cell division and fertilization interact to help maintain the species chromosome number. [1]

Base your answers to questions 25 and 26 on the information in the following paragraph and on your knowledge of biology.

It is possible to collect human sperm and to use this sperm later to fertilize eggs in a process called artificial insemination. The collected sperm samples are frozen and stored in a sperm bank until needed. When a woman makes use of a sperm bank, she requests sperm from a donor with the physical features she wants. The name of the donor is not revealed. The artificial insemination process involves placing the sperm in the woman's body and allowing fertilization to occur in the normal manner.

25. A woman whose husband cannot produce sperm becomes pregnant through artificial insemination. How will the baby's DNA compare with the DNA of the woman and her husband? [2]

26. If the woman were given sperm from the same donor for three different pregnancies and she had three daughters, would the three girls look alike or would they be different? Support your answer with a biological explanation. [1]

Base your answers to questions 27–29 on the following paragraph and on your knowledge of biology.

In the United States, between 65% and 95% of pregnant women take over-the-counter (OTC) drugs. OTC drugs are available to anyone without a prescription. They include pain relievers, cough medicine, allergy medications, and laxatives. While both pregnant women and their physicians are extremely careful about taking prescription medications during pregnancy, the same caution does not seem to apply to OTC drugs.

Researchers fear that some disorders, especially of the nervous system, may result from using OTC drugs during pregnancy. Some damage may not become apparent until the affected children are 12 years old or older. As a result, it is often difficult to pinpoint the cause of the problem.

Imagine that you are an independent researcher studying whether or not OTC drugs taken by the mother during pregnancy affect the development and/or health of the child. As a part of your research, you will collect data through a mail survey.

27. List two things all of the people in your survey study group should have in common in order for you to obtain meaningful information. [2]

28. To get meaningful data for your research, what are two specific questions that you should ask the survey participants? Do not include anything you used in your answer to question 27. [2]

29. Twenty-five people respond to your survey. Some of those responses suggest problems that may be connected with OTC drugs. What would be the next step to take with your research project? Explain why this action would be appropriate. [2]

Evolution

VOCABULARY		
adaptive value	genetic variation	overproduction
evolution	geologic time	theory
extinction	mutation	
fossil record	natural selection	

Extensive evidence indicates that life on Earth began more than three billion years ago. Fossils found in ancient rocks have given us many clues to the kinds of life that existed long ago. The first living organisms were simple, single-celled organisms. Over time, more complex single-celled creatures developed. Then, about a billion years ago, increasingly complex, multicellular organisms began to appear. The idea that explains how this change in species has occurred over time is known as **evolution.**

The Theory of Evolution

The theory of evolution is accepted as the central theme of modern biology. It helps biologists understand how the variations among individuals can lead to changes in an entire species of organism. Since it was first suggested by Charles Darwin, the concept of evolution has been refined by massive amounts of evidence offered by thousands of scientists. So much evidence has been collected that evolution now has the stature of a **theory,** which is a concept that has been tested and confirmed in many different ways and can be used by scientists to make predictions about the natural world.

The theory of evolution helps biologists understand the similarities (such as bone structure and biochemistry) among different organisms. It also helps to explain the history of life that is revealed by the **fossil record,** which is a collection of fossils that provides clues to the history of Earth's organisms.

The fossil record spans much of **geologic time**—the billions of years of Earth's history—revealing many changes in environments as well as species. Figure 5-1 shows examples from the fossil record through geologic time.

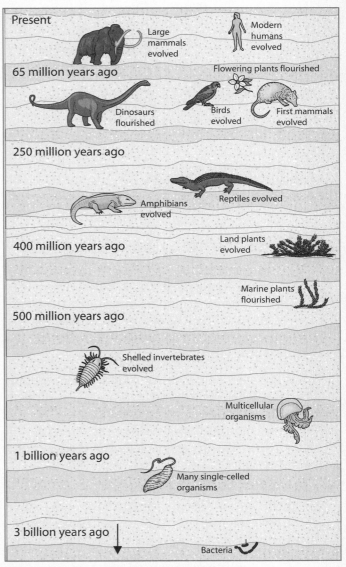

Figure 5-1. Examples from the fossil record

Evolution does NOT necessarily produce long-term progress in any set direction. Instead, evolutionary change appears to be more like the growth of a bush. Notice in Figure 5-2 that some branches survive from the beginning with little or no change. Some die out altogether. Others branch repeatedly, with each new branch representing a new species.

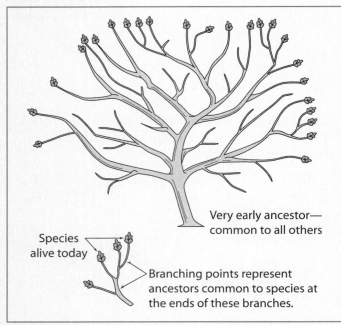

Species alive today

Very early ancestor—common to all others

Branching points represent ancestors common to species at the ends of these branches.

Figure 5-2. Evolution modeled as the growth of a bush: Evolutionary changes in species are like the growth of a bush in which some twigs grow and branch, while others die. The tips of the living twigs represent species that are alive now.

Review Questions

1. Evolution is the process of the (1) development of one-celled organisms from mammals (2) change in species over long periods of time (3) embryonic development of modern humans (4) changing energy flow in food webs

2. Which phrase best defines evolution? (1) an adaptation of an organism to its environment (2) a sudden replacement of one community by another (3) the isolation of organisms from each other for many years (4) a process of change in species over a period of time

3. Evolution is often represented as a branching tree similar to the one shown in the diagram at the top of the next column. The names shown represent different groups of organisms alive today; the lines represent their evolutionary histories.

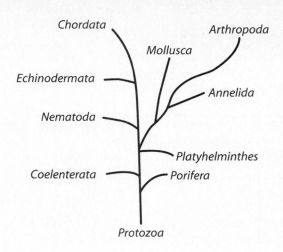

The statement that is best supported by the diagram is that (1) *Annelida* and *Arthropoda* have an ancestor in common (2) *Echinodermata* are more closely related to *Mollusca* than they are to *Chordata* (3) *Mollusca* and *Arthropoda* probably evolved before *Porifera* (4) *Annelida* and *Arthropoda* evolved from *Echinodermata*

4. The study of fossils has allowed scientists to (1) describe past environments and the history of life (2) study present ocean temperatures at different depths (3) analyze the chemical composition of sedimentary rocks and minerals (4) describe the details of the process by which life began on Earth

5. The following diagram represents possible lines of the evolution of primates.

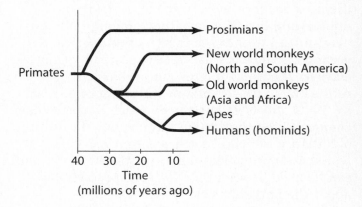

Which inference can best be made based on the diagram? (1) Adaptations for living in trees are inherited by all primates. (2) Humans and apes have a common ancestor. (3) The embryos of monkeys and apes are identical. (4) The period of development is similar in most primates.

The Mechanics of Evolution

Darwin did not only suggest that species evolved. He also suggested how that evolution might have occurred. Darwin thought that the mechanism of evolution was like the process of <u>artificial selection</u> practiced by breeders of plants and animals. (See Figure 5-3.) He used the term **natural selection** to indicate that the process of evolution was controlled by "nature" rather than by people. In the process of natural selection, individuals that survive are able to breed and pass their genetic information to the next generation. Those that are not as successful in the environment often die without leaving any offspring.

Figure 5-3. Racehorses are bred for speed and stamina: When humans breed plants or animals, they select specific traits, such as speed, flower color, or resistance to insects. In a similar way, "nature" selects any trait that increases an organism's ability to survive and reproduce.

Overview of Evolution

Darwin's ideas are easy to understand: In any environment, an individual may be born with a characteristic that makes it stronger, faster—any sort of advantage that will help it survive and reproduce. The individuals that prove to be the best adapted to their environment will be more likely to survive. If they do survive, their favorable characteristics will be passed on to many of their offspring. As a result, these useful adaptations, which first appeared randomly, are likely to become more and more common with each generation. Similarly, characteristics that reduce an individual's chance of surviving and reproducing will tend to decrease over time.

The long-term result of natural selection is a change in the frequency of certain traits in a population. Beneficial traits tend to become more common; harmful traits tend to become less common. As the frequency of a trait in a population increases or decreases over time, it can be said that the species is evolving. Note that the population—not the individual—changes as a result of evolution. An individual does not evolve; each is born with genetic information that may or may not help it survive and reproduce. As natural selection leads to changes in the composition of a population, that population may have more individuals with a certain favorable characteristic than it did earlier.

Interactions and Evolution

The driving force behind evolution is the interaction between individual organisms and their environment. Conditions that are vital to the process of evolution include

- the potential for a species to increase its numbers, known as **overproduction**
- the <u>finite</u> (limited) supply of resources needed for life
- the genetic variation of offspring due to mutation and genetic "shuffling"
- the selection by the environment of those offspring better able to survive and reproduce

All of these conditions, which are explained below, are involved in the process of evolutionary change.

OVERPRODUCTION In each generation, a species has the potential to produce more offspring than can possibly survive. Species with high reproductive potential include bacteria, insects, dandelions, and rabbits. (See Figure 5-4 on the next page.) If all the offspring of these organisms survived, they would overrun Earth. However, that does not happen. Scientists have learned that, in stable environments, the population of a species remains about the same from one year to the next. For example, no matter how many deer are born in one year, at the same time the next year, there will be about the same number of deer as there were the year before. Similarly, some fish species lay millions of eggs, but by the next year, the population of that species is the same as it was the previous year. This happens because not all of the new individuals that are born or hatched will survive to adulthood.

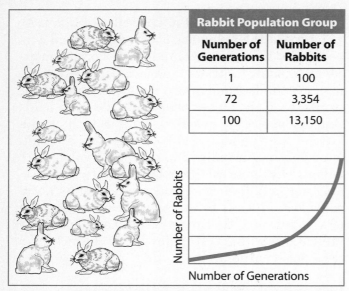

Rabbit Population Group	
Number of Generations	Number of Rabbits
1	100
72	3,354
100	13,150

Figure 5-4. Overproduction: Rabbits are known for their high reproductive potential.

THE STRUGGLE FOR SURVIVAL Overproduction leads to competition among the members of a species. Not all offspring survive long enough to reproduce. In many cases, chance determines which offspring survive. For example, wind may blow a dandelion seed to a patch of fertile soil or into a lake. A deer may be born in a wildlife preserve or in the path of a forest fire.

But chance is not the only factor that determines which offspring will survive and which will die. The offspring all have to cope with environmental conditions, such as temperature, disease, parasites, and predators. They also need resources, such as oxygen, water, food, and shelter. However, the supply of these resources is finite. If they are to survive, organisms of the same species must compete for limited resources. Depending on their success as competitors, individuals will get the resources they need to survive, or they will not. Those that are the best suited to their environment are more likely to survive. Many of the losers in this struggle for resources will die before they have a chance to reproduce.

VARIATION The new traits that can lead to evolution come from normal variation within species. As shown in Figure 5-5, organisms within a species are never exactly alike. For example, some adult grasshoppers have longer legs than others; some have a lighter body color. In any group of gray squirrels, some have sharper or longer claws, lighter or darker fur, bigger or smaller ears, and so on. The differences among offspring are due to **genetic variation**—the unique combination of traits each organism inherits from its parents.

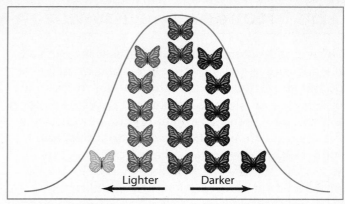

Figure 5-5. Genetic variation: In this example, a species of green butterflies might have individuals that vary in color from very dark green to very light green.

Some variations give individuals an advantage over others in their struggle for resources. Any trait that helps an organism survive and reproduce under a given set of environmental conditions is said to have **adaptive value.** For example, a rabbit's ability to blend in with its surroundings may allow it to escape capture by a fox. The coloration it inherited has adaptive value for the rabbit, allowing it to escape predators and survive. When the fox population is high, this adaptation may be especially valuable to rabbits that inherited it.

SELECTION BY THE ENVIRONMENT As Darwin proposed with his idea of natural selection, traits with an adaptive value in a specific environment give individuals in that environment a competitive advantage. If the beneficial trait is passed to the offspring, they, too, are more likely to survive and reproduce. The proportion of individuals with these advantageous characteristics will increase because they are better able to compete than individuals without the beneficial trait. Eventually, nearly all the individuals in the population will have the beneficial trait. This change in the characteristics present in population over time is evolution.

Although some evolution may occur without much change in the environment, it is usually the adaptation of a species to changes in its environment that brings about evolution. Therefore, a changing environment is often the driving force for evolutionary change.

Review Questions

6. The process of natural selection is based on the assumption that (1) environmental changes will cause changes in body structure in individuals (2) most changes from generation to generation are the result of mutations (3) part of the population of organisms always remains stable (4) different traits inherited by offspring have different survival value.

Base your answers to questions 7–8 on the following information and on your knowledge of biology.

A study of beetles on an isolated oceanic island formed by volcanic action and far from any other land shows that all of the beetles that are presently on the island are incapable of flying. A study of fossils from different rock layers of the island shows that the island was once populated with flying beetles. The graph shows the probable change over the last 5,000 years.

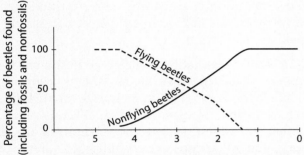

7. The loss of flying ability by the beetle is most probably the result of (1) predators eating the beetles' wings (2) beetles not using their wings (3) genetic changes in the beetles (4) lack of vegetation for the beetle to feed on

8. The graph indicates that the non-flying beetles probably (1) were better adapted to the environment (2) arrived from other islands 5000 years ago (3) mutated and produced flying beetles (4) became extinct about 1.5 thousand years ago

9. When lions prey on a herd of antelope, some of the antelope are eliminated. Which part of the theory of evolution can be used to describe this situation? (1) asexual reproduction of the fittest (2) isolation (3) survival of the best adapted (4) new species development due to mutation

10. Every spring, each mature female fish of a particular species produces several million eggs. However, the total population of this species remains at around 10,000 from one year to the next. State two reasons why the fish population remains approximately the same from one generation to the next.

Base your answers to questions 11–12 on the following diagram and on your knowledge of biology.

The diagram represents a small island divided by a mountain range. The mountain range prevents populations A and B from making contact with each other. At one time in the past, however, lowlands existed in the area indicated, and the ancestors of population A and population B were members of the same population.

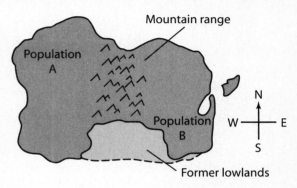

11. The organisms of population A and population B are now incapable of interbreeding and producing offspring. Which biological process most likely caused this situation to occur? (1) artificial selection (2) cloning (3) natural selection (4) asexual reproduction

12. Over many years, the climate on the west side of the island has undergone drastic changes while the climate on the east side has remained the same. It is most likely that population B will (1) migrate and intermix with population A (2) become extinct (3) have evolved more than population A (4) have evolved less than population A

Base your answers to questions 13–14 on the following information and graph and on your knowledge of biology.

Scientists studying a moth population in a wooded area of New York State recorded the distribution of moth wing color as shown in the following graph. While observing the moths, scientists noted that the moths spent most of the day resting on trees and looking for food during the night. The woods contained trees with a bark color that was predominantly brown.

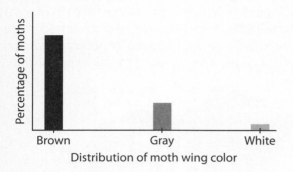

13. A fungus infection affected nearly all trees in the woods so that the color of the tree bark was changed to a gray-white color. Which graph shows the most probable results that would occur in the distribution of wing color in this moth population after a long period of time?

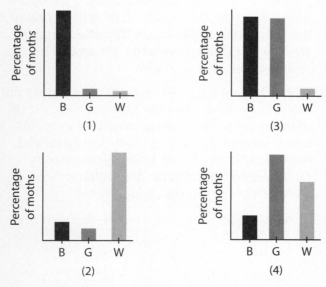

14. As a result of the fungus infection, the change in moth wing color distribution would most probably occur by the (1) production of sex cells by mitosis
(2) natural selection of favorable variations
(3) eating of pigments in fungus spores
(4) production of mutations as a result of eating the fungus

Sources of Variation

As you may recall from Topic 3, the arrangement of an individual's DNA bases determines all the inherited characteristics of that individual. Any change in bases or their sequence may bring about a change in the individual. But not all of those changes can be passed on to the individual's offspring. In sexually reproducing organisms, only changes in the genes of sex cells can be passed on to the next generation and become the basis for evolutionary change. Other types of variation (such as changes to body cells) die with the individual. For example, a father who has built huge muscles due to exercise does NOT pass those large muscles to his offspring.

There are two major ways an organism can wind up with genes that differ from those of its parents. Some genetic variations arise because of mutations in the genes of an organism. Others are due to "genetic shuffling," the routine sorting and recombination of genes that occurs during sexual reproduction.

MUTATION A **mutation** is a change in the base sequence of a DNA molecule. Mutations occur as random, chance events that cannot be predicted. Some mutations occur as errors in DNA as cells function, but radiation and some chemicals can also cause them. Mutations are an important source of totally new forms of genes.

When mutations occur in body cells, they affect only that individual. The mutation dies with the individual. However, a mutation in a single-celled organism or in the sex cells of a multicellular organism can be passed on to the offspring. In organisms that reproduce sexually, only mutations in the genes of sex cells can become the basis for evolutionary change.

Nearly all mutations are harmful and may affect the offspring so severely that it cannot survive. A few mutations benefit the individual, however, and can increase its chance of surviving, reproducing, and passing the mutation to the next generation. A beneficial mutation may lead to the evolution of a new species. For example, the ancestors of polar bears probably had dark fur. If a mutation resulted in a bear with white fur, that bear probably would have died young. However, if the mutation occurred in a snowy environment, the white fur would be a useful mutation, allowing the bear to stalk its prey more effectively.

GENETIC SHUFFLING The sorting and random recombining of genes during meiosis and fertilization results in new and different combinations of genes. These genes can be passed on to individual offspring. The process is similar to shuffling and dealing cards. The deck stays the same, but nearly every hand will be slightly different because of mixing and rearranging during shuffling. At fertilization, even more variety is introduced because now cards from "two decks" are combined. Although mutations provide new genetic instructions, genetic shuffling is the main source of the variation that exists among the members of any sexually reproducing species.

MEMORY JOGGER

Recall that at the beginning of meiotic cell division, the chromosomes line up and can exchange parts. What ends up in each gamete is the result of chance, just as any hand of cards dealt to you after shuffling is the result of chance. As a result of this shuffling, the gametes (sperm and egg) each contain a unique combination of genetic information. Since any sperm may combine with an egg, the number of possible combinations becomes enormous.

 Review Questions

15. Which statement is basic to the theory of evolution by natural selection? (1) In general, living organisms maintain a constant population from generation to generation. (2) Changes in living organisms are almost completely the result of mutations. (3) Natural variations are inherited. (4) There is little competition between species.

16. Which statement is NOT included as part of our modern understanding of evolution? (1) Sexual reproduction and mutations provide variation among offspring. (2) Traits are transmitted by genes and chromosomes. (3) More offspring are produced than can possibly survive. (4) New organs are formed when organisms need them.

17. The modern theory of evolution states that a basis for variation within a species is provided by (1) mutations (2) asexual reproduction (3) cloning (4) overproduction

18. Sexual reproduction is related to evolution because sexual reproduction (1) occurs only in more recently evolved forms of animal life (2) increases the chances of extinction of different species (3) increases the chances for variations to occur (4) is the more usual kind of reproduction

19. Genetic variations are the raw material of evolution. These variations will not be acted upon by natural selection unless they (1) produce unfavorable characteristics (2) produce favorable characteristics (3) are found in the fossil record (4) affect the organisms' appearance or functioning

20. Which of the following is produced by mutation and is essential for evolution to occur? (1) stability in the genetic code of organisms (2) additional DNA in an organism (3) a struggle for existence (4) variations in organisms

21. Which two factors provide the genetic basis for variation within many species? (1) asexual reproduction and meiosis (2) mutations and sexual reproduction (3) competition and the synthesis of proteins (4) ecological succession and mitosis

22. The sudden appearance of a light-colored moth in a large population of dark-colored moths was probably the result of (1) a mutation (2) random mating (3) non-random mating (4) isolation of the moth population

23. Mutations can be transmitted to the next generation if they are present in (1) hormones (2) gametes (3) body cells (4) muscle cells

The Results of Genetic Variation

The changes that result from mutation or genetic shuffling in the sex cells may affect the offspring in several ways. Most of the changes can be categorized as structural, functional, or behavioral.

STRUCTURAL CHANGE The structure of any organism is the result of its species' entire evolutionary history. There are millions of examples of variations that have resulted in structural changes. For example, the polar bear (like other bears) has thick fur that keeps it warm in its cold environment. Polar bears, however, have evolved an extra protection from the cold. The soles of their feet are also mostly covered with thick fur. This extra fur not only keeps their skin off the ice but also improves traction.

The theory of evolution has helped scientists explain many of the structural variations and similarities found in organisms. For example, in Figure 5-6, notice that each limb has one thick "long" bone, two thinner "long" bones, and a "hand" with five digits. The ancestor of these mammals most likely had a similar limb structure. At one point, however, limbs began to vary, evolving into arms, legs, wings, or flippers.

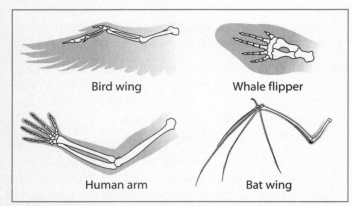

Figure 5-6. Similar bone structure of different species: The limbs shown above are from different species and have different functions, but they share many structural similarities. They are all made of the same type of bones and are attached in a similar way. The whale flipper is actually MUCH larger than the other limbs. Notice that the ulna and radius of the bat wing are almost fused.

Structures that are no longer used by modern organisms give scientists clues to the evolutionary history of a species. Some snakes, for example, have tiny, nonfunctional leg bones—an indication that they probably evolved from four-legged, lizardlike ancestors.

FUNCTIONAL CHANGE Molecular or biochemical changes affect how an organism works. These are functional changes. For example, all working muscles emit an extremely tiny electrical output. In some eels, however, that electrical output has evolved into an adaptation that helps it find and capture food. The muscles of these eels can produce a massive shock that stuns or kills its prey.

Changes in DNA often lead to functional changes. One example is a mutation in the DNA of certain one-celled organisms that led to their ability to make enzymes that digest wood. Another is the evolution of the ability of some snakes to make a poisonous venom.

BEHAVIORAL CHANGE Behaviors have also evolved through natural selection. Many of the specific behaviors we find in species today have become common because they resulted in greater reproductive success.

- Fighting among the males of a walrus population for a harem of females is one evolved behavior. Because of the fighting, the stronger, healthier male mates with the most females.

- The correct rate of "blinking" allows males and females of firefly species to find each other. A different pattern or rate of blinking would isolate the individual from potential mates.

The Importance of Variation

If environmental conditions change, organisms that have adapted to those conditions may die. If all the members of the species had exactly the same combination of characteristics, an environmental change could be disastrous, wiping out the entire species. The variation of organisms within a species increases the likelihood that at least some members of the species will survive in a changed environment. Once the diversity present in a species is lost, it is next to impossible to get it back. Today's endangered species have such small populations that biologists worry that they may not have the genetic diversity to adapt to even slight changes in their environment.

 **Review Questions**

24. The changes in the foot structure in a bird population over many generations are shown in the following diagram.

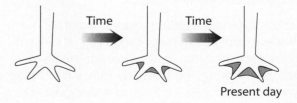

These changes can best be explained by the concept of (1) natural selection (2) extinction (3) stable gene frequencies (4) cloning

25. How might the lack of genetic diversity found in populations of endangered species hinder their recovery?

26. Possible explanations for the origin of differences in structure, function, and behavior among organisms are contained in the (1) modern cell membrane model (2) theory that genes are on chromosomes (3) model for DNA replication (4) modern theory of evolution

27. In most populations, the individuals that produce the greatest number of offspring are (1) always the strongest (2) usually the best adapted (3) those that have only inheritable traits (4) those that are the most intelligent

28. Even though the American toad and the Fowlers toad are often found living in the same habitat, they do not breed with each other. Which conclusion can best be drawn from this information? (1) The two types of toads do not interbreed because they are geographically isolated. (2) The two types of toads do not interbreed due to differences in mating behavior. (3) Adaptive mutations occurred more often during the evolution of the American toad. (4) Fowlers toad has a higher rate of survival than the American toad does.

29. The best scientific explanation for differences in structure, function, and behavior found in different species of organisms is provided by (1) carbohydrate electrophoresis (2) population chromatography (3) the theory of carrying capacity (4) the theory of evolution

30. Which of the following could be used as evidence to show that two different species of organisms most likely developed from a single, common ancestor? (1) They eat the same types of food. (2) They have different digestive enzymes (3) They lived during the same time period. (4) They contain similar amino acid sequences.

Patterns of Change

Evolution appears to follow certain patterns that appear repeatedly in the fossil record. For example:

- Changes in species are often related to environmental change.

- Species with short reproductive cycles that produce many offspring tend to evolve more quickly than species with long lifespans and few offspring.

- The failure to adapt to a changing environment may result in the death of the species.

The Rate of Evolution

Most of the diversity of life on Earth today is believed to be the result of natural selection occurring over a vast period of geologic time. The amount of change seems to be linked to changes in the environment. Minimal environmental change often results in stable populations. Rapid environmental change often leads to rapid changes in species. However, for any species, it may take millions of years to accumulate enough differences from its ancestors to be classified as a new or different species. As shown in Figure 5-7, some species have hardly changed in many millions of years. Others have changed so much that the relationships may not be obvious.

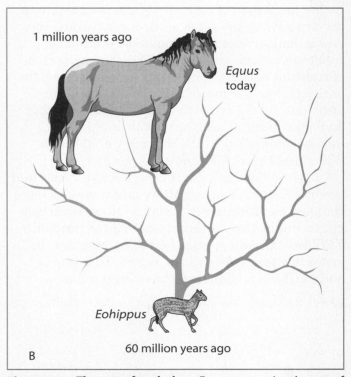

Figure 5-7. The rate of evolution: For some species, the rate of evolutionary change has been very slow. For example, the horseshoe crab (A) has shown little change from fossils of its ancestors that lived 300 million years ago. However, the horse (B) has evolved tremendously over the past 60 million years.

The rate of evolutionary change may also be influenced by the number of offspring produced by a species. Those that have few offspring and live a long time generally evolve quite slowly. Those that have brief lifespans and numerous offspring can change so quickly that evolution may occur in just a few years.

One example of rapid change involves the evolution of antibiotic resistance by pathogenic bacteria. When a population of millions of bacteria is exposed to an antibiotic, there is a chance that a few might have a gene that makes them resistant to the antibiotic. (This gene probably occurred as a chance mutation at some earlier time. It was most likely present in some of the bacteria before the antibiotic was used, and its appearance was totally unrelated to the presence of the antibiotic.) The antibiotic could kill almost all of the bacteria except for a few that escape exposure to the antibiotic. The ones with the resistance gene would also survive.

Because most of the competition is eliminated by the antibiotic, the few survivors, including the resistant ones, reproduce quickly, giving rise to a new population of the bacteria. In this new population, a higher proportion of individuals is now resistant to the drug. When the same antibiotic is used on the descendants of this new population, even more resistant bacteria will survive. Now the proportion of resistant bacteria is even higher. In this case, the antibiotic has become an agent of selection. The antibiotic did not cause the original mutation that made the bacteria resistant to the antibiotic. It merely determined which bacteria would live to reproduce. Figure 5-8 shows the process.

Insects also have short reproductive cycles and produce many offspring. Many insect species have changed significantly in response to pesticide use. For example, the widespread use of the pesticide DDT led to insect species becoming resistant in just a few years. As was the case with bacteria and antibiotics, there may have been a few DDT-resistant insects in the population before the chemical was ever used. They probably had a random mutation that had no adaptive value before the use of DDT. Once the DDT was sprayed, nearly all of the nonresistant insects were killed, leaving a high proportion of resistant insects to repopulate the area. Later, if DDT was sprayed again, it was less effective against the resistant offspring of the survivors of the earlier spraying.

As a result of these kinds of rapid evolutionary events, we are finding more and more bacteria that are resistant to antibiotics and more and more insect species that are resistant to our pesticides. This has created many problems in the fields of medicine and agriculture and will continue to be a problem in the future.

Extinction

Extinction is the disappearance of an entire species. Any time the death rate of individuals within a species is greater than the birth rate, extinction is a possibility. Generally, extinction occurs when the environment changes. Temperatures change; sea levels rise and fall. Grasslands become deserts; clear lakes become polluted. The variation of organisms within a species increases the likelihood that at least some members of the species will survive the changing environmental conditions. However, when the adaptive characteristics of a species are insufficient to allow its survival in a new environment, the species will become extinct.

The fossil record shows that throughout geologic time, millions of species have evolved, survived for a while, then failed to adapt successfully, and finally became extinct. It is a surprisingly common process. In fact, from the number of fossils of extinct organisms found, it is apparent that a majority of the species that ever lived on Earth is now extinct.

◖◀— Has genetic mutation making it resistant to antibiotic X   ◔◀— Has no genetic resistance to antibiotic X

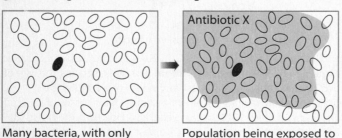

Many bacteria, with only one resistant to antibiotic X

Population being exposed to antibiotic X

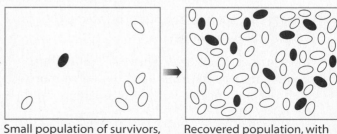

Small population of survivors, with one resistant

Recovered population, with many resistant bacteria

Figure 5-8. How resistance to antibiotics can develop

Review Questions

31. The shark has changed very little in the last 50 million years. Which statement best explains why this is the case? (1) The shark is well adapted to its relatively unchanged environment. (2) Sharks have a high reproductive rate and show little change in their genetic makeup from one generation to the next. (3) Sharks need to change only if humans are present in their environment. (4) Sharks have a high mutation and genetic recombination rate.

32. Many animals exist today in a form that is almost identical to the form they had a million years ago. What is the most probable explanation for this lack of evolutionary change? (1) Genetic mutations have occurred among these animals. (2) The environment of these animals remained about the same. (3) These animals reproduce by sexual reproduction. (4) Complex organisms evolved into simpler ones.

Base your answers to questions 33–34 on the following information and on your knowledge of biology.

Joshua Lederberg discovered that, in a large population of *Escherichia coli,* about 1 in 10 million of the offspring was naturally resistant to the antibiotic streptomycin. When these naturally resistant bacteria were isolated and grown separately, they soon formed a larger population. The entire population so formed was also naturally resistant to streptomycin.

33. The formation of the large streptomycin-resistant population is based on (1) variations and survival of the fittest (2) mutations and asexual reproduction (3) sexual reproduction and no mutations (4) survival of the fittest and cloning

34. According to modern evolutionary theory, the resistance to streptomycin probably resulted directly from (1) culturing the *Escherichia coli* (2) changes in temperature under which *Escherichia coli* are grown (3) a change in the DNA of *Escherichia coli* (4) the presence of streptomycin

35. A large population of cockroaches was sprayed with a newly developed, fast-acting insecticide. The appearance of some cockroaches that are resistant to this insecticide supports the concept that (1) species traits tend to remain constant (2) variation exists within a species (3) insecticides cause mutations (4) the environment does not change

36. Compounds like the pesticide DDT may bring about the evolution of new strains of organisms by (1) destroying food producers (2) acting as a natural selecting agent (3) mixing two different sets of genes (4) creating new ecological niches

37. A population of mosquitoes is sprayed with a new insecticide. Most of the mosquitoes are killed, but a few survive. In the next generation, the spraying continues, but still more mosquitoes hatch that are immune to the insecticide. How could these results be explained according to the present concept of evolution? (1) The insecticide caused a mutation in the mosquitoes. (2) The mosquitoes learned how to fight the insecticide. (3) A few mosquitoes in the first population were resistant and transmitted this resistance to their offspring. (4) The insecticide caused the mosquitoes to develop an immune response, which was inherited.

38. Throughout the history of Earth, which factor has probably been the chief cause of the extinction of various species? (1) people's interference with nature (2) failure to adapt to environmental changes (3) warfare within the species (4) volcanic eruptions

39. Fossil evidence indicates that many species have existed for relatively brief periods of time and have then become extinct. Which statement best explains the reason for their short existence? (1) These organisms lacked the energy to produce mutations. (2) Humans modify plant and animal species through the knowledge of genetics. (3) These organisms lacked variations having adaptive value. (4) Within these species, increasing complexity reduced their chances of survival.

Questions for Regents Practice

Part A

1. How does natural selection operate to cause change in a population?
   (1) The members of the population are equally able to survive environmental change.
   (2) The members of the population differ so that only some survive when the environment changes.
   (3) The members of the population cause environmental changes and adapt to them.
   (4) All the members of the population adapt to environmental changes.

2. Which mutation could be passed on to future generations?
   (1) a gene change in a liver cell
   (2) cancer caused by excessive exposure to the sun
   (3) a chromosomal alteration during gamete formation
   (4) random breakage of a chromosome in a leaf cell of a maple tree

3. A trait with low survival value to the members of a population will most likely
   (1) undergo a series of mutations in succeeding generations
   (2) cause the reproductive rate of the individual to increase
   (3) decrease in frequency from one generation to the next
   (4) remain unchanged in frequency through many generations

4. The process by which a species passes out of existence is known as
   (1) endangerment
   (2) deforestation
   (3) extinction
   (4) adaptation

5. A change in the genetic material that produces variation in a species may be the result of
   (1) the struggle for survival
   (2) the overproduction of a species
   (3) a mutation
   (4) competition

6. The diagram below illustrates the change that occurred in the frequency of body pattern traits shown by an insect population over ten generations.

First generation

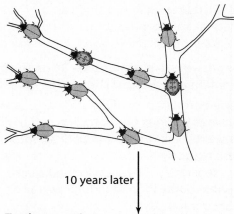

10 years later

Tenth generation

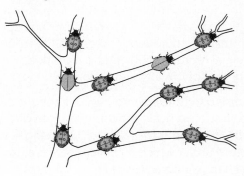

A probable explanation for this change would be that over time there was
   (1) a decrease in the adaptive value of the spotted trait
   (2) an increase in the adaptive value of the spotted trait
   (3) an increase in the population of the insect
   (4) a decrease in the mutation rate of the gene for body pattern

7. The fact that a healthy deer can outrun a timber wolf is an example of

(1) mutation

(2) isolation

(3) non-random mating

(4) natural selection

8. A maple tree releases hundreds of seeds in a single season. This is an example of

(1) a mutation

(2) isolation

(3) overproduction

(4) non-random mating

9. The DNA sequences found in two different species are 95% the same. This suggests that these species

(1) are evolving into the same species

(2) contain identical proteins

(3) may have similar evolutionary histories

(4) have the same number of mutations

Part B

Base your answers to questions 10 through 13 on the paragraph below.

Two different species of crickets inhabited a meadow. One species of cricket had a straw-colored body and made up 90% of the total cricket population. The other species of cricket had a dark red body and made up 10% of the population. This proportion between the species had been constant for many years. A new variety of grass with purple blades appeared in the meadow. The purple grass was better adapted to the meadow environment than the native green grass and replaced the green grass within a period of 50 years.

10. The appearance of the purple grass was most likely the result of

(1) asexual reproduction

(2) genetic engineering

(3) cloning

(4) mutation

11. What is the most likely reason for the large proportion of straw-colored crickets in the original population?

(1) The straw-colored crickets were larger and killed off most of the red crickets.

(2) Few natural enemies of the straw-colored crickets lived in the meadow.

(3) More straw-colored crickets than red were able to survive in the green grass.

(4) Red-colored crickets were not a part of the fossil record for the meadow.

12. Which graph most likely indicates the percentages of the straw-colored crickets (%S) over the 50-year period?

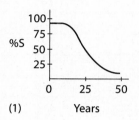

(1)

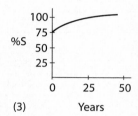

(3)

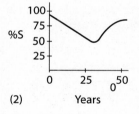

(2)

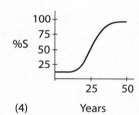

(4)

13. The evolutionary concept that would explain the changes taking place during the 50-year period in both the crickets and grasses is called

(1) common ancestry

(2) natural selection

(3) homeostatic balance

(4) selective breeding

Base your answers to questions 14 through 20 on the information below and on your knowledge of biology.

The bark of trees around Manchester, England, was mostly light in color before the Industrial Revolution. Light-colored peppered moths that rested on the trees were camouflaged from bird predators, while dark-colored peppered moths were easily preyed upon. After a few years of industrialization, the tree bark became darkened from pollution. The table below represents a change in the number of light- and dark-colored moths within the peppered moth population over a period of six years from the beginning of industrialization.

End of Year	Number of Light Moths	Number of Dark Moths
1	556	64
2	237	112
3	484	198
4	392	210
5	246	281
6	225	357

Using the information in the data table, construct a line graph on the grid provided. Follow the instructions below.

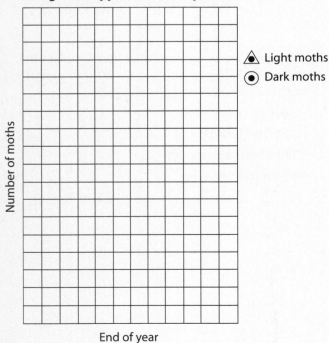

Changes in Peppered Moth Population

△ Light moths
◉ Dark moths

Number of moths

End of year

14. Mark an appropriate scale on the axis labeled End of year.

15. Mark an appropriate scale on the axis labeled Number of moths.

16. Plot the data for the number of dark moths on the grid. Surround each point with a small circle and connect the points.

Example: ◉—◉—◉

17. Plot the data for the number of light moths on the grid. Surround each point with a small triangle and connect the points.

Example: △—△—△

18. At the end of which year of study was the number of dark-colored moths closest to the number of light-colored moths?

(1) 1   (3) 5
(2) 2   (4) 6

19. An aspect of the evolutionary process that is suggested by the information provided is that

(1) the light-colored moths will eventually increase in number

(2) the darker moths appeared when the tree trunks became lighter

(3) the changing environment caused a darkening of the pigments of the moths

(4) the darker moths increased in number when the environment became more favorable for their traits

20. The biological concept that is most closely associated with the changes in the peppered moth population in England is known as

(1) natural selection

(2) positive feedback

(3) asexual reproduction

(4) homeostatic control

Part C

21. Genetic variation is the raw material of evolution. State two different sources of genetic variation in a plant or animal population. [2]

Base your answers to questions 22 through 24 on the information below and on your knowledge of biology.

Humans have modified some animal species by breeding only those that possess certain desirable traits. As a result, we have racehorses and greyhounds that are faster than their ancestors.

In a similar way, many animals have been modified naturally. The giraffe has long forelegs and a long neck, head, and tongue, which make it well adapted for browsing (feeding) in the higher branches of trees. Therefore, the giraffe can obtain food that is beyond the reach of other animals, especially during droughts. Ancient populations of giraffes varied in the relative lengths of their body parts. Those giraffes that were able to browse the highest were more likely to survive. They mated, and their offspring often inherited the structural characteristics suitable for high browsing. The giraffes that could not reach the food supply most likely died of starvation and therefore did not produce as many offspring as those that could reach higher.

22. Describe how the type of selection for traits in animals such as greyhounds and racehorses is different from the type of selection for traits that is occurring in animals such as giraffes. [1]

23. Describe two specific events of sexual reproduction that can be the source of the variations selected for in both giraffes and racehorses. [2]

24. Variation, a struggle for existence, and the survival of the fittest are all important to the evolution of species. Provide an example of each of these from the passage above. Record your information in the form of a chart that has two columns and four rows. The top row should include a heading for each column. [4]

Base your answers to questions 25 through 27 on the reading passage below.

Evolution is the process of change in species through time. Theories of evolution attempt to explain the diversification of species existing today. The essentials of Darwin's theory of natural selection serve as a basis for our present understanding of the evolution of species. Recently, some scientists have suggested two possible explanations for the time frame in which the evolution of species occurs.

Gradualism proposes that evolutionary change is continuous and slow, occurring over many millions of years. New species evolve through the accumulation of many small changes. Gradualism is supported in the fossil record by the presence of transitional forms in some of the evolutionary pathways.

Punctuated equilibrium is another possible explanation for the diversity of species. This explanation proposes that species exist unchanged for long geological periods of stability, typically several million years. Then, during geologically brief periods of time, significant changes occur and new species may evolve. Some scientists use the apparent lack of intermediate forms in the fossil record in many evolutionary pathways to support punctuated equilibrium.

25. Identify one major difference between gradualism and punctuated equilibrium. [1]

26. According to the concept of gradualism, what may result from the accumulation of small variations? [1]

27. What fossil evidence indicates that evolutionary change may have occurred within a time frame known as gradualism? [1]

Base your answers to questions 28 and 29 on the information below and on your knowledge of biology.

Scientists have observed thousands of female leatherback turtles during egg laying. Every female leatherback exhibits the same remarkable behavior. When she first comes up on the beach to lay her eggs, she digs a deep hole, lays her eggs in the hole, and then covers the eggs with sand. She then travels about 100 meters away from the first hole and digs another. She doesn't lay any eggs in this hole, but goes through the same process of covering the hole just as if there had been eggs present.

28. Write a hypothesis to explain why the female leatherback digs two holes. [1]

29. In the past, some leatherbacks may have only dug one hole and laid their eggs in it. In terms of evolution, how can this modern behavior be explained? [1]

Base your answers to questions 30 and 31 on the information below and on your knowledge of biology.

Cockroaches that are resistant to many common household insecticides are more numerous than those that are killed by these same insecticides. Scientists explain the increased numbers of insecticide-resistant cockroaches with the following statement: Variations that have a high survival value tend to be passed on to the next generation of organisms in greater number than those variations that have low survival value.

30. Identify the variation that is present in the cockroach population and describe how this variation most likely came about. [2]

31. Explain how the use of insecticides is associated with the fact that the resistant cockroaches outnumber the nonresistant cockroaches. [1]

Base your answer to questions 32 through 34 on the paragraph below and on your knowledge of biology.

A scientist discovered that in a large population of *E. coli* bacteria, a few were resistant to the antibiotic streptomycin. By adding streptomycin to the population, she soon obtained a large population that was resistant to streptomycin.

32. Explain how this experiment supports the concept of evolution by natural selection. Your explanation should include the concepts of
- selective agent [1]
- resistance [1]
- reproduction [1]
- offspring [1]

33. Identify the chemical substance in the bacteria that provides the resistance to streptomycin and makes this resistance inheritable. [1]

34. The evolutionary changes described here occurred in a relatively short period of time rather than requiring millions of years. State one reason why it is possible for *E. coli* to evolve so rapidly. [1]

Base your answers to questions 35 and 36 on the information below and on your knowledge of biology.

Over a period of 28 million years, various genera (related groups) of hoofed mammals called *Titanotheres* showed a continuous change in body and horn size before they eventually became extinct.

35. Provide a description of how gradual changes in the environment might have resulted in the changes observed in *Titanotheres*. [2]

36. Explain how environmental changes could have led to the extinction of *Titanotheres*. [1]

Ecology

VOCABULARY

abiotic	decomposer	herbivore
autotroph	ecology	heterotroph
biodiversity	ecological niche	host
biosphere	ecological succession	limiting factors
biotic	ecosystem	parasite
carnivore	energy pyramid	population
carrying capacity	environment	predator
community	food chain	prey
competition	food web	producer
consumer	habitat	scavenger

Our Earth is home to trillions of different organisms. None of these organisms can survive alone. All organisms—including humans—must interact with both the living and nonliving things that surround them. **Ecology** is the study of how organisms interact with the living and nonliving things that surround them.

Organisms and Their Environment

As you read this book, you are surrounded by your environment, which includes this book and perhaps your chair, light streaming through the window, a dog barking outside, and a pretzel on the table. If you're in class, your environment may include other students squirming nearby, your teacher pacing the aisles, the drone of an airplane, the smell of the lunchroom, and the unseen mite picking skin flakes off your arm. In short, the **environment** is every living and nonliving thing that surrounds an organism.

Parts of an Ecosystem

Ecosystem is a short way of saying "ecological system." Scientists use the term to describe any portion of the environment. An ecosystem is made up of all the living things, such as bacteria, plants, and animals, that interact with one another. These interacting living things are termed **biotic** factors. When scientists study ecosystems, they also study the nonliving things, such as soil, water, physical space, and energy, that influence the organisms. Nonliving influences are termed **abiotic** factors.

A decaying log, a pond, a field of corn, and even a fish tank are ecosystems. In each of these ecosystems, organisms interact with both the biotic and abiotic parts of their environment. For example, frogs in a pond ecosystem may interact with insects, fish, hawks, and children chasing them with nets. They are also affected by abiotic factors, such as rainfall, the acidity of their pond, temperature, and the amount of light. Some biotic and abiotic parts of an ecosystem are shown in Figure 6-1 on page 88.

Environment

Biotic Factors

Abiotic Factors

Figure 6-1. Parts of an ecosystem: The biotic part of the ecosystem includes all the living things that make up the community.

Because the world contains a wide variety of physical conditions, many different kinds of environments are available to organisms. Some are shown in Figure 6-2 on page 89. Most species, however, have a specific environment that is their "home." That specific environment is known as the species' **habitat.** Familiar habitats include fields, forests, oceans, streams, and deserts.

All the organisms of a species that live in the same area make up a **population.** Ants in a single anthill would be one population. All the different populations are combined to form a **community.**

Collectively, all of Earth's ecosystems make up the **biosphere**—the biologically inhabited portions of the planet. Earth's biosphere extends from the deepest ocean troughs to high above the surface of the planet. It includes all the water, land, and air in which organisms thrive. Throughout the biosphere, organisms interact and compete for vital resources, such as food, space, and shelter.

The fundamental concept of ecology is that all living organisms are interdependent, and they interact with one another and with the physical environment. These interactions result in a flow of energy and a cycling of materials essential for life.

Figure 6-2. Some ecosystems in Earth's biosphere: In each ecosystem, the organisms interact with one another and with their environment. The degree to which each abiotic factor is present determines the type of organisms that can live there.

Environmental Limits on Population Size

In any ecosystem, the growth and survival of organisms depends on the physical conditions and on the resources available to the organism. If they had unlimited resources, living things could produce populations of <u>infinite</u> (unlimited) size. Within any ecosystem, however, resources, such as oxygen and carbon dioxide, water, nutrients, space, and sunlight, are <u>finite</u> (limited). This has a profound effect on the interactions among organisms: Because the resources are finite, organisms must compete with one another to survive.

Competition is the struggle for resources among organisms. Within any one species, competition keeps the size of that species' population in check. In established ecosystems, populations tend to increase or decrease depending on the resources that are available at the time. This variation in population size tends to follow a predictable cycle. Many populations, for example, vary with the seasons. Over time, however, the size of the population remains stable.

Factors in the environment that limit the size of populations are known as **limiting factors.** Some

limiting factors are abiotic; others are biotic. For example, abiotic factors, such as the amount of dissolved oxygen in a pond, may limit the kinds and numbers of fish that can live there; the amount of sunlight filtering through a forest may limit the number of green plants living on the forest floor. Some other specific limiting factors include the intensity of light, the temperature range in the environment, minerals that are available in the water or soil, the type of rock or soil in the ecosystem, and the relative acidity (measured according to the pH scale).

An important biotic factor that limits population sizes is the relationship between **predators,** which kill and eat other organisms, and **prey,** which are killed for food. As predators kill and eat their prey, they limit the growth of the prey population. If too many prey animals are killed, predators begin to starve, and their population is reduced. With fewer predators, the size of the prey population begins to recover.

The number of organisms of any single species that an ecosystem can support is referred to as its **carrying capacity.** It is determined not only by the available energy, water, oxygen, and minerals (and the recycling of such minerals), but also by the interactions of its organisms. For example, a field's carrying capacity for a population of foxes is affected not only by the climate, but also by the number and kinds of other populations present. If there are many mice for the foxes to eat, the fox population may boom. If there are many viruses affecting the health of the foxes, their population may crash. Figure 6-3 shows the population increase that normally occurs until the carrying capacity is reached.

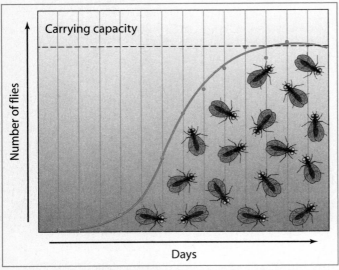

Figure 6-3. **Carrying capacity:** This population of insects increased until it neared its carrying capacity. Then the population became approximately stable.

 Review Questions

1. All of the Earth's water, land, and atmosphere within which life exists is known as (1) a population (2) an ecosystem (3) the biosphere (4) a biotic community

2. In the biosphere, what are some of the major abiotic factors that determine the distribution and types of plant communities? (1) temperature, sunlight, and rainfall (2) humidity, location, and humans (3) soil type, soil bacteria, and soil water (4) insects, carbon dioxide, and nitrogen in the air

3. The fact that an organism cannot live without interacting with its surroundings is a basic concept in the field of study known as (1) ecology (2) evolution (3) behavior (4) technology

4. When two different species live in the same area and use the same limited resources, which of the following will occur? (1) competition (2) succession (3) parasitism (4) industrialization

5. This graph shows the changes in two populations of herbivores in a grassy field.

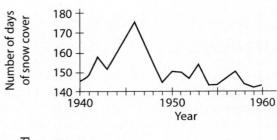

A possible reason for these changes is that (1) all of the plant populations in this habitat decreased (2) population B competed more successfully for food than population A did (3) population A produced more offspring than population B did (4) population A consumed members of population B

Base your answers to questions 6–7 on the two graphs shown and on your knowledge of biology. The first graph shows the number of days of snow cover from 1940–1960. The second graph shows the percentage of white mice in a population that was sampled during the same period.

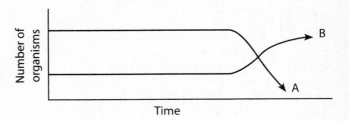

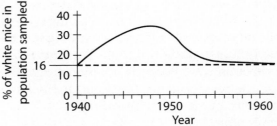

6. The appearance of the greatest percentage of white mice occurred (1) before the maximum number of days of snow cover (2) at the same time as the maximum number of days of snow cover (3) after the maximum number of days of snow cover (4) both before and after the maximum number of days of snow cover

7. Which statement is supported by the data in the graphs? (1) The percentage of brown mice was greatest during the years of longest snow cover. (2) The percentage of mice with white fur was greatest during the years of longest snow cover. (3) The actual number of white mice was greatest during the years of least snow cover. (4) The actual number of brown mice was greatest during the years of longest snow cover.

8. Which term includes all of the interactions that occur between the organisms and the physical factors in a pond environment? (1) population (2) ecosystem (3) abiotic (4) competition

9. The amount of salt in the air and water of coastal areas determines which species can exist there. In these areas, salt functions as a (1) source of energy (2) biotic factor (3) food source (4) limiting factor

Population Interactions

There is a wide diversity of interacting species in most ecosystems. Most of the interactions occur as organisms obtain their food. Every population is linked, directly or indirectly, with all of the other populations in the ecosystem. Each population has one or more specific roles in the ecosystem. As a result, maintaining the ecosystem's diversity is essential to its stability.

Roles in the Ecosystem

The role that each species plays in the ecosystem is called its **ecological niche.** Only one species at a time can occupy a particular niche. If two species attempt to fill the same role in an ecosystem, competition results. Usually, one species will be more suited to the niche, which forces the other species to move on or face elimination. Eventually, only one species will occupy each niche.

Sometimes it appears as if different populations occupy the same niche. For example, deer and moose often live in the same area and seem to eat the same plants. A closer examination reveals that the deer and moose have different food preferences and only compete when food is very scarce. Similarly, several bird species may seem to nest and feed in the same tree. In reality, it is more probable that the birds are nesting in different parts of the tree and eating different insects. For example, the northeastern United States is home to several species of warblers. Five of those species feed on the insects that live in spruce trees. As shown in Figure 6-4, each species feeds in a different part of the tree.

Competition for a particular ecological niche often occurs when a foreign species enters an area. The new species may be more successful than the native species, partly because the newcomer may not have any natural enemies to control its population. Humans frequently bring foreign species into an area either on purpose or accidentally. One example is the zebra mussels that were brought to the Great Lakes on cargo ships. The zebra mussel has become a major problem in New York waterways.

Figure 6-4. Feeding patterns among warblers: Several warbler species feed in spruce trees, but they actually occupy different niches because each species feeds in a different part of the spruce tree.

Relationships in an Ecosystem

In every ecosystem, populations of different species are linked together in a complex web of interactions. Sometimes these relationships are competitive; occasionally they are cooperative. For example, termites have one-celled organisms in their intestinal tracts. These unicellular organisms help the termites digest their food. The tiny organisms gain a place to live and plenty of food, and the termites can make use of a food supply that they would not be able to digest without this cooperative relationship.

Other relationships benefit one organism and have no effect on the other. For example, when a shark attacks and eats its prey, small pieces of the food drift downward. Smaller fish swimming below the shark feed on these scraps. The small fish benefit, but the shark is unaffected.

FOOD CHAINS Among the most common relationships in any ecosystem are the predator-prey relationships. **Food chains,** such as those shown in Figure 6.5, illustrate the relationships between prey and predator. In simple terms, the food chain shows what eats what.

Organism's niches are defined by how they obtain their food. For example, photosynthetic organisms make their own food and in the process, store the sun's energy. They are known as **autotrophs** (self-feeders) or **producers.** They provide a source of food energy for almost all other living things.

Heterotrophs must acquire food by consuming other organisms. **Herbivores** are heterotrophs that survive on plant tissues; **carnivores** are heterotrophs that eat other animals. Heterotrophs are also known as **consumers.** The wastes and dead

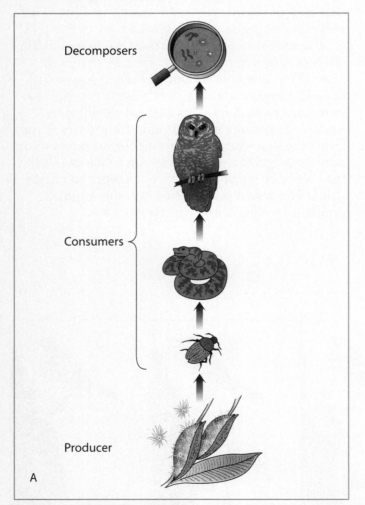

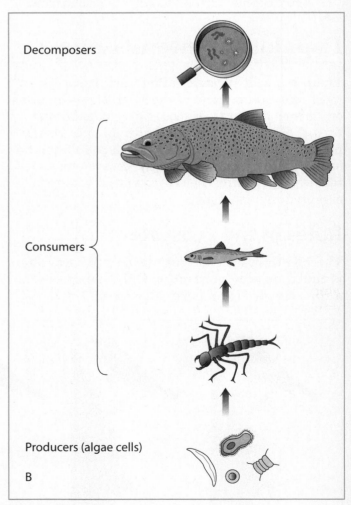

Figure 6-5. **Typical food chains:** A field ecosystem (A) and a pond ecosystem (B)

bodies of all these organisms are consumed by the **decomposers.** The decomposers recycle materials that can then be reused by producers.

Two other feeding relationships between organisms do not fit into the typical predator-prey categories. These organisms are similar to predators in that they feed on other organisms, but different in that they do not kill the organisms for food. **Scavengers,** such as vultures, are consumers that eat dead organisms. They are nature's "clean-up crew." Scavengers, however, are not decomposers. Dead bodies and wastes still have to be broken down by decomposers. **Parasites** are organisms that attack other live organisms (called **host** organisms), but rarely kill them. Parasites usually live on or in the body of their host. Ticks, for example, may live on a dog and also feed on its blood.

Notice in Figure 6-5 that all food chains begin with autotrophs—the photosynthetic producers—and end with decomposers. The intermediate heterotrophs (the herbivores and carnivores that rely on others for food) are often, but not always, part of food chains. A food chain may be as simple as: grass → decay bacteria.

Decomposers may be included at the end of a food chain, but it is important to remember that they actually consume and break down the chemical materials in all dead organisms and in the wastes of all living organisms.

FOOD WEBS Normally, each organism feeds on more than one kind of organism. Because organisms normally have more than one food source, food chain diagrams are oversimplified. **Food webs,** as shown in Figure 6-6, are diagrams that show the more complex feeding relationships among producers, consumers, and decomposers. The food web shows the many interconnected food chains that exist in the ecosystem. Because organisms have several food choices, ecosystems often remain stable even when one population shows a major decline in numbers. The organisms that feed on the declining population simply rely more heavily on one of their other food choices until the declining population recovers.

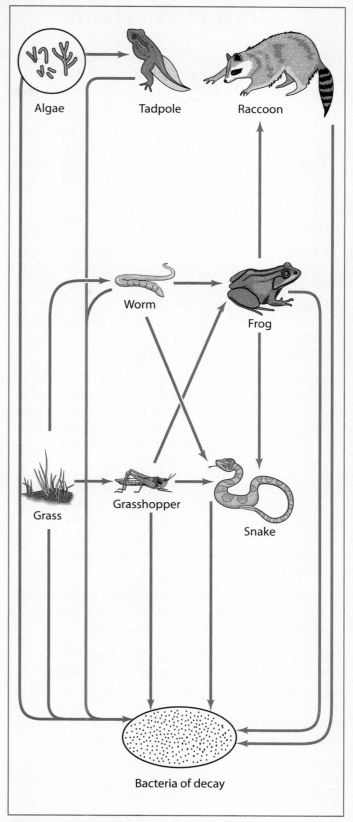

Figure 6-6. A simplified food web near a pond

Review Questions

10. The following diagram illustrates the feeding areas of two populations in the same ecosystem during the summer and fall. Both populations feed on oak trees.

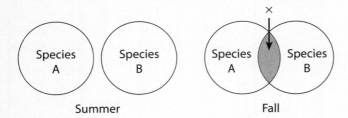

The portion of the diagram labeled X most likely indicates that (1) these populations compete for food in the fall, but not in the summer (2) the species are separated by a geographic barrier in the summer (3) the supply of oxygen is greater in the summer than in the fall (4) mating occurs between the species in the fall, but not in the summer

11. An earthworm lives and reproduces in the soil. Through its feeding, excretion, and tunneling activities, the worm adds nutrients and allows air to enter the soil. Together, these statements describe the earthworm's (1) habitat (2) nutrition (3) niche (4) environment

12. Among the populations of any natural community, the basic food supply is always a critical factor because it is (1) produced by all organisms of the community (2) synthesized from oxygen (3) a means of transferring energy (4) present in surplus amounts

13. A consumer–producer relationship is best illustrated by (1) foxes eating mice (2) leaves growing on trees (3) rabbits eating clover (4) fleas living on a cat

Base your answers to questions 14–16 on the following food chain and on your knowledge of biology.

rosebush→aphid→beetle→spider→toad→snake

14. Which organism in this food chain can transform light energy into chemical bond energy?

15. At which stage in this food chain will the population with the smallest number of organisms probably be found? (1) spider (2) aphid (3) rosebush (4) snake

16. If all of the aphids were killed off due to the spraying of pesticides, what would happen to the number of toads this ecosystem could support?

17. Which group of organisms is NOT represented in the following food web diagram?

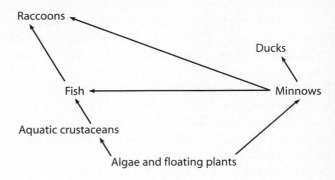

(1) consumers (2) carnivores (3) producers (4) decomposers

18. Which organisms are chiefly responsible for the recycling of dead matter? (1) parasites (2) viruses (3) decomposers (4) producers

19. In a natural community in New York State, the producer organisms might include (1) bacteria, fungi, and viruses (2) deer, rabbits, and squirrels (3) grasses, maple trees, and weeds (4) trout, peas, and earthworms

20. Which sequence illustrates a generalized food chain in a natural community?
(1) autotroph → herbivore → carnivore
(2) autotroph → herbivore → autotroph
(3) heterotroph → herbivore → carnivore
(4) consumer → autotroph → carnivore

21. In a food chain consisting of photosynthetic organisms, herbivores, carnivores, and organisms of decay, the principal function of the photosynthetic organisms is to (1) capture energy from the environment (2) provide material for decay (3) prevent erosion of the topsoil (4) release energy from organic compounds

22. A characteristic shared by both predators and parasites is that they (1) feed on decomposing plant material (2) capture and kill animals for food (3) live inside their hosts (4) attack a living food source

23. As you drive down the highway, you may see crows feeding on dead animals. As a result of this nutritional pattern, crows may be classified as (1) scavengers (2) predators (3) herbivores (4) producers

24. In the following diagram of a food chain, what do the arrows indicate?

(1) the direction in which organisms move in the environment (2) the direction of energy flow through a series of organisms (3) the order of importance of the various organisms (4) the return of chemical substances to the environment

25. When the food relationships in a habitat are illustrated by means of a diagram, the result is always a complicated weblike pattern. This is due to the fact that (1) many consumers are adapted to use more than one food source (2) producer organisms always outnumber the consumer organisms (3) matter is lost in an ecosystem as it moves from producers to consumers (4) both producers and consumers require oxygen for metabolic processes

26. Although three different butterfly species all inhabit the same flower garden in an area, competition between the butterflies rarely occurs. The most likely explanation for this lack of competition is that the butterflies (1) occupy different niches (2) have a limited supply of food (3) share food with each other (4) are able to interbreed

27. In the diagram below, which organisms are components of the same food chain?
(1) trees, mountain lion, snake, and hawk (2) trees, rabbit, deer, and shrubs (3) grasses, cricket, frog, and mouse (4) grasses, mouse, snake, and hawk

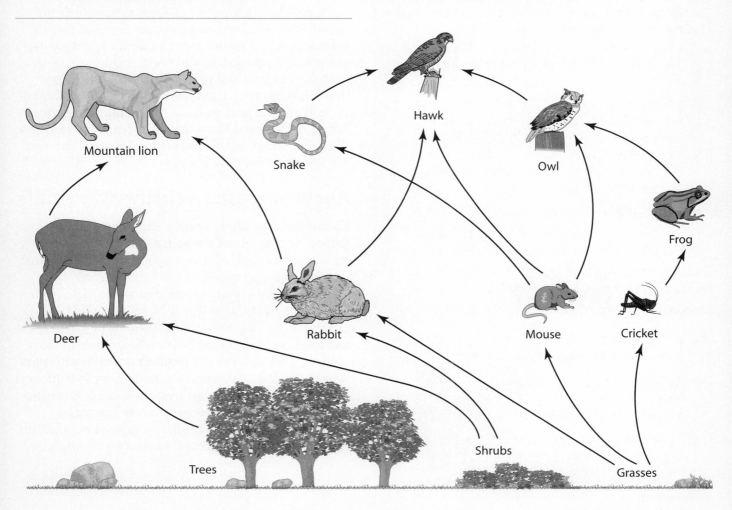

Energy Flow Through an Ecosystem

Almost all organisms use the solar energy stored in food to power their life processes. That energy, however, does not remain in the organism forever. Every second of every day, an animal that is not eating has less energy in its tissues than it had a few seconds before. This energy loss occurs because the organism is continually breaking the chemical bonds in food to use the energy to live. As it is released to make ATP and then used in the cells, much of the energy is converted to heat and is lost to the environment. Only a small amount can actually be used by the cells. As a result, each next step in the food chain has less of the original solar energy available to it.

Figure 6-7 shows how the energy is lost. Only the energy stored in the body tissues of each organism is passed to the next consumer in the chain. Because of the energy loss described above, most of the original stored energy is lost in just a few steps of the food chain. For this reason, food chains are usually quite short.

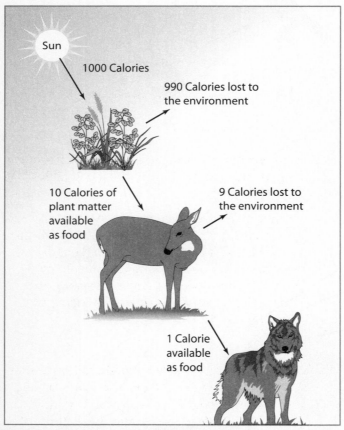

Figure 6-7. As energy is transferred, much of it is lost to the environment.

An **energy pyramid,** shown in Figure 6-8, is a diagram that illustrates the transfer of energy through a food chain or web. Each block of the energy pyramid represents the amount of energy that was obtained from the organisms below it. Only this amount of energy is available to the organisms in the next higher block. Notice that each level is smaller due to the loss of heat as the organisms carry on their life activities.

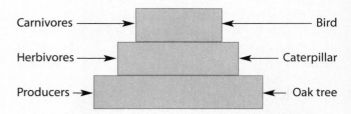

Figure 6-8. An energy pyramid: Each block in the energy pyramid illustrates the amount of energy available for use by organisms at the next level above it. (Energy for decomposers actually comes from organisms at all the levels, so they are not shown in this simplified pyramid.)

A continual input of energy, typically from the sun, is required to start the process and to keep it going. Producer organisms capture this energy and store it in the chemical bonds of the food molecules they make. The flow of energy that accompanies the transfer of the food shown in food chains and webs is essential to life on Earth. In spite of this constant drain of energy to the environment, life continues because the sun continues to provide energy.

Recycling and Reusing Materials

The parts of dead organisms that are not consumed during one of the other steps in the food chain are not wasted. Decomposers extract the last bit of energy contained in the dead organisms (as well as the energy in the waste products from living organisms) and use it to sustain their life processes. As they do so, they return the raw materials contained in the once-living matter to the soil. This process of breaking down dead organisms, as well as the wastes produced by living organisms, into their raw materials and returning those materials to the ecosystem is known as decomposition. Two examples of organisms that fill the role of decomposers are bacteria and fungi.

Because of the actions of decomposers, the atoms and molecules in living things cycle through both the nonliving and living parts of the biosphere. As they do, chemical elements, such as carbon, hydrogen, oxygen, and nitrogen, that make up the bodies of living things pass through food webs and are combined and recombined in different ways in different living organisms. For example, plants trap carbon dioxide and water molecules in energy-rich compounds (such as glucose and starch) during photosynthesis. When plants need energy to power their cell processes or are eaten by a consumer, these molecules may be broken down and used by the organism. During respiration, the molecules are released by the cells and returned to the environment.

Much of the cycling of materials in ecosystems is carried out by decomposers. Figure 6-9 shows some of the ways matter cycles throughout the ecosystem.

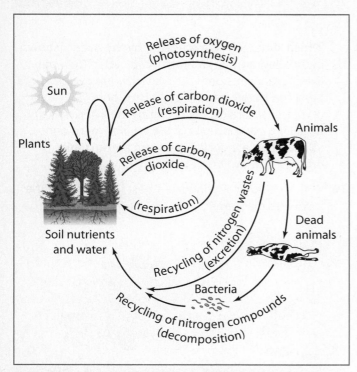

Figure 6-9. The recycling of materials in ecosystems: Dead organisms and wastes must be recycled in ecosystems so that their raw materials can be made available for re-use by producer organisms. The gas exchanges of photosynthesis and respiration, along with the action of decomposers, are crucial to the recycling process.

28. Decomposition and decay of organic matter are accomplished by the action of (1) green plants (2) bacteria and fungi (3) viruses and algae (4) scavengers

29. Which statement best describes energy transfer in a food web? (1) Energy is transferred to consumers, which convert it to nitrogen and use it to make amino acids. (2) Energy from producers is converted into oxygen and transferred to consumers. (3) Energy from the sun is stored in green plants and transferred to consumers. (4) Energy is transferred to consumers, which use it to produce food.

30. Organisms that eat goats obtain less energy from the goats than the goats obtain from the plants they eat. This is because the goats (1) pass on most of the energy to their offspring (2) convert solar energy to food energy (3) store all of their energy in milk (4) use energy for their own metabolism

Base your answers to questions 31–32 on the following energy pyramid and on your knowledge of biology.

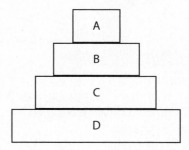

31. If birds eat insects that feed on corn, which level on this pyramid would birds occupy? (1) A (2) B (3) C (4) D

32. Which statement concerning the energy in the pyramid is correct? (1) The producer organisms contain the least amount of energy. (2) Stored energy decreases as it is passed from consumer to consumer. (3) Consumers contain more energy than producers. (4) Decomposers are the source of energy for this pyramid.

33. Most green algae are able to obtain carbon dioxide from the environment and use it to synthesize organic compounds. This activity is an example of (1) cellular respiration (2) autotrophic nutrition (3) heterotrophic nutrition (4) heterotrophic respiration

Base your answers to questions 34–37 on the activities described in the following paragraphs and on your knowledge of biology.

A tomato plant was placed under a sealed bell jar and exposed to light. Carbon dioxide containing radioactive carbon was introduced into the bell jar as shown in the following diagram. After an hour, the inlet valve was closed. Later, the entire plant was removed from the soil and cleaned by rinsing it in water. A Geiger counter indicated radioactivity in the roots. These roots were then dried and chopped into very small pieces. The chopped roots were sprinkled into an aquarium containing a very hungry goldfish that was NOT radioactive. Four days later, the fish was removed from the aquarium and a tissue section of the fish was tested with the Geiger counter. The counter indicated an above-normal level of radioactivity in the fish tissues.

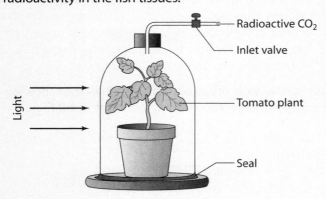

34. Which cycle is primarily being studied by means of this investigation? (1) oxygen (2) carbon (3) nitrogen (4) water

35. A control setup for this investigation would be identical to the one described except for the replacement of the (1) tomato plant with a geranium plant (2) goldfish with a tadpole (3) radioactive carbon dioxide with atmospheric carbon dioxide (4) soil with distilled water

36. By which process was the radioactivity incorporated into the material that was transported to the roots? (1) growth (2) mitosis (3) photosynthesis (4) respiration

37. This investigation suggests that when plants are eaten by animals, some of the plant materials may be (1) changed to animal tissue (2) separated into smaller molecules before being digested (3) eliminated by the animal in a form that allows the plant to grow again (4) used in regulating the animal's digestive processes

38. A cycling of materials is represented in the following diagram.

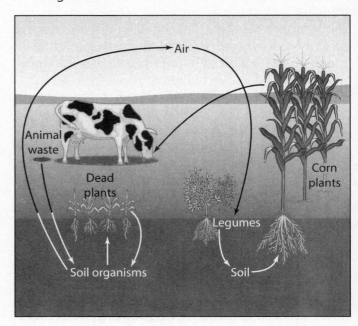

Which statement is supported by the events shown in the diagram? (1) Materials are cycled between living organisms only. (2) Materials are cycled between heterotrophic organisms only. (3) Materials are cycled between the living and nonliving components of the environment only. (4) Materials are cycled between autotrophic organisms only.

39. Which ecological principle is best illustrated by the following diagram?

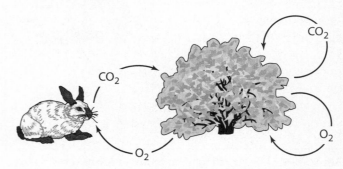

(1) In an ecosystem, material is cycled among the organisms and the environment. (2) In an ecosystem, the number of producers and consumers is equal. (3) Competition within a species results in natural selection. (4) An ecosystem requires a constant source of energy.

Diversity Benefits Species and Habitats

As a result of evolution, there is a great diversity of species on Earth. Almost every ecosystem is populated by many species, each occupying its own special niche. The interrelationships and interdependencies of these species help to keep ecosystems stable, and the diversity of species increases the chance that at least some organisms will survive in the face of large environmental changes.

Biodiversity is a measurement of the degree to which species vary within an ecosystem. There is a strong connection between biodiversity and the stability of an ecosystem. A natural forest, for example, contains many different species of trees. If disease or insects attack one population, nearby trees of another species are likely to survive. The mix of species in the ecosystem also makes it difficult for the disease organisms to move quickly through this environment. Here, biodiversity serves as a barrier to the spread of disease or insect attack. In contrast, on a tree farm where all of the trees are planted and are of a single species, the entire population could be seriously damaged by a single disease or insect attack.

The interactions between organisms may allow an ecosystem to remain stable for hundreds or thousands of years. In established, stable ecosystems, populations tend to increase and decrease in size in a predictable pattern. Over time, however, the size of the population remains relatively stable. For example, when the prey population increases, a large food supply causes the size of the predator population to rise. Because each predator requires many prey to meet its energy needs, the prey population rapidly decreases. Soon, with the decline in a prey population, some of the predators begin to starve. When only a few predators remain alive, the prey population reproduces and greater numbers of prey survive. The cycle begins anew. Figure 6-10 illustrates the seasonal change in a rabbit population.

The loss of biodiversity in an ecosystem upsets its stability. Removing species from an environment often causes instability due to the loss of organisms that were filling critical ecological niches.

Many species may be lost when natural disasters or human activities cause large-scale destruction to habitats. Clearing large areas of tropical

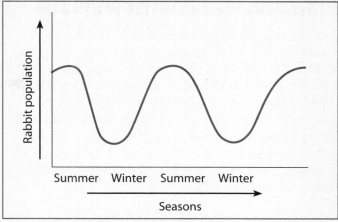

Figure 6-10. Rabbit populations: Rabbit populations may rise and fall over the course of a year, but from year to year they follow the same pattern if the environment is stable.

rain forest, for example, has disrupted many ecosystems; some may never recover. Although some species may be able to return to a damaged ecosystem, others with critical roles may be totally lost. The interdependencies between populations in the original ecosystem may have been so great that if biodiversity is lost, the ecosystem may never be restored to its original state.

Species can also be lost when humans do not consider the environmental impact of their actions. For example, offering bounties for the removal of predatory mountain lions from some environments sounded like a good idea at one time, but it led to population explosions of deer herds. Soon the deer overpopulated the area, and their overgrazing reduced the food supply so much that many deer starved. The overgrazing also led to soil erosion that caused permanent environmental damage. The negative effects begun by the removal of the mountain lions were evident for many years.

When humans clear land for agricultural purposes, the loss of biodiversity may also lead to an unstable environment. Disease and insect pests present major problems to farmers whose crops are genetically similar. For these farmers, any disruption threatens to affect the entire crop. Farmers are constantly in search of ways to control insect pests and diseases in their crops, because they have created an environment that is always in danger of serious disruption. In natural ecosystems, the diversity of species provides no such concentration of one kind of food, making it far less likely that any single pest or disease will cause problems.

Biodiversity Benefits Humans

Biodiversity also represents one of the greatest resources known to humans. It ensures the availability of a rich variety of genetic material, some of which may prove valuable to humans. Though still largely untapped, the genetic diversity found in rain forests has provided humans with medicines, insecticides, and other useful resources. If we destroy ecosystems, we lose much of the biodiversity they hold. As diversity is lost, potentially valuable resources are lost with it.

 Review Questions

Use the following information and graph to answer questions 40–41.

During the 1970s, Canadian forests in New Brunswick were heavily sprayed to control the spruce budworms that were damaging the spruce trees. Ecologists discovered that, along with the budworm, bees of many species—including sweat bees and bumblebees—had also been killed. All of the bees were important for pollinating flowers so the plants could produce fruit. Miles away from the spruce forests, blueberry growers were devastated when their blueberry yield declined by 75 percent over the same time period as the spraying was taking place. The graph shows the biodiversity present in the Canadian spruce forests prior to, during, and after the spraying.

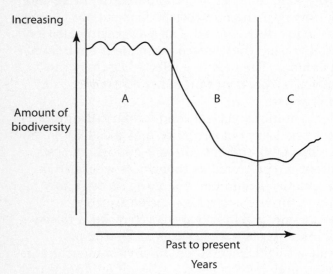

40. As the number of insect species declined due to spraying, the blueberry production decreased. Explain how these two events might be related even though the pesticide did not land directly on the blueberry plants.

41. On the graph provided, draw a line that shows the relationship of ecosystem stability to changes in biodiversity.

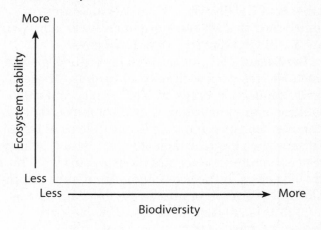

Base your answer to question 42 on the graph below and on your knowledge of biology.

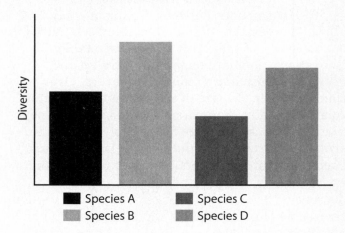

42. If the environment were to change dramatically or if a new plant disease were to be introduced, which plant species would be the most likely to have individuals that could survive the disease? (1) Species A (2) Species B (3) Species C (4) Species D

43. Explain why medical researchers are concerned when the biodiversity of an ecosystem decreases.

44. The color, taste, and juiciness of a particular variety of strawberry makes it very popular. Growers are able to plant hundreds of acres of this variety, and all the plants will be exactly the same, since they reproduce asexually. Explain why this lack of diversity in the strawberry field could prove to be a problem for the growers.

45. A forest community is made up of thousands of species of organisms and can exist practically unchanged for hundreds of years. This stability is due to the (1) diversity of organisms present (2) abundance of insects that feed on plants (3) changes in the climate of the area (4) lack of decomposers in the forest

Environmental Changes

Many environments, such as the bare rock on a mountaintop, have few resources that can provide homes for living organisms. Through natural processes, these environments will change over long periods of time to become habitats for many diverse species. The series of changes by which one habitat changes into another is called **ecological succession.**

In the process of ecological succession, each community causes modifications to its environment. The modifications result in changes that make it more suitable for another community. The original species that lived there may find it harder to adapt to these changes, while the new species coming in may be able to compete more successfully for the new niches.

For example, as grasses grow in an area with very shallow soil, they add organic matter, making the soil deeper and more fertile. Shrubs are then able to live in this modified environment and will eventually produce enough shade to eliminate the grasses growing below them. Over a period of many years, these gradual changes may result in the formation of a stable forest community that can last for hundreds or even thousands of years. (In dry or cold climates, succession may not advance to the forest stage, but the final stage will be a stable ecosystem that can last for many years.)

Climatic changes, natural disasters, and the activities of animals (including humans) can alter stable ecosystems. These changes may occur rapidly, perhaps due to a forest fire or flood, or slowly, as when a long-term drought or climate change occurs. Altered environments undergo a slow series of successional changes that return them to a point where long-term stability is possible. In this process, an existing community of organisms is replaced by different communities over a period of time ranging from a few decades to thousands of years.

There are two commonly observed patterns of succession. A community of mostly bare rock will gradually accumulate soil, leading to a progression of vegetation types from grasses to shrubs, and eventually a forest. This process is seen in Figure 6-11.

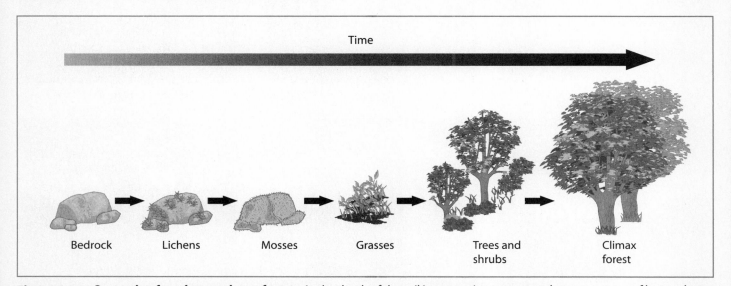

Time

Bedrock   Lichens   Mosses   Grasses   Trees and shrubs   Climax forest

Figure 6-11. Succession from bare rock to a forest: As the depth of the soil increases, it can support the root systems of larger plants.

Another commonly observed example of ecological succession is the change from a lake community to a forest. The lake will gradually accumulate sediments from erosion and the buildup of organic debris from plants and dead organisms. As the lake fills in, it becomes shallower. After many years, it may become a swamp. The filling-in continues, and eventually a mature forest may result. Successional changes from lake to forest are shown in Figure 6-12.

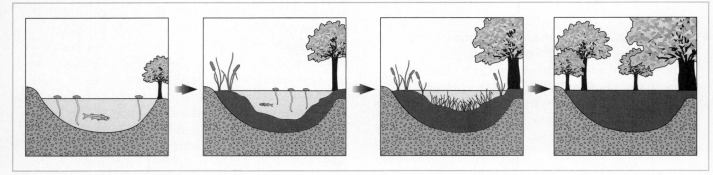

Figure 6-12. **Succession from a lake to a forest**

 # Review Questions

Base your answers to questions 46–49 on the following sequence of diagrams.

46. This sequence of diagrams best illustrates (1) succession (2) evolution (3) the effects of acid rain (4) a food chain

1840

1870

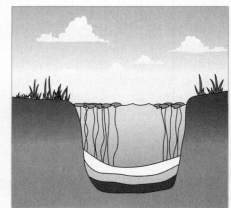

1900

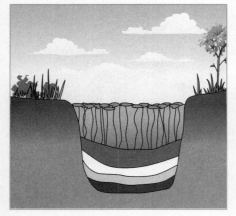

1930

1960

1990

47. If no human intervention or natural disaster occurs, by the year 2050 this area will most likely be a (1) lake (2) swamp (3) desert (4) forest

48. The natural increase in the amount of vegetation from 1840 to 1930 is related to the (1) decreasing water depth (2) increasing amount of sunlight (3) presence of bottom-feeding fish (4) use of the pond for fishing

49. Describe what would happen over the following fifty years if a fire burned off all of the vegetation in the area.

Base your answers to questions 50–51 on the information provided and on your knowledge of biology.

If you travel inland from the shores of the present Lake Michigan, which was once much larger than it is today, you would travel through the following areas:

1. the present sandy beach   2. grasses

3. a cottonwood forest   4. a pine forest

5. an oak forest   6. a beech-maple forest (where the original shoreline was located)

50. The above sequence of plant growth is an illustration of (1) succession (2) a food chain (3) evolution (4) an autotroph pyramid

51. Describe why the plants growing in the area of the old shoreline are beech and maple trees and no longer the grasses observed near the new shoreline.

52. When a stable forest community is destroyed by fire, the community usually is (1) not restored (2) restored in a series of successive changes (3) restored only if humans reforest the area (4) changed into a permanent grassland

53. In a pond, which change would most likely lead to land succession? (1) a decrease in the amount of particles suspended in the water of the pond (2) an increase in the speed of the water currents in the pond (3) a decrease in the number and diversity of organisms inhabiting the shallow water of the pond (4) an increase in the amount of sediment, fallen leaves, and tree limbs accumulating on the bottom of the pond.

54. The conditions that existed in a forest before a fire will be established mainly by (1) the water cycle (2) the carbon cycle (3) succession (4) evolution

55. When Mount St. Helens erupted in 1980, a portion of the surrounding area was covered by lava, which buried all of the vegetation. Four months later, *Anaphalis margaritacea* plants were found growing out of lava rock crevices. The beginning of plant regrowth in this area is a part of the process known as (1) species preservation (2) evolution (3) biotic competition (4) succession

 Questions for Regents Practice

Part A

1. The members of an animal community are usually similar in

(1) size

(2) structure

(3) food requirements

(4) environmental requirements

2. Which is a biotic factor that affects the size of a population in a specific ecosystem?

(1) the average temperature of the ecosystem

(2) the number and kinds of soil minerals in the ecosystem

(3) the number and kinds of predators in the ecosystem

(4) the concentration of oxygen in an ecosystem

3. An overpopulation of deer in a certain area will most likely lead to

(1) a decrease in the number of predators of the deer

(2) an increase in the number of autotrophs available for food

(3) a decrease in the incidence of disease

(4) an increase in competition between the deer

4. A farmer abandons one of his fields, and over the years, he notices that one field community is replaced by another community. This replacement represents part of

(1) a food chain

(2) an abiotic community

(3) an energy pyramid

(4) an ecological succession

5. An ecosystem, such as an aquarium, is self-sustaining if it involves the interaction between organisms, a flow of energy, and the presence of

(1) an equal number of plants and animals

(2) more animals than plants

(3) material cycles

(4) organisms undergoing succession

6. In order to be self-sustaining, an ecosystem must contain

(1) a large number of organisms

(2) a warm, moist environment

(3) a constant source of energy

(4) organisms that occupy all of the niches

Part B

Base your answers to questions 7 through 9 on the graph and on your knowledge of biology. The graph illustrates a comparison between pH conditions and species survival rates in certain Adirondack lakes.

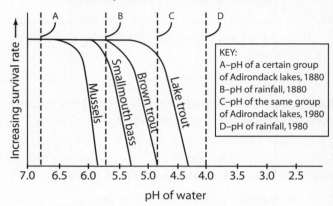

The Effect of ph on Survival Rates of Selected Species in Certain Adirondack Lakes

–*National Geographic* (adapted)

7. Which species can tolerate the highest level of acidity in its water environment?

(1) mussels

(2) smallmouth bass

(3) brown trout

(4) lake trout

8. In the years between 1880 and 1980, which species would most likely have been eliminated FIRST due to the gradual acidification of Adirondack lakes?

(1) mussels

(2) smallmouth bass

(3) brown trout

(4) lake trout

9. What was the total change in pH in the rainwater from 1880 to 1980?

(1) 1.3

(2) 1.7

(3) 5.3

(4) 9.7

10. Which types of organisms must be present in an ecosystem if the ecosystem is to be maintained?

(1) producers and carnivores

(2) producers and decomposers

(3) carnivores and decomposers

(4) herbivores and carnivores

11. Although three different bird species all inhabit the same type of tree in an area, competition between the birds rarely occurs. The most likely explanation for this lack of competition is that these birds

(1) have different ecological niches

(2) eat the same food

(3) have a limited supply of food

(4) are unable to interbreed

12. Producer organisms function to

(1) store more energy than they use

(2) use more energy than they store

(3) store energy but not use it

(4) use energy but not store it

13. Which foods are derived from organisms that occupy the level that contains the greatest amount of energy in an energy pyramid?

(1) bread and tomatoes

(2) shrimp and rice

(3) hamburger and French fries

(4) chicken and lettuce

14. Which organism shown in the following food web would most likely be adversely affected by a continuous decrease in the population of mice?

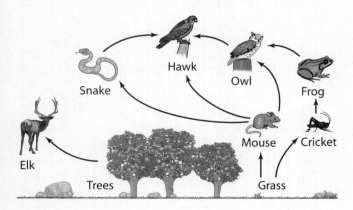

(1) grass   (3) crickets

(2) elk   (4) hawks

15. Which pair of terms would most likely apply to the same organism?

(1) heterotroph and herbivore

(2) heterotroph and autotroph

(3) autotroph and parasite

(4) producer and predator

16. In the following diagram of a food web, which organisms are most likely to be competitors?

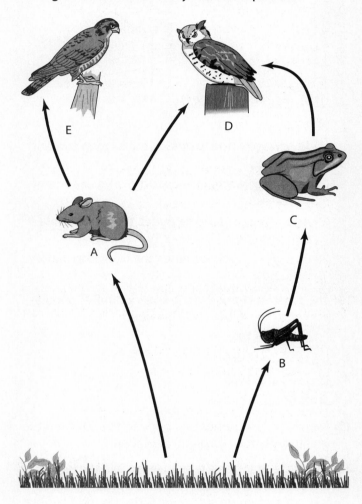

(1) A and C   (3) B and C

(2) B and D   (4) D and E

17. In the following food chain, which are the most abundant organisms?

corn plants → field mice → garter snakes → red-tailed hawks

(1) corn plants   (3) garter snakes

(2) field mice   (4) red-tailed hawks

Base your answers to questions 18 through 21 on the following graphs that show data on some environmental factors affecting a large New York lake.

18. Which relationship can be correctly inferred from the data present?

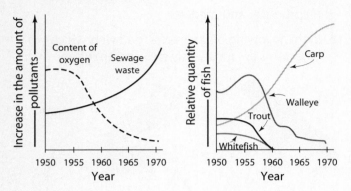

(1) As sewage waste increases, the oxygen content decreases.

(2) As sewage waste increases, the oxygen content increases.

(3) As oxygen content decreases, the carp population decreases.

(4) As oxygen level decreases, the trout population increases.

19. The greatest change in the lake's whitefish population occurred in the years between

(1) 1950 and 1955

(2) 1955 and 1960

(3) 1960 and 1965

(4) 1965 and 1970

20. Name the fish species that appears to withstand the greatest degree of oxygen depletion.

21. Using the graph as a reference, explain the impact of increased sewage levels on the biodiversity of the lake ecosystem. Be sure to provide specific examples from the graph to support your answer.

Base your answers to questions 22 through 25 on the following information and data table.

A field study was conducted to observe a deer population in a given region over time. The deer were counted at different intervals over a period of 40 years. During this period, both ranching and the hunting of deer and their predators increased in the study region. A summary of the data is presented in the table.

Deer Population Changes 1900-1940

Year	Deer Population (thousands)
1900	3.0
1910	9.5
1920	65.0
1924	100.0
1926	40.0
1930	25.0
1940	10.0

Using the information in the data table and the directions on the next page, construct a line graph on the following grid.

Deer Population Changes 1900–1940

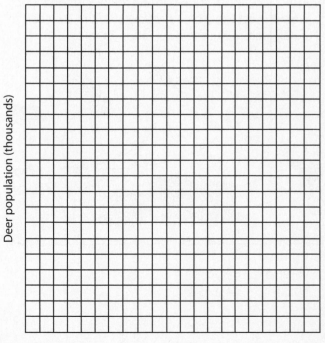

Year

22. Mark an appropriate scale on each labeled axis.

23. Plot the data for the deer population on the grid. Surround each point with a small circle and connect the points.

24. During which 10-year period did the greatest increase in the deer population occur?

(1) 1900–1910   (3) 1920–1930

(2) 1910–1920   (4) 1930–1940

25. State one possible action that could have been taken to help maintain a more stable population of deer in the area.

Base your answers to questions 26 through 29 on the information provided and on your knowledge of biology.

For 25 years, hay was cut from the same 10 acres on a farm. During these years, shrews, grasshoppers, spiders, rabbits, and mice were seen in this hayfield. After the farmer retired, he no longer cut the hay, and the field was left unattended.

26. Which description best matches the events in the former hayfield over the next few decades?

(1) The plant species will change, but the animal species will remain the same.

(2) The animal species will change, but the plant species will remain the same.

(3) Neither the plant species nor the animal species will change.

(4) Both the plant species and the animal species will change.

27. The grasshoppers, spiders, shrews, and other organisms, along with the soil minerals, amount of rainfall, and other factors, constitute

(1) an ecosystem

(2) a species

(3) a biosphere

(4) a food web

28. Just before he retired, the farmer determined the population size of several of the field species during the months of May, July, and August. The results are recorded in the table.

Field Species	Number of Organisms		
	May	July	August
Grasshoppers	1,000	5,000	1,500
Birds	250	100	100
Grasses	7,000	20,000	6,000
Spiders	75	200	500

Draw a food chain that represents the most likely feeding relationships among four of the organisms (grasshopper, birds, grasses, and spiders) that live in the field.

29. Which graph best represents the relative population size of the field species for May?

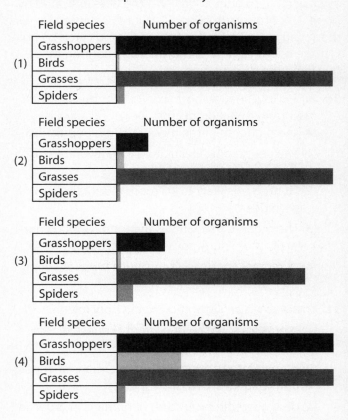

Base your answers to questions 30 and 31 on the information below and on your knowledge of biology.

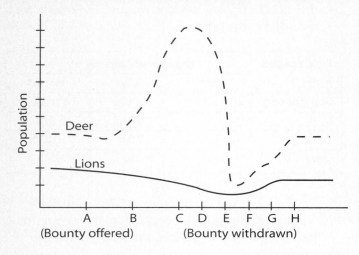

The graph shows the relative populations of mountain lions and deer in a certain geographic area that is generally favorable to both animals. At the time indicated by point A, hunters were offered a bounty payment for each mountain lion killed. Later, at the time indicated by point E, these bounties were withdrawn and hunting mountain lions was discouraged.

30. Which explanation best accounts for the fact that, according to the graph, the deer population is always higher than the mountain lion population?

(1) The geographic location is more favorable for deer than for mountain lions.

(2) Hunters are likely to kill more mountain lions than deer.

(3) The organism serving as the food supply is normally more numerous than its predator.

(4) Mountain lions usually produce more offspring than deer.

31. The graph is an illustration of the principle that

(1) predators serve an important purpose in a balanced ecosystem

(2) human intervention has little permanent impact on the survival of animal species

(3) deer need the protection of humans in order to survive the attacks of their natural enemies

(4) mountain lions do not pose the greatest danger to deer in their struggle for survival

Part C

32. Provide two reasons why it is important to preserve biodiversity. [2]

33. Explain the difference between a habitat and a niche. [2]

34. A predator affects the population of its prey, but a parasite may not have the same effect on its host population. Explain why. [2]

35. Predict what would happen to a community if the number of carnivores present suddenly doubled. [1]

36. If you introduced a population of rabbits into a huge field and then made sure that they had all of the food and water they needed, would the population continue to increase in size forever? Support your answer with an explanation. [1]

37. Imagine that you are stuck on a deserted island and will not be rescued for weeks. The only food you have available is two chickens and a bushel of corn. Due to environmental conditions, it is impossible for you to grow the corn. The only way to keep the chickens alive is to feed them the corn. Read the following choices, and then select the choice that provides you with the best chance of surviving until rescuers arrive. Identify your choice, and then explain your selection, addressing the pros and cons of all three choices. [4]

Choice A: You and the chickens eat the corn first, and then you eat the chickens.

Choice B: You eat the chickens first, and then eat the corn.

Choice C: You feed the corn to the chickens and eat the eggs. Later, you eat the chickens.

Human Impact on Ecosystems

VOCABULARY

carrying capacity	industrialization	renewable resource
deforestation	nonrenewable	technology
direct harvesting	resource	trade-off
energy flow	nuclear fuel	water cycle
fossil fuel	ozone shield	
global warming	pollution	

All living things affect the environment around them. Porcupines chew the bark from trees; squirrels break twigs as they leap from branch to branch. Generally, the changes to the environment are small. Humans, however, have made impressive technological achievements in the past few hundred years. As a result, we are now making significant changes in Earth's diverse environments. As the human population grows and our need for the resources to sustain our technology expands, the possibility that we will harm Earth's ecosystems increases. Our decisions about how to use—or misuse—Earth's resources will have a profound impact on all the organisms that depend on those resources.

Need for Awareness and Understanding

Human activities can create ecological problems that must be avoided or corrected. If we are to find solutions to those problems, we must encourage everyone to become environmentally literate. That means people need to understand the causes and effects of environmental problems as well as the possible solutions that could lead to environmental stability. Because environmental issues often concern many countries, resolving environmental issues frequently requires global awareness, cooperation, and action.

Our Environment

Like all living things, humans are part of Earth's natural ecosystems. We depend on our ecosystem to supply the food we eat, the water we drink, and the air we breathe. As long as our ecosystem functions normally, those essential resources will be available. We can continue to depend on the plants in the ecosystem to provide food and oxygen and to recycle the carbon dioxide we exhale. We will also be able to rely upon our ecosystem to maintain the quality of our water.

Limited Resources

Earth has a finite supply of resources. Some of Earth's resources, such as our food supply and solar energy, are renewable. Given sufficient time, **renewable resources** can be replaced. Other resources, such as fossil fuels and minerals, are **nonrenewable resources.** Once they're used, they cannot be replaced. Decisions we make today and tomorrow will determine whether or not we increase our consumption of Earth's limited resources. One way to reduce our use of resources is to control the growth rate of our population. An ever-increasing human population accelerates the use of Earth's limited resources. Making the right decisions about these issues will affect you as well as the future generations of all the organisms that share the biosphere.

RENEWABLE RESOURCES Although many resources are renewable, they must be used carefully. Increased consumption can stress the natural processes that renew some resources. As a result, the resource might be unable to renew itself. For example, the fish we eat are a renewable resource. Even if many fish are captured, over time the fish populations can reproduce and recover their losses. Today, however, modern, commercial fishing can remove so many fish so quickly that specific populations may not have time to recover. In some cases, the reduction can be so severe that the fish population may fail to reproduce. At that point, the fish would no longer be a renewable resource.

NONRENEWABLE RESOURCES Our increasing consumption of resources that cannot be replaced naturally is becoming a serious problem. Most metals, such as the aluminum we use for packaging, and other minerals, such as the silicon we use for computer chips, are nonrenewable resources. Fossil fuels, such as the gas that runs our cars and the coal that powers many factories, are also nonrenewable resources. Using too many nonrenewable resources will cause their <u>depletion</u> (serious reduction) within a relatively short time.

PRESERVING OUR RESOURCES Individuals can help maintain our supply of both renewable and nonrenewable resources by practicing the three R's: Reducing, Reusing, and Recycling. Suggestions are included in Table 7-1.

Table 7-1. How Individuals Can Preserve Resources		
The 3 R's	**Action**	**Example**
Reduce	Avoid using the resource.	Use energy efficiently; walk, bike or carpool instead of driving.
Reuse	Use the same product over and over, instead of throwing it away after one use.	Use dishes rather than paper plates. Instead of discarding your paper lunchbag, take it home and use it again.
Recycle	Don't throw it in the trash. Instead, discard the product in a way that it can be used to make another product.	Paper, metal, plastic, and glass are all easily recycled.

Natural Processes in Ecosystems

Several natural processes that occur in ecosystems affect the life and health of humans as well as all the other organisms that rely on the ecosystem. Some activities of humans affect these processes, and most of the changes are likely to be <u>detrimental</u>, or damaging, to the ecosystems. For example, if **pollution**—a harmful change in the chemical makeup of the soil, water, or air—spreads to a particular habitat, some of the species that live in that habitat will suffer. The stability of the ecosystem and the variety of species that live in it might be threatened.

MAINTAINING ATMOSPHERIC QUALITY Throughout the biosphere, animals take in oxygen during respiration and release carbon dioxide. Plants and algae take in carbon dioxide during photosynthesis and release oxygen. Through the biotic processes of respiration and photosynthesis, the levels of carbon dioxide and oxygen in the atmosphere are kept in the range that is suitable for life.

Abiotic factors also help maintain the quality of the atmosphere. For example, as it falls, rain cleans the air of particles and soluble gases. The rainfall also helps maintain humidity in the atmosphere.

SOIL FORMATION Soils form when weathering breaks down rocks and when organic materials from decaying plants and animals accumulate. Such soils support the growth of many producer organisms and serve as a habitat for decomposers. The root systems of plants hold the soil in place. If the vegetation that covers the ground is removed, the soil can be washed away by rain or blown away by wind. Soil erosion sometimes occurs during a drought when many plants die, leaving bare soil.

THE WATER CYCLE Water continuously evaporates from the surface of the land and water and from the leaves of plants. The water vapor rises into the atmosphere and collects as clouds that can move long distances through the atmosphere. Eventually, the vapor condenses as precipitation, which is distributed over many areas of Earth. The water collects as runoff or groundwater or evaporates, continuing the water cycle. Because of this process, which is known as the **water cycle** and shown in Figure 7-1, many ecosystems maintain a supply of fresh water, which is available to all organisms, including humans.

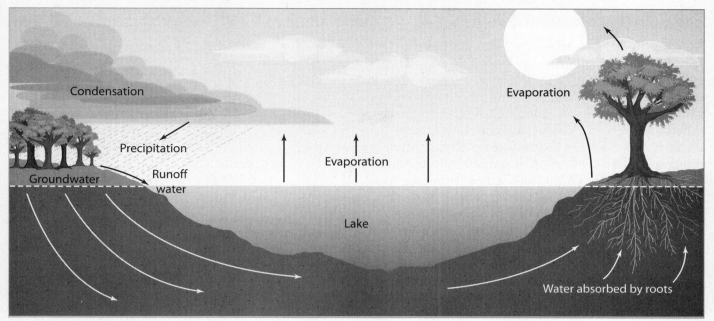

Figure 7-1. **The water cycle**

WASTE REMOVAL AND THE RECYCLING OF NUTRIENTS Plants that live in the soil use the soil's minerals as they grow. The nutrients are transported from one organism to another through the food chains in the ecosystem. Those that are not released into the atmosphere are eventually contained in the dead bodies and wastes of organisms. Decomposers break down the wastes and the dead bodies of organisms, removing the nutrients in the process. The nutrients are then restored to the soil, where they can then be used by other plants, continuing the cycle.

Without this natural recycling, much of the abiotic materials needed by living organisms would remain "locked up" in the bodies of dead organisms. Minerals and other nutrients would not be available for new organisms. In tropical forests, where heavy rains are frequent, decomposition and the recycling process must take place rapidly. Otherwise, the frequent rains strip the land of minerals before new plants can absorb and use them. In areas where the Amazon rain forest has been cleared and burned for planting, many nutrients have been washed away, leaving the soil unfertile.

Humans sometimes make use of this natural recycling process when they mix decaying lawn and garden wastes to make compost, which is a natural fertilizer and soil conditioner. Adding compost to the soil recycles wastes naturally and reduces the need for chemical fertilizers. It also reduces the amount of waste material in landfills and eliminates the need to burn yard waste, which pollutes our atmosphere.

THE FLOW OF ENERGY Food chains, food webs, and energy pyramids illustrate the **energy flow** through ecosystems. (See Figure 6-7 and 6-8.) Each organism has a role in the process and contributes to the overall stability of the ecosystem. As a result, losing all or most of the members of any species of an ecosystem could upset the stability of the whole.

Unlike nutrients, energy is passed through the environment, but it does NOT recycle. Instead, at each feeding level in an energy pyramid, organisms lose large amounts of energy (as heat) to the environment. This energy cannot be recaptured by living things. Because of this constant energy loss, ecosystems need a constant source of new energy. That energy source is usually the sun.

People and the Environment

Because humans are part of Earth's ecosystems, they affect the way ecosystems function. They also are affected by changes in the ecosystem. Once the ecosystem is damaged, people may suffer from that damage just like any other species.

Population Growth

Most species in new environments can have a period of rapid population growth. The population increase levels off as it approaches the ecosystem's **carrying capacity,** which is the number of individuals the environment can support. For example, as rabbits move into a field, their population may boom. Eventually, the food supply dwindles, and the scarcity of food leads to a reduction in the population of rabbits. Those that do not get enough to eat may become too weak to escape predators or recover from diseases. Some may even die of starvation. The population growth levels off when the number of rabbits is balanced by the availability of food and the presence of limiting factors, such as predators. The relationship between population and the carrying capacity of an environment is shown in Figure 7-2.

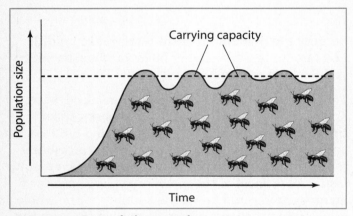

Figure 7-2. A population growth curve: In a new environment, the population usually increases quickly, but it stabilizes when it reaches the carrying capacity of that environment.

Earth can only support a certain number of people. Our planet has a carrying capacity for humans just as it does for other species. The more people there are, the more resources they need. These resources come from the environment. More people also produce more waste, which must be disposed of or recycled. Overcrowding and lack of food also become problems when populations are very large.

For thousands of years, the human population grew slowly. Then about 300 years ago, our food supply began to increase, and improvements in health care and hygiene led to dramatic increases in our population. At present, the population curve inclines steeply upward. To many population scientists, the sharp increase suggests that the human population is growing at a dangerously fast rate.

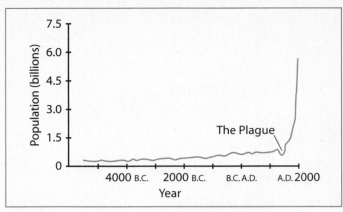

Figure 7-3. Growth curve for the human population worldwide

Compare Figure 7-3, the growth curve for the human population, with Figure 7-2, the growth curve typical for animals in an ecosystem.

If the human population continues to grow at the rate shown in Figure 7-3, Earth's carrying capacity could be reached soon. That result could be catastrophic. With no controls, the human population might even overshoot Earth's carrying capacity for our species. There might not be enough food, water, space, and oxygen for anyone. The resulting deaths from famine, disease, or wars over resources could reduce the human population to a small fraction of its present level. Finding ways to slow our population growth so that the growth rate levels off BEFORE Earth's carrying capacity is reached could save future generations from suffering the consequences of unlimited population growth.

Review Questions

1. Which of the following is a renewable resource? (1) wood (2) oil (3) iron (4) coal

2. The best way to ensure that there will be enough aluminum for all future needs is to (1) dig more mines and process more aluminum ore (2) buy more aluminum from other countries and save our own (3) recycle and reuse aluminum (4) increase space exploration and search for new sources of aluminum

3. Some ecologists are concerned that the human population has outgrown the capacity of many of Earth's ecosystems. The natural limiting factor that will most likely prevent further human population growth in many parts of the world is (1) habitat destruction (2) political intervention (3) food supply (4) social intervention

4. Which of these human activities is quite often responsible for the other three human activities? (1) increasing demand on limited food production (2) rapid increase of loss of farmland due to soil erosion (3) rapid increase of human population (4) increasing levels of air pollution

5. The following graphs show the size of the human population in relation to food production per acre in four different countries over the same period of time.

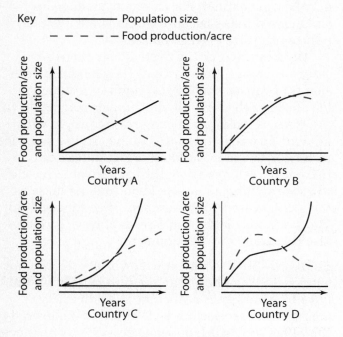

Which country's population appears to have reached—and is now maintaining—its population close to its carrying capacity? Using one or more sentences, explain how you can tell.

Human Activities and the Loss of Diversity

Some human activities that destroy habitats and degrade ecosystems do far more than damage individual organisms. They also destroy diversity in both the living and nonliving parts of the environment. For example, when humans use land to build a parking lot, the organisms that lived on that land are likely to die. Other organisms that ate the plants, burrowed through the ground, or nested in the nearby trees are also affected. There will be fewer resources available for a variety of species.

Many deliberate human activities, such as clearing land to plant a single crop, can change the equilibrium in an ecosystem. So can some accidents, such as inadvertently or unknowingly adding a species to an ecosystem.

DIRECT HARVESTING The destruction or removal of species from their habitats is known as **direct harvesting.** It can sometimes lead to the extinction of a species. For example, some species that live in distant parts of the world (rain forests or deserts) are removed from their native habitats and sold to people who want them as unusual pets, ornaments, or house or garden plants. That cute monkey or beautiful parrot in the pet shop may not have been born in captivity. Instead, it may have been captured in the wild and shipped here. Many animals die in the process.

Other organisms are killed to collect a specific body part. For example, baby harbor seals are killed for their pelts, and elephants are killed for the ivory in their tusks, which people carve into jewelry or other trinkets. Direct harvesting can threaten the existence of the entire population of a species. Due to over-harvesting, so many of some species of plants and animals have been taken from their native habitats that those species are now endangered. So many whales have been slaughtered that some species are now in danger of extinction.

In the past, humans have caused the extinction of several species. For example, in the early 1800s, billions of passenger pigeons lived in North America. (See Figure 7-4.) Each year hunters shot millions, until the population was greatly reduced. By the time people realized that the species was endangered, it was too late to save it. The last passenger pigeon died in a zoo in Cincinnati, Ohio, in 1914. Today, some endangered species are protected by law. However, because there may be a demand for products made from endangered species, poaching (illegally capturing or killing an organism) is a continuing problem.

Figure 7-4. The passenger pigeon: The passenger pigeon, once present in huge numbers, is now extinct because of uncontrolled hunting.

LAND USE As human populations grow, we use more resources to make the things we need or want, such as clothes, homes, refrigerators, radios, and cars. We also need more space for places to live. More land is needed to grow food, to build roads and factories, and even to provide parks and recreational areas. As human populations and needs increase, our use of land decreases the space and resources available for other species.

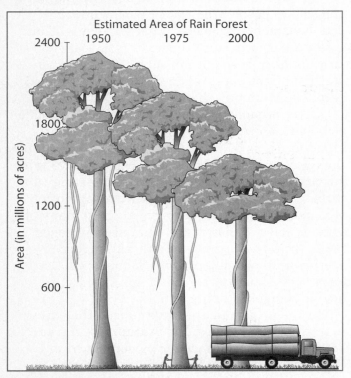

Figure 7-5. Habitat destruction: The destruction of rain forests, an example of deforestation, eliminates many ecosystems.

HABITAT DESTRUCTION Many people think that when a habitat is destroyed, the organisms simply find a new home. However, because other parts of the ecosystem are already occupied, displaced animals seldom find a new place to live. Habitat destruction occurs when people take over land for their own use. It is an important way that species can become endangered: They simply have nowhere to live! As habitats are destroyed, whole ecosystems can be damaged and entire species may become extinct. For example, pandas are endangered today because humans have greatly reduced the size of their habitat.

Deforestation, or the destruction of forests resulting from human activity, is a land use decision that causes widespread habitat destruction. People clear the forest by burning or cutting down the trees. Deforestation can provide people with land for farming and places to live. It also provides resources to use in building or manufacturing. Because of deforestation, the area covered by the world's rain forests is only about half as large as the area covered 150 years ago. (See Figure 7-5.) The wetlands, fields, and forests of New York are also threatened by development.

BIODIVERSITY When a wide variety of different species live together in an ecosystem, it is said to have biodiversity. A reduction in biodiversity occurs when species are lost. This lost biodiversity can affect the health of whole ecosystems and food webs. It can even affect the proportion of gases in the atmosphere. Our future ability to find new medicines for treating diseases or to discover new

Figure 7-6. Loss of biodiversity: The corn in this field provides habitats for only a few species. The meadow that once grew here was home for hundreds of species of birds, flowers, shrubs, trees, insects, and small animals.

sources of genes that could be genetically engineered into more productive and pest-resistant crops is threatened when biodiversity is lost.

Habitat destruction, such as deforestation, can lead to loss of biodiversity, but it is not the only way that human activities threaten biodiversity. For example, a farmer might plow under a meadow that is home to many species. Then the farmer might plant a single crop, such as corn or wheat, on many continuous acres of land. This practice greatly reduces the biodiversity of the area. (See Figure 7-6.) In addition, it creates an ideal environment for insects that feed on that crop. To control the insects, the farmer may need to use pesticides, which could harm other organisms living in the same or nearby environments.

IMPORTED SPECIES Biodiversity is often reduced when people import and release a species from one environment into another. The release may be inadvertent or intentional. For example, before 1859, there were no rabbits in Australia. Then two dozen rabbits were released in Australia. By 1953, more than a billion rabbits occupied 1.2 million square miles of the continent. These rabbits ate massive amounts of vegetation ordinarily available to the native species

Many species become pests when they are added to a new environment. Because the new organisms are not part of an existing food web in the area, they often have no natural enemies in their new environment and rapidly overpopulate the area. They then crowd out, feed on, or otherwise eliminate native species. Two examples are Japanese beetles and gypsy moths, which were accidentally released in the U.S. (See Figure 7-7.) Now they are serious pests in New York.

Once an imported species becomes a pest, it is very difficult to solve the problem. If another species is imported to control it, the second species may choose to feed on native organisms, adding another problem. Using pesticides or poisons can kill other organisms in addition to the imported one. Sometimes scientists find a disease organism that only affects the imported species. The rabbits that overran Australia were eventually controlled by a disease organism. However, there is always a risk that the species may become resistant to the disease and overpopulate again.

Because imported species are such a problem, many states and countries have laws to restrict the transport of fruits or vegetables. The goal of these laws is to avoid introducing diseases or insects that might damage local crops. Some countries require the <u>quarantine</u> (confined isolation) of certain animals and plants until officials are sure they are free of any pests that could escape into the new environment.

Scientists are working to find safer methods of pest control. One safe pest control method is setting traps that use chemical scents to attract insects. With this method, no other species are harmed and the population of the pest species can be reduced to a safe level. Breeding and releasing native predators of a pest species has also sometimes been used successfully and without harm to other species.

 # Review Questions

6. Ladybugs were introduced as predators into an agricultural area of the United States to reduce the number of aphids feeding on grain crops. This action is an example of (1) preservation of endangered species (2) conservation of natural resources (3) protection of watershed areas (4) use of a nonchemical means of insect control

7. An example of a human activity that has had a positive effect on the environment is the (1) disruption of natural habitats through deforestation (2) capture and sale of rare South American birds (3) use of reforestation to control erosion in the mountains (4) hunting of endangered species of animals

8. The trees in a forest aid in reducing flood damage chiefly because their (1) branches store water in the form of sap (2) leaves absorb moisture from the air (3) root systems hold the soil in place (4) stems serve to store food

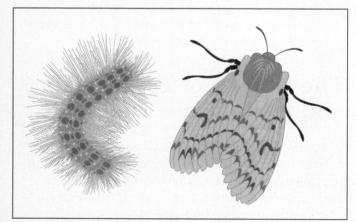

Figure 7-7. Imported species: During the larval stage, the gypsy moth consumes vast quantities of leaves. The adult moth lays hundreds of eggs, continuing the problem.

9. The creation of wildlife refuges and the enforcement of game laws are conservation measures that promote increased (1) use of chemicals to control pests (2) preservation of species (3) use of natural controls to limit pest populations (4) exploitation of wildlife species

10. When land is cleared for agriculture or home construction, small isolated sections of the original habitat may remain. How might this reduction in habitat size and the isolation of small sections of habitat lead to species endangerment?

11. A method of agriculture presently used in many regions of the world where one crop is grown on many acres of land has created serious insect problems. This is primarily because this method (1) increases soil erosion (2) provides concentrated areas of one kind of food for insects (3) increases the effectiveness of insecticides used over long periods of time (4) involves the growing of crops in former desert areas

12. The least ecologically damaging method for controlling the mosquitoes that spread the diseases malaria and encephalitis is by (1) draining the swamps where mosquitoes breed (2) spraying swamps with chemical pesticides (3) spreading oil over swamps (4) introducing local fish species to the swamps where mosquitoes breed

13. Many people place bat boxes on their property to provide housing that attracts insect-eating bats. Explain how this activity has a positive effect on the environment.

14. Which human activity would most likely result in the addition of an organism to the endangered species list? (1) the use of cover crops to prevent soil erosion (2) the use of pollution controls by industry (3) the use of erosion prevention measures by road construction crews (4) habitat destruction by shopping mall developers

15. Humans are responsible for some of the negative changes that occur in nature because they (1) have controlled the use of many pesticides and other environmentally damaging chemicals (2) have passed laws to preserve the environment (3) are able to preserve scarce resources (4) are able to modify their physical environment to provide for human needs

16. Which of the following human activities would be the most likely to prevent certain species from becoming extinct? (1) Pass laws to place all endangered species in zoos. (2) Increase the hunting of predators. (3) Increase wildlife management and habitat protection. (4) Mate organisms from different species to create new and stronger organisms.

17. In the Cochella Valley in California, much of the desert has been converted into golf courses, housing developments, and hotels. The habitat of the Cochella Valley fringe-toed lizard is rapidly being lost. This lizard is adapted to life on fine, windblown sand. Environmentalists want to save the lizard, and developers want to continue construction. Which action would be the best long-term solution?
(1) Land in the Cochella Valley should be purchased and set aside as a preserve for the lizards. (2) The fringe-toed lizards should be crossed with a species adapted for survival in a different habitat. (3) The land should be developed as planned and the lizards relocated to a different valley. (4) The land should be developed as planned and the lizards monitored to see if they can adapt to the new conditions.

18. Refer to the chart below, which illustrates some methods of pest control.

Methods of Insect Pest Control
Insect pests can be repelled or attracted with sex hormones.
Insect populations can be controlled by releasing males sterilized with X-rays.
New plant varieties can be produced and grown that are resistant to insect pests.
Insect pests can be controlled by introducing their natural enemies.

One likely effect of using these methods of pest control will be to (1) prevent the extinction of endangered species (2) increase water pollution (3) reduce pesticide contamination of the environment (4) harm the atmosphere

The Impact of Technology and Industrialization

Humans modify ecosystems through population growth, consumption, and technology. As human populations grow, they take up more space, consume more resources, and produce more wastes. The expansion of **technology** (using scientific knowledge and technical processes to meet human needs) also increases the quantity of resources people use. All these activities lead to changes in ecosystems, including the way they function. The equilibrium of ecosystems can be upset by human actions.

Industrialization

Industrialization is the development of an economy in which machines produce many of the products people use. These products may add to the quality of life, but their manufacture can harm the environment. In addition to contributing to pollution of the air and water, industrialization increases the demand for energy, water, and other resources, including fossil and nuclear fuels.

The higher energy demands in an industrialized society mean that more power plants must be built. Additional power plants—especially those that burn coal—add to the pollution of our air and water. **Nuclear fuel** is an energy source that results from splitting atoms. Nuclear power plants do not pollute the air or water with toxic chemicals, but they can cause thermal pollution of waterways. Also, the disposal of radioactive nuclear wastes presents a huge environmental problem.

Another problem with increased industrialization is that most factories use a lot of water. Large wells drilled for factories sometimes dry up the nearby smaller wells that individuals use to supply their homes. In some cases, withdrawing large quantities of water allows the ground to collapse, forming sinkholes. In dry climates, reducing the supply of groundwater can have serious consequences for native plants and the consumers that depend on them for food.

Just as conservation (the three R's) can help preserve our resources, it can also help to limit the negative impact of industrialization. We can REDUCE our demand for energy and manufactured goods that we don't really need. We can REUSE manufactured products rather than discard them, and we can RECYCLE as many products as possible, conserving both energy and resources in the process.

Water Pollution

Rivers, lakes, and oceans are easy places for people to dispose of wastes, including sewage, wastes from homes and factories, and animal wastes from farms. The addition of pollutants to natural environments causes water pollution, which can

change the abiotic conditions in ecosystems. For example, sewage and animal wastes can act as fertilizer, increasing the growth of plants, algae, and bacteria in aquatic systems. Plants consume oxygen all the time, day and night. However, photosynthesis, the primary source of oxygen, stops at night because it requires light. As a result, oxygen production also stops. Then, oxygen levels drop and many organisms suffocate. When these organisms die, oxygen-using decomposers begin their decay activity, which further decreases the oxygen supply. Eventually, all the organisms in this oxygen-reduced ecosystem may be lost. Figure 7-8 shows several ways water pollution can affect a natural habitat.

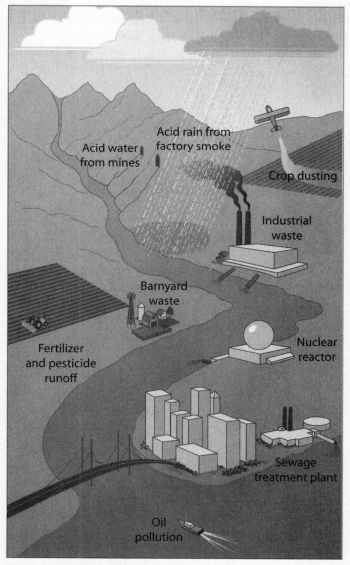

Figure 7-8. Water pollution: Water pollution, which can damage an ecosystem, comes from many sources.

TOXIC WASTES Many wastes dumped into waterways from cities, farms, or industries can be toxic (poisonous) to the organisms that use or live in the water. Chemical fertilizers and weed and insect killers can be washed off farmlands into streams or rivers. The chemicals can collect in the cells of organisms living in the water and along the shore. These toxic materials then move through the food chain and eventually damage or kill many kinds of organisms.

Although the level of toxic substances in the water might be low, scientists have learned that the concentration of a toxin increases as it moves through the food chain. For example, small quantities of toxic substances are absorbed into the cells of algae and other producers living in the water. When those producers are eaten by small herbivores, the toxins are stored in the herbivore's fatty tissue. There it stays until the herbivore is eaten by the next consumer in the food chain. At each level of the chain, larger and larger amounts of toxic material collect in the fatty tissue. Organisms at or near the top of the food chain are most likely to accumulate enough of these chemicals in their bodies to cause them harm.

For example, farmers used to spray the pesticide DDT on their crops. Rain washed some of the DDT off the land and into streams and rivers. In the water, the DDT moved up through the food chain. Soon, fish-eating birds at the top of the food chain produced eggs with very thin shells. The shells were so thin that they broke easily, which killed the next generation of birds before it even hatched.

THERMAL POLLUTION Some power plants and industries use water to cool their machines or materials. The warmed water is then released into a river or lake, and the water temperature in the river or lake rises. Because warm water cannot hold as much dissolved oxygen as cold water, the oxygen level in the river or lake drops as the water temperature rises. Some species may suffocate as a result of thermal pollution; others may be forced to try to find a new home.

The solution to most of these problems is to find better ways to deal with wastes and to reduce the need for power. Sewage can be treated before it is discharged into waterways. Toxic wastes can be separated from other materials and either recycled or stored safely. People could conserve energy by using less power. Methods could be developed for cooling industrial processes that would reduce their damage to the environment.

Air Pollution

Just as wastes dumped into rivers and oceans cause water pollution, harmful substances released into the air cause air pollution. Early in the industrial age, people thought that burning wastes just disappeared into the atmosphere, and that they didn't have to worry any more about the wastes. We now know this is not true! Most of the pollutants released into the atmosphere eventually wind up in the water cycle and return to the water or land. Like water pollution, air pollution can damage habitats and harm the organisms that live in them. Figure 7-9 shows how air pollution can affect a natural habitat.

Figure 7-9. Air pollution: Trees can be damaged—or killed—by polluted air.

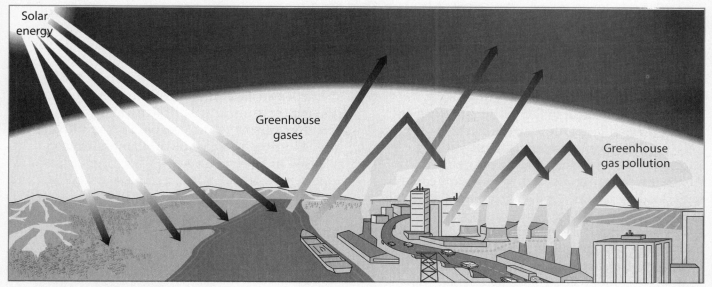

Figure 7-10. Global warming: Pollution caused by human activity is increasing the amount of greenhouse gases in the atmosphere. This increase can intensify the greenhouse effect, causing global warming.

BURNING FOSSIL FUELS Fuels such as the coal and gas that formed from the remains of organisms that lived millions of years ago are known as **fossil fuels.** Factories, cars, and most electrical power-generating plants burn fossil fuels. When fossil fuels are burned, carbon dioxide and other gases—some containing sulfur and/or nitrogen—are added to the air.

Acid Precipitation Sulfur and nitrogen compounds that are produced when fossil fuels burn can combine with moisture in the atmosphere. When this moisture falls to Earth as <u>acid rain</u>, snow, or other precipitation, it has a low pH level and is much more acidic than normal precipitation. Some acid precipitation can be as acidic as lemon juice. When highly acidic rain or snow touches plants, it may damage them and disrupt the way they function. The damaged plants may be more susceptible to attacks by fungi or insects.

Acid precipitation can also fall into lakes and streams or run off the land into the water. In lakes, the lower pH levels can be deadly to algae, the eggs of some fish, and other organisms. Producer organisms, such as algae, are killed. Without algae suspended in it, the water looks crystal clear and pure. However, the food chains in the ecosystem have been disrupted, and populations of fish and other organisms have died. Some lakes have become so acidic that nothing can live in them.

Smog Other air pollutants are produced by automobile exhaust and by industrial processes. Some of these pollutants can be toxic when inhaled. This kind of pollution becomes more serious when weather conditions trap the gases in an area for hours or even days. <u>Smog</u> is a kind of air pollution that results when certain pollutants react with sunlight. It looks like a gray or brown haze and contains many airborne pollutants. People with respiratory diseases are especially sensitive to air pollution and may be in danger when air pollution is intense.

Global Atmospheric Changes

Some pollutants in the air harm living things directly, like the trees in Figure 7-9. Others can cause worldwide atmospheric changes that threaten many habitats and the organisms that live in them.

GLOBAL WARMING Sunlight passes through the gases in the atmosphere to reach Earth. But some of these atmospheric gases, called <u>greenhouse gases,</u> also trap and absorb the infrared radiation that bounces off Earth's warmed surface. For thousands of years, this process—called the <u>greenhouse effect</u>—has kept Earth warm. In recent years, however, the amount of greenhouse gases in the atmosphere has increased. As Figure 7-10 shows, the increased amount of greenhouse gases in Earth's atmosphere traps some of the heat that would normally radiate into space. The result is that Earth's average temperature is rising. This increase in temperature, called **global warming,** could lead to changes in climate patterns and even to the melting of the ice caps at the North and South Poles. Most of the recent increase in greenhouse gases have been caused by burning fuel for transportation and industry.

Carbon dioxide, a major greenhouse gas, is released when fossil fuels are burned. (See Figure 7-11.) If the greenhouse effect causes climate change, the world's food supply may suffer. Another effect could be that the ice caps could melt, leading to a rise in sea level and flooding in many coastal habitats.

Finding and using energy sources that do not add carbon dioxide to the atmosphere is one way to prevent further global warming. Because trees remove large quantities of carbon dioxide during photosynthesis and store it in their tissues as carbon compounds, growing more long-lived trees could also help solve the problem.

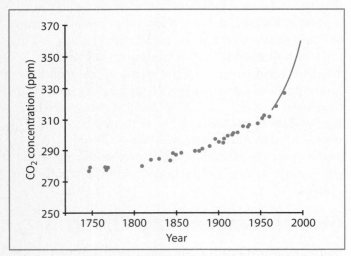

Figure 7-11. Carbon dioxide in the atmosphere from 1750 to 2000: The amount of carbon dioxide in the atmosphere has increased greatly since the beginning of the Industrial Revolution. The dots are data from ice core samples; the solid line represents direct measurements.

OZONE DEPLETION Ozone depletion is another atmospheric problem that we must solve. Like global warming, ozone depletion is a worldwide problem, and international cooperation is needed to find an effective long-term solution.

The release of certain industrial gases into the atmosphere has led to destruction of much of the **ozone shield,** the layer of ozone gas in the upper atmosphere that protects Earth from some of the sun's radiation. (See Figure 7-12.) The thinning "hole" in the ozone shield allows above normal amounts of ultraviolet radiation from the sun to reach Earth's surface. Ultraviolet radiation can cause genetic mutations and can kill cells that are exposed to it. An increase in ultraviolet radiation at Earth's surface could result in more cases of skin cancer. It could also destroy many of the producer organisms in the oceans. This would disrupt food chains and reduce the amount of oxygen released by the producers.

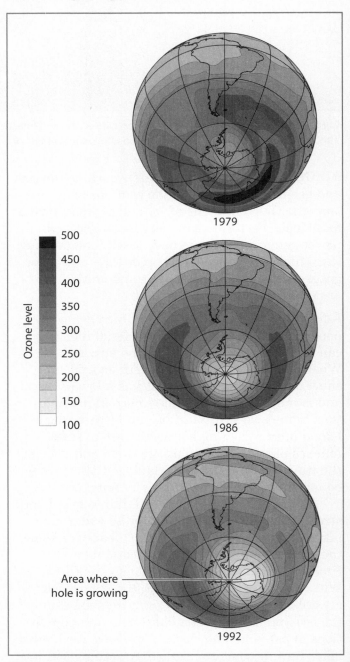

Figure 7-12. The "hole" in the ozone shield: These satellite maps show how much the "hole" in the ozone shield above the South Pole grew in just over a decade.

The main cause of ozone depletion is the release of gases called chlorofluorocarbons, or CFCs, into the atmosphere. CFCs have been used as coolants in refrigerators and air conditioners, as propellants in aerosol cans, and in the manufacture of plastic foam. Some steps have been taken to reduce the release of these gases: Researchers have found alternatives to the products that cause the most damage, and international agreements to reduce emissions of the harmful gases have been made.

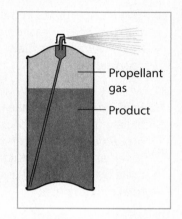

Figure 7-13. **CFCs:** Aerosol cans no longer use ozone-destroying CFCs as propellants. Safer alternatives have been found.

Propellant gas

Product

Individual Choices and Societal Actions

Many people hope technology will help solve some of our environmental problems. In fact, technology has led to some improvements. For example, advances in technology have allowed farmers to greatly increase the crop yield of an acre of land. Larger crop yields mean a greater supply of food. However, some kinds of technology, such as pesticides and fertilizers, can cause pollution and have other harmful effects on the environment.

If technology cannot solve all our environmental problems, people will need to take some difficult steps to save our ecosystem. For some problems, solutions are now available, but they affect our quality of life. For example, we know how to reduce the air and water pollution caused by factories, power-generating plants, and automobiles, but the solutions are expensive and would make the products we buy cost more. We also know how to conserve energy, but many people are unwilling to give up their large cars, brightly lit neighborhoods, and air-conditioned comfort and to turn off their radios, computers, and televisions.

For each environmental problem, people must learn to assess the risk to the ecosystem. For each solution, they must learn to analyze the costs and benefits. Then they must determine which **trade-off,** or compromise, is acceptable and which is simply too dangerous to the welfare of future generations.

The Impact of New Technologies

New laws restrict the introduction of certain new technologies or major construction projects. The individual or company seeking permission to make a change that affects the environment must prepare a statement known as an <u>environmental impact statement</u>. This statement includes an analysis of how the project or technology will affect the environment and is usually discussed at public hearings. Then members of the public or their elected representatives vote on whether or not to allow the new technology or construction project to go forward. Appropriate decisions can be made only if the public is environmentally literate and has a clear understanding of the ecological issues. If an incorrect decision is made, it may be impossible to undo the damage that might result.

Figure 7-14. **Public hearings:** Discussions can be held to consider environmental issues.

Today's Decisions Affect the Next Generation

The decisions we make today can have a huge impact on our environment. Those decisions, right or wrong, will affect the people living today as well as future generations.

The loss of some species may seem unimportant. However, the loss of that single species might have a huge impact on the ecology of an area. If the loss of species continues, large-scale destruction of natural environments will result, with serious consequences for the future. For example, the destruction of large forests or the loss of algae in ocean waters affects not only the organisms that live in those ecosystems now. Those losses may also compromise Earth's ability to produce enough oxygen and remove enough carbon dioxide to maintain an atmosphere that meets the needs of all of its inhabitants, including humans.

Many important decisions about the environment are made by states and nations, but a surprising number of important decisions are made each day by individuals. For example, individuals decide whether to burn their garden waste or turn it into compost, whether to toss the soda can into the trash or recycle it, whether to grab a fresh sheet of paper or write a note on an old envelope.

Figure 7-15. Recycling: Decisions on recycling are made by individuals and their communities.

Much of the impact of our technology and population growth on Earth's ecosystems has been detrimental. If our environmental problems are not recognized and solved, the long-term damage will be irreversible and severe. On the other hand, cooperation by individuals and nations can help maintain the stability of the ecosystems upon which all life depends. Making people aware of the successful results of the collective actions of many separate individuals may be the most promising approach to solving ecological problems.

Review Questions

19. Plants help maintain the quality of the atmosphere by (1) storing carbon dioxide (2) opening holes in the ozone shield (3) causing global warming (4) storing oxygen

20. Greenhouse gases in the atmosphere (1) keep Earth warm (2) are released mostly from greenhouses (3) are valuable as fuels (4) reduce holes in the ozone shield

21. Which human activity has probably contributed MOST to lake acidification in the Adirondack region of New York State? (1) passage of environmental protection laws (2) reforestation projects in lumbered areas (3) production of chemical air pollutants by industry (4) use of biological insect controls to eliminate pests

22. What is one part of the water cycle that the burning of fossil fuels, such as coal and oil, directly affects? Explain your answer.

23. How might the runoff waters from farm land and golf courses be dangerous to organisms living in ponds, rivers, or streams?

24. Why are there frequently water shortages in parts of New York State even though the water supply is nearly constant?

25. The number of industries along New York State's rivers is increasing. What is the most likely consequence of increased industrialization? (1) a decrease in the amount of water needed by industry (2) a decrease in the amount of water pollution (3) an increase in the destruction of natural ecosystems (4) an increase in the amount of water available for recreational use

26. To preserve the biosphere for future generations, humans must (1) make use of technology to develop new pesticides (2) put all wild animals in game preserves (3) explore ways to drain and fill wetlands along the seacoast (4) understand how living things interact with their environment

27. The use of technology often alters the equilibrium in ecosystems. With which of the following statements would most scientists agree? (1) Humans should use their knowledge of ecology to consider the needs of future generations of humans and other species. (2) Humans should develop new technology to expand the influence of humans in natural communities. (3) Humans should learn how to control every aspect of the environment so that damage due to technology will be spread evenly. (4) Humans should develop the uninhabited parts of Earth for human population expansion.

28. Which illustrates the human population's increased understanding and concern for ecological interrelationships? (1) importing organisms in order to disrupt existing ecosystems (2) allowing the air to be polluted only by those industries that promote technology (3) removing natural resources from the Earth at a rate equal to or greater than the needs of an increasing population (4) developing animal game laws in order to limit the number of organisms that may be killed each year

Base your answers to questions 29–31 on the following passage and on your knowledge of biology.

Polychlorinated biphenyls (PCBs) are microcontaminants that are found in some water. Microcontaminants do not change the appearance, smell, or taste of the water, yet they affect parts of the surrounding ecosystem. After PCBs get into water, they are absorbed by some algae, which concentrate them. Then fish, which feed on the algae, concentrate the PCBs many more times. The PCBs are thousands of times more concentrated in fish than they are in the water in which the fish live. At this level of contamination, the survival of some species in the food web is threatened. The health of other species, including humans who may consume some predator fish, such as salmon, is also threatened.

29. In which of the following are PCBs usually most concentrated? (1) dissolved oxygen (2) water (3) algae (4) fish species

30. Which is a harmful effect of microcontaminants on an aquatic ecosystem? (1) They decrease the density of the water. (2) They cause water used for human consumption to have an unpleasant taste. (3) They accumulate in some organisms, making them toxic to other organisms. (4) They cause water to appear cloudy.

31. Name the producer organisms described in the passage.

 # Questions for Regents Practice

Part A

1. Today's lifestyles have led to increased demands for disposable products. The packaging of these products has caused environmental problems most directly associated with
   (1) food web contamination
   (2) atmospheric depletion
   (3) solid waste disposal
   (4) the use of nuclear fuels

2. Some modern agricultural methods have created serious insect problems, primarily because these methods
   (1) increase soil loss
   (2) provide concentrated areas of food for insects
   (3) aid in the absorption of water
   (4) grow crops in areas where formerly only insects could live

3. The decline and extinction of many predatory animal species is most probably the result of
   (1) an overabundance of prey species
   (2) the introduction of a new species of animal into an area
   (3) the disruption of natural food chains
   (4) the decreased use of chemical pesticides

4. Modern methods of agriculture have contributed to the problem of soil depletion because many of these methods
   (1) require smaller amounts of mineral and fertilizer application
   (2) interfere with the natural cycling of elements
   (3) use many varieties of cloned plants
   (4) depend on the practice of planting and harvesting

5. Which action that humans have taken in attempting to solve an ecological problem has had the most negative effect?

   (1) seeking better means of birth control in the human population

   (2) applying scientific farming techniques to oceans

   (3) producing stronger and more effective pesticides

   (4) developing new techniques for the disposal of sewage and industrial and chemical wastes

6. Japanese beetles, a major insect pest in the United States, do relatively little damage in Japan because they

   (1) are kept in check by natural enemies

   (2) are kept in check by effective pesticide sprays

   (3) hibernate during the winter months

   (4) have gradually adapted to the environment

7. Gypsy moths were accidentally introduced into North America. The most probable reason these insects have become serious pests in North America is that they

   (1) were bred by research scientists and are resistant to all pesticides

   (2) are protected by environmental laws and feed on other insect species

   (3) have few natural enemies and reproduce successfully

   (4) are affected by natural controls and feed on plants

8. The survival of many plants and animals has been aided most by

   (1) increasing the height of industrial smokestacks to spread air pollutants away from the immediate vicinity of combustion

   (2) reduction in the number of restrictive pollution control laws

   (3) heavy use of pesticides to kill all of the insect pests that compete with humans for food sources

   (4) development of research aimed toward the preservation of endangered species

9. DDT is an insecticide that accumulates in the fatty tissues of animals and is transferred through food chains. Its concentration increases at each link of a food chain. Which organism in a food chain is most likely to accumulate the highest concentration of DDT?

   (1) rabbit (a herbivore)

   (2) corn (a producer)

   (3) field mouse (a consumer)

   (4) owl (a predator)

10. What is the most likely cause of the change in life expectancy shown in the graph?

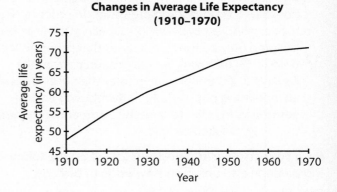

Changes in Average Life Expectancy (1910–1970)

   (1) poor land-use management that has affected the quality of the topsoil

   (2) technological oversights that have had an impact on air quality

   (3) a decrease in natural checks, such as disease, on the population

   (4) widespread use of pesticides, such as DDT, in water supplies

11. A desired outcome derived from an understanding of the principles of ecology would be

   (1) the elimination of most predatory species

   (2) an increase in world human population

   (3) a decrease in disruptions of existing wildlife habitats

   (4) an increase in the amount of industrialization

Part B

Base your answers to questions 12 through 14 on the paragraph below.

A scientist studied a river and forest area downstream from a large city with an increasing human population. During the study, the scientist made observations that could be classified as:

(A) Most likely a negative result of human activity

(B) Most likely a positive result of human activity

(C) Probably not influenced by human activity to any extent

Select the letter of the phrase from the list above that best fits the observation for each question. A letter may be used more than once or not at all.

12. Measurement of the levels of nitrates and phosphates (fertilizer chemicals from sewage) in the river that flows through the forest showed the following results:

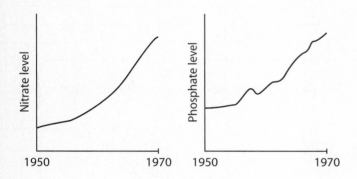

Which phrase from the choices listed above best fits this observation?

13. After 1970, measurements showed that the concentration of dissolved oxygen in the river increased, while the concentration of suspended particles decreased. Which phrase from the choices listed above best fits this observation?

14. The population of hawks declined, while their food sources increased. High levels of pesticides were found in the reproductive tissues of the hawks. Which phrase from the choices listed above best fits this observation?

Base your answers to questions 15 through 18 on the diagram, which represents the growth rate of a mouse population introduced into an abandoned field ecosystem.

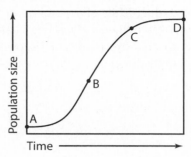

15. At what points is food most likely a limiting factor in the rate of mouse population growth?

(1) A and B

(2) B and C

(3) C and D

(4) B and D

16. At what point is the rate of population growth the greatest?

(1) A

(2) B

(3) C

(4) D

17. At what point would the mouse population be the greatest in the ecosystem?

(1) A

(2) B

(3) C

(4) D

18. Compare the growth rate of the mouse population in the abandoned field to the growth rate of the human population. In your comparison be sure to identify

• how it is similar

• how it is the same

Base your answers to questions 19 and 20 on the following information and graph and on your knowledge of biology.

The screw-worm fly is a destructive parasite of livestock. The graph shows the results of an experiment in which one population of screw-worm flies was treated with pesticides and another group of equal size was treated with ionizing radiation, which made the male flies sterile.

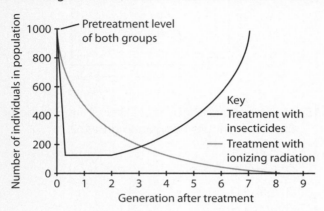

19. At what point after treatment will the group treated with pesticide probably reach its pretreatment population?

(1) first generation

(2) seventh generation

(3) third generation

(4) eighth generation

20. At what point after treatment will the sterility method be more successful against screw-worm flies than the pesticide method?

(1) immediately

(2) second generation

(3) third generation

(4) sixth generation

Base your answers to questions 21 and 22 on the information in the paragraph provided and on your knowledge of biology.

A single protist (a one-celled organism) was placed in a large test tube containing nutrient broth. The tube was kept at room temperature for 24 hours. Samples from the tube were observed periodically during the 24 hours, using the low power of a compound light microscope. The data are summarized in the table below.

Age and Number of Protists in Culture	
Age of the Population in Hours	**Number of Protists in the Population**
0	1
6	2
8	3
10	4
13	8
16	16
18	32
20	64
22	128
24	256

21. Which graph best represents the data given in the table?

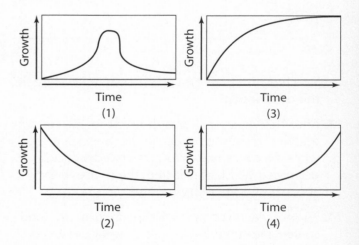

22. Which graph most resembles the growth of the human population at the present time?

(1) 1

(2) 2

(3) 3

(4) 4

Base your answers to questions 23 through 26 on the following information and on your knowledge of biology.

The gypsy moth, *Pothetria dispar,* is a defoliator (an agent that removes leaves) of both deciduous trees and conifers in New York State. The gypsy moth undergoes complete metamorphosis from egg to larva (caterpillar) to pupa to adult moth. The gypsy moth larvae cause the most damage to trees. The heaviest defoliations occur in oak forests, because these trees are highly favored as food plants by all larval stages. The adult moths do not feed; their only function is to reproduce.

The male moth is a fairly strong daytime flier and tends to fly upwind in a zigzag pattern. The female is so heavily laden with eggs that she is unable to fly. Egg laying occurs soon after the moths mate, usually within a day or so after the female reaches the adult stage. Moths die soon after egg-laying is completed.

The best means of controlling gypsy moths in the forests of New York State is through the development and use of biological methods of pest control. The most important of these are *Ooencytrus kuwanae,* a tiny wasp that parasitizes the upper layers of eggs in a cluster and is normally effective on about three fourths of the eggs; and *Calosoma sycophanta,* a ground beetle that preys on both gypsy moth larvae and pupae.

An important natural agent that causes gypsy moth populations to collapse is a viral disease that affects the larvae. Affected caterpillars are seen hanging from trees. The virus is always present in gypsy moth colonies in a dormant form and becomes activated when outside stress is applied. The viral disease, starvation, stress-induced diseases, and parasitism may cause a population to collapse after a forest has undergone two or three years of defoliation.

23. Which method is the best way to eliminate gypsy moth populations from the Adirondack and Catskill Mountains of New York State?

(1) Spray oak, beech, and maple trees with a pesticide.

(2) Apply DDT and other pesticides to the trunks of spruce, fir, and pine trees.

(3) Introduce a species of ground beetle that preys upon gypsy moth larvae.

(4) Apply a phosphate fertilizer to the soil to prevent larval attack against conifer and deciduous root systems.

24. Which factor is *not* likely to cause a population of gypsy moths to decline after two or three years of heavy defoliation?

(1) parasitism

(2) starvation

(3) viral disease

(4) climate-resistant eggs

25. Which statement concerning the gypsy moth is true?

(1) Adult gypsy moths die shortly after the completion of egg-laying.

(2) Adult gypsy moths heavily defoliate oak forests in New York State.

(3) Gypsy moth larvae can survive the cold winters in New York State.

(4) The male gypsy moth is not a very good daytime flier.

26. Identify which diagram represents the stage of development of the gypsy moth in which it destroys the most deciduous trees and conifers in New York State. Support your choice with a biological explanation.

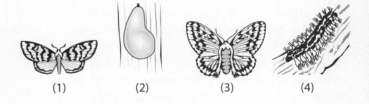

(1)   (2)   (3)   (4)

Base your answers to questions 27–31 on the reading passage that follows and on your knowledge of biology.

The ecological balance of the Great Lakes has been seriously altered by human civilization, which has disrupted species in food chains from the producers (microscopic plankton) to the predator fish. This disruption has caused a reduction in the natural game fish populations of the lakes.

For example, the Atlantic salmon was formerly found in Lake Ontario. The salmon's passage to Lake Erie was blocked by Niagara Falls. The fish was a prize catch for fishermen, but no Atlantic salmon have been caught in Lake Ontario since 1890. Soil that eroded from farmland covered the salmon's gravel spawning grounds with silt, trees that shaded the streams where the young salmon lived were torn down as forests were cleared, and dams built for sawmills prevented the salmon from traveling upstream to spawn.

As the population of Atlantic salmon and other deepwater fish declined, two alien marine species— the alewife and the sea lamprey—appeared in Lake Ontario. These intruders most likely entered by way of the Hudson River, the Erie Canal, and the Oswego River. Lack of predators and the abundant food supply led to a rapid increase in the populations of these species until they were the dominant species in the lake. Furthermore, the completion of the Welland Canal, linking Lake Erie with Lake Ontario, in 1932 gave these species access to the remainder of the Great Lakes. By the early 1970s, about half the fish caught throughout the Great Lakes were alewives. The lamprey's increasing population devastated the desirable fish in the lakes, harming the fishing industry.

Government agencies, such as the United States Fish and Wildlife Service, took action at this point to restore game fish to the lakes and return sport fishing to this region. They developed a lampricide that proved fatal to the young sea lampreys, but had no harmful effects on other species. They also started stocking the lakes with predator game fish such as Coho salmon, Chinook salmon, and steelhead trout. As a result of these actions, the populations of the alewife and the sea lamprey have both decreased, and sport fishing has returned to Lake Ontario.

27. Which would be most likely to have occurred if microscopic plankton had been removed from Lake Ontario when Atlantic salmon were abundant?

(1) Predator fish would have thrived.

(2) Game fish would have increased their spawning activities.

(3) Food chains would have been disrupted.

(4) The water level in the lake would have increased.

28. Which fish species was not introduced into the Great Lakes for sport fishing?

(1) Coho salmon

(2) Chinook salmon

(3) alewife

(4) steelhead trout

29. Which graph represents the effect of the spread of human civilization on the population of Atlantic salmon in Lake Ontario?

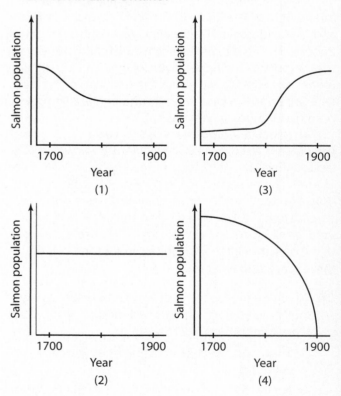

30. State one way humans contributed to the change in the Atlantic salmon population in Lake Ontario.

31. Explain the role humans played in the appearance of the alewife and the sea lamprey in Lake Erie.

Part C

32. The use of ionizing radiation in an attempt to control the screw-worm fly is a form of a pest control method referred to as biological control. The use of ladybugs to control aphids, milky spore disease to reduce Japanese beetle populations, and sex attractants to lure pest insects into traps are also examples of biological control strategies used against insect pests. Using one or more complete sentences, give one reason why the use of biological control methods is often better than the use of chemical pesticides. [1]

33. Cattail plants that grow in freshwater swamps in New York State are being replaced by an imported species of plant called purple loosestrife. The two species have very similar environmental needs. Using one or more complete sentences, answer the following questions.

    (a) Since cattails and loosestrife occupy the same niche, it is predicted that eventually only one of the two species will exist in New York freshwater swamps. Provide one reason why loosestrife will probably out-compete the cattails and be more successful. [1]

    (b) Why would loosestrife plants replacing the native cattails potentially cause a decrease in many swamp wildlife populations and perhaps even lead to the elimination of some species from New York State?

34. Scientists have discovered a link between deforestation and global warming. Write a paragraph that explains what is meant by the terms *deforestation* and *global warming,* then describe the connection between the two. [3]

35. A developer clears all of the plants, including the trees and grasses, from a hillside before building many new homes, roadways, and sidewalks. After several windy, rainy springs, a homeowner in the new development decided to plant a garden. What is the best explanation for why the garden grew poorly? [1]

36. Describe two ways in which the destruction of the rainforest in South America could affect a hospital patient in New York State? Use one or more complete sentences in your answer. [2]

37. Humans have the ability to modify nearly any environment on Earth, but in the process they may have a negative impact on the species living there. On a number of occasions this has happened. Select one such instance and write a paragraph in which you name a particular modification, describe the reason for the modification, and identify one specific negative impact on natural ecosystems that occurred as a result. [3]

38. Burning coal and oil can lead to global warming. Write a paragraph to describe what global warming is and provide a specific example of its likely effects on organisms or ecosystems. [2]

39. Plankton is the name given to the algae and microscopic life that grow in great numbers on and near the surface of the ocean. Plankton serve as the basis of food chains for oceanic life. Scientists have become concerned with the increase in ultraviolet (UV) radiation reaching the surface of the Earth in recent years. They fear that UV rays may negatively impact the plankton.

    Write a paragraph to explain why the amount of UV radiation reaching the surface may be on the increase, especially near the North and South Poles. Also describe the effect any large-scale plankton destruction will have on larger species living in these same areas of the ocean where the UV levels have been increasing. [3]

40. Global warming is generally considered a negative aspect of human involvement with the ecosystem. Using one or more complete sentences,

    (a) explain how solving this problem will require increasing global awareness and cooperation [1]

    (b) identify two trade-offs that may have to be considered in decisions regarding what to do about the problem [2]

Base your answers to question 41 on the following diagram which represents part of a food web in a Long Island ecosystem.

41. The numbers show the concentration of the insecticide DDT in parts per million (ppm) in the body tissues of the various organisms. Write a paragraph to explain:

- why the water plant contains the pesticide DDT [1]

- why the amounts of DDT in the three bird species are so much higher than in the other organisms of this food web [2]

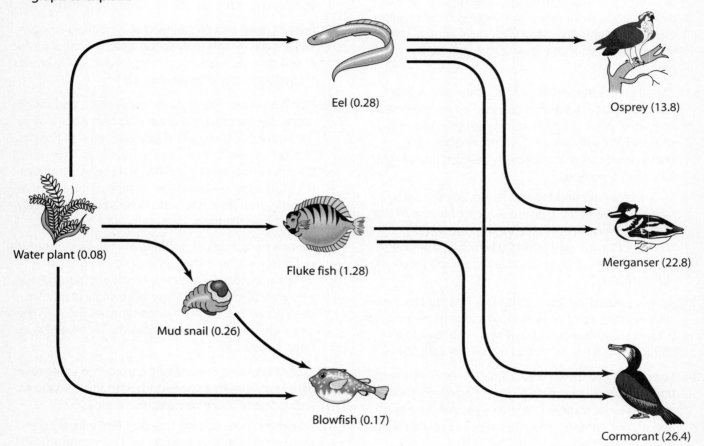

Eel (0.28)

Osprey (13.8)

Water plant (0.08)

Fluke fish (1.28)

Merganser (22.8)

Mud snail (0.26)

Blowfish (0.17)

Cormorant (26.4)

Scientific Inquiry and Skills

VOCABULARY		
assumption	dependent variable	model
bias	evidence	observation
conclusion	experiment	opinion
control	hypothesis	peer review
controlled experiment	independent variable	research plan
data	inference	scientific literacy

What Is Science?

Science is both a body of knowledge and a way of knowing things. Through intellectual and social activities, human thinking is applied to discovering and explaining how the world works. Science originates when people ask questions. At one time, "scientific" knowledge was just a collection of opinions and unrelated ideas attempting to explain observations. For example, many people gazing out over the ocean were certain that Earth was flat. A few individuals were equally sure that Earth was round. The topic was hotly debated. Those believing that Earth was flat offered for **evidence** (support for the idea that something is true) the fact that some ships never returned home. They believed that these ships had been destroyed when they sailed over Earth's edge. Those who believed that Earth was round also had evidence. They had observed boats approaching land and noticed that the tops of the sails were visible before the hull of the boat.

Another common idea once was that living organisms could come from nonliving things. Some people believed that when conditions were just right, frogs formed from the mud, water, and gases in the bottom of a pond. People also thought that if you left some grain and a dirty shirt in a wooden box, mice would develop after a period of time. Many people were certain that reproduction was not necessary for life to form. This idea, too, was discussed and debated.

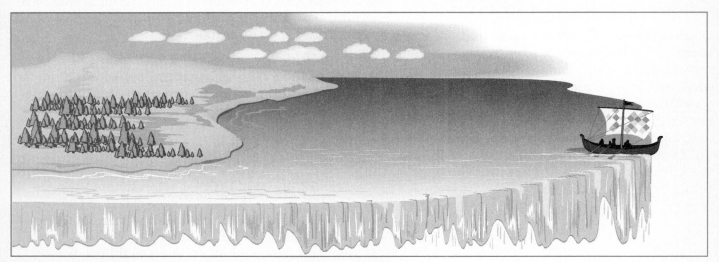

Figure 8-1. Ships at sea: At one time a flat Earth seemed to make sense.

Today, scientists do more than debate whether or not a new opinion or idea seems to make sense. They develop explanations using observations as evidence. New information is combined with what people already know. Learning about the historical development of scientific concepts and about the individuals who have contributed to scientific knowledge helps people understand the thinking that has taken place. At first, it might seem silly to believe that Earth is flat, but based on observations made at the time and the tools available at the time, it's not surprising that many people believed in a flat Earth. The emergence of life from pond mud seemed equally reasonable.

Scientific Inquiry

Scientific investigation involves the following:

- questioning
- observing and inferring
- experimenting
- collecting and organizing data
- finding evidence and drawing conclusions
- repeating the experiment several times
- peer review

Questioning is at the heart of science. Progress in science depends on people who not only wonder how the world works but who also take the time to develop questions that can be tested and answered.

Observations and Inferences

Observations are things or events that are made using any of the senses or tools, such as thermometers, graduated cylinders, balances, or rulers. As more and better tools are developed, the ability of scientists to observe the natural world increases. For example, the invention of both the microscope and, later, the electron microscope increased our ability to observe the structure of living organisms. This led to the realization that all living things are composed of cells.

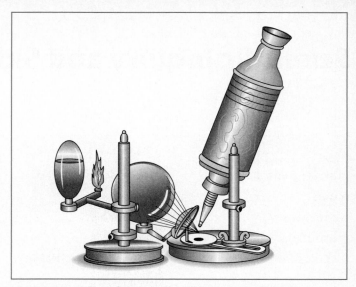

Figure 8-2. The microscope: With the invention of the microscope, scientists could finally observe microorganisms.

INFERENCES Conclusions or deductions based on observations are **inferences.** Inferences may be very subtle. An inference can also be thought of as an idea or conclusion based on the results of an experiment or observation. For example, you may infer that a slug that remains motionless for several hours is dead.

Assumptions A good experiment keeps assumptions to a minimum. An **assumption** is the belief that something is true. Assumptions also may be very subtle, and at first you may be unaware you are making them. For example, when doing a seed germination experiment, you might assume that all 100 seeds planted will germinate when watered and kept under favorable conditions. The idea that 100% of the seeds will grow is an assumption. An assumption that could be made during a slug feeding experiment is that slugs will eat every day if provided with desirable food.

Opinions Ideas people have that may or may not have any basis in fact are **opinions.** Opinions are often **biased,** or influenced by an assumption that may or may not be correct. Although everyone has opinions, which should be respected, a good way to avoid bias is to leave opinions out of data collection and analysis.

THE SCIENTIFIC VIEW Understanding the scientific view of the world is essential to personal, societal, and ethical decision making. To think scientifically, you must critically analyze events, explanations, and ideas. You should use these skills—as well as ideas from other disciplines—to develop personal explanations of natural events. You should also create visual models and mathematical formulations to represent your thinking.

Keep in mind that asking questions to develop an explanation is a continuing and creative process. Sometimes conflicting explanations arise from the same body of evidence. For example, plants seem to grow better when talked to daily. Some explain this by crediting the voice or words. Others point out that simply breathing carbon dioxide on the plant helps it grow. Science is a search for the truth. Scientific thinking can keep you from being misled and making poor judgments.

Review Questions

1. A student performed an experiment involving two strains of microorganisms, strain A and strain B, cultured in various temperatures for 24 hours. The results of this experiment are shown in the following data table.

Microorganism Growth and Temperature		
Temperature (°C)	Microorganism Growth (Number of Colonies)	
	Strain A	Strain B
25	10	11
28	10	7
31	11	3
34	12	0

Based on the results of the experiment, the student inferred that strain A was more resistant to higher temperatures than strain B was. What, if anything, must the student do for this inference to be considered a reasonable conclusion?
(1) nothing, because this inference is a valid scientific fact (2) repeat this experiment several times and obtain similar results (3) repeat this experiment several times using different variables (4) develop a new hypothesis and test it

2. The following graph represents the results of an investigation of the growth of three identical bacterial cultures incubated at different temperatures.

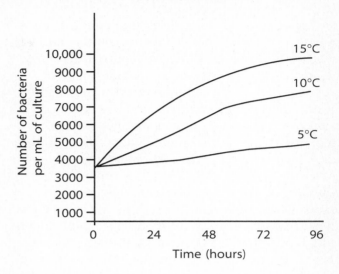

Which inference can be made from the graph?
(1) Temperature is unrelated to the reproductive rate of bacteria. (2) Bacteria cannot grow at a temperature of 5°C. (3) Life activities in bacteria slow down at high temperatures. (4) Refrigeration will most likely slow the growth of these bacteria.

3. A student prepared the following list of steps for performing a laboratory investigation. She omitted one important step for completing the investigation. Using one or more complete sentences, state the procedure that is missing in the chart.

Steps to Follow in an Experiment
Define a problem.
Develop a hypothesis.
Select suitable lab materials and perform a controlled experiment to test the hypothesis.
Collect, organize, and graph the experimental data.
?

4. When heavy rains occur while apple orchards are in bloom, the apple crop the following fall is much smaller than normal. This information can best be described as (1) an inference (2) a hypothesis (3) a prediction (4) an observation

5. Which of the steps listed below would be first in a scientific investigation? (1) Perform the experiment. (2) Analyze the experimental data. (3) Formulate a hypothesis. (4) Define the problem to be investigated.

Inquiry Skills and Understandings

Everyone needs to understand certain concepts about science and inquiry. **Scientific literacy** involves applying critical thinking skills to everyday life, particularly to claims related to health, technology, and advertising. For example, imagine you are watching a television commercial with your family. The advertiser claims its company has developed a cream that makes hair grow when applied to the scalp. According to the commercial, people with thin hair or no hair have both used the cream with success. Before rushing out to buy this product, you should think about the claims and begin to question some of what you heard. Next, think about how you can get answers to your questions. Then you should evaluate whether or not the information is to be believed. Here is a way to approach the problem:

1. *Inquiry involves asking questions, and locating, interpreting, and processing information from a variety of sources.*

You may begin by thinking about the following questions:
- How many people were tested?

- What is in the product?

- How long do you have to use it to get results?

- Does it have any side effects?

Next, you ask your friends, and no one knows anything about the product. You also find that your state's consumer product information agency has no information about the company or the hair growth product. Then, you may go to the Internet and find that the company has a Web page that claims 50% of the people using the product grew a full head of hair after ten applications.

Now ask yourself: Are you ready to use the product based on the information you have found? Do you know enough about the product to make an informed decision? You might want to find answers to more questions.

- How many people actually took part in the study? In other words, 50% of how many people grew hair?

- What caused the participants to have thinning hair or to be bald? Did they have a medical condition that needed attention?

- How long has the company been in business?

- Why hasn't the consumer information agency heard of them and their product?

- Was the cream tested scientifically with careful experimental techniques and design?

Keep in mind that careful scientific inquiry involves doing research to find answers to questions and explanations of natural phenomena. Much of the research in the hair product example was done by finding information without actually doing a laboratory investigation.

2. *Inquiry involves making judgments about the reliability of the source and relevance of information: Scientific explanations are accepted when they are consistent with experimental and observational evidence.*

When evaluating evidence and making decisions about how useful your information is, keep the following in mind.

- All scientific explanations are tentative. They can be changed or updated as new evidence emerges. What seems to be true today may be disproved tomorrow.

- Each new bit of evidence can create more questions than it answers. This leads to an increasingly better understanding of how things work.

- Good scientific explanations can be used to make accurate predictions about natural phenomena.

- Beyond the use of reasoning and consensus, scientific inquiry involves the testing of proposed explanations using conventional techniques and procedures. In other words, logic is not enough. Questions should be answered using a good experimental design and thoughtful interpretation.

For example, suppose you read in a magazine about a newly developed HIV vaccine that is said to be effective on monkeys. You should ask:

- Are these results preliminary and tentative, or are they the final results of extensive studies?

- How was the testing done? How many animals were used? For how long have they remained healthy?

- Is HIV in monkeys the same as HIV in humans? Is this the solution to the HIV epidemic in humans or just an early step?

3. *Answers can be found through a research plan and hypothesis testing.*

DEVELOPING A RESEARCH PLAN A **research plan** involves finding background information, developing a hypothesis, and devising an experimental process for testing a hypothesis. Before investing time and resources on research, it is important to find out what others have already learned. Most research plans begin with a thorough library search. This search may include the use of electronic information retrieval (the Internet and library databases), a review of the literature (scientific journals), and feedback from the investigator's peers. This background work is done so that the researcher has a thorough understanding of the major concepts being investigated and any similar investigations.

Figure 8-3. Research: A review of the literature must be done before the investigation can be designed. Useful resources include primary science journals, professional Web sites, and library databases.

MAKING HYPOTHESES Inquiry involves developing and presenting proposals, including formal hypotheses, to test explanations. A good **hypothesis** attempts to explain what has been observed in a way that can be tested. It is a tentative answer to a question. Experiments cannot prove a hypothesis; they can only either support the hypothesis or fail to support it.

Most hypotheses would make sense if the words "I think that" were added to the beginning of the statement. Try adding "I think that" to the beginning of each hypothesis in the following chart.

Examples of Hypothesis Statements
This hormone will make plants grow faster.
The presence of this chemical in our drinking water does not harm us.
If this hormone is applied to plant leaves, then the plant will grow faster.
If this chemical is safe, then it will not harm us when it is added to our drinking water.

A good hypothesis can also help determine the organization of an experiment as well as what data to collect and how to interpret those data. Testing a hypothesis is valuable even when the hypothesis is not supported by experimental results, since new information is gained in the process of testing any hypothesis.

Designing an Experiment

Once the background work has been done and the hypothesis developed, the actual experiment must be designed. An **experiment** is a series of trials or tests that are done to support or <u>refute</u> (disprove) a hypothesis.

Let's say that you suspect that applying the chemical IAA (a growth hormone) to plant leaves will increase the growth rate of the plant. Your hypothesis might read as follows: *If IAA is applied to the leaves of plants, then the plants will grow more rapidly than those that do not have IAA applied to their leaves.* Once you have written your hypothesis, you must make decisions about variables and experimental techniques.

THE DEPENDENT VARIABLE What is it that you will measure? In the above experiment, you will measure the effect of IAA on plants. What you will measure is called the **dependent variable,** since it depends on what you do to the plants. Since you asked about how the plants will grow, you will need to measure how large the plants are at the beginning as well as at regular intervals until the conclusion of the experiment. You will also have to decide how to make the measurements. Will you measure only the height of the stem, or will you also measure the size of the leaves? What units will you use?

INDEPENDENT VARIABLES Factors that might influence the dependent variable are **independent variables.** This is the variable the investigation manipulates. If you are investigating the effect of IAA's being applied to the leaves, you must decide on the concentration of IAA. How often will it be applied to the leaves, and how will you apply it? You may even decide to test several concentrations of IAA. In this example, the frequency of applications and the concentration of IAA are independent variables.

CONTROLLING VARIABLES How will you control the independent variables that might affect your interpretation of the results? A **control** is an established reference point used as a standard of comparison. It allows you to make comparisons that generate valid information. For example, you should start with plants that are of the same kind and are about the same age and size. All of the plants should be healthy, grown in the same kind of soil, and provided with the same amount of water and light. If you neglect to control all independent variables, one or more of them may affect plant growth, and you may reach a false conclusion concerning IAA. A **controlled experiment** is one in which the possible variables have been carefully considered and regulated so the results are due only to the independent variable you are testing.

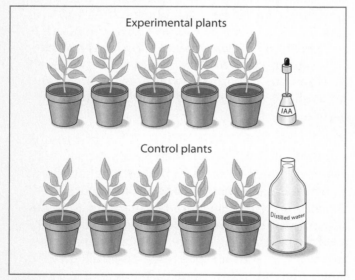

Figure 8-4. Experimental controls: The control group will have distilled water applied to their leaves in place of IAA. It is important to apply something to the leaves of the control group or they would be treated differently in two ways from the experimental group. The plants will be the same type, size, and age as those in the experimental group. They will be grown in the same soil, with the same amount of light and water.

Keep in mind that there should only be one variable being tested at one time. You can test different concentrations of IAA, or you can test the frequency of applying IAA, but you cannot test both on the same plants at the same time. You also cannot test both the impact of fertilizer AND the impact of IAA on the same plants at the same time.

DEVELOPING EXPERIMENTAL TECHNIQUES Selecting, acquiring, and building apparatus, as well as considering safety precautions and planning how to avoid bias, are important parts of this stage in the development of the research plan. For example, in the IAA study, you need to decide how many plants to use. Would one plant for each concentration of IAA be enough? Should you use 100 plants for each concentration? Think about these possibilities. With only one plant, genetic differences could cause variations in growth. Could one of the plants have been infected with a fungus while still an embryo? Would using multiple plants help to cancel out this type of problem? How many trials will you need? Is one trial enough, or would five or six trials be better? Large sample sizes with repeated trials provide much more accurate information, and there is less probability of error due to chance. Large sample sizes and multiple trials are more likely to produce valid results.

When designing an experiment, think of the steps in the following Experimental Design Guide as a way to assist you in your planning. Remember that you should first formulate the question you want to answer or the problem you want to solve. Then review the literature to learn about the topic you are investigating.

Experimental Design Guide	
What is your hypothesis?	The hypothesis should suggest a possible answer to the question you are investigating.
What is your dependent variable?	What should change and/or be measured as a result of the experiment? Make a data table to record the data as they are collected.
What is your independent variable?	What is the treatment? Are you only changing one factor at a time to see its effect? Will there be several groups with more than one treatment—such as several pH values, colors of light, or temperatures?
Describe how you will control the experiment.	What other possible factors may vary that could also affect the results and make your experiment inconclusive?
What steps will you take to conduct this experiment?	Make a list of procedures and materials needed to conduct the experiment.

Review Questions

6. A drug company tested a new medication before putting it on the commercial market. Pills without medication were given to 500 test subjects in group A, and pills with medication were given to 500 subjects in group B. In this experiment, the individuals in group A served as the (1) host group (2) dependent variable (3) control (4) hypothesis

7. In order to find the percentage of organic matter in soil from several different locations, a student collected the samples, weighed them immediately, roasted them for several minutes in the flame of a Bunsen burner to burn off organic matter, and weighed them again. The student concluded that the difference between the first and second weights represented the weight of the organic matter in the soil. The most serious mistake that the student made in this experiment was in (1) taking large samples (2) weighing the samples before roasting them (3) failing to dry the samples before first weighing them (4) assuming that roasting could remove the organic matter

8. In an investigation to determine the effects of environmental pH on the germination of dandelion seeds, 25 dandelion seeds were added to each of five petri dishes. Each dish contained a solution that differed from the others only in its pH, as shown below. All other environmental conditions were the same. The dishes were covered and observed for 10 days. The data table the student designed is shown below.

Using one or more complete sentences, state the independent variable in this investigation.

The Effect of pH on Seed Germination		
Petri Dish	pH of Solution	Number of Seeds Germinated
1	9	
2	8	
3	7	
4	6	
5	5	

Base your answers to questions 9–11 on the information below.

A student placed five geranium plants of equal size in five environmental chambers. Growing conditions were the same for each plant except that each chamber was illuminated by a different color of light of the same intensity. At the end of 20 days, plant growth was measured.

9. State a possible hypothesis for this experiment.

10. What control should be used in this experiment?

11. Using one or more complete sentences, describe one modification you would make in the design of this experiment to make the results more reliable.

12. A student wants to shorten the ripening time for tomatoes. He predicts that the more water the seedlings receive, the faster their tomatoes will ripen. To test this prediction, he grows 20 tomato plants in a garden in full sunlight that has dry soil and 20 in a garden in a shadier location where there is greater moisture content in the soil. He then records the time it takes for fruit to develop and ripen on the plants in each garden location. Using one or more complete sentences, state a serious error the student made with the design of this experiment.

13. In attempting to demonstrate the effectiveness of a new vaccine, a scientist performed these experimental procedures:

- One hundred genetically similar rats were divided into two groups of 50 rats each (group A and group B).

- Each rat in group A was given an injection of the vaccine in a glucose-and-water solution.

- Each rat in group B was given an injection of the glucose-and-water solution containing no vaccine.

- After several weeks, all rats in both groups were exposed to the disease for which the vaccine was developed.

What dependent variable was studied in this experiment?

14. A new drug for the treatment of asthma is tested on 100 people. The people are evenly divided into two groups. One group is given the drug, and the other group is given a glucose pill. The group that is given the glucose pill serves as the (1) experimental group (2) limiting factor (3) control (4) indicator

15. As part of a laboratory experiment, a thin slice of peeled raw potato weighing 10 grams is placed in an oven at 80°C. After 5 hours, the potato sample is removed from the oven and weighed again. The purpose of this experiment might be to (1) test for the presence of starch in living tissues (2) isolate cells in various stages of cell division (3) determine the water content of potato tissue (4) study the rate of photosynthesis in potatoes

16. What is the function of a control group in an experiment?

17. Scientists breed mice to be as genetically alike as possible to use in experiments. What is the advantage of using such mice compared to mice that are not genetically similar? Why would cloned mice be even better?

Collecting and Organizing Data

In science, **data** generally refers to the results of trials, or tests, completed during experiments. Scientific inquiry involves the ability to use various methods of recording, representing, and organizing data. Data can be organized into diagrams, tables, charts, graphs, equations, and matrices. Scientists must then be able to interpret the organized data and make inferences, predictions, and conclusions based on those data.

A data table is an important initial stage in making sense of the information you will collect while doing an experiment. When constructing a table to record your data, keep the following checklist in mind.

Figure 8-5. **Data collection:** Making measurements and carefully recording data are important parts of doing an experiment.

Data Table Checklist
✔ Title the table in a way that relates the independent variable to the dependent variable. For example: The Effect of Fertilizer Concentration (the independent variable) on Plant Growth (the dependent variable).
✔ Column headings include the dependent and independent variables. They may also include trial or setup numbers or other information.
✔ Column headings need to indicate units of measurement.
✔ The independent variable is typically recorded in increasing order.
✔ The dependent variable is recorded to correspond with the independent variable.

The next step is to construct a graph that allows you to see trends or patterns in your mathematical data. Almost every day you interpret graphs. Television, newspapers, and other media often use graphs to illustrate ideas. Advertisers use graphs to convince us to use their pain reliever or allergy medication. They know that a carefully constructed graph can provide us with a large amount of information quickly. Examining columns of numbers in a data table is time consuming and sometimes difficult. Looking at a graph allows us to form opinions and to make comparisons quickly.

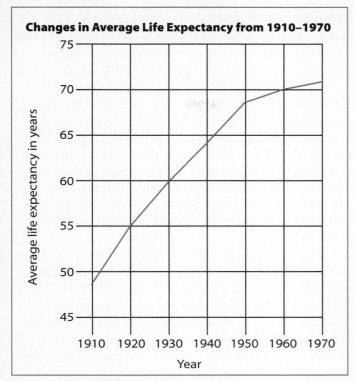

Changes in Average Life Expectancy from 1910–1970

Figure 8-6. Everyday use of graphs: Interpreting graphs like this one is part of everyday life.

There are four basic types of graphs:

- pie or circle graph
- bar graph
- histogram
- line graph

A scientist must decide which type of graph will be the most effective for presenting data so that the conclusion will be clear. Different rules are used in drawing each type of graph. However, there are a few rules common to all line and bar graphs.

Rule 1: The dependent variable is plotted on the vertical, or *y*-axis. Remember that the dependent variable is what you find out as a result of doing the experiment. It is what you measure during the experiment.

Rule 2: The independent variable is plotted on the horizontal, or *x*-axis. This is the factor you varied to find its effect on the test organisms or situation.

Rule 3: The spacing between the numbers on both axes must be in equal increments. Figure 8-7 shows how to apply the three rules to a line graph. Use the Graph Construction Checklist when constructing a graph.

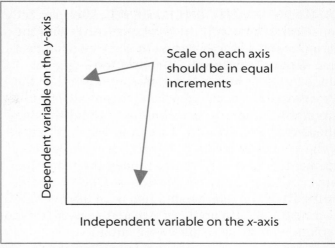

Figure 8-7. Rules for a line graph

Graph Construction Checklist

✔ Title your graph so that the reader knows what it is illustrating. You can often use the same title you used on the data table.

✔ Dependent variable is on the vertical axis.

✔ Vertical axis is labeled, including units of measure.

✔ Scale on the vertical axis is appropriate and spaced at even intervals.

✔ Independent variable is on the horizontal axis.

✔ Horizontal axis is labeled, including units of measure.

✔ Scale on the horizontal axis is appropriate and spaced at even intervals.

✔ Points are plotted accurately.

✔ Data points are connected, and the line does not go beyond. (You only know what you measured; beyond that is speculation.)

✔ Legend indicates the meaning of each line if there is more than one. Often you are expected to surround data points with small circles or triangles.

The Results

A careful examination of the experimental results involves the ability to look at relationships between the predicted result contained in the hypothesis and the actual result.

DRAWING VALID CONCLUSIONS After carefully considering how well the predicted result and the actual result of the experiment correspond, a decision about the outcome—a **conclusion**—can be made. A scientist needs to determine whether the hypothesis has been supported. Scientists often use statistical analysis techniques to find the likelihood that their results were produced by chance. If the results differ only slightly, errors in measurement, genetic differences among the test organisms, or chance may be the reason. Once a significant pattern or relationship has been discovered as a result of data analysis, a scientist next tries to explain why these results were obtained.

A **model** can often be used to explain the results of an experiment. A model is a way of explaining or demonstrating what might be happening and to predict what will occur in new situations. A model explains how DNA carries the genetic code and how traits are passed from one generation to the next. As more is learned about the structure and function of DNA, parts of the model are confirmed or changed.

REPORTING RESULTS One assumption of science is that other individuals could arrive at the same explanation if they had access to similar evidence. Experiments that cannot be repeated exactly with the same results have little worth. Research must be shared in such a clear manner that other scientists can repeat the investigation and try to get the same results. When reporting the results of an experiment, a scientist must pay close attention to details. The experimental results may be used by hundreds of other scientists to repeat the experiment. Thus, each step of the experiment must be described accurately and in exact detail.

If you wanted to repeat an experiment done by a friend, would you be able to do it if your friend told you to heat the mixture "for a little while"? Or if you had to add some soap powder to the mixture, would it be acceptable for your friend to tell you to "add two pinches"? If you expect to obtain the same results, your friend must provide precise instructions, such as to heat the mixture at a temperature of 75°C for 5 minutes, and then add 2 grams of a certain kind of soap powder.

Scientific inquiry also requires the ability to develop a written report for public scrutiny. Scientists report their findings in scientific journals or during presentations at professional meetings. The report describes the hypothesis, including a literature review of previous studies, the experiment performed, its data and the scientist's conclusion, and suggestions for further study.

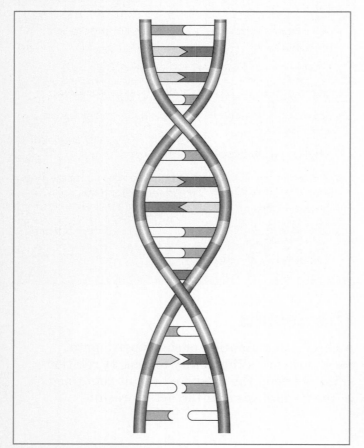

Figure 8-8. A model of DNA

Figure 8-9. Peer review: Scientists examine one another's work to ensure that the results are correct.

Based on the results of the experiment and public discussion and review, inquiry may also require the scientist to revise the explanation and think about additional research.

A **peer review,** in which several scientists examine the details of an experiment, is an important part of the scientific process. Scientists are expected to question explanations proposed by other scientists. Peers analyze the experimental procedures, examine the evidence, identify faulty reasoning, point out statements that go beyond the evidence, and suggest alternative explanations for the same observations. Peer review is one of the systems of checks and balances in science.

Keep in mind that all scientific explanations are subject to change as more is learned. Scientists know and accept this as a part of the way they work. With new information, they must be willing to change their thinking and, therefore, their explanations.

Evidence is a collection of facts offered to support the idea that something is true. Scientists accept evidence when it is supported by many facts. Until they have a large collection of evidence to support their thinking, scientists must remain neutral.

Sometimes claims are made that are not supported by actual evidence. Scientific claims should be questioned if

- the data are based on samples that are very small, biased, or inadequately controlled

- the conclusions are based on the faulty, incomplete, or misleading use of numbers

For example, enough organisms must be used in an experiment and the difference in data between the control and experimental group must be significant enough so that genetic differences, random chance, and inaccuracies in measurement cannot be responsible for the results. Wherever appropriate, a statistical analysis of the results should be done. This could be something as simple as finding the average, calculating the percentage of difference, or determining the frequency. Claims should also be questioned if

- fact and opinion are intermingled

- adequate evidence is not cited

- conclusions do not follow logically from the evidence given

Further Science Understandings

Well-accepted scientific theories are supported by many different scientific investigations, often involving the contributions of individuals from different disciplines. In developing a theory, scientists carry out many investigations. They may vary in degree of complexity, scale, and focus. Research by different scientific disciplines can bring to light multiple views of the natural world. The resulting theory can encompass many different aspects of natural events. For instance, the theory of evolution began with the observations of one naturalist. But over the years scientists—including botanists, biologists, geologists, oceanographers, and others—researched numerous aspects of the theory to reach one general scientific idea.

 Review Questions

18. A student conducted an original, well-designed experiment, carefully following proper scientific procedure. In order for the conclusions to become generally accepted, the experiment must (1) contain several experimental variables (2) support the original hypothesis (3) be repeated to verify the reliability of the data (4) be conducted by a scientist

19. A student tossed a coin five times and observed results of four tails and one head. He concluded that when a coin is tossed, there is an 80% chance of getting a tail and a 20% chance of getting a head. The conclusion would be more valid if (1) only two tosses of the coin had been used (2) the weight of the coin had been taken into consideration (3) a greater number of tosses had been used (4) the surface the coin landed on had been taken into consideration

Base your answers to questions 20–22 on your knowledge of biology and the experiment described in the paragraphs and graphs below.

A group of 24 frogs was separated into two equal groups. Group A was placed in an environment in which the temperature was a constant 35°F. Group B was placed in a similar environment, except the temperature was a constant 65°F.

Equal amounts of food were given to each group at the start of the experiment and again every 24 hours. Immediately before each daily feeding, the excess food from the prior feeding was removed and measured. This allowed the scientist to determine the daily amount of food each group of frogs consumed. Each day, the heart rate and breathing rate of the frogs were checked. At the end of the experiment, the following bar graphs were prepared:

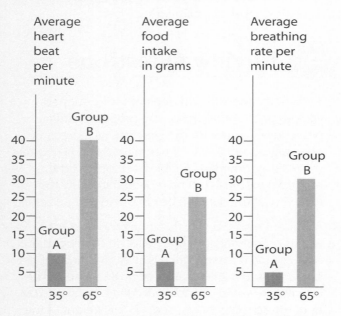

20. Using one or more complete sentences, state the hypothesis the scientist was most likely investigating in this experiment.

21. After examining the graphs, the scientist could reasonably assume that at a low temperature the frogs would (1) become more active (2) produce less carbon dioxide (3) eat more food (4) use more oxygen

22. The independent variable in this experiment was (1) heart rate (2) breathing rate (3) amount of food consumed (4) temperature of the environment

Base your answers to questions 23–25 on the experiment below and on your knowledge of biology.

After watching the behavior of earthworms in soil, a biology student suggested that the penetration of air into the soil promotes the root development of plants. The student then set up the following experiment.

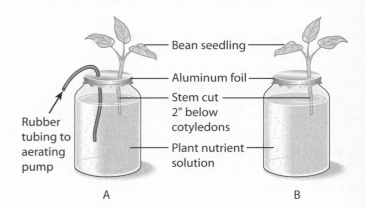

23. The important data to be recorded in this experiment will come from the observation of the increase in (1) leaf size (2) stem size (3) number of leaves (4) number of roots

24. State the hypothesis being tested in this experiment.

25. Describe what the student could do to this experiment to improve the reliability of the student's conclusions. Use one or more complete sentences.

Base your answers to questions 26–29 on the information below and on your knowledge of biology.

A student was working on an investigation to measure the relative activity of an enzyme at various pH values. He collected the following data: pH 2, enzyme activity 10; pH 8, enzyme activity 50; pH 12, enzyme activity 10; pH 4, enzyme activity 20; pH 6, enzyme activity 40; pH 10, enzyme activity 40

26. What is the independent variable in this experiment?

27. Organize the data above by filling in the data table provided on the next page. Follow these directions when completing your data table.

- Provide an appropriate title for the data table.
- Fill in the first box in each column with an appropriate heading.
- Arrange the data so that pH values are in increasing order.

Title:	

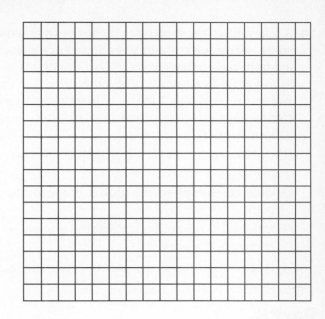

28. Construct a graph using the information in the data table, the following directions, and the grid provided in the next column.

  • Provide an appropriate title for the graph.

  • Make and label an appropriate scale on each axis.

  • Plot and connect the points. Surround each data point with a circle.

29. According to the data, this enzyme would probably work best at what pH values? (1) 7 and 8 (2) 2 and 12 (3) 6 and 7 (4) 4 and 10

Questions for Regents Practice

Part A

1. One ounce each of protein, carbohydrate, and fat are burned separately in a calorimeter to determine Caloric content. The results are shown in the data table.

Caloric Content of Substances	
Organic Compound	**Number of Calories Produced**
Protein	147
Fat	271
Carbohydrate	152

Which statement represents a valid conclusion based on the data?

(1) An ounce of fat contains about twice as many Calories as an ounce of protein.

(2) Protein is a better energy food than carbohydrate.

(3) Carbohydrates, fats, and proteins all yield approximately the same number of Calories per unit of weight.

(4) Proteins and carbohydrates provide the most Calories per ounce.

2. Which laboratory procedure would be best for demonstrating the effect of light intensity on the production of chlorophyll in pea plants?

(1) using 10 plants of different species, each grown in the same intensity of light

(2) using 10 plants of different species, each grown in a different intensity of light

(3) using 10 plants of the same species, each grown in the same intensity of light

(4) using 10 plants of the same species, each grown in a different intensity of light

3. In an early trial of the Salk vaccine for polio, 1,830,000 school children participated. This original trial was an attempt to determine whether the Salk vaccine was effective in preventing polio. Of the 1,830,000 children involved, only 440,000 received the vaccine. The remainder were not given the vaccine because they

(1) had a natural immunity

(2) already had polio

(3) served as a control

(4) were allergic to the vaccine

4. A scientific study showed that the depth at which some microscopic plants were found in a lake varied from day to day. On clear days, the plants were found as far as 6 meters below the surface of the water but were only 1 meter below the surface on cloudy days. Which hypothesis would these observations support?

(1) Light intensity affects the growth of microscopic plants.

(2) Wind currents affect the growth of microscopic plants.

(3) Nitrogen concentration affects the growth of microscopic plants.

(4) Precipitation affects the growth of microscopic plants.

Part B

Identify the Steps of Development that best correspond to the statements below (questions 5 through 8). The steps are in no particular order and may be used more than once or not at all.

Steps of Development

A. *Test the hypothesis with an experiment.*

B. *State the results.*

C. *Draw a conclusion from the results.*

D. *Form a hypothesis.*

5. Beans will grow faster if you fertilize them at regular intervals than if you only fertilize the ground once before you plant them.

6. If I add more catalyst to the reaction, the reaction will speed up.

7. A scientist took saliva from his dog's mouth and mixed it with a solution of starch and warm water. He took the same amount of saliva from his own mouth and mixed it with the contents of a second tube of starch and warm water. One hour later, the contents of both tubes were checked for sugar.

8. In an experiment, caterpillars consumed 8 grams of lettuce leaves and 0.4 grams of tomato leaves.

9. A scientist performed an experiment using the steps below. State the directions that belong in box X.

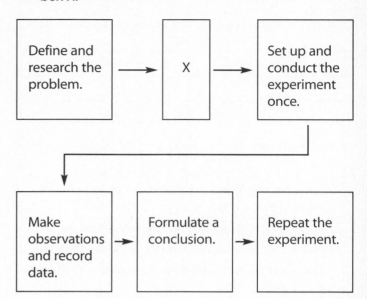

10. To investigate the effect of a substance on plant growth, two bean plants of the same species were grown under identical conditions with Substance X added to the soil of one of the plants. At the end of 2 weeks, the plant grown with Substance X added was 12.5 centimeters tall, and the plant grown without Substance X was 12.2 centimeters tall. The researcher concluded that the presence of Substance X causes plants to grow taller. State one reason why this conclusion may not be valid.

Part C

11. You have discovered a new chemical that you think will kill harmful bacteria. You exposed four groups of the same bacteria species to the chemical and counted how many cells were alive after the application of the chemical. Four identical groups of bacteria did not receive the chemical. At the end of a certain period of time, you also counted how many cells were alive in these groups. You are invited to present your findings at a professional meeting. During the peer review process, you indicate that at the end of the study, only 10% of the bacteria in the groups treated with the new chemical were still alive; so your antibiotic is effective at killing bacteria. Identify one specific question about your experiment the peer reviewers would need to ask to determine whether your conclusion is valid. [1]

Use the information provided and your knowledge of biology to answer questions 12 through 14.

A biology student wanted to investigate the effects of fish oil fertilizer on the growth of plants. A month ago, she planted 10 bean plants. Five of the plants were fertilized once a week with 1 mL of the fertilizer mixed in 10 mL of water. The other five plants were given 11 mL of water each week in place of the fertilizer. All other conditions were kept exactly the same for both groups of plants.

The information the biology student collected during the experiment appears in Tables 1 and 2.

Table 1: Height Gain in Centimeters — Fertilizer Added — Experimental Plants

Plant	Height (cm) on Day 1	Growth (cm)				Total Growth (cm)	Average Growth per Week (cm)
		Week 1	Week 2	Week 3	Week 4		
A	15.0	2.6	1.4	3.0	2.5	9.5	2.4
B	10.0	1.1	1.5	2.0	2.5	7.1	1.8
C	17.0	3.0	2.0	1.9	1.9	8.8	2.2
D	12.0	2.1	2.2	1.8	2.3	8.4	2.1
E	16.0	2.3	2.0	1.7	2.4	8.4	2.1
Totals	—	11.1	9.1	10.4	11.6	42.2	10.6

Table 2: Height Gain in Centimeters — No Fertilizer Added

Plant	Height (cm) on Day 1	Growth (cm)				Total Growth (cm)	Average Growth per Week (cm)
		Week 1	Week 2	Week 3	Week 4		
F	16.0	2.0	1.0	2.0	1.2	6.2	1.6
G	11.0	1.0	1.1	1.0	1.5	4.6	1.2
H	18.0	2.0	1.2	1.1	1.3	5.6	1.4
I	11.0	1.1	1.4	1.2	1.3	5.0	1.2
J	17.0	1.3	1.0	1.4	1.4	5.1	1.3
Totals	—	7.4	5.7	6.7	6.7	26.5	6.7

12. The student wrote the following hypothesis before designing the experiment: "Adding fish oil fertilizer to the soil will affect the growth of bean plants." Do the results of the experiment support her hypothesis? Use data from the two tables to support your answer. [1]

13. Explain why the student should compare average plant height gain instead of comparing individual plants. [1]

14. Explain why the extra water was used in place of the fertilizer in the No Fertilizer group of the plant growth experiment. [1]

15. In experiments designed to test new drugs on human patients, doctors usually give one group the new drug while the other group is given a sugar pill—or placebo—instead. Explain why it is important to give the placebo to the second group rather than giving them no pill at all. [1]

Base your answers to questions 16 through 18 on the illustration and reading passage below and on your knowledge of biology.

In an experiment to determine how salmon find their way back to their home stream, a biologist captured 50 salmon from the South Bend River. She then blocked the nostrils (chemical sensors) of one half of them (the experimental group), and did nothing to the other half of the captured salmon (the control group).

She then tagged all of the captured salmon and transported them downstream to the location indicated by the X on the following map, and then released them. The scientist then returned to point Y on the South Bend River (upstream from the release site) and netted salmon as they swam up the river. A total of 50 salmon were caught at the recapture site: 22 from the control group and 12 from the experimental group. She also caught 16 salmon that were not tagged at all.

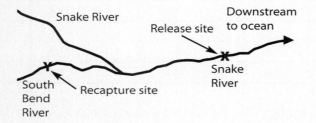

16. State the hypothesis that the biologist is testing. [1]

17. State the dependent variable in the biologist's experiment. [1]

Use data provided in the passage to create two data tables. Both tables must have a heading for each column that describes the data in that column.

18. The first table should indicate the numbers of experimental and control fish released at point X. [2]

19. The second data table should summarize the fish counts referred to in the paragraphs above that indicate the categories and numbers of fish caught at the recapture site. [2]

Laboratory Skills

VOCABULARY

balance	electronic balance	metric ruler
chromatography	electrophoresis	microscope
compound light microscope	graduated cylinder	stain
dichotomous key	indicator	stereoscope
dissection	magnification	triple-beam balance
	mass	volume

Tools for Measurement

During laboratory investigations, you are often required to make measurements of length, mass, and volume. You need to know the proper pieces of equipment to select and the appropriate procedures and units to use.

MEASURING LENGTH Typically a **metric ruler** is used to determine the length of an object. To measure length, use either centimeters (cm) or millimeters (mm). You should know how to convert millimeters to centimeters and vice versa.

The metric ruler shown in Figure 9-1 is calibrated—or scaled—in centimeters (cm). The lines indicated by the numbers 1, 2, 3, and so on each represent a distance of 1 centimeter. The smaller divisions each equal 1 millimeter (10 mm = 1 cm). A line equal to 5 cm is shown above the ruler in Figure 9-1.

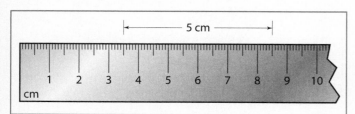

Figure 9-1. Metric ruler: The tool used for measuring length in centimeters and millimeters

Micrometers (μm), are very tiny units that are used to measure objects through the microscope. One thousand micrometers equal one millimeter.

Figure 9-2 shows a metric ruler as seen under the low-power objective of a microscope. The distance across the field of view is approximately 3.2 millimeters, or 3,200 micrometers (since 1.0 mm = 1,000 μm). If the cells observed on the slide in Figure 9-3 are being viewed through the same low-power objective, the field of view is still 3.2 millimeters. The approximate length of each cell is therefore about 1 millimeter or 1,000 micrometers, since about 3 cells fit across the diameter (widest part) of the field.

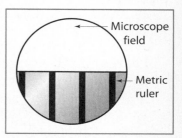

Figure 9-2. Microscope field with metric ruler

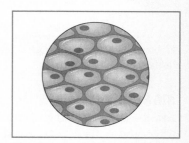

Figure 9-3. Microscope field with cells

MEASURING VOLUME A **graduated cylinder** is often used to measure a liquid's **volume,** or the space it occupies. Liters and milliliters are typically used to indicate volume in the metric system, while quarts and ounces are used in the English system. Graduated cylinders are calibrated in milliliters (mL).

Water and many other fluids form a meniscus (curving surface) when placed in the narrow tube of a graduated cylinder. To correctly read the volume of the liquid, place the cylinder on a flat surface. Then read from the bottom of the curved meniscus at eye level. The volume of liquid in the graduated cylinder in Figure 9-4 is 13 mL.

MEASURING TEMPERATURE

In the biology laboratory, temperature is often measured in degrees Celsius. The freezing point of water is 0°C; the boiling point is 100°C. Human body temperature is 37°C, which is the temperature indicated on the thermometer in Figure 9-5.

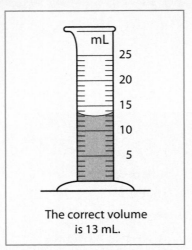

Figure 9-4. Graduated cylinder: You can find the volume of a liquid using a graduated cylinder.

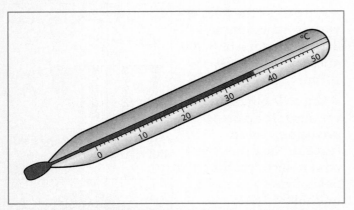

Figure 9-5. Thermometer: This Celsius thermometer shows human body temperature.

MEASURING MASS

In the biology laboratory, **mass**—the quantity of matter in something—is often measured with a **balance,** which is a tool that works by comparing an object of unknown mass with an object of known mass. The triple-beam balance or an electronic balance is typically found in a high school laboratory.

A **triple-beam balance** (Figure 9-6) has a single pan and three bars (beams) that are calibrated in grams. One beam, the 500-gram beam, is divided into five 100-gram units. Another beam is divided into ten units of 10 grams totaling 100 grams. The front beam is divided into 10 major units of 1 gram each. Each of these divisions is further divided into 0.1-gram units.

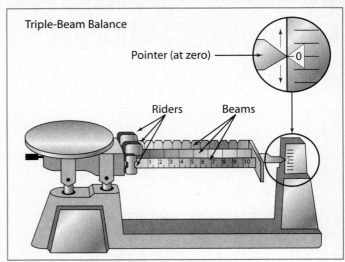

Figure 9-6. Triple-beam balance

Before using a balance, make sure that the pan is empty and that the pointer and all of the riders (devices that are moved along the beams) are on zero. To determine the mass of an object, it is first placed on the pan. Then, starting with the 500-gram beam, the masses on the beams are adjusted until the pointer is again pointing to zero. The mass of the object is equal to the sum of the readings on the three beams.

An **electronic balance** measures mass automatically. To use an electronic balance, first turn it on and wait until it shows a zero mass. (This may require using the re-zero button shown on Figure 9-7.) Place the object with the unknown mass on the pan. Read the mass.

Figure 9-7. Electronic balance

Never place a substance directly on a balance pan. Instead, protect the balance with a weighing paper or dish. With a triple-beam balance, first find the mass of the weighing paper. Then find the mass of the substance AND the weighing paper. Subtract the mass of the weighing paper from the total mass of the paper plus the substance. The remainder is the mass of the substance.

For an electronic balance, put the weighing paper on the balance and then use the re-zero button to set the balance to zero. Next, put the substance on the paper and read the mass. The re-zero button automatically subtracts the mass of the weighing paper from the total. The reading on the balance is the actual mass of the substance.

Review Questions

1. The crab shown in the following illustration has four pairs of walking legs and one pair of pincer legs. The crab is shown in its normal walking position.

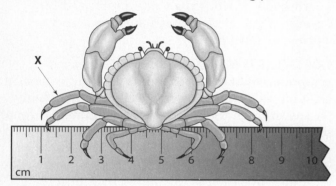

In this position, what is the distance between the ends of the front pair of walking legs? (One of the front pair of walking legs is identified with an "X" in the illustration.) (1) 8.5 cm (2) 85 cm (3) 7.5 cm (4) 75 cm

2. State which piece of laboratory equipment you would use to accurately measure 10 grams of glucose.

3. Which piece of laboratory equipment would be used to most accurately measure the volume of a liquid? (1) beaker (2) balance (3) test tube (4) graduated cylinder

4. A student measured a larva using a metric ruler, as represented in the following diagram.

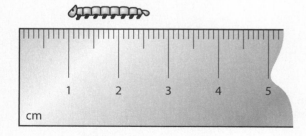

What is the length of the larva? (1) 26 cm (2) 26 mm (3) 16 cm (4) 16 mm

5. Draw a meniscus to represent a water level of 6 mL on the adjacent diagram of a graduated cylinder.

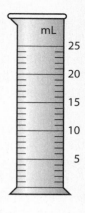

6. Which of the following graduated cylinders contains a volume of liquid closest to 15 mL?

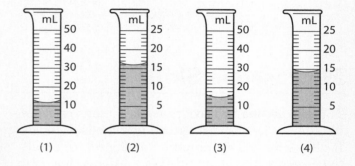

(1)   (2)   (3)   (4)

7. Which of the following diagrams shows a correct measurement?

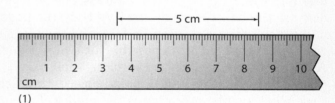

(1)

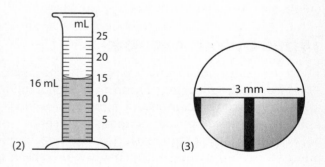

(2)   (3)

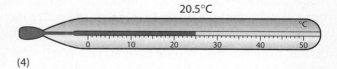

(4)

8. The following diagram shows a triple-beam balance with a mass on the pan. With the riders in the positions indicated, what is the mass of the object on the pan of the balance? (1) 9 grams (2) 200 grams (3) 249 grams (4) 942 grams

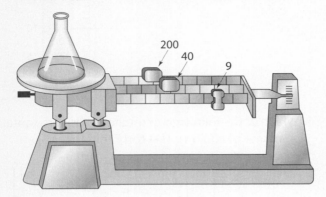

Microscope Skills

The **microscope** is a tool that uses a lens or a combination of lenses to make an object easier to see. It allows for the examination of objects too small to be seen with the unaided eye. Microscopes also permit the close observation of fine details. For example, without a microscope you can see the legs and wings of a fly. With a microscope you can also see the hairs covering the fly's body, the pads and clawlike structures on its feet, and the framework of its wings. This is possible for two reasons. A microscope magnifies the specimen and also allows you to distinguish between objects that are close together. **Magnification** is the ability of a microscope to make an object appear larger.

Types of Microscopes

There are many different types of microscopes. The two most commonly found in a high school laboratory are the compound light microscope and the stereoscope. The primary difference between the two is that with a compound light microscope, light must pass through or reflect off the specimen being examined.

STEREOSCOPES With a stereoscope (Figure 9-8), light is reflected off the specimen. A **stereoscope,** sometimes called a dissecting microscope, has two <u>ocular</u> eyepiece lenses, one for each eye, and one or more <u>objectives</u> (the other lenses of the microscope). The amount of magnification is low, but the image is three-dimensional and is not reversed as it would be with a compound

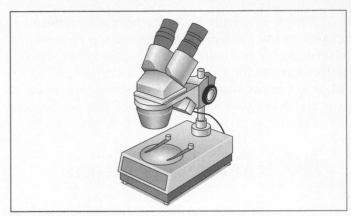

Figure 9-8. A stereoscope

microscope. Stereoscopes are often used to observe parts of specimens such as insects, worms, or flowers.

COMPOUND MICROSCOPES The typical **compound light microscope** has one ocular lens, at least one objective lens, and a light source. Light passes through the object being examined, through the objective lens, and then through the eyepiece.

The image you see is magnified by both lenses—the ocular lens and the objective lens. The total magnification is calculated by multiplying the magnification of the ocular by the magnification of the objective. For example, if you use a microscope that has a 10x eyepiece and a 40x objective, the magnification of a specimen would be 400x.

Eyepiece	x	Objective	= Total Magnification
10x	x	40x	= 400x

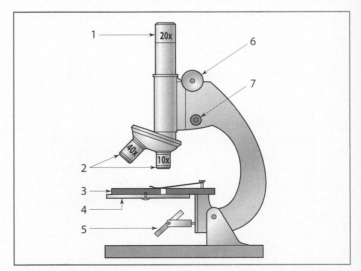

Figure 9-9. A compound microscope: Each part is labeled with a number. The names and functions of the parts are given in Table 9-1.

Microscope lenses may get dirty from contact with fingers, specimens, stains, and so on. Do not use paper towels or your shirt to clean them! Only use lens paper to clean the lenses of a microscope. Lens paper will not scratch the soft glass of the lens.

Table 9-1. Names and Functions of Parts of a Compound Microscope	
1 Eyepiece or Ocular Lens	• lens nearest the eye and used to "look through" • usually magnifies 10x
2 Objective Lenses	• lenses located closest to specimen • usually 2 or 3 • commonly magnify at 4x, 10x, and 40x
3 Stage	• flat surface (platform) on which the slide is placed • stage clips hold the slide in place
4 Diaphragm	• located under the stage • controls the amount of light passing up through the specimen
5 Light Source	• might be a mirror or a light bulb • provides light that passes up through the specimen and makes it visible
6 Coarse Adjustment	• used to focus only under low power (up to 100x) • never used when the high-power objective is in place for viewing • usually the larger knob; causes a large amount of movement of the lenses
7 Fine Adjustment	• the only focus you should use with high power • used to sharpen the image under low power • also used to see different layers of a specimen • usually the smaller of the focus knobs; causes a small amount of movement of the lenses

Techniques for Using Microscopes

Due to the action of microscope lenses, there are a number of things you need to remember when viewing objects through a compound light microscope.

• The image will be upside-down and backwards, as shown in Figure 9-10.

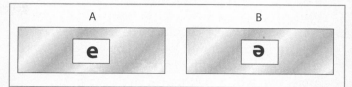

Figure 9-10. Microscope view: The letter "e" as seen on a slide (A) and as seen through the microscope (B). (Only the change in position of the letter is shown, not magnification.)

• You must move the slide in the direction that is opposite the way the organism appears to be moving. In other words, if the organism appears headed toward the upper right side of your field of view, you must move the slide down and to the left to keep it in view. See Figure 9-11.

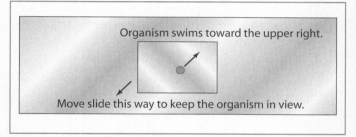

Organism swims toward the upper right.

Move slide this way to keep the organism in view.

Figure 9-11. Moving the slide to follow a moving object

• The field becomes darker as you increase the magnification. You will need to increase the amount of light passing through the specimen as you go from low power to high power. The diaphragm, located under the stage, can be used to do this.

• Since the field becomes smaller under high power, center the object you are viewing before switching to a higher power. Otherwise the object may be outside of the field of view.

FOCUSING When observing specimens through the compound light microscope, first use the low-power objective. Do this even if higher magnification is needed to make your observations.

1. First, place the slide on the stage of your microscope. Position the slide so that the specimen is over the opening in the stage. Anchor the slide with the stage clips.

2. Move the coarse adjustment so that the low-power objective is as close to the slide as you can get it without touching the slide. Some microscopes have a built-in "stop" that prevents you from getting the objective lens too close to the slide. You should look at the objective and the slide while doing this. Never lower the objective while looking through the eyepiece.

3. Look through the eyepiece with both eyes open and turn the coarse adjustment so that the low-power objective and slide move apart. The specimen should come into view.

4. Next, turn the fine adjustment to bring the specimen into sharp focus.

5. To focus the specimen under higher magnification after locating it under low power, move the slide so that what you are interested in seeing is located in the center of your field of view. Remember that as you increase the magnification, the object appears larger, but you see less of its edge. The field of view becomes smaller when you switch from low power to a higher power. See Figure 9-12.

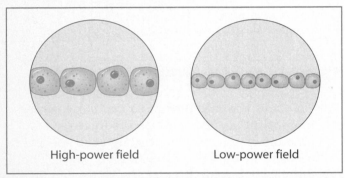

High-power field   **Low-power field**

Figure 9-12. Specimen under low and high power: Note that the high power field is narrower (only 4 cells can be seen), but the cells appear larger, and more detail is visible.

6. Watch from the side of the microscope and slowly turn the high-power objective into place. Be sure that the high-power objective is not going to touch the slide. High-power objectives are longer than low-power objectives and can easily hit the slide—be careful.

7. If the objective is not going to hit the slide, click it into position. As you look through the eyepiece, the specimen should be visible. Use the fine adjustment to sharpen the focus. Remember never to use the coarse adjustment when using the high-power objectives. You could damage the microscope lens and break the slide.

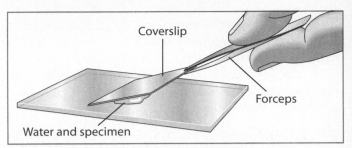

Coverslip

Forceps

Water and specimen

Figure 9-13. Preparing a wet-mount slide

PREPARING WET-MOUNT SLIDES Only specimens that are small and thin can be seen through a compound light microscope. However, thin slices may quickly dry and shrivel. To avoid this, a temporary wet-mount slide can be prepared by using the following steps:

1. Using a <u>pipette</u> (eye dropper), add a small drop of water to the center of a clean, glass slide.

2. Place the object to be viewed in the water. (It should be lying flat rather than folded over.)

3. Use <u>forceps</u> to position a <u>coverslip</u>, as shown in Figure 9-13. Using forceps will keep you from getting fingerprints on the coverslip. Fingerprints could interfere with your ability to view the image clearly.

4. Lower the coverslip slowly. This technique will prevent the formation of air bubbles under the coverslip.

STAINING SPECIMENS When you examine cells and cell parts through a microscope, they often appear to be transparent. You need to adjust the light and the focus so that you can see differences in thickness and density. Although adjusting the amount of light passing through the specimen may help, stains are often used to create greater contrast. Different types of cells and cell parts vary in their ability to soak up various stains. For example, certain cell parts turn darker in the presence of iodine stain. Other parts do not become darker.

To add a stain, such as methylene blue, to a wet-mount slide, place a drop of the stain beside one edge of the coverslip. Next touch a small piece of paper towel to the opposite edge of the coverslip. The towel absorbs water and draws the stain across the slide under the coverslip. This technique allows you to keep the slide on the stage of the microscope. You do not need to prepare a new slide. See Figure 9-14.

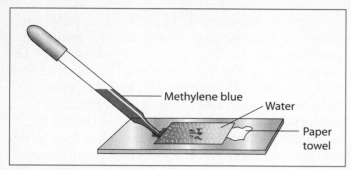

Figure 9-14. Staining a wet-mount slide

IDENTIFYING AND COMPARING CELL PARTS

It is important to remember that cells have specific structures that perform specific jobs. Many of these structures are visible through a compound light microscope. Some of the parts you can either expect to see or see evidence of are the following:

- **Nucleus**—usually observed as a rounded, dense, dark-staining structure. It can be located anywhere in the cell, not just in the middle.

- **Cytoplasm**—typically fills the cell. It appears to be clear in some cells and very grainy in others. Cell organelles, which may or may not be visible, are suspended in the cytoplasm.

- **Cell membrane**—found surrounding the cytoplasm. It is the outer boundary of animal cells and is located between the cell wall and the cytoplasm in plants and some other organisms.

- **Cell wall**—The nonliving cell wall on the outside of the cell membrane in plant cells is a supportive structure. Many bacteria form a different type of protective cell wall.

- **Chloroplasts**—green, oval structures found in the cytoplasm of some plant cells and photosynthetic one-celled organisms.

- **Vacuoles**—often seen as clear areas in the cytoplasm. Plant cells contain very large fluid-filled vacuoles that occupy much of the inside of the cell. Some single-celled organisms may contain specialized vacuoles for digestion and for regulating water balance.

- **Chromosomes**—most easily observed in cells undergoing mitosis or meiosis. They are usually dark-staining and threadlike.

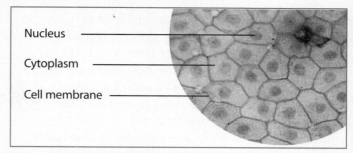

Figure 9-15. Animal cells: As seen through a compound light microscope

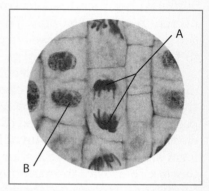

Figure 9-16. Plant cells undergoing mitotic cell division: A indicates chromosomes, and B indicates a nucleus before the cell undergoes mitosis.

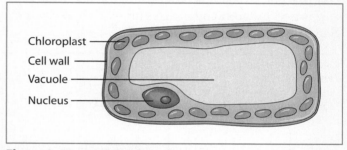

Figure 9-17. Typical plant cell: Structures that can be seen through a microscope

Additional Laboratory Techniques

There are many techniques that are useful in the biology laboratory. Some of the most common are electrophoresis, chromatography, and the application of stains and indicators. Dichotomous keys are especially useful for field research.

ELECTROPHORESIS Gel **electrophoresis** is a very powerful tool and is widely used by scientists in many disciplines—not just biologists. It allows scientists to separate mixtures of large molecules according to size. DNA and proteins are the two types of molecules most often separated by gel electrophoresis.

When setting up a protein gel, a sample of biological material containing proteins is prepared by breaking open the cells in order to release the proteins. Next, the proteins are treated with both chemicals and heat. One of the chemicals used coats the protein molecules and gives them a negative charge. Then, very small amounts of the prepared sample are placed in wells at the top of a special gel positioned in a gel electrophoresis apparatus. (The wells are similar to the holes you would get by pressing the teeth of a comb part way into a block of gelatin dessert.) The gel is placed between two electrodes that are connected to a power supply. This causes one end of the gel to take on a positive charge and the other to take on a negative charge.

Positively charged molecules in the sample move toward the negative electrode, while negatively charged protein molecules move toward the positive electrode. The type of gel used in protein electrophoresis is made up of long molecules that form a tangled mesh. Smaller molecules are able to work their way through the gel more quickly than larger molecules. Therefore, molecules are separated by both their size and electrical charge. See Figure 9-18.

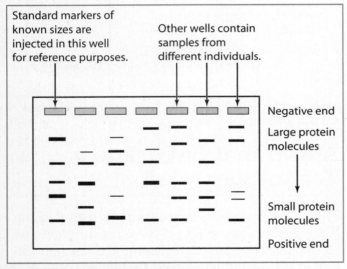

Figure 9-18. Protein gel electrophoresis: Protein gels are typically run vertically.

DNA gel electrophoresis is a little different. The analysis of an individual's DNA begins with the use of special enzymes to cut the DNA at specific points in the sequence of bases. This produces fragments of DNA that are of different lengths. These pieces of DNA will vary in size and number from one individual to another due to the uniqueness of each genetic code.

Next, small amounts of the DNA samples are placed in wells located on one side of a semisolid gel. Typically the DNA gel is made of <u>agarose</u>—the same gelatine-like substance used to culture bacteria but without the nutrients. The gel is located between two electrodes that are connected to a power supply. This causes one end of the gel to take on a positive charge and the other to take on a negative charge when the current is turned on. The negatively charged DNA fragments move toward the positive electrode.

As with the protein gel, the smaller the fragment, the more rapidly it moves through the gel. Small pieces of DNA will travel farther and be located farther from the well where they were initially injected. This allows the DNA fragments to form a distinct pattern that becomes visible through staining or a variety of other techniques.

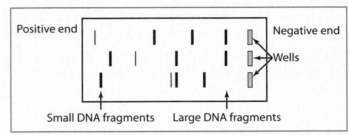

Figure 9-19. DNA gel electrophoresis: DNA gels are typically run horizontally.

The information provided by both DNA and protein gels looks very much like a bar code. The patterns formed from different protein samples or the DNA of different individuals can provide information about relatedness. DNA has been used to determine who the father and/or mother of a child actually is in paternity cases or in instances where a couple suspects that the child given to them in the hospital is not their child. It has also been used to determine guilt or innocence during criminal investigations. The source of blood, semen, or skin can be identified with this technique. DNA left at a crime scene can be compared to a suspect's DNA to determine if the suspect was at the crime scene.

In the case of endangered species, scientists can use DNA electrophoresis to learn which groups are being devastated by poachers, since skins from members of the same group will have similar DNA patterns. Gel electrophoresis can also be used to determine and to identify the genes responsible for specific genetic diseases such as sickle cell disease.

CHROMATOGRAPHY Like gel electrophoresis, **chromatography** is a technique used for separating mixtures of molecules. In one type of chromatography commonly used in the biology laboratory, the mixture being separated is placed on a paper to which it sticks. For example, chlorophyll extract from plant leaves is placed on filter paper or special chromatography paper. It is done by placing a small dot of the concentrated chlorophyll extract near one end of a strip of the paper. Then, the end of the paper nearest the dot of extract is placed in a <u>solvent</u>. In the case of chlorophyll, the solvent could be alcohol. The solvent cannot touch the dot when it is initially set up, or the chlorophyll would simply wash away into the solvent.

As the solvent soaks into the paper and moves upward, substances in the mixture that do not stick tightly to the paper will be picked up by the solvent and moved along quickly. Substances that are more tightly held to the paper and less attracted to the solvent will also be picked up but will move along more slowly. This results in the formation of bands of the different substances on the chromatography paper. If the substances in the mixture are colorless, they can be viewed by combining them with reactive chemicals that will give them color. The chlorophyll extract consists of several plant pigments that are very colorful and easy to distinguish.

In summary, the rate at which a substance moves along the paper in a given solvent can be used to separate it from other substances. By comparing the distances moved with those of known substances in the same solvent, the unknowns can be identified. See Figure 9-20.

Figure 9-20. Chlorophyll chromatography

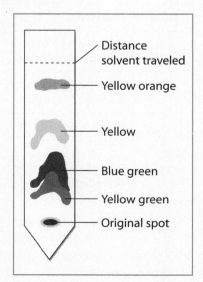

- Distance solvent traveled
- Yellow orange
- Yellow
- Blue green
- Yellow green
- Original spot

STAINS AND INDICATORS **Stains** can be used to make cell structures more visible. In fact, chromosomes were so named for the fact that they are easily stained. Commonly used stains are iodine and methylene blue. Iodine darkens certain cell structures. It is especially useful when examining plant cells through the microscope. Methylene blue stains structures in the nucleus. It is useful when observing many types of cells.

An **indicator** is a substance that changes color when it contacts certain chemicals. The examples in Table 9-2 represent only a few of the indicators commonly used in the biology laboratory.

Table 9-2. Indicators Used in the Biology Laboratory	
Indicator	**What It Tests**
pH paper	A piece of pH paper is dipped in the solution to be tested. Its color is then matched to a color scale. Specific colors indicate whether the solution is acidic (pH values from 0 to 6), neutral (pH 7), or basic (pH values from 8 to 14).
Iodine (Lugol's) solution	A color change from golden brown to blue-black indicates the presence of starch in the tested solution.

Other indicators can be used to determine how much sugar there is in a solution or the amount of carbon dioxide present. Swimming pool owners use indicators to tell them how much chlorine is in the water. Some of the pregnancy test kits that pharmacies sell also use indicators.

DICHOTOMOUS KEYS A key is used to sort, name, and/or classify a particular organism. By working through a series of steps, organisms are eliminated until the one of interest is finally identified. Each step of a **dichotomous key** typically consists of two statements that divide the things being identified/classified into two groups. Each statement is followed by a direction that indicates either what step to go to next or the name of the organism.

To make your own dichotomous key, you would need to start out with two statements that divide the organisms being classified into two groups. Each statement would be followed with a direction about the next step to take. At the next step, you again divide the organisms into two groups that are again followed by directions about the next step to go to or the identity of the organism or object.

For example, this is how you might construct a key to classify the following objects: bicycle, car, jet, and motorcycle.

1a	Requires petroleum fuel	go to Step 2
1b	Requires only muscle power	bicycle
2a	Has wings and flies	jet
2b	Has no wings and does not fly	go to Step 3
3a	Has two wheels	motorcycle
3b	Has more than two wheels	car

Pretend that you do not know a motorcycle from a bicycle from a jet, from a car. All you could do is examine each one of the objects, make observations, and determine how they work. Once you did that, you would be ready to place names on each of the four items. Notice that if you did not work through the key step by step, it would be very easy to misname an object. If you thought about a bicycle as having two wheels and scanned down the list with no attention to following the steps, you could easily mistake the bicycle for a motorcycle. You would spot step 3a, which says, "Has two wheels" and say to yourself, "Yep, that's the bicycle." You would totally miss the fact that the object in step 3a must run on petroleum fuel. Always start at the beginning of a key.

 Review Questions

Base your answers to questions 9–11 on the following diagram and information and on your knowledge of biology.

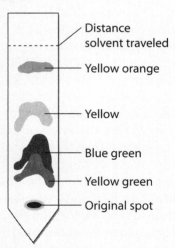

Distance solvent traveled

Yellow orange

Yellow

Blue green

Yellow green

Original spot

Several drops of concentrated green pigment extract obtained from spinach leaves were placed near the bottom of a strip of highly absorbent paper. When the extract dried, the paper was suspended in a test tube containing solvent so that only the tip of the paper was in the solvent. As the solvent was absorbed and moved up the paper, the various pigments within the extract became visible, as shown in the diagram.

9. A valid conclusion that can be drawn from this information is that spinach leaves (1) contain only chlorophyll (2) contain pigments in addition to chlorophyll (3) contain more orange pigment than yellow pigment (4) are yellow-orange rather than green

10. The technique used to separate the parts of the extract in the diagram is known as (1) staining (2) dissection (3) chromatography (4) electrophoresis

11. In which organelle would most of these pigments be found? (1) nucleus (2) mitochondrion (3) ribosome (4) chloroplast

12. To test for the presence of glucose, a student added the same amount of Benedict's solution to each of four test tubes. (Benedict's is a glucose indicator that is a royal blue color when no glucose is present. To determine if glucose is present, Benedict's must be mixed in the unknown solution and heated for several minutes.) Two of the test tubes contained unknown solutions. The other two test tubes contained known solutions. The chart below shows the color results obtained after the solutions were heated in the four test tubes in a hot water bath.

Data Table		
Tube	**Contents**	**Color After Heating**
1	Unknown solution + Benedict's solution	Royal blue
2	Unknown solution + Benedict's solution	Red orange
3	Water + Benedict's solution	Royal blue
4	Glucose + water + Benedict's solution	Red orange

The student could correctly conclude that (1) all of the tubes contained glucose (2) tubes 1 and 2 contained glucose (3) tube 1 did not contain glucose, but tube 2 did (4) tube 2 did not contain glucose, but tube 1 did

13. A student viewing a specimen under the low-power objective of a compound light microscope switched to high power and noticed that the field of view darkened considerably.

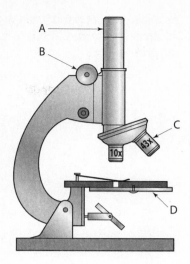

Which microscope part identified on this microscope would the student adjust to brighten the field of view?

14. A student observed a one-celled organism in the field of view of a compound light microscope as shown in the adjacent diagram.

On the diagram, draw an arrow to indicate the direction the organism would seem to move if the student moved the slide on the stage to the left and down.

15. A student studied the upper layer of cells of a tissue sample on a slide, using the high-power objective of the compound microscope shown.

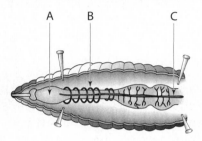

Which part of the microscope should the student adjust to observe the lower layer of the sample?
(1) A   (3) C
(2) B   (4) D

16. What is the purpose of using stains in a wet-mount slide preparation?

17. The eyepiece of a compound light microscope has a magnification of 10X and the low-power objective and high-power objective lenses have magnifications of 10X and 30X, respectively. If the diameter of the low-power field measures 1500 micrometers, the diameter of the high-power field will measure either 4500 micrometers or 500 micrometers. Select the correct diameter and explain your answer.

Base your answers to questions 18–19 on the following diagram of some internal structures of an earthworm and on your knowledge of biology.

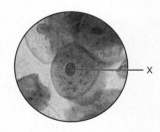

18. Which laboratory equipment should be used to observe the surface details of structures A, B, and C of the earthworm? (1) stereoscope (2) compound light microscope (3) graduated cylinder (4) triple-beam balance

19. Structure A has a diameter of 3 millimeters. What is the approximate diameter of the blood vessel indicated by C? (1) 2.5 mm (2) 2.0 mm (3) 1.5 mm (4) 0.5 mm

---

Base your answers to questions 20–21 on the illustration and on your knowledge of biology. The image shows an animal cell as viewed with the high power lens of a compound light microscope.

20. Name the organelle indicated by the letter X.

21. What technique could be used to make the organelle indicated by letter X more visible?

---

22. While focusing a microscope on high power, a student crushed the coverslip. The student probably (1) shut the light off (2) turned up the light intensity (3) rotated the eyepiece (4) used the coarse adjustment

23. The following chart shows the total magnification produced by the ocular and objective lenses in compound light microscopes. What is the total magnification of microscope D? (1) 60x (2) 20x (3) 600x (4) 800x

Microscope	Ocular Lens Magnification	Objective Lens Magnification	Total Magnification
A	10x	10x	100x
B	10x	20x	200x
C	20x	20x	400x
D	20x	40x	?

Base your answers to questions 24–27 on the photograph below and on your knowledge of biology. The photograph shows onion root-tip tissue viewed under the high-power objective of a compound light microscope.

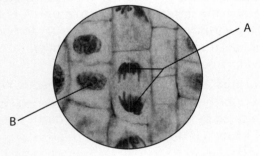

24. The photograph illustrates stages in the process of (1) meiosis in root tips (2) mitotic cell division in plants (3) water conduction in onions (4) chlorophyll production in chloroplasts

25. Identify the structure indicated by arrow A.

26. Identify the structure indicated by arrow B.

27. Describe one adjustment that could be made to the microscope to make the field of view brighter.

28. When viewed with a compound light microscope, which letter would best illustrate the way in which the microscope inverts and reverses the image? (1) A (2) W (3) F (4) D

29. Pieces of pH paper were used to test the contents of three test tubes. The results are shown in the diagram below.

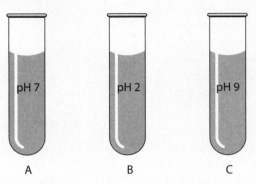

Which statement about the tubes is correct? (1) Tube A contains a base. (2) Tube B contains a base. (3) Tube B contains an acid. (4) Tube C contains an acid.

30. Gel electrophoresis is a technique used to (1) cut DNA into pieces of various sizes (2) separate DNA fragments by charge and size (3) move DNA fragments from one species to another (4) make copies of chromosomes

Observing Plant and Animal Specimens

Classroom experiences involving plants and animals range from observation to dissection. Opportunities to observe plants and animals require consideration and appreciation for the organism. The abuse of any live organism for any purpose is intolerable.

Dissection and Preserved Specimens

The dissection of plant and animal specimens provides a framework upon which to organize biological knowledge. **Dissection** (or the examination of preserved specimens) provides a way to

- observe similarities and differences that exist among species
- understand the relationship between biological form and function
- expose and identify the internal structures of organisms

To dissect a specimen correctly, you need:

• the knowledge of what equipment to use and how to use it properly

• a work area that is clean and well organized both before and after the activity

Equipment commonly used during dissection activities is described in Table 9-3.

Table 9-3. Dissection Equipment

Equipment	Use
Dissecting pan	Resembles a cake pan but has a wax or a rubber-like substance in the bottom. The specimen is placed on the waxy surface.
Dissecting pins	Large pins with a "T" shape used to anchor the specimen during the dissection
Scalpel	A sharp instrument used to slice open the specimen so that the internal parts can be observed
Scissors	Used for cutting open the specimen and to remove parts. May have two sharp points or one blunt and one sharp point.
Probe/ Teasing needle/ Dissecting needle	Used to move structures around while they are still intact. The probe can be used to lift some organs so that others located below them are observable. The probe or dissecting needle is also used to point out different structures when showing specific features to someone else. Another function is to "tease" or gently tear apart structures such as muscle tissue.
Tweezers/ Forceps	Used to lift out small parts, to move structures, and to pry parts open
Safety goggles	Wrap-around shatter-proof glasses used to protect eyes from accidental splashes of preservative when dissecting as well as in other lab situations.

 Review Questions

31. State one scientific purpose for dissecting an organism.

32. For what purpose would the equipment in the following illustration most likely be used? (1) dissecting an earthworm (2) removing cell organelles (3) identifying and classifying a single-celled organism (4) observing mitosis on prepared slides

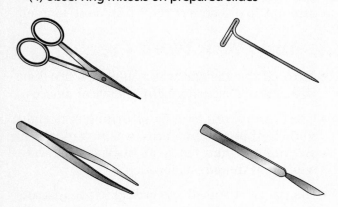

33. Along with a dissecting pan, which group of equipment would be most useful to a student planning to dissect a preserved specimen? (1) dissecting pins, compound light microscope, and pH paper (2) pH paper, eye dropper, and safety goggles (3) safety goggles, scissors, and compound light microscope (4) safety goggles, stereoscope, and scissors

34. What is the best use for the dissection instrument illustrated in the following diagram? (1) cutting through bones (2) spreading apart muscle tissue (3) cutting through thick muscles (4) removing blood plasma

Laboratory Safety

Laboratory investigations are, for some students, the most exciting part of the Living Environment course. However, they sometimes involve potentially dangerous activities and materials. As a result, careful attention to safety procedures is critical.

Using Safety Equipment

You should know how to properly use the safety equipment located in your biology laboratory. It is critical to be aware of the location in your laboratory of each of these:

- fire extinguisher
- safety shower
- eye wash station
- fire blanket
- emergency gas shutoff

Use the safety equipment provided for you. Goggles should be worn whenever a lab calls for the use of chemicals, preserved specimens, or dissection. If indicated by your teacher, you should also wear a safety apron when using chemicals. Some activities, such as those involving chemicals or live or preserved organisms, also require the use of special gloves.

Safety in the Laboratory

Read all of the directions for an investigation before you start to work. If you are unsure about any part of the lab procedures, check with your teacher. As a general rule, do not perform activities without permission; do only what the instructions and your teacher direct you to do.

- Do NOT eat or drink in the laboratory.

- When you are heating a test tube, always slant it so that the open end of the tube points away from you and others. Never heat a closed container, such as a test tube that has been closed with a stopper.

- Never inhale or taste any of the chemicals you are using in a laboratory. This includes the specimens you are dissecting.

- If you spill a chemical or get any on your skin, wash it off immediately. Also, report the incident to your teacher.

- Tell your teacher about any personal injury no matter how minor it may seem.

- Tie back long hair, and keep loose clothing away from laboratory equipment, chemicals, and sources of heat and fire.

- Never expose flammable liquids to an open flame. Use a hot water bath (such as a large beaker of water heated on a hot plate) if you need to heat flammable liquids (such as alcohol). See Figure 9-21.

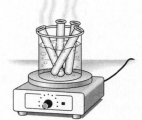

Figure 9-21. Hot water bath: A hot water bath is used to heat test tubes that contain a flammable liquid such as alcohol.

- Know what equipment to use when handling hot glassware. Do not use bare fingers to pick up hot test tubes or beakers. Use test tube holders and beaker tongs.

- Do not use glassware that has cracks or large chips. Tell your teacher about the damage and get a replacement.

- Do not pour chemicals back into stock bottles or exchange stoppers on the stock bottles.

- Use laboratory apparatus as it is intended to be used. For example, do not stir a solution using a thermometer, plastic ruler, or your pen.

- Do not use electrical equipment around water. If electrical cords seem to have exposed wires or if you get a shock handling electrical equipment, notify your teacher immediately. Do not attempt to disconnect the equipment yourself.

Cleaning Your Work Area

- Turn off the gas and water after you are done with them. Disconnect any electrical devices.

- Clean your work area by returning materials to their appropriate places, washing glassware according to your teacher's instructions, and wiping off the lab surface.

- Dispose of chemicals according to the instructions provided by your teacher.

- Wash your hands thoroughly!

Review Questions

35. A student performing an experiment noticed that the beaker containing the water being heated had a small crack. It was not leaking. What should the student do? (1) Stop heating the beaker and try to fix the crack. (2) Stop heating the beaker and report the crack to the teacher. (3) Stop heating the beaker and immediately take the beaker to the teacher. (4) Continue heating as long as the liquid does not start to leak out of the crack.

36. An UNSAFE procedure for heating a nutrient solution in a flask would be to (1) heat the solution at the lowest temperature on a hot plate (2) stopper the flask tightly to prevent evaporation of the solution (3) use a Bunsen burner to heat the solution (4) stir the solution while it is heating

37. The following diagram shows a student conducting a laboratory experiment. Describe one safety procedure the student should be following that is NOT represented in the diagram.

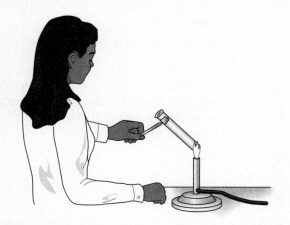

38. If a student spills nitric acid on her arm, she should FIRST (1) report the accident to the school nurse (2) report the spill to her teacher (3) rinse her arm with water (4) allow the acid to evaporate

39. When they are not being used during a laboratory investigation, electrical devices should be (1) put away (2) turned off (3) unplugged (4) covered

40. The following diagram shows a student heating some test tubes with chemicals in them during a laboratory activity. Using one or more complete sentences, describe one error in the laboratory procedure shown in the diagram.

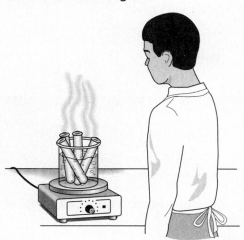

41. Chlorophyll can be removed from leaves by boiling them in alcohol, a flammable solvent. In addition to wearing safety goggles, which is the safest procedure to follow? (1) A stoppered test tube of leaves and alcohol should be held over the Bunsen burner. (2) A stoppered test tube of leaves and alcohol should be placed in a large beaker of alcohol and heated on a hot plate. (3) A beaker of leaves and alcohol should be placed on a tripod over a Bunsen burner. (4) A beaker of leaves and alcohol should be placed into a larger beaker of water and heated on a hot plate.

42. Which safety procedure should a student follow during a dissection? (1) The student should wear gloves and hold the specimen in the palm of her hand while cutting the specimen open. (2) The student should cut the specimen open while holding it under running water. (3) The student should apply additional preservative to the specimen. (4) The student should direct the cutting motion away from her body.

Questions for Regents Practice

Part A

1. The following diagram shows a wasp positioned next to a centimeter ruler.

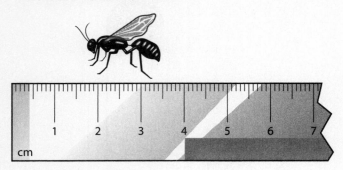

What is the approximate length of a WING of this wasp?
(1) 10 mm
(2) 1.4 cm
(3) 3.5 cm
(4) 35 mm

2. When preparing a wet-mount slide of onion cells, a student put a drop of Lugol's iodine stain on the slide. Lugol's iodine stain was added to
(1) prevent the formation of air bubbles
(2) make cell structures more visible
(3) increase the magnification
(4) increase the rate of photosynthesis in the cells

3. A student views some cheek cells under low power. Before switching to high power, the student should
(1) adjust the eyepiece
(2) center the image being viewed
(3) remove the slide from the stage
(4) remove the coverslip from the slide

4. Which statement describes two unsafe laboratory practices represented in the following diagram?

(1) The flame is too high, and the test tube is unstoppered.
(2) The opening of the test tube is pointed toward the student, and the student is not wearing goggles.
(3) The test tube is unstoppered, and the student is not wearing goggles.
(4) The beaker has water in it, and the flame is under the tripod.

5. Bromthymol blue turns yellow in the presence of carbon dioxide. This characteristic makes it possible for bromthymol blue to function as
(1) a measure of volume
(2) an indicator
(3) a catalyst
(4) an energy source

6. A student sees the following image when observing the letter "f" with the low-power objective lens of a microscope.

f

Which of the four following diagrams most closely resembles the image the student will see after switching to high power?

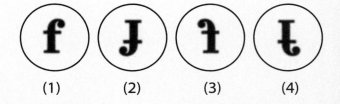

(1)   (2)   (3)   (4)

Part B

7. The diagram represents the field of view of a compound light microscope. Three single-celled organisms are located across the diameter of the field.

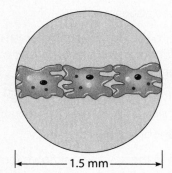

|← 1.5 mm →|

Knowing that 1 mm = 1000 micrometers, what is the approximate length of each single-celled organism?

(1) 250 micrometers

(2) 500 micrometers

(3) 1000 micrometers

(4) 1500 micrometers

8. When stained with certain dyes, cell structures known as nucleoproteins appear black. These dyes would most likely be used to

(1) identify specific nucleoproteins within cells

(2) stain all types of cell organelles

(3) determine the chemical composition of nucleoproteins

(4) indicate the presence of nucleoproteins

9. A student, not wearing safety goggles, gets some unknown chemical in his eye. What is the most appropriate action he should take?

(1) Put on safety goggles immediately.

(2) Ask his lab partner to see if his eye looks OK .

(3) Go to the eyewash station and use it to rinse his eye thoroughly.

(4) Rub the eye gently and see if it hurts or stings.

10. The following diagram represents part of the process of

(1) gel electrophoresis

(2) genetic engineering

(3) homeostatic control

(4) cell culturing

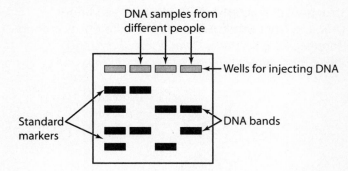

11. A student is viewing a single-celled organism under the low-power objective of a compound light microscope. Describe an adjustment the student would need to make to see the organism clearly AFTER switching from low power to high power. In your description include the name of the part of the microscope that would be used to make the adjustment.

12. A student is heating a test tube containing an indicator solution and glucose. The student is wearing safety goggles and a laboratory apron. Describe another safety procedure that this student should be following.

13. While she is using a Bunsen burner, a student's sleeve catches fire. State two things the student should have done to avoid this kind of accident.

Base your answers to questions 14 through 16 on the information below, the key, and your knowledge of biology.

Biologists use keys to accurately classify unknown organisms such as the unidentified female mosquito shown in the following diagram. These keys are designed to categorize organisms according to structural characteristics. The key shows various characteristics used to identify the differences among *Anopheles, Deinocerites, Culex, Psorophora,* and *Aedes* mosquitoes.

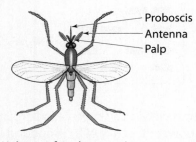

— Proboscis
— Antenna
— Palp

Unknown female mosquito

1a Antennae very bushy — Male mosquito	**1b** Antennae not bushy — Go to 2
2a Palps much shorter than proboscis — Go to 3	**2b** Palps as long as proboscis — Female *Anopheles*
3a Tip of abdomen blunt, without points — Go to 4	**3b** Tip of abdomen with points — Go to 5
4a Antennae much longer than proboscis — Female *Deinocerites*	**4b** Antennae shorter than proboscis — Female *Culex*
5a Many long scales present on hind legs — Female *Psorophora*	**5b** Hind legs without long scales — Female *Aedes*

14. According to the key, which feature distinguishes male from female mosquitoes?
(1) palp length
(2) leg scales
(3) abdomen points
(4) antennae appearance

15. According to the key, which characteristics are necessary to identify a female *Anopheles* mosquito?
(1) antennae, palps, and proboscis
(2) wings, proboscis, and scales on legs
(3) eyes, scales on legs, and abdomen tip
(4) palps, abdomen tip, and wings

16. According to the key, the unknown female mosquito belongs to the group known as
(1) *Deinocerites*
(2) *Culex*
(3) *Psorophora*
(4) *Aedes*

Part C

17. Some students did a lab to test the vitamin C content of several fruits. They squeezed the juice from some of the fruits and cut others up and placed them in a blender to obtain a juice sample. Juice for each fruit was kept in a clean, labeled beaker. Pipettes were used to transfer the juices to test tubes for analysis. During the laboratory cleanup, one student drank some of the juice left in one beaker. State why this was an unsafe procedure. [2]

18. Below is a drawing of a hypothetical electrophoresis gel. Included on the gel are some bands for several different individuals.

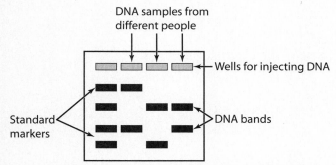

- Decribe where the smallest fragments of DNA would be located on the gel in the illustration. [1]

- Discuss two practical applications of information that can be obtained through this process. [2]

19. The dichotomous key begun below should allow users to classify the organisms illustrated. Complete the key using only information shown in the illustration. [3]

Cat   Cow   Spider   Fly

Dichotomous Key	
1a. Wings present ·· Fly	
1b. No wings present ·································· go to 2	

Appendix A: Strategies for Answering Test Questions

This appendix provides strategies to help you answer various types of questions on The Living Environment Regents Examination. Strategies are provided for answering multiple-choice and constructed-response questions as well as for questions based on diagrams, data tables, and graphs. For each type of question, practice questions are provided to show you how to apply the strategies to answer specific questions.

Strategies for Multiple-Choice Questions

Multiple-choice questions account for more than 50 percent of The Living Environment Regents Examination. Part A is totally made up of multiple-choice questions, and Part B includes some. Therefore, it is important to be good at deciphering multiple-choice questions. Here are a few helpful strategies. For any one question, not all strategies will need to be used. The numbers are provided for reference, not to specify an order (except for Strategies 1 and 2).

1. Always read the entire question, but wait to read the choices. (See Strategy 4.)

2. Carefully examine any data tables, diagrams, or photographs associated with the question.

3. Underline key words and phrases in the question that signal what you should be looking for in the answer. This will make you read the question more carefully. This strategy applies mostly to questions with a long introduction.

4. Try to think of an answer to the question before looking at the choices given. If you think you know the answer, write it on a separate piece of paper before reading the choices. Next, read all of the choices and compare them to your answer before making a decision. Do not select the first answer that seems correct. If your answer matches one of the choices, and you are quite sure of your response, you are probably correct. Even if your answer matches one of the choices, carefully consider all of the answers, because the obvious choice is not always the correct one. If there are no exact matches, re-read the question and look for the choice that is most similar to your answer.

5. Eliminate any choices that you know are incorrect. Lightly cross out the numbers for those choices on the exam paper. Each choice you can eliminate increases your chances of selecting the correct answer.

6. If the question makes no sense after reading through it several times, leave it for later. After completing the rest of the exam, return to the question. Something you read on the other parts of the exam may give you some ideas about how to answer this question. If you are still unsure, go with your best guess. There is no penalty for guessing; but answers left blank will be counted as wrong. If you employ your best test-taking strategies, you just may select the correct answer.

Practice Questions

1. Most of the oxygen that enters the atmosphere results from the process of (1) respiration (2) photosynthesis (3) excretion (4) digestion

Explanation of Answer Use strategy 5. Eliminating choices 3 and 4 may be easy, but think about the other two choices carefully before choosing your final answer. Be sure that you are not confusing respiration with photosynthesis. The correct answer is choice (2), photosynthesis.

---

2. Cellular respiration in humans occurs in (1) red blood cells, only (2) the cells of the lungs, only (3) the cells of the digestive system, only (4) all the cells of the body

Explanation of Answer Use strategy 4. Note that the question is asking where cell respiration occurs in humans. Your answer before reading the choices should say that respiration occurs in all of the cells of the body or that respiration occurs in the mitochondria. All of the choices are different types of cells. Think about what cell respiration is, and why cells respire. Lung cells and red blood cells help obtain and carry oxygen, but cell respiration is a process that releases energy in ALL cells. Therefore, the correct answer is choice (4), all the cells of the body.

---

3. A number of white potato plants are grown by placing pieces of one potato in the ground. This method of reproduction is most similar to (1) sexual reproduction (2) cloning (3) genetic engineering (4) zygote formation

Explanation of Answer Use strategy 5. You should be able to eliminate choices 1 and 4, since both are related to the same form of reproduction. The fusion of sex cells results in the formation of a zygote. Since there can be only one correct answer, these will not work. Genetic engineering refers to the manipulation of genes leading to the development of new combinations of traits and new varieties of organisms. Since only one parent (potato) is involved, the genetic makeup of the new potato plants will be the same as the original plant. Therefore, cutting up a potato and planting the pieces is most like choice (2), cloning. This is a form of asexual reproduction in which all offspring are genetic copies.

---

4. Overexposure of animals to X-rays is dangerous, because X-rays are known to damage DNA. A direct result of this damage is cells with (1) unusually thick cell membranes (2) no organelles located in the cytoplasm (3) abnormally large chloroplasts (4) changes in chromosome structure

Explanation of Answer Use strategy 3. As you read this question, underline key words: Overexposure of <u>animals</u> to <u>X-rays</u> is dangerous, because X-rays are known to <u>damage</u> <u>DNA</u>. A <u>direct</u> <u>result</u> of this damage is cells with (4) changes in chromosome structure. You should know that chromosomes are composed of DNA

molecules and that X-rays can cause mutations, which are changes in DNA and/or chromosome structure. Choices 1, 2, and 3 can be eliminated, since even if they could occur, it would not be a <u>direct</u> <u>result</u> of the <u>DNA's</u> being <u>damaged</u>.

Strategies for Constructed–Response Questions

Some questions in Part B and all questions in Part C of The Living Environment Regents Examination require a constructed response. Some of these questions require you to write one or two sentences, while others require several paragraphs. No matter which type of answer is requested, the following strategies will help you write constructed responses. Some Part B questions may not require complete sentences. However, students who use complete sentences tend to have more organized answers. As a result, they uusually get higher scores.

1. Always read through the entire question.

2. Underline key words and phrases in the question that signal what you should be looking for in the answer. This will make you read the question more carefully.

3. Write a brief outline, or at least a few notes to yourself, about what should be included in the answer.

4. Pay attention to key words that indicate how to answer the question and what you need to say in your answer. Several of these words are very common. For example, you might be asked to discuss, describe, explain, define, compare, contrast, or design. The table on the next page lists key words and directions for your answers.

5. When you write your answer, don't be so general that you are not really saying anything. Be very specific. You should use the correct terms and clearly explain the processes and relationships. Be sure to provide details, such as the names of processes, names of structures, and, if it is appropriate, how they are related. If only one example or term is required, do not give two or more. If one is correct and the other is wrong, your answer will be marked wrong.

Key Word	What Direction Your Answers Should Take
Analyze	• Break the idea, concept, or situation into parts, and explain how they relate. • Carefully explain relationships, such as cause and effect.
Compare	• Relate two or more topics with an emphasis on how they are alike. • State the similarities between two or more examples.
Contrast	• Relate two or more topics with an emphasis on how they are different. • State the differences between two or more examples.
Define	• State the exact meaning of topic or word. • Explain what something is or what it means.
Describe	• Illustrate the subject using words. • Provide a thorough account of the topic. • Give complete answers.
Discuss	• Make observations about the topic or situation using facts. • Thoroughly write about various aspects of the topic or situation.
Design	• Plan an experiment or component of an experiment. Map out your proposal, being sure to provide information about all of the required parts.
Explain	• Clarify the topic of the question by spelling it out completely. • Make the topic understandable. • Provide reasons for the outcome.
State	• Express in words. • Explain or describe using at least one fact, term, or relationship.

6. If a question has two or three parts, answer each part in a separate paragraph. This will make it easy for the person scoring your paper to find all of the information. When writing your answer, don't shortchange one part of the question by spending too much time on another part.

7. If sentences are called for in the answer, be sure that you write sentences. A sentence should always have a subject and a verb, and a good answer should not start with the word *because*. Note that you will not lose points for incorrect grammar, spelling, punctuation, or poor penmanship. However, such errors and poor penmanship could impair your ability to make your answer clear to the person scoring your paper. If that person cannot understand what you are trying to say, you will not receive the maximum number of points.

8. When the question calls for you to write the answer in paragraphs, do not write a "standard" essay such as you would write for social studies. Do not spend time writing an introduction, several short paragraphs, and a conclusion. Write your outline, then answer the question directly.

Practice Questions

5. Using one or more complete sentences, state a safety precaution that a student should use when heating liquid in a test tube.

Sample Answer When heating liquid in a test tube, the student should wear safety goggles.

6. The following diagram shows the setup of an experiment.

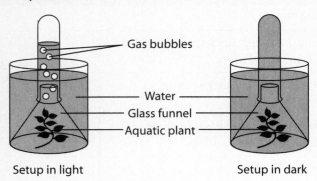

Setup in light Setup in dark

Using one or more complete sentences, state a problem that could be investigated using this experimental setup.

Sample Answer Is light needed for photosynthesis?

Tip Note that "State a problem" here really means to state a question. You are not expected to describe a fault with this setup.

---

7. The diagram below shows two ways in which grains, such as wheat or corn, can provide food for humans.

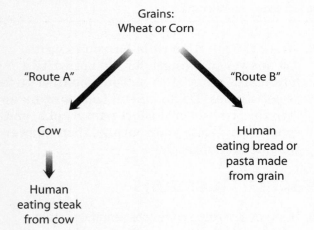

Using one or more complete sentences, <u>select which "Route,"</u> A or B, involves the least energy loss and <u>explain why</u> this is true. [2]

Hint Note the key words that have been underlined to indicate two things you must do: (1) select a route and then (2) explain why it is your choice. Note that this question is worth two points, one point for each correct answer.

Scoring Guide Teachers are provided with Scoring Guides and Sample Answers to use when rating your answers. Often there are several correct answers to a question. Here is an example of what teachers would use to score question 7: Award one point for identifying Route B as the one with the least energy loss, and one point for a correct explanation. A possible explanation would be that Route B involves the least energy loss because some energy is lost at each step in a food chain. Since Route A involves two transfers, it would lose more energy than Route B where there is only one transfer. Maximum of two points.

---

8. Provide two reasons why it is important to preserve biodiversity. [2]

Scoring Guide and Sample Answers Award one point for each correct reason given—maximum of two points. Possible answers include the following:

- Biodiversity ensures the availability of a variety of genetic material.
  OR
- Biodiversity may allow us to find plants or animals that could be used as new medicines.
  OR
- Biodiversity helps an ecosystem remain stable.
  OR
- A lot of tropical plants may contain chemicals people can use to cure cancer or HIV.
  OR
- Loss of species from an ecosystem could disrupt the food web.

Base your answers to questions 9–12 on the information in the paragraph below and on your knowledge of biology.

It is possible to collect human sperm and to use this sperm later to fertilize eggs in a process called *artificial insemination*. The collected sperm samples are frozen and stored in a sperm bank until needed. When a woman makes use of a sperm bank, she requests sperm from a donor with the physical features she wants for her baby. The name of the donor is not revealed. The artificial insemination process involves placing the sperm in the woman's body and allowing fertilization to occur in the normal manner.

9. Suppose a woman whose husband cannot produce sperm becomes pregnant through artificial insemination. How will the baby's DNA compare with the DNA of the woman and her husband? [1]

10. If a woman were given sperm from the same donor for three different pregnancies, and she had three daughters, would the three girls look alike, or would they be different? Provide at least one scientific fact that supports your answer. [1]

11. The production of a normal baby also involves protecting the developing embryo from harmful environmental factors. Explain three ways in which the pregnant woman could avoid exposing the developing embryo to environmental risks. [1]

12. Artificial insemination is also used on animals. State two benefits farmers or animal breeders gain from using artificial insemination. [1]

Scoring Guide For questions 9 through 12:

9. Award one point for an answer that recognizes that the baby received DNA from the mother, but none from her husband. A possible acceptable answer would be: The baby's DNA sequence would have much (one half) in common with the mother's DNA sequence, but it would have no specific resemblance to the DNA of the woman's husband.

10. Award one point for an answer that states the girls would not look alike, and one point for a correct explanation of why they would not look alike. Award no credit for stating they would all look alike. A possible correct answer: The girls would look different from each other, since they came from different eggs and sperm, each containing unique DNA information. (Equivalent correct answers are also acceptable.) Maximum of two points.

11. Award one point for each correct way the pregnant woman could avoid environmental risks to the embryo. Fully correct answers should include three of the following (or other equivalent correct ways to avoid environmental risks to the embryo): The woman should not drink alcohol, smoke, take drugs, expose herself to a disease such as HIV, or eat an unhealthy diet. Maximum of three points.

12. Award one point for an answer that identifies one benefit that artificial insemination provides to farmers or breeders. Correct

responses could include reference to being able to breed animals that live far apart without transporting them to the same location, being able to select desirable traits from animals you do not own and cannot afford to buy, not needing to maintain large numbers of both sexes on a farm (bulls along with cows, or roosters with chickens), or that one male individual with very desirable characteristics being able to father many, many offspring in many locations, and so on.

Strategies for Questions Based on Diagrams

Both multiple-choice and extended-response questions frequently include diagrams or pictures. Usually the diagrams provide information needed to answer the question. The diagrams may be realistic, or they may be a schematic. Schematic drawings show the relationships among parts and sometimes the sequence of events that occur in a system.

Practice Questions

Base your answer to questions 13–14 on the following diagram and on your knowledge of biology.

The diagram illustrates one possible scheme of evolution among various groups of organisms.

- **First, study the diagram.** Ask yourself what the diagram is about and what it shows you. Read the title or description provided, if there is one.

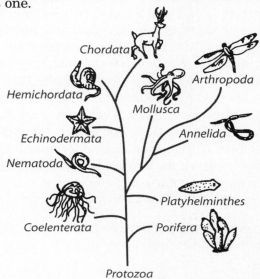

You are told that the diagram represents a possible sequence of events in the evolution of a number of organisms. Based on the illustration, you see that *Protozoa* are the common ancestor of all the other animals shown. It also indicates that *Porifera, Platyhelminthes, Nematoda,* and *Coelenterata* existed before *Echinodermata, Hemichordata, Chordata, Arthropoda, Annelida,* and *Mollusca*. The diagram also shows that *Platyhelminthes* and *Nematoda* are very closely related, as are *Arthropoda, Annelida,* and *Mollusca*. You need to know that the closer the point of branching, the more closely related the organisms. The farther apart the point of branching, the more distant the relationship.

• **Second, read the question.**

13. Which inference does the diagram best support?

For this type of question, it is difficult to try to anticipate what the correct answer might be. Carefully read each of the choices, one at a time, and see if they make sense by looking back at the diagram. As you do this, eliminate any choices you can.

(1) Members of the animal kingdom are more complex than members of the plant kingdom.
(2) Members of the animal kingdom and members of the plant kingdom share common ancestry.
(3) Chordates are more closely related to arthropods than to echinoderms. (4) Members of the group *Echinodermata* and the group *Annelida* share common ancestry.

Explanation of Answer There is no information provided about plants by the diagram; you can eliminate choices 1 and 2 based on what you see here or even on what you have learned during the year. According to the diagram, chordates are more closely related to *Echinodermata* than they are to *Arthropoda*—the opposite of what choice (3) states—because *Echinodermata* branches off the same line that chordates are on. Arthropod ancestors branched before that. The correct answer is (4), Members of the group *Echinodermata* and the group *Annelida* share common ancestry. All of the animals on this evolutionary diagram share a common ancestor—*Protozoa*.

14. Which two groups of organisms in the diagram are shown to be the most closely related?

Before reading the choices provided, think about how you could tell which organisms are most closely related (by two organisms being close together on one branch). Then apply this to eliminate obviously wrong choices. Do not select the first answer that seems correct.

(1) Porifera and Echinodermata (2) Chordata and Platyhelminthes (3) Mollusca and Annelida (4) Arthropoda and Coelenterata

Explanation of Answer Choices 1, 2, and 4 have separate branches and are widely separated. Therefore, these choices can be eliminated. *Mollusca* and *Annelida* are the only two groups that share a common side branch on the diagram. Therefore, the correct answer is (3), *Mollusca* and *Annelida*.

• **First, study the diagram for Question 15.** This illustration shows a rabbit and a plant giving off CO_2 and taking in O_2 from the environment. This analysis of the illustration indicates that materials are being cycled through the environment.

• **Second, read the question.**

15. Which ecological principle is best illustrated by the following diagram?

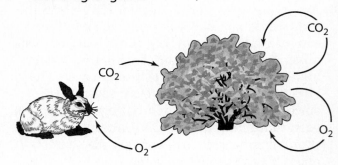

Before reading the choices provided, think about the diagram and what the question is asking. It seems that the ecological principle illustrated here has something to do with cycles in the environment. As you read the choices, eliminate any choices that you can.

(1) In an ecosystem, material is cycled among the organisms and their environment. (2) In an ecosystem, the number of producers and consumers is equal. (3) Competition within a species results in natural selection. (4) An ecosystem requires a constant source of energy.

Explanation of Answer Since an ecosystem requires more producers than consumers, choice 2 is incorrect. Choices 3 and 4 are not addressed by the illustration. It does not show competition within the rabbit species. There is no energy source shown in the diagram, nor is the ecosystem requirement for a constant energy source illustrated. Therefore, you would probably select the correct answer as being choice (1), In an ecosystem, material is cycled among the organisms and their environment.

- **First, study the diagram for Question 16.** Ask yourself what the diagram is about and what it shows you. It shows CO_2 and H_2O entering, and sugar and O_2 leaving. The illustration seems to have something to do with photosynthesis, since CO_2 and H_2O are raw materials and sugar and O_2 are products.

- **Second, read the question.**

16. The diagram represents some events that take place in a plant cell. With which organelle would these events be most closely associated?

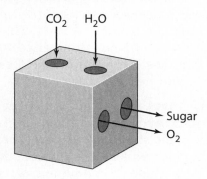

Before reading the choices provided, write what you think the answer should be on a separate piece of paper. Then compare your answer to the choices provided.

   (1) mitochondrion (2) chloroplast (3) ribosome
   (4) vacuole

Explanation of Answer Mitochondria are associated with cellular respiration, ribosomes with protein synthesis, and vacuoles with storage. Since this diagram illustrates photosynthesis, which occurs in chloroplasts in plant cells, the correct answer is choice (2), chloroplast.

Note: If you realized that the process was either photosynthesis or respiration but weren't sure

which one, you at least could narrow your choices to 1 and 2 and improve your chances of guessing the right one.

Base your answers to questions 17–18 on the following information, the map, and your knowledge of biology. Each question is worth one point.

The map was drawn by an ecologist. It represents the vegetation around a small pond in a forest located in New York State.

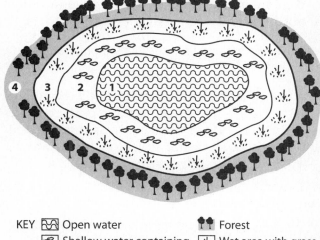

KEY   Open water   Forest
      Shallow water containing   Wet area with grass
      pond plants   and cattails

- **First, study the diagram.** Think about what the diagram shows you. Did you read the information at the top of the illustration? If you were approaching the pond from the forest, you would walk through trees, then wet areas with tall plants, such as cattails and grasses. The ground would be wet and squashy. Next, you would enter shallow water in which many rooted plants grow. From this point, open water would be visible. The water would be much deeper, and you would probably not be able to walk but would need to swim or use a boat. There are many different questions you could be asked about this diagram.

- **Second, read the questions.**

17. Using one or more complete sentences, describe one specific way this environment would be likely to change if it were left undisturbed by humans for 100 years. [1]

Sample Answers The pond environment will probably fill in, leaving mostly forest.

OR

The species present in the nonforest communities will disappear, and forest plants and animals will replace them.

Explanation of Answers Both answers relate to the idea of ecological succession. All ecosystems progress through a series of changes during which one community modifies the environment, making it more suitable for another community. The organic matter from decaying vegetation will gradually fill the pond.

18. Name two organisms in this ecosystem that are producers. [1]

Sample Answers and Scoring Guide Sample answers: cattails and grass. Scoring guide: Any two of the following or their equivalent are acceptable: cattails, pond plants, grass, or trees. Award one point for naming two correctly. Award no points for naming only one correctly.

Explanation of Answer Producers are organisms that are capable of taking inorganic raw materials from the environment and synthesizing their own food. Plants are producers.

Strategies for Questions Based on Data Tables

Most data tables contain information that summarizes a topic. A table uses rows and columns to condense information and to present it in an organized way. Rows are the horizontal divisions going from left to right across the table, while columns are vertical divisions going from top to bottom. Column headings name the type of information included in a table. Sometimes different categories of information are listed down the left-hand column of the table.

Examine the sample data table at the right. It provides information collected during an old study of the death rates of policy holders of a large life insurance company.

Deaths as a Result of Disease

Cause of Death	Deaths per 100,000 People	
	1911	**1957**
Tuberculosis	224.6	6.7
Communicable disease	58.9	0.1
Cancer	69.3	136.2
Heart disease	156.4	256.2

Before attempting to answer any questions based on the data, go through the following steps:

1. Find the title of the table. It is usually located across the top. What is the title of the sample table? (Answer: Deaths as a Result of Disease)

2. Determine the number of columns in the table and their purpose. Do this for the sample table. (Answer: There are three columns. They show the causes of death and deaths per 100,000 people during the years of 1911 and 1957.)

3. Determine the number of rows and their purpose. Do this for the sample table. (Answer: There are four rows. The rows provide you with the number of deaths due to tuberculosis, communicable diseases, cancer, and heart disease.)

4. Read across the rows and down the columns to determine what the relationships are. Do this for the table shown. Notice how the numbers of deaths changed for each disease between 1911 and 1957. Some decreased and some increased.

Now you are ready to read the question with the sample data table and answer it.

19. The study most clearly indicated that during the time period examined (1) cancer of the lungs was increasing (2) people were living longer (3) children were safer from communicable diseases (4) better housing reduced deaths from tuberculosis

Explanation of Answer Choice 1 doesn't work because even though cancer death rates increased from 69.3 to 136.2 per 100,000, there is no way to tell what type or types of cancer caused the difference. Choice 2 is not correct because you have no information about how long old people were living in either 1911 or 1957. Choice 4 is not correct because no information is provided about what caused the decrease in deaths due to tuberculosis. You only know that the death rate decreased from 224.6 in 1911 to 6.7 per 100,000 in 1957. The correct answer is choice (3), children were safer from communicable diseases. The number of deaths decreased from 58.9 per 100,000 in 1911 to 0.1 per 100,000 in 1957.

Practice Questions

Base your answers to questions 20–21 on the following information and on your knowledge of biology.

A dog was placed in a special room free of unrelated stimuli. On repeated trials, a tone was sounded for 5 seconds; approximately 2 seconds later, the dog was given food. Trials 1, 10, 20, 30, 40, and 50 were test trials; that is, the tone was sounded for 30 seconds and no food was given. The following data were collected:

Data Table		
Test Trial Number	**Drops of Saliva Secreted**	**Number of Seconds Between Onset of the Tone and Salivation**
1	0	----
10	6	18
20	20	9
30	60	2
40	62	1
50	59	2

20. The greatest increase in the number of drops of saliva secreted occurred between test trials (1) 1 and 10 (2) 10 and 20 (3) 20 and 30 (4) 30 and 40

Explanation of Answer The increase for choice 1 amounted to 6 drops, since it increased from 0 drops to 6 drops between Test Trial Numbers 1 to 10. Choice 2 resulted in an increase of 14 drops, since Test Trial Number 10 resulted in 6 drops, while Test Trial Number 20 resulted in 20 drops. The difference is 14 drops. Choice (4) only resulted in an increase of 2 drops. The correct answer is choice (3), 20 to 30. The number of drops of saliva secreted increased from 20 in Test Trial 20 to 60 in Test Trial 30, for an increase of 40 drops of saliva.

21. At test trial 60, the number of drops of saliva secreted would probably be closest to (1) 75 (2) 55 (3) 35 (4) 25

Explanation of Answer Choice 1 is wrong, since it shows a large increase. Choices 3 and 4 are incorrect, because the decrease in number of drops is very large. These numbers do not fit the trend shown in the data table. The correct answer is choice 2, because the number of drops of saliva secreted between trials 30 and 50 has been changing slowly and at trial 50 has started to go down.

Strategies for Questions Based on Graphs

Graphs represent relationships in a visual form that is easy to read. Three different types of graphs commonly used on science Regents examinations are line graphs, bar graphs, and circle graphs. Line graphs are the most common, and they show the relationship between two changing quantities, or variables. When a question is based on any of the three types of graphs, the information you need to correctly answer the question can usually be found on the graph.

When answering a question that includes a graph, first ask yourself these questions:

- What information does the graph provide?

- What are the variables?

- What seems to happen to one variable as the other changes?

After a careful analysis of the graph, use these strategies along with the other strategies you have learned:

- Read the question.

- Read each of the possible answers and consider which is the correct choice by referring to the graph.

Practice Questions

Use the following graph to answer questions 22–23.

Genetic Diversity in Corn and Wheat Varieties

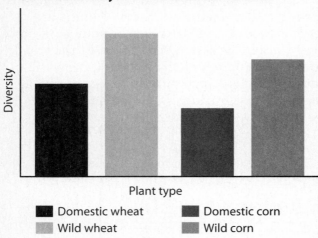

Domestic wheat   Domestic corn
Wild wheat   Wild corn

22. Which types of plants represented on the graph have the greatest diversity? (1) wild wheat and wild corn (2) wild wheat and domestic corn (3) domestic wheat and wild corn (4) domestic wheat and domestic corn

Explanation of Answer Choices 2, 3, and 4 do not work, because they each contain one or more of the domestic plant types that do not extend as high on the diversity scale. The correct choice is (1), wild wheat and wild corn. The bars for wild wheat and corn extend higher on the diversity scale than the others.

23. If the environment were to change dramatically or a new plant disease affecting both corn and wheat were to strike, which of the plant types would be most likely to survive? (1) wild wheat (2) domestic wheat (3) wild corn (4) domestic corn

Explanation of Answer To be able to answer this question correctly, you need to know two things. First, biodiversity increases the stability of an ecosystem. Second, the diversity of species increases the chance that some will survive in the face of environmental changes. Therefore, the bar representing the plant with the greatest diversity would be the best choice for an answer. For that reason, the correct answer is choice (1), wild wheat.

24. Which statement best describes the relationship between enzyme action and temperature shown in the following graph?

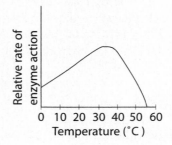

Remember to first study the graph in order to determine what it is about and what information it gives you about the variables. Then read the question and analyze the choices by referring to the graph.

(1) Enzyme synthesis begins at 30°C. (2) Enzyme activity constantly increases with increasing temperature. (3) The pH has a greater effect on this enzyme than temperature does. (4) Enzyme activity increases as the temperature increases from 32°C to 34°C.

Explanation of Answer Choice 1 is not correct since the graph tells you nothing about enzyme synthesis. The graph starts to show data at 30°C, but shows nothing about synthesis. Choice 2 is wrong, because enzyme activity does not continue to increase. It starts to decrease rapidly at about 37°C. Choice 3 is incorrect, since there is no mention of pH anywhere on the graph. The correct answer is choice 4. If you follow the graph line, it does show an increase in relative rate of enzyme activity as the temperature increases from 32°C to 34°C.

Appendix B: NY State Required Laboratory Activities

As of June 2004, the Living Environment Regents examination consists of four parts. The type and numbers of questions on Parts A, B, and C continues mostly unchanged from previous examinations. The fourth part, Part D, is composed of multiple-choice and/or open-ended constructed response questions, based on the NY State-required laboratory activities for that year. *Because the tested laboratory activities change from year-to-year with the January examination, always check so you know which ones are required for a particular examination.*

Part D of the Living Environment Regents Examination—Questions and answers:

1. **How important are the required laboratory activities?** Everyone taking the Living Environment examination is expected to have satisfactorily met the laboratory requirement, and completed the four laboratory activities required for that year. Questions on Part D of the Regents Examination will assess content and skills related to those required laboratory activities. Everyone who has completed these activities should have available for review, the *Student Laboratory Packet* for each of the labs. The packet contains background information, procedures, questions, and answers that were filled in as you carried out the laboratory activity. These packets should be used for review purposes, along with the information provided in this Appendix of *Brief Review in Living Environment.*

2. **How do the required labs help me in the Living Environment course?** Performing the required laboratory activities accomplishes two basic things. First, you learn and/or practice important laboratory skills associated with the biological sciences. Second, the lab activities are each associated with specific concepts contained in the *Living Environment Core Curriculum,* helping you better learn, understand, and apply those concepts.

3. **How can this Appendix help me prepare for the Part D questions?** To best prepare for the questions on Part D, you need to review your completed *Student Laboratory Packet* for each required laboratory activity along with the information presented here. You should have all four completed packets (with correct answers) available as you work through this Appendix.

4. **What should I know about each of the Required Laboratory Activities?** The most critical thing is that you have actually completed each activity and observed firsthand the results of each part. The next thing is to review the content and skills associated with each activity by working through the rest of this Appendix. In many cases, the content or skills are already found elsewhere in this book. References and notes are provided to show you where to look. Specific information and skills related to each activity is provided in this section.

The questions on Part D may be *applications* of the skills and content associated with the activity. For example, although red onion cells are used in the diffusion laboratory activity, a question involving the basic concepts of diffusion using another kind of plant cell would be appropriate as a Part D question.

It is important to note that you do *not* have to know, for test purposes, all of the content information provided with each activity. Much of it is included in the activity so that you can understand the important concepts. Only a few concepts in the required labs that are not in the Core Curriculum are actually testable. Each of these will be clearly noted in this Appendix.

Laboratory Activity #1, *Relationships and Biodiversity*
(This lab is required for and subject to testing on examinations from June 2004 through August 2005)

In this activity, you conducted a number of tests to compare various characteristics of a hypothetical "endangered plant species" with 3 other species that were related to it. From the data, you then determined which species might be the most likely to produce the substance "Curol" that has important medical uses. The final segment of the activity focused on biodiversity; both its benefits and how the loss of biodiversity can be an environmental problem.

Skills and/or content associated with the laboratory activity	Procedures and suggestions for review **Note:** Pages noted below are either in *Brief Review in the Living Environment (BR)* or in your *Student Lab Packet (SLP)*.
Making/recording observations of plant tissues	See pages 131–132, and page 158 (BR) for information about observations, inferences, assumptions, and opinions.
Making/recording observations of tissue samples with a microscope	Review focusing and other microscope skills on pages 150–153 (BR). In this section you examined plant tissues with the microscope to look for similarities and differences.
Comparing samples to determine similarities and differences	You compared the flowers, leaves, seeds, and stem cross sections in an attempt to determine which one was most closely related to *Botana curus (B. curis)*. If a Regents question illustrates parts of specific organisms, you could be asked to use your observations to determine relationships between them.
Use of paper chromatography	Review what you did during the laboratory activity on pages 2–3 (SLP). Review the process on page 155 (BR). Be prepared to answer questions about why goggles were required or about correct vs. incorrect technique related to chromatography, such as: What if the water level was above the pigment spots when the paper was put in the cup? (answer: the pigment would wash away and not go up the paper)
Use of an indicator (to test for enzyme M)	You were testing for an enzyme that was present in *B. curis* to see if any of the other plants also produced it. The presence of this enzyme in any of the other plants might suggest a closer relationship to *B. curis*. Review information about indicators on page 155 (BR).
Use of simulated gel electrophoresis of DNA from plant samples.	Review what you did during the laboratory activity on pages 3–4 (SLP), then review the technique of electrophoresis on pages 153–154 (BR). Be prepared to answer questions about how enzymes are used to cut the DNA into fragments as described in the lab activity. Also know how to interpret gel electrophoresis results: e.g., what do the bands represent and what information do they convey?
Translating the DNA code to a particular protein sequence	Review what you did during the laboratory activity on page 7 (SLP). You first used the base pairing "rule" for DNA to RNA transcription—G goes with C, and A goes with U (not T) to get the mRNA sequences. Then you used the universal genetic code table provided by your teacher to look up which amino acid each three-letter mRNA sequence represented. This enabled you to get a particular amino acid sequence for each species, so that you could compare them and determine possible genetic relationships. Similar DNA suggests common ancestry. Review the information on pages 42–3 (BR) regarding proteins and DNA in cells.
Using branching tree diagrams to show relationships	Review question 6 on page 6 (SLP), then review Figure 5.2 on page 72 (BR). Read pages 77–78 (BR). Read the information about Practice Questions 13–14 on pages 171–172 (BR).
Human actions and biodiversity	Re-read the passage on page 7 (SLP), then review your answers to questions 8–10. Review pages 99–100 (BR), and pages 113–115 (BR) regarding the benefits of biodiversity, and the section: *Extinction,* on page 80 (BR).

Review questions and comments regarding Laboratory Activity #1

After reviewing your Student Lab Packet and the sections of this book as noted above, check yourself by answering the following questions found in this book on the pages noted.

p. 43; 8, 9

p. 44; 13, 16, 17, 18, 20, 21, 22

p. 48; 41

p. 49; 1, 6

p. 50; 8

p. 72; 3, 5

p. 79; 29, 30

p. 81; 38

p. 82; 4

p. 83; 9

p. 100; 40, 41, 42, 43, 45

p. 108; 32

p. 112; 2, 4

p. 115; 7

p. 116; 15, 16

p. 129; 36, 37

p. 133; 1, 2, 4

p. 156; 9, 10, 11, 12

p. 157; 13, 15, 22

p. 158; 28, 30

p. 162; 3

p. 163; 10, 11

p. 165; 18

You should also be able to:

- explain how you used your lab data to determine which plant species is the closest relative to *B. curus*.

- explain why finding a close relative to *B. curus* is important.

- list several forms of structural evidence that can be used to indicate biological relationships (such as similarities in embryos, flower form, or leaf shape).

- explain why structural evidence is often less useful than molecular evidence to determine biological relationships.

- use a genetic code table to convert a DNA sequence, to a mRNA sequence, to an amino acid sequence. (Ask your teacher for a copy of the table you used in the activity and practice with it.)

- explain why closely related species often share many molecular/biochemical similarities.

- answer questions related to why and how biodiversity may be lost, why such a loss is important, and how human activities often play a role in the loss of biodiversity.

- discuss why tradeoffs must be considered when the destruction of habitats/native species is involved.

Laboratory Activity #2, *Making Connections*
(This lab is required for and subject to testing on examinations from June 2004 through August 2005, and tentatively, thrugh August 2006)

In Part A of this activity, you learned to take your pulse rate. Then you compared pulse rate data for the class. You next experienced muscle fatigue by rapidly squeezing a clothespin. In Part B, you designed a controlled experiment to determine which of two claims about exercise and pulse rate is correct.

Skills and/or content associated with the laboratory activity	Procedures and suggestions for review **Note:** Pages noted below are either in *Brief Review in the Living Environment (BR)* or in your *Student Lab Packet (SLP)*.
Taking pulse rate	You should be familiar with the procedure to find a person's pulse rate on page 2. (SLP) Review the information on human systems on pages 8–11 (BR).
Data tables and graphs	Review the data table and histogram you prepared on page 3 (SLP). Also review the questions and your answers on page 4 (SLP). Review the information about collecting and organizing data on pages 138–139 (BR).
Muscle fatigue	Review the information, questions, and your answers to them on pages 5 and 6 (SLP).
Designing a controlled experiment and a report on the findings	Review the background information on page 7 (SLP) to help you recall how you determined the hypothesis your experiment tested. Review the steps for the design of a controlled experiment and how to organize the final report on pages 8–9 (SLP), then read over your final laboratory report for this activity, noting how you addressed each step of the design and report organization. Review the information on pages 134 through 141 (BR) regarding experimental design and the reporting of results and conclusions.

Review questions and comments regarding Laboratory Activity #2

After reviewing your Student Lab Packet and the sections of this book as noted above, check yourself by answering the following questions found in this book on the pages noted.

p. 12; 40
p. 14; 15
p. 133; 3, 5
p. 137; 6, 8, 9, 10, 11, 12, 14
p. 138; 16

p. 141; 18, 19
p. 142; 20, 21, 22, 26, 27, 28
p. 144; 5, 6, 7, 8, 9
p. 146; 15

You should also be able to:

- explain what your pulse rate tells you about activities occurring within your body.
- explain why a higher level of activity would affect a person's pulse rate. Be sure to state specifically how the functioning of muscle cells is affected by blood flow through various parts the body including the respiratory and digestive systems.

- explain what muscle fatigue is, what happens to cause it, and how it can eventually be overcome—see page 5 (SLP).
- explain why different individuals may have different resting pulse rates and that not all people experience muscle fatigue with the same amount of muscle activity.
- explain why evidence is important in determining whether or not a claim someone makes is true.
- describe your actual experiment, including the question, hypothesis, independent and dependent variables, and your conclusions. You should also be able to suggest at least one additional experiment that could be done to answer a question that came about as a direct result of the experiment you conducted. (Such a question might involve the effect of more activity on the test subjects, having more test subjects, or choosing a greater variety of test subjects.)

Laboratory Activity #3, *The Beaks of Finches*
(This lab is required for and subject to testing on examinations from June 2004 and August 2004)

The Beaks of Finches lab is a simulation of how natural selection works. Various tools are used in this activity to represent some beak variations that might be present in a population. Competition between participants leads to finding which tool(s) are best suited for obtaining an enough food for the individuals with that tool (beak variation) to survive. The activity concludes with data about actual beak variations present today in different species of finches—the result of competition over many years on the Galapagos Islands.

Skills and/or content associated with the laboratory activity	Procedures and suggestions for review **Note:** Pages noted below are either in *Brief Review in the Living Environment (BR)* or in your *Student Lab Packet (SLP)*.
Predicting	Review the procedures and questions on page 2 (SLP) to recall why you could expect a particular tool to be useful for the job specified.
Collecting and organizing data, making predictions	Review what you did during the Round One competition on page 3 (SLP). You could be asked to place data in a data table provided, as you did in this activity. Review the information on p. 138–140 (BR).
Analyzing and interpreting data	Review what you did during the Round Two competition on page 3 (SLP). The competition in Round Two was expected to make it harder to collect as many seeds in the same time interval as you had in Round One. State whether or not your results supported this expectation. Include data from the table in your answer. Read the introduction to The Mechanics of Evolution and Overview of Evolution on page 73 (BR) and on pages 174–175 (BR) about data table question strategies.
Summarizing results	Review questions 1–9 and your answers on pages 4–6 (SLP). Read the information on page 73 (BR), then on page 74 (BR) read the three sections and review the information in figures 5–4 and 5–5. Read pages 89–91 (BR); *Environmental Limits on Population Size*.

Skills and/or content associated with the laboratory activity	Procedures and suggestions for review **Note:** Pages noted below are either in *Brief Review in the Living Environment (BR)* or in your *Student Lab Packet (SLP)*.
Galapagos Island Finches— Interpreting charts	Review the chart on page 6 (SLP), noting the "design" of each beak compared with the way it functions and the preferred food. Review the questions about the chart along with your responses to them. Be prepared to answer similar questions in association with this chart or a similar chart or diagram.

Review questions and comments regarding Laboratory Activity #3

After reviewing your Student Lab Packet and the sections of this book as noted above, check yourself by answering the following questions found in this book on the pages noted.

p. 75; 6, 11, 12   p. 90; 4, 5

p. 77; 16   p. 94; 10

p. 82; 1, 3, 6   p. 141; 19

You should also be able to:

- identify a specific procedure or action you carried out in this lab that is directly associated with *each* of the following concepts associated with evolution: variation, competition, survival, adaptation, and the role of the environment as an agent of natural selection. For help, see question #9 on page 6 (SLP).

- describe how being assigned a tool is more like how adaptations occur in nature than being allowed to choose a particular tool for the task.

- predict how the addition of small pebbles to the dish (that could not be used as food) could affect the results as the (food) seeds were being collected.

- explain how the characteristics of a particular bird's beak could affect its survival.

- explain why a bird has no control over the type of beak it has.

- explain how a particular beak could be useful in one environment and nearly useless in another.

- explain why migration to a new environment may enable an individual who cannot successfully compete in its original location to survive.

- explain why an individual with a beak that does not enable it to compete successfully for food cannot simply get a new beak that would make it better adapted.

- describe two characteristics of a bird, other than its beak, that would vary among individuals in the population and be a factor in the ability of individual birds to survive. Select one of these characteristics and state how it would specifically be important to the individual's survival.

- name two species on the beak chart, on page 6 (SLP), that would be likely to compete when food is scarce. Explain the basis for your answer.

Laboratory Activity #5, *Diffusion Through a Membrane*
(This lab is required for and subject to testing on examinations from June 2004 through August 2005, and tentatively, through August 2007)

The *Diffusion Through a Membrane* activity initially focuses on making a model "cell" and determining how certain materials move through the membrane surrounding it. Indicators are then used to test various solutions to determine which materials moved and where they ended up. Red onion cells were treated with salt solution and distilled water to determine the effect of such substances on live cells.

Skills and/or content associated with the laboratory activity	Procedures and suggestions for review **Note:** Pages noted below are either in *Brief Review in the Living Environment (BR)* or in your *Student Lab Packet (SLP)*.
Making a model "cell"	Review the procedures by which you made a model "cell" out of dialysis tubing (or a plastic bag). The "cell" contained both glucose and starch while the beaker contained starch indicator solution and water—see p. 2 (SLP). Read pages 3–6 (BR) regarding cell organelles, including the cell membrane. Read p. 147–149 (BR), *Tools for Measurement*.
Using starch and glucose indicator solutions	Review the procedures (p. 3 SLP, Table One) for testing for starch and glucose using the indicator. Notice that, in each case, a color change indicated the presence of the substance, and that the glucose test required heating before a result could be observed.
Determining indicator results	Table 2 (p. 3 SLP) summarizes the tests and results for each indicator. Be sure you can explain why it is necessary to test both the substance you want the indicator to "find" and any other substances that are also present. Read p. 155 (BR); *Stains and Indicators*.
Observing and interpreting results	Review your Model Cell Observations (p. 4 SLP) and the diagrams you filled in. Then carefully review your answers to questions 1–7 on pages 4–5 (SLP). Be sure you now understand which molecules moved through the membrane and know how you could tell. Also be sure you know how this information was used to determine the relative sizes of the molecules.
Making a wet-mount slide (of onion cells)	Review the procedures for making a wet mount slide. (p. 6 SLP) Read pages 150–153 (BR); *Microscope Skills*.
Drawing and labeling microscope images	Review the drawings you made for questions 6, 10 and 15. (p. 7 SLP) Note the differences in each drawing and review what you did each time to cause the changes you observed and drew.
Adding liquids to wet-mount slides	Review the procedure for this technique. (p. 6 SLP) You should be able to describe this process and predict the effect a substance being added would have on the cells.
Applying skills and concepts	Review the Analysis Questions and your answers to them. (p. 8–9 SLP) Just as you did for these questions, you should be able to apply the main concepts from this activity to questions like these if they appear on Part D of the Regents examination.

Review questions and comments regarding Laboratory Activity #5

After reviewing your Student Lab Packet and the sections of this book as noted above, check yourself by answering the following questions found in this book on the pages noted.

p. 4; 11
p. 7; 22, 23, 25, 26, 27
p. 8; 28, 30, 31, 32, 33, 35
p. 13; 4, 5, 6, 7, 8, 9
p. 14; 10

p. 16; 28, 29
p. 149; 3, 4, 5, 6, 7
p. 156; 12
p. 157; 13, 14, 15, 16, 17, 22
p. 162; 2, 5

You should also be able to:
- explain why dialysis tubing or a plastic bag could be used to simulate a cell membrane in this activity.
- identify a particular indicator and explain how it is used to indicate whether or not a specific substance is present.
- explain why it was important to keep the onion skin material as flat as possible when making the wet-mount slide.
- describe the direction that particles move during the process of diffusion relative to the concentration of a substance or substances.
- describe how the size of a molecule can affect whether or not it can pass across (through) a membrane.
- provide several examples of cells being affected by the process of diffusion. The effects may be on the appearance of the cell, the contents of the cell, and/or the functioning of the cell.
- provide several specific examples of the process of diffusion occurring within the human body. For each example be able to identify the substance(s) diffusing and the effect of this process on body functioning.

- describe the effect of salt on the water content of cell cytoplasm.
- describe how distilled water can be used to counteract the effect of salt on living cells on a wet-mount microscope slide.
- predict the effect of an error in procedure by students doing this particular laboratory activity, such as putting a substance in the wrong place, using salt solution instead of water, using the wrong indicator, and so on.

- Understand that osmosis, the diffusion of water through a membrane, is a kind of diffusion and therefore follows the same general "rules" as for the diffusion of other substances.
- explain how the process of digestion is related to the process of diffusion—see question 6 on p. 9 (SLP).

Regents Examinations

The following examinations were prepared by the New York State Education Department to give teachers and students an idea of what to expect from the format and content of the new Regents Examination for The Living Environment. The tests were given to students taking The Living Environment Pilot Course. Since then, a few changes have been made in the core content, so there may be several slight changes in the actual content you are responsible for knowing. However, the content of this book is up-to-date and provides specifically what you need to review for The Living Environment Regents Examination.

The best way to use these examinations is to take the entire test after you have reviewed the course content. Taking these tests as practice before your review may be both discouraging and of little value. Instead, use the tests to determine if you have reviewed enough to do well on the Regents Examination and to determine where further review will be most helpful.

Do not look up any information or answers while you take the examinations. Answer each question just as you would during a real test. As you take the Examination, use the margin of the paper to note any question where you are just guessing. Leave the more difficult questions for last, but be sure to answer each question. Every point counts so do not skip over a long question that is only worth a point or two. A long question could be easier than it looks and may make the difference between an A or a B or between passing or failing.

When you finish, have your teacher score your Examination and help you determine the areas where you need the most work. Also review the "guesses" you noted in the margin to find out what you need to study to ensure that you will be able to answer similar questions on the next test. Once you have determined your weaknesses, you can focus your review on those topics in this book.

Reviewing the areas where you know the least will give you the best chance of improving your final score. Spending time on areas where you are doing quite well will not produce much improvement in your total score, but it is still important if time permits.

Part A

Answer all questions in this part.   [35]

Directions (1–35): For *each* statement or question, write on the separate answer sheet the number of the word or expression that, of those given, best completes the statement or answers the question.

1 A student observes that an organism is green. A valid conclusion that can be drawn from this observation is that

(1) the organism must be a plant
(2) the organism cannot be single celled
(3) the organism must be an animal
(4) not enough information is given to determine whether the organism is a plant or an animal

2 Why do scientists consider any hypothesis valuable?

(1) A hypothesis requires no further investigation.
(2) A hypothesis may lead to further investigation even if it is disproved by the experiment.
(3) A hypothesis requires no further investigation if it is proved by the experiment.
(4) A hypothesis can be used to explain a conclusion even if it is disproved by the experiment.

3 Which letter indicates a cell structure that directly controls the movement of molecules into and out of the cell?

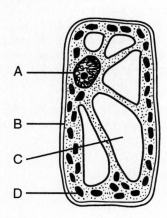

(1) *A*   (3) *C*
(2) *B*   (4) *D*

4 A great deal of information can now be obtained about the future health of people by examining the genetic makeup of their cells. There are concerns that this information could be used to deny an individual health insurance or employment. These concerns best illustrate that

(1) scientific explanations depend upon evidence collected from a single source
(2) scientific inquiry involves the collection of information from a large number of sources
(3) acquiring too much knowledge in human genetics will discourage future research in that area
(4) while science provides knowledge, values are essential to making ethical decisions using this knowledge

5 The diagram below represents one metabolic activity of a human.

Metabolic Activity A

Protein

Letters *A* and *B* are best represented by which row in the chart?

Row	Metabolic Activity A	B
(1)	respiration	oxygen molecules
(2)	reproduction	hormone molecules
(3)	excretion	simple sugar molecules
(4)	digestion	amino acid molecules

6 When a person does strenuous exercise, small blood vessels (capillaries) near the surface of the skin increase in diameter. This change allows the body to be cooled. These statements best illustrate

(1) synthesis   (3) excretion
(2) homeostasis   (4) locomotion

7 Which ecological term includes everything represented in the illustration below?

(1) ecosystem
(2) community
(3) population
(4) species

8 Which sequence represents the correct order of levels of organization found in a complex organism?

(1) cells → organelles → organs → organ systems → tissues
(2) tissues → organs → organ systems → organelles → cells
(3) organelles → cells → tissues → organs → organ systems
(4) organs → organ systems → cells → tissues → organelles

9 Scientific studies show that identical twins who were separated at birth and raised in different homes may vary in height, weight, and intelligence. The most probable explanation for these differences is that

(1) original genes of each twin increased in number as they developed
(2) one twin received genes only from the mother while the other twin received genes only from the father
(3) environments in which they were raised were different enough to affect the expression of their genes
(4) environments in which they were raised were different enough to change the genetic makeup of both individuals

10 When DNA separates into two strands, the DNA would most likely be directly involved in

(1) replication
(2) fertilization
(3) differentiation
(4) evolution

11 The instructions for the traits of an organism are coded in the arrangement of

(1) glucose units in carbohydrate molecules
(2) bases in DNA in the nucleus
(3) fat molecules in the cell membrane
(4) energy-rich bonds in starch molecules

12 Which statement is true regarding an alteration or change in DNA?

(1) It is always known as a mutation.
(2) It is always advantageous to an individual.
(3) It is always passed on to offspring.
(4) It is always detected by the process of chromatography.

13 In heterotrophs, energy for the life processes comes from the chemical energy stored in the bonds of

(1) water molecules
(2) oxygen molecules
(3) organic compounds
(4) inorganic compounds

14 The diagram below represents the chemical pathway of a process in a human liver cell.

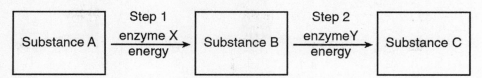

A particular liver cell is unable to make substance C. One possible explanation for the inability of this cell to make substance C is that

(1) excess energy for step 2 prevented the conversion of substance B to substance C
(2) an excess of enzyme X was present, resulting in a decrease in the production of substance B
(3) nuclear DNA was altered resulting in the cell being unable to make enzyme Y
(4) a mutation occurred causing a change in the ability of the cell to use substance C

15 The diagram below shows a process that can occur during meiosis.

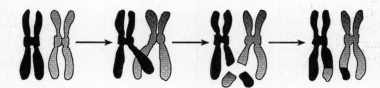

The most likely result of this process is

(1) a new combination of inheritable traits that can appear in the offspring
(2) an inability to pass either of these chromosomes on to offspring
(3) a loss of genetic information that will produce a genetic disorder in the offspring
(4) an increase in the chromosome number of the organism in which this process occurs

16 Structures in a human female are represented in the diagram below.

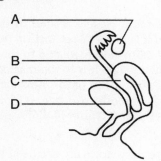

A heavy dose of radiation would have the greatest impact on genetic information in future offspring if it reached gametes developing within structure

(1) A   (3) C
(2) B   (4) D

17 Organism X appeared on Earth much earlier than organism Y. Many scientists believe organism X appeared between 3 and 4 billion years ago, and organism Y appeared approximately 1 billion years ago. Which row in the chart below most likely describes organisms X and Y?

Row	Organism X	Organism Y
(1)	simple multicellular	unicellular
(2)	complex multicellular	simple multicellular
(3)	unicellular	simple multicellular
(4)	complex multicellular	unicellular

18 The sequence of diagrams below represents some events in a reproductive process.

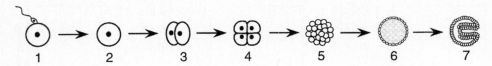

To regulate similar events in human reproduction, what adaptations are required?

(1) the presence of genes and chemicals in each cell in stages 1 to 7
(2) an increase in the number of genes in each cell in stages 3 to 5
(3) the removal of all enzymes from the cells in stage 7
(4) the elimination of mutations from cells after stage 5

19 Which statement best describes human insulin that is produced by genetically engineered bacteria?

(1) This insulin will not function normally in humans because it is produced by bacteria.
(2) This insulin is produced as a result of human insulin being inserted into bacteria cells.
(3) This insulin is produced as a result of exposing bacteria cells to radiation, which produces a mutation.
(4) This insulin may have fewer side effects than the insulin previously extracted from the pancreas of other animals.

20 Which population of organisms would be in greatest danger of becoming extinct?

(1) A population of organisms having few variations living in a stable environment.
(2) A population of organisms having few variations living in an unstable environment.
(3) A population of organisms having many variations living in a stable environment.
(4) A population of organisms having many variations living in an unstable environment.

21 In animals, the normal development of an embryo is dependent on

(1) fertilization of a mature egg by many sperm cells
(2) production of new cells having twice the number of chromosomes as the zygote
(3) production of body cells having half the number of chromosomes as the zygote
(4) mitosis and the differentiation of cells after fertilization has occurred

22 The relationship of some mammals is indicated in the diagram below.

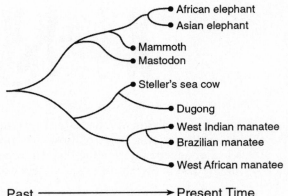

Past ⟶ Present Time

Which statement about the African elephant is correct?

(1) It is more closely related to the mammoth than it is to the West African manatee.
(2) It is more closely related to the West Indian manatee than it is to the mastodon.
(3) It is not related to the Brazilian manatee or the mammoth.
(4) It is the ancestor of Steller's sea cow.

23 Which process normally occurs at the placenta?

(1) Oxygen diffuses from fetal blood to maternal blood.
(2) Materials are exchanged between fetal and maternal blood.
(3) Maternal blood is converted into fetal blood.
(4) Digestive enzymes pass from maternal blood to fetal blood.

24 Individual cells can be isolated from a mature plant and grown with special mixtures of growth hormones to produce a number of genetically identical plants. This process is known as

(1) cloning
(2) meiotic division
(3) recombinant DNA technology
(4) selective breeding

25 A single-celled organism is represented in the diagram below. An activity is indicated by the arrow.

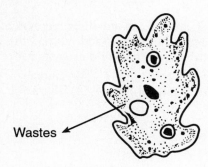

Wastes

If this activity requires the use of energy, which substance would be the source of this energy?

(1) DNA   (3) a hormone
(2) ATP   (4) an antibody

26 Which activity would stimulate the human immune system to provide protection against an invasion by a microbe?

(1) receiving antibiotic injections after surgery
(2) choosing a well-balanced diet and following it throughout life
(3) being vaccinated against chicken pox
(4) receiving hormones contained in mother's milk while nursing

27 In an ecosystem, the presence of many different species is critical for the survival of some forms of life when

(1) ecosystems remain stable over long periods of time
(2) significant changes occur in the ecosystem
(3) natural selection does not occur
(4) the finite resources of Earth increase

28 The most immediate response to a high level of blood sugar in a human is an increase in the

(1) muscle activity in the arms
(2) blood flow to the digestive tract
(3) activity of all cell organelles
(4) release of insulin

29 Which ecological term best describes the polar bears in the cartoon below?

"I lift, you grab....Was that concept just a little too complex, Carl?"

(adapted)

(1) herbivores   (3) carnivores
(2) parasites   (4) producers

30 A new island formed by volcanic action may eventually become populated with biotic communities as a result of

(1) a decrease in the amount of organic material present
(2) decreased levels of carbon dioxide in the area
(3) the lack of abiotic factors in the area
(4) the process of ecological succession

31 Certain microbes, foreign tissues, and some cancerous cells can cause immune responses in the human body because all three contain

(1) antigens   (3) fats
(2) enzymes   (4) cytoplasm

32 Decomposers are important in the environment because they

(1) convert large molecules into simpler molecules that can then be recycled
(2) release heat from large molecules so that the heat can be recycled through the ecosystem
(3) can take in carbon dioxide and convert it into oxygen
(4) convert molecules of dead organisms into permanent biotic parts of an ecosystem

33 An environment can support only as many organisms as the available energy, minerals, and oxygen will allow. Which term is best described by this statement?

(1) biological feedback
(2) carrying capacity
(3) homeostatic control
(4) biological diversity

34 Communities have attempted to control the size of mosquito populations to prevent the spread of certain diseases such as malaria and encephalitis. Which control method is most likely to cause the *least* ecological damage?

(1) draining the swamps where mosquitoes breed
(2) spraying swamps with chemical pesticides to kill mosquitoes
(3) spraying oil over swamps to suffocate mosquito larvae
(4) increasing populations of native fish that feed on mosquito larvae in the swamps

35 Which animal has modified ecosystems more than any other animal and has had the greatest negative impact on world ecosystems?

(1) gypsy moth   (3) human
(2) zebra mussel   (4) shark

Answer all questions in this part. [30]

Directions (36–62): For those questions that are followed by four choices, circle the number of the choice that best completes the statement or answers the question. For all other questions in this part, follow the directions given in the question and record your answers in the spaces provided.

36 The map below shows the movement of some air pollution across part of the United States.

Movement of Air Pollution

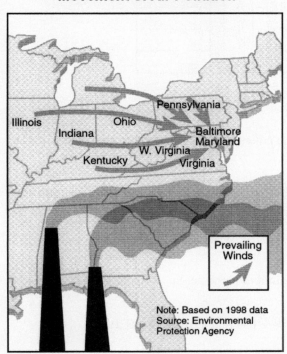

Note: Based on 1998 data
Source: Environmental Protection Agency

Which statement is a correct inference that can be drawn from this information?

(1) Illinois produces more air pollution than the other states shown.

(2) The air pollution problem in Baltimore is increased by the addition of pollution from other areas.

(3) There are no air pollution problems in southern states.

(4) The air pollution problems in Virginia clear up quickly as the air moves toward the sea.

36 ☐

Base your answers to questions 37 and 38 on the graph below and on your knowledge of biology. The graph illustrates a single species of bacteria grown at various pH levels.

Number of Colonies of Bacteria Present at Various pH Levels

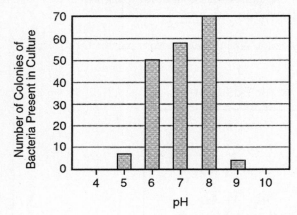

37 The most likely reason there are no colonies in cultures of this species at pH 4 and at pH 10 is that

(1) these bacteria could successfully compete with other species of bacteria at these pH values

(2) there are more predators feeding on these bacteria at pH 4 and pH 10 than at other pH levels

(3) at pH 4 and pH 10 the environment is too acidic or too basic for the bacteria to grow

(4) fertilization cannot occur in these bacteria at pH 4 or pH 10

37 ☐

38 Which statement is supported by data from this graph?

(1) All species of bacteria can grow well at pH 7.

(2) This type of bacterium would grow well at pH 7.5.

(3) This type of bacterium would grow well at pH 2.

(4) Other types of bacteria can grow well at pH 4.

38 ☐

39 In an experiment, DNA from dead pathogenic bacteria was transferred into living bacteria that do not cause disease. These altered bacteria were then injected into healthy mice. These mice died of the same disease caused by the original pathogens. Based on this information, which statement would be a valid conclusion?

(1) DNA is present only in living organisms.

(2) DNA functions only in the original organism of which it was a part.

(3) DNA changes the organism receiving the injection into the original organism.

(4) DNA from a dead organism can become active in another organism.

40 Dodder is a creeping vine that is parasitic on other plants. Which characteristic does dodder share with all other heterotrophs?

(1) It produces nutrients by photosynthesis.

(2) It must grow in bright locations.

(3) It consumes preformed organic molecules.

(4) It remains in one place for its entire life.

41 In a forest community, a shelf fungus and a slug live on the side of a decaying tree trunk. The fungus digests and absorbs materials from the tree, while the slug eats algae growing on the outside of the trunk. These organisms do not compete with one another because they occupy

(1) the same habitat, but different niches

(2) the same niche, but different habitats

(3) the same niche and the same habitat

(4) different habitats and different niches

42 Studies of fat cells and thyroid cells show that fat cells have fewer mitochondria than thyroid cells. A biologist would most likely infer that fat tissue

(1) does not require energy

(2) has energy requirements equal to those of thyroid tissue

(3) requires less energy than thyroid tissue

(4) requires more energy than thyroid tissue

Base your answers to questions 43 and 44 on the diagram below and on your knowledge of biology. Letters *A* through *J* represent different species of organisms. The vertical distances between the dotted lines represent long periods of time in which major environmental changes occurred.

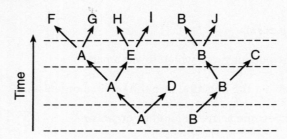

43 Which species was the first to become extinct?

(1) *E*

(2) *J*

(3) *C*

(4) *D*

43 ☐

44 Which species appears to have been most successful in surviving changes in the environment over time?

(1) *A*

(2) *B*

(3) *C*

(4) *H*

44 ☐

45 The graph below shows the growth of two populations of paramecia grown in the same culture dish for 14 days.

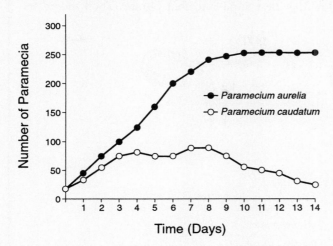

Which ecological concept is best represented by the graph?

(1) recycling

(2) equilibrium

(3) competition

(4) decomposition

45 ☐

46 Two different types of cells from an organism are shown below.

Explain how these two different types of cells can function differently in the same organism even though they both contain the same genetic instructions. [1]

_____

_____

_____

46 ☐

Directions (47–49): The diagrams below represent organs of two individuals. The diagrams are followed by a list of sentences. For each phrase in questions 47 through 49, select the sentence from the list below that best applies to that phrase. Then record its *number* in the space provided.

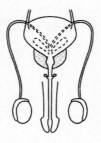
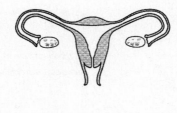

Individual A   Individual B

Sentences

1. The phrase is correct for both Individual *A* and Individual *B*.
2. The phrase is not correct for either Individual *A* or Individual *B*.
3. The phrase is correct for Individual *A*, only.
4. The phrase is correct for Individual *B*, only

47 Contains organs that produce gametes   [1]

_____

48 Contains organs involved in internal fertilization   [1]

_____

49 Contains a structure in which a zygote divides by mitosis   [1]

_____

47 ☐

48 ☐

49 ☐

Base your answers to questions 50 and 51 on the information below and on your knowledge of biology.

Amphibians have long been considered an indicator of the health of life on Earth. Scientists are concerned because amphibian populations have been declining worldwide since the 1980s. In fact, in the past decade, twenty species of amphibians have become extinct and many others are endangered.

Scientists have linked this decline in amphibians to global climatic changes. Warmer weather during the last three decades has resulted in the destruction of many of the eggs produced by the Western toad. Warmer weather has also led to a decrease in rain and snow in the Cascade Mountain Range in Oregon, reducing the water level in lakes and ponds that serve as the reproductive sites for the Western toad. As a result, the eggs are exposed to more ultraviolet light. This makes the eggs more susceptible to water mold that kills the embryos by the hundreds of thousands.

50 The term used to identify the worldwide climatic changes referred to in the passage is

(1) global warming

(2) deforestation

(3) mineral depletion

(4) industrialization

50 ☐

51 State *two* ways the decline in amphibian populations could disrupt the stability of the ecosystems they inhabit.   [2]

1. _____

_____

_____

2. _____

_____

_____

51 ☐

52 The diagram below represents reproduction of single-celled organism A, which has a normal chromosome number of 8.

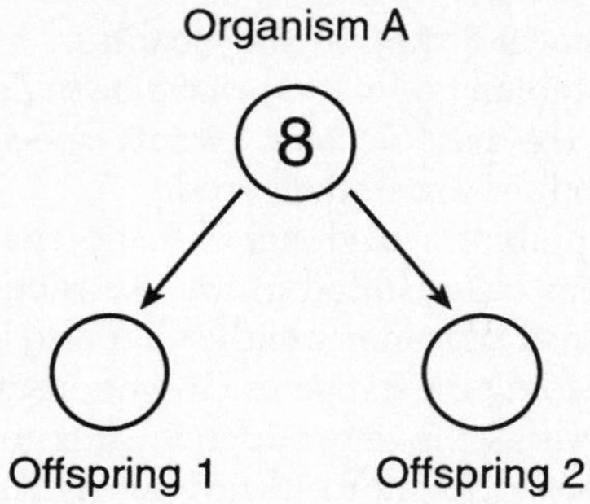

Organism A

Offspring 1   Offspring 2

In the circles representing offspring 1 and offspring 2, write the number of chromosomes that result from the normal asexual reproduction of organism A.   [1]

Base your answers to questions 53 and 54 on the structures in the diagram of human blood below that help to maintain homeostasis in humans.

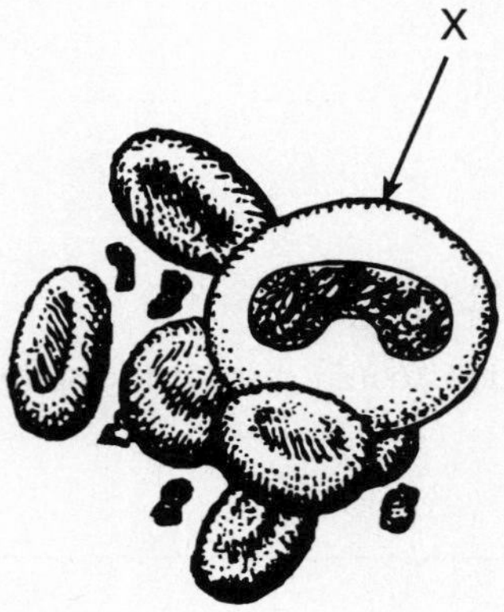

53 Identify the cell labeled X.   [1]

_____

54 State *one* way a cell such as cell X helps to maintain homeostasis.   [1]

_____

_____

_____

Base your answers to questions 55 and 56 on the diagram below, which represents a unicellular organism in a watery environment. The ▲s represent molecules of a specific substance.

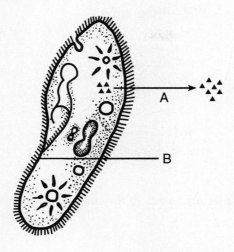

55 Arrow *A* represents active transport. State *two* ways that active transport is different. from diffusion. [2]

1. _____

   _____

   _____

2. _____

   _____

   _____

55 ☐

56 In cells of multicellular organisms, structure *B* often contains molecules involved in cell communication. What specific term is used to identify these molecules? [1]

_____

_____

56 ☐

57 Diagram *A* below represents a microscopic view of the lower surface of a leaf. Diagram *B* represents a portion of the human body.

Diagram A **Diagram B**

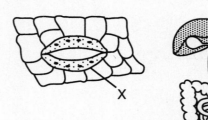

X   X

a Choose *one* diagram and record its letter, *A* or *B,* in the space provided.

Diagram: _____

b Identify the structure labeled *X* in the diagram you chose.   [1]

_____

c State *one* problem for the organism that would result from a malfunction of the structure you identified.   [1]

_____

_____

_____

57 ☐

Base your answers to questions 58 through 62 on the information below and on your knowledge of biology.

In an investigation, plants of the same species and the same initial height were exposed to a constant number of hours of light each day. The number of hours per day was different for each plant, but all other environmental factors were the same. At the conclusion of the investigation, the final height of each plant was measured. The following data were recorded:

8 hours, 25 cm; 4 hours, 12 cm; 2 hours, 5 cm; 14 hours, 35 cm; 12 hours, 35 cm; 10 hours, 34 cm; 6 hours, 18 cm

58 Organize the data by completing both columns in the data table provided, so that the hours of daily light exposure *increase* from the top to the bottom of the table.   [1]

Data Table

Daily Light Exposure (hours)	Final Height (cm)

59 State *one* possible reason that the plant exposed to 2 hours of light per day was the shortest.   [1]

_____

_____

_____

58 ☐

59 ☐

Directions (60–61): Using the information given, construct a line graph on the grid provided, following the directions below.

Effect of Light Exposure on Plant Growth

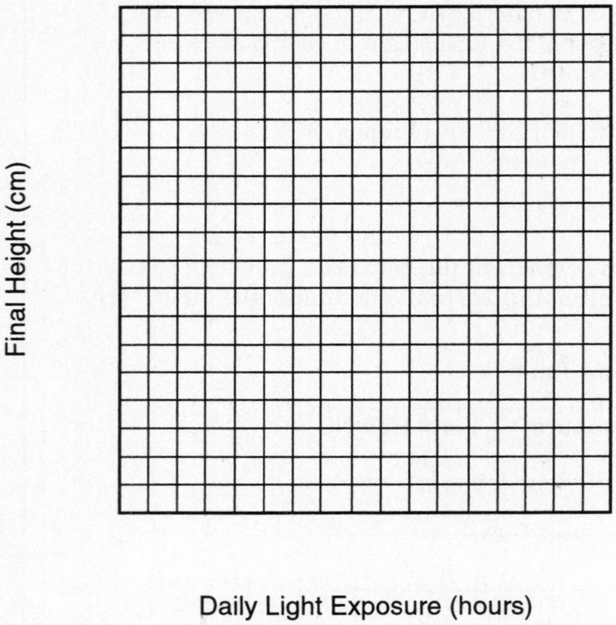

Final Height (cm)

Daily Light Exposure (hours)

60 Mark an appropriate scale on each axis. [1]

61 Plot the data for final height on the grid. Surround each point with a small circle and connect the points. [1]

Example:

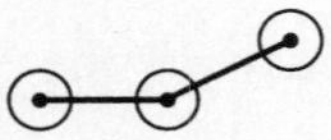

62 If another plant of the same species had been used in the investigation and exposed to 16 hours of light per day, what would the final height of the plant probably have been? Support your answer. [1]

_____

_____

_____

Part C

Answer all questions in this part. [20]

Directions (63–72): Record your answers in the spaces provided in this examination booklet.

Base your answers to questions 63 through 65 on the article below which was written in response to an article entitled "Let all predators become extinct."

Predators Contribute to a Stable Ecosystem

In nature, energy flows in only one direction. Transfer of energy must occur in an ecosystem because all life needs energy to live, and <u>only certain organisms can change solar energy into chemical energy.</u>
<u>Producers are eaten by consumers that are, in turn, eaten by other consumers.</u> Stable ecosystems must contain predators to help control the populations of consumers.

Since ecosystems contain many predators, exterminating predators would require a massive effort that would wipe out predatory species from barnacles to blue whales. Without the population control provided by predators, some organisms would soon overpopulate.

63 Draw an energy pyramid in the space below that illustrates the information underlined in the second paragraph. Include *three* different, specific organisms in the energy pyramid. [1]

63 ☐

64 Explain the phrase "only certain organisms can change solar energy into chemical energy," in the underlined portion of the first paragraph. In your answer be sure to identify:

- the type of nutrition carried out by these organisms   [1]
- the process being carried out in this type of nutrition   [1]
- the organelles present in the cells of these organisms that are directly involved in changing solar energy into chemical energy   [1]

_____

_____

_____

_____

_____

_____

_____

_____

64 ☐

65 Explain why an ecosystem with a variety of predator species might be more stable over a long period of time than an ecosystem with only one predator species.   [1]

_____

_____

_____

65 ☐

Base your answers to questions 66 and 67 on the information and data table below and on your knowledge of biology.

Trout and black bass are freshwater fish that normally require at least 8 parts per million (ppm) of dissolved oxygen (O_2) in the water for survival. Other freshwater fish, such as carp, may be able to live in water that has an O_2 level of 5 ppm. No freshwater fish are able to survive when the O_2 level in water is 2 ppm or less.

Some factories or power plants are built along rivers so that they can use the water to cool their equipment. They then release the water (sometimes as much as 8°C warmer) back into the same river.

The Rocky River presently has an average summer temperature of about 25°C and contains populations of trout, bass, and carp. A proposal has been made to build a new power plant on the banks of the Rocky River. Some people are concerned that this will affect the river ecosystem in a negative way.

The data table below shows the amount of oxygen that will dissolve in fresh water at different temperatures. The amount of oxygen is expressed in parts per million (ppm).

Data Table

Temperature (°C)	Fresh Water Oxygen Content (ppm)
1	14.24
10	11.29
15	10.10
20	9.11
25	8.27
30	7.56

66 State *one* effect of temperature change on the oxygen content of fresh water. Support your answer using specific information from the data table.   [2]

_____

_____

_____

_____

_____

66 ☐

67 Explain how a new power plant built on the banks of the Rocky River could have an environmental impact on the Rocky River ecosystem downstream from the plant. Your explanation must include the effects of the power plant on:

- water temperature [1]
- dissolved oxygen [1]
- fish species [1]

_____

_____

_____

_____

_____

_____

_____

_____

68 Enzyme molecules are affected by changes in conditions within organisms.

Explain how a prolonged, excessively high body temperature during an illness could be fatal to humans. Your answer must include:

- the role of enzymes in a human [1]
- the effect of this high body temperature on enzyme activity [1]
- the reason this high body temperature can result in death [1]

_____

_____

_____

_____

_____

_____

_____

67 ☐

68 ☐

Base your answers to questions 69 through 71 on the quotation below and on your knowledge of biology.

"Today I planted something new in my vegetable garden — something very new, as a matter of fact. It's a potato called the New Leaf Superior, which has been genetically engineered — by Monsanto, the chemical giant recently turned "life sciences" giant — to produce its own insecticide. This it can do in every cell of every leaf, stem, flower, root, and (here's the creepy part) spud [the potato]."

Source: *New York Times Sunday Magazine,*
Michael Pollan, 10/25/98

69 State *two* reasons that a gardener might choose to grow this new variety of plant.   [2]

1. _____

_____

_____

2. _____

_____

_____

69 ☐

70 State *one* possible *disadvantage* of the synthesis of an insecticide by potatoes.   [1]

_____

_____

_____

70 ☐

71 Explain why every cell in the New Leaf Superior potato plant is able to produce its own insecticide.   [1]

_____

_____

_____

71 ☐

72 Select *one* of the following ecological problems.

Ecological Problems

Acid rain
Increased amounts of nitrogen and phosphorous in a lake
Loss of biodiversity

For the ecological problem that you selected, briefly describe the problem and state *one* way to reduce it. In your answer be sure to:

- state the ecological problem you selected
- state how humans have caused the problem you selected [1]
- describe *one* specific effect that the problem you selected will have on the ecosystem [1]
- state *one* specific action humans could take to reduce the problem you selected [1]

_____

_____

_____

_____

_____

_____

_____

_____

_____

_____

_____

_____

72 ☐

Part A

Answer all questions in this part. [35]

Directions (1–35): For *each* statement or question, write on the separate answer sheet the number of the word or expression that, of those given, best completes the statement or answers the question.

1 A biologist reported success in breeding a tiger with a lion, producing healthy offspring. Other biologists will accept this report as fact only if

(1) research shows that other animals can be crossbred
(2) the offspring are given a scientific name
(3) the biologist included a control in the experiment
(4) other researchers can replicate the experiment

2 The diagram below represents a pyramid of energy in an ecosystem.

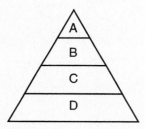

Which level in the pyramid would most likely contain members of the plant kingdom?

(1) *A*   (3) *C*
(2) *B*   (4) *D*

3 Which condition would cause an ecosystem to become *unstable*?

(1) only heterotrophic organisms remain after a change in the environment
(2) a slight increase in the number of heterotrophic and autotrophic organisms occurs
(3) a variety of nonliving factors are used by the living factors
(4) biotic and abiotic resources interact

4 Nerve cells are essential to an animal because they directly provide

(1) communication between cells
(2) transport of nutrients to various organs
(3) regulation of reproductive rates within other cells
(4) an exchange of gases within the body

5 Certain bacteria produce a chemical that makes them resistant to penicillin. Since these bacteria reproduce asexually, they usually produce offspring that

(1) can be destroyed by penicillin
(2) mutate into another species
(3) are genetically different from their parents
(4) survive exposure to penicillin

6 A sudden change in the DNA of a chromosome can usually be passed on to future generations if the change occurs in a

(1) skin cell   (3) sex cell
(2) liver cell   (4) brain cell

7 A change in the order of DNA bases that code for a respiratory protein will most likely cause

(1) the production of a starch that has a similar function
(2) the digestion of the altered gene by enzymes
(3) a change in the sequence of amino acids determined by the gene
(4) the release of antibodies by certain cells to correct the error

8 Many vaccinations stimulate the immune system by exposing it to

(1) antibodies   (3) mutated genes
(2) enzymes   (4) weakened microbes

9 The data in the graph below show evidence of disease in the human body.

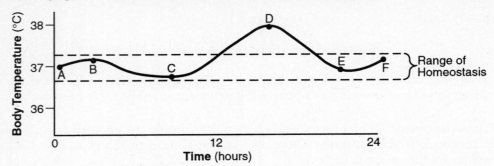

A disruption in dynamic equilibrium is indicated by the temperature change between points

(1) A and B

(3) C and D

(2) B and C

(4) E and F

10 The diagram below represents events involved as energy is ultimately released from food.

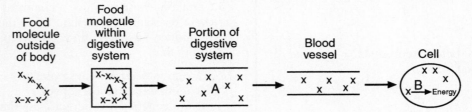

Which row in the table below best represents the chain of Xs and letters A and B in the diagram?

X-X-X-X-X-X-X	A and B
(1) nutrient	antibodies
(2) nutrient	enzymes
(3) hemoglobin	wastes
(4) hemoglobin	hormones

11 In the diagram below, the dark dots indicate small molecules. These molecules are moving out of the cells, as indicated by the arrows. The number of dots inside and outside of the two cells represents the relative concentrations of the molecules inside and outside of the cells.

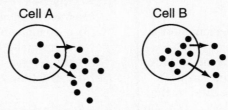

ATP is being used to move the molecules out of the cell by

(1) cell A, only

(3) both cell A and cell B

(2) cell B, only

(4) neither cell A nor cell B

12 The diagrams below represent some steps in a procedure used in biotechnology.

Bacterial DNA

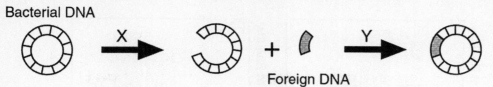

Letters *X* and *Y* represent the

(1) hormones that stimulate the replication of bacterial DNA
(2) biochemical catalysts involved in the insertion of genes into other organisms
(3) hormones that trigger rapid mutation of genetic information
(4) gases needed to produce the energy required for gene manipulation

13 According to some scientists, patterns of evolution can be illustrated by the diagrams below.

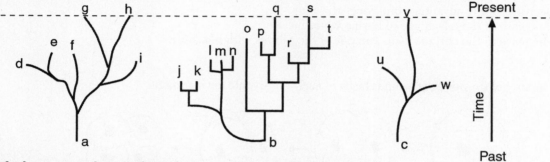

Which statement best explains the patterns seen in these diagrams?

(1) The organisms at the end of each branch can be found in the environment today.
(2) The organisms that are living today have all evolved at the same rate and have undergone the same kinds of changes.
(3) Evolution involves changes that give rise to a variety of organisms, some of which continue to change through time while others die out.
(4) These patterns cannot be used to illustrate the evolution of extinct organisms.

14 Which statement best illustrates a rapid biological adaptation that has actually occurred?

(1) Pesticide-resistant insects have developed in certain environments.
(2) Scientific evidence indicates that dinosaurs once lived on land.
(3) Paving large areas of land has decreased habitats for certain organisms.
(4) The characteristics of sharks have remained unchanged over a long period of time.

15 During meiosis, crossing-over (gene exchange between chromosomes) may occur. Crossing-over usually results in

(1) overproduction of gametes
(2) fertilization and development
(3) the formation of identical offspring
(4) variation within the species

16 The diagram below illustrates the change that occurred in the physical appearance of a rabbit population over a 10-year period.

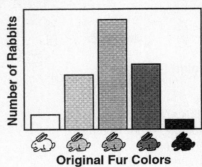 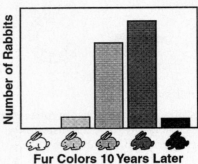

Which condition would explain this change over time?

(1) a decrease in the mutation rate of the rabbits with black fur
(2) a decrease in the advantage of having white fur
(3) an increase in the advantage of having white fur
(4) an increase in the chromosome number of the rabbits with black fur

17 The diagram below represents some stages of early embryonic development.

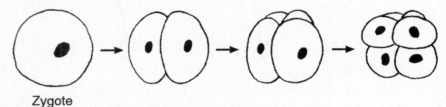

Zygote

Which process is represented by the arrows in the diagram?

(1) meiosis
(2) fertilization
(3) mitosis
(4) evolution

18 The reproductive system of the human male produces gametes and

(1) transfers gametes to the female for internal fertilization
(2) produces enzymes that prevent fertilization
(3) releases hormones involved in external fertilization
(4) provides an area for fertilization

19 Blood can be tested to determine the presence of the virus associated with the development of AIDS. This blood test is used directly for

(1) cure
(2) treatment
(3) diagnosis
(4) prevention

20 The equation below represents a summary of a biological process.

carbon dioxide + water → glucose + water + oxygen

This process is completed in

(1) mitochondria
(2) ribosomes
(3) cell membranes
(4) chloroplasts

21 In a stable, long-existing community, the establishment of a single species per niche is most directly the result of

(1) parasitism
(2) interbreeding
(3) competition
(4) overproduction

22 The diagram below represents a developing bird egg.

What is the primary function of this egg?

(1) food supply for predators to preserve predator populations
(2) adaptation to allow maximum freedom for parent birds
(3) continuation of the species through reproduction
(4) preservation of the exact genetic code of the parent birds

23 The diagram below represents part of the human female reproductive system.

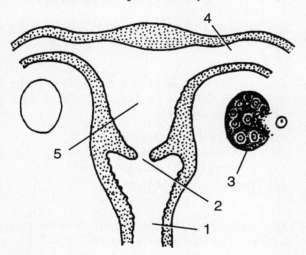

Fertilization and development normally occur in structures

(1) 1 and 5   (3) 3 and 1
(2) 2 and 4   (4) 4 and 5

24 The flow of energy through an ecosystem involves many energy transfers. The diagram below summarizes the transfer of energy that eventually powers muscle activity.

Sun $\xrightarrow[A]{}$ Food $\xrightarrow[B]{}$ ATP $\xrightarrow[C]{}$ Muscle Activity

The process of cellular respiration is represented by

(1) arrow A, only   (3) arrow C, only
(2) arrow B, only   (4) arrows A, B, and C

25 The presence of parasites in an animal will usually result in

(1) an increase in meiotic activity within structures of the host
(2) the inability of the host to maintain homeostasis
(3) the death of the host organism within twenty-four hours
(4) an increase in genetic mutation rate in the host organism

26 In Texas, researchers gave a cholesterol-reducing drug to 2,335 people and an inactive substitute (placebo) to 2,081. Most of the volunteers were men who had normal cholesterol levels and no history of heart disease. After 5 years, 97 people getting the placebo had suffered heart attacks compared to only 57 people who had received the actual drug. The researchers are recommending that to help prevent heart attacks, all people (even those without high cholesterol) take these cholesterol-reducing drugs. In addition to the information above, what is another piece of information that the researchers must have before support for the recommendation can be justified?

(1) Were the eating habits of the two groups similar?
(2) How does a heart attack affect cholesterol levels?
(3) Did the heart attacks result in deaths?
(4) What chemical is in the placebo?

27 What is represented by the sequence below?

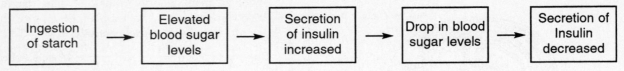

(1) a feedback mechanism in multicellular organisms
(2) an immune response by cells of the pancreas
(3) differentiation of organic molecules
(4) the disruption of cellular communication

28 In an ecosystem, which component is *not* recycled?

(1) water
(2) energy
(3) oxygen
(4) carbon

29 Vultures, which are classified as scavengers, are an important part of an ecosystem because they

(1) hunt herbivores, limiting their populations in an ecosystem
(2) feed on dead animals, which aids in the recycling of environmental materials
(3) cause the decay of dead organisms, which releases usable energy to herbivores and carnivores
(4) are the first level in food webs and make energy available to all the other organisms in the web

30 "Natural ecosystems provide an array of basic processes that affect humans."

Which statement does *not* support this quotation?

(1) Bacteria of decay help recycle materials.
(2) Trees add to the amount of atmospheric oxygen.
(3) Treated sewage is less damaging to the environment than untreated sewage.
(4) Lichens and mosses living on rocks help to break the rocks down, forming soil.

31 The carrying capacity of a given environment is *least* dependent upon

(1) recycling of materials
(2) the available energy
(3) the availability of food and water
(4) daily temperature fluctuations

32 Increased efforts to conserve areas such as rain forests are necessary in order to

(1) protect biodiversity
(2) promote extinction of species
(3) exploit finite resources
(4) increase industrialization

33 Which practice would most likely deplete a non-renewable natural resource?

(1) harvesting trees on a tree farm
(2) burning coal to generate electricity in a power plant
(3) restricting water usage during a period of water shortage
(4) building a dam and a power plant to use water to generate electricity

34 Changes in the chemical composition of the atmosphere that may produce acid rain are most closely associated with

(1) insects that excrete acids
(2) runoff from acidic soils
(3) industrial smoke stack emissions
(4) flocks of migrating birds

35 One way to help provide suitable environments for future generations is to urge individuals to

(1) apply ecological principles when making decisions that will have an environmental impact
(2) control all aspects of natural environments
(3) agree that population controls have no impact on environmental matters
(4) work toward increasing global warming

Directions (36–64): For those questions that are followed by four choices, circle the number of the choice that best completes the statement or answers the question. For all other questions in this part, follow the directions given in the question and record your answers in the spaces provided.

36 As the depth of the ocean increases, the amount of light that penetrates to that depth decreases. At about 200 meters, little, if any, light is present. The graph below illustrates the population size of four different species at different water depths.

For Teacher Use Only

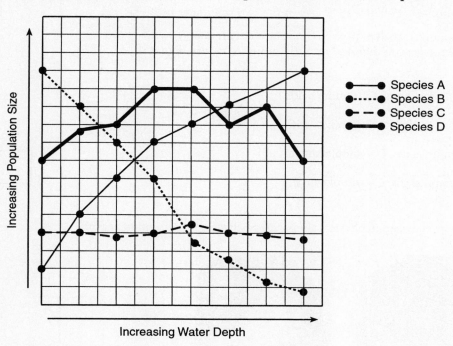

Which species most likely performs photosynthesis?

(1) A

(2) B

(3) C

(4) D

36 ⬚

37 Which structure is best observed using a compound light microscope?

  (1) a cell

  (2) a virus

  (3) a DNA sequence

  (4) the inner surface of a mitochondrion

38 Which words best complete the lettered blanks in the two sentences below?

   Organic compounds, such as proteins and starches, are too _A_ to diffuse into cells. Proteins are digested into _B_ and starches are digested into _C_ .

  (1) A—large, B—simple sugars, C—amino acids

  (2) A—small, B—simple sugars, C—amino acids

  (3) A—large, B—amino acids, C—simple sugars

  (4) A—small, B—amino acids, C—simple sugars

38

39 The photographs below show some physical similarities between John Lennon and his son Julian.

Lewis, Ricki *Life* 3rd edition WCB/McGraw Hill

Which conclusion can be drawn regarding these similarities?

  (1) The DNA present in their body cells is identical.

  (2) The percentage of their proteins with the same molecular composition is high.

  (3) The base sequences of their genes are identical.

  (4) The mutation rate is the same in their body cells.

39

Base your answers to questions 40 through 43 on the information below and on your knowledge of biology.

A decade after the Exxon Valdez oil tanker spilled millions of gallons of crude [oil] off Prince William Sound in Alaska, most of the fish and wildlife species that were injured have not fully recovered.

Only two out of the 28 species, the river otter and the bald eagle, listed as being injured from the 1989 spill are considered to be recovered said a new report, which was released by a coalition of federal and Alaska agencies working to help restore the oil spill region.

Eight species are considered to have made little or no progress toward recovery since the spill, including killer whales, harbor seals, and common loons [a type of bird].

Several other species, including sea otters and Pacific herring, have made significant progress toward recovery, but are still not at levels seen before the accident the report said.

More than 10.8 million gallons of crude oil spilled into the water when the tanker Exxon Valdez ran aground 25 miles south of Valdez on March 24, 1989.

The spill killed an estimated 250,000 seabirds, 2,800 sea otters, 300 harbor seals, 250 bald eagles, and up to 22 killer whales.

Billions of salmon and herring eggs, as well as tidal plants and animals, were also smothered in oil.

Reuters

40 Identify *two* species that appear to have been *least* affected by the oil spill.   [1]

(1) _____

(2) _____   40 ⬚

41 The oil spilled by the Exxon Valdez tanker is an example of a

(1) nonrenewable resource and is a source of energy

(2) renewable resource and is a source of ATP

(3) nonrenewable resource and synthesizes ATP

(4) renewable resource and is a fossil fuel   41 ⬚

42 The impact that the oil spill made on the environment is still being experienced. State information from the reading passage that supports this statement. [1]

For Teacher Use Only

42

43 Which autotrophic organisms were *negatively* affected by the oil spill? [1]

43

44 Although paramecia (single-celled organisms) usually reproduce asexually, some have developed a method by which they exchange genetic material with each other in a simple form of sexual reproduction. State *one* advantage this simple form of sexual reproduction would provide over asexual reproduction for the survival of these single-celled organisms. [1]

44

45 Identify a specific structure in a single-celled organism. State how that structure is involved in the survival of the organism. [2]

45

Base your answers to questions 46 and 47 on the diagram below and on your knowledge of biology.

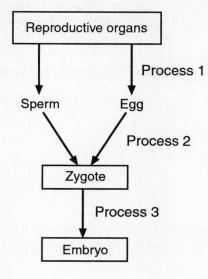

46 State why Process 2 is necessary in sexual reproduction.   [1]

_____

_____

_____

46 ☐

47 State *one* difference between the cells produced by Process 1 and the cells produced by Process 3.   [1]

_____

_____

_____

47 ☐

_____

Base your answers to questions 48 and 49 on the diagram of a slide of normal human blood below and on your knowledge of biology.

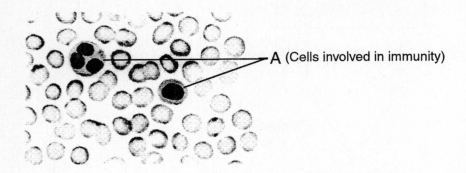

A (Cells involved in immunity)

48 An increase in the production of the cells labeled *A* is a response to an internal environmental change. State a change that might cause this response.   [1]

_____

_____

_____

48 [   ]

49 Describe *one* possible immune response, other than an increase in number, that one of the cells labeled *A* would carry out.   [1]

_____

_____

_____

49 [   ]

Base your answers to questions 50 through 53 on the diagram of a food web below and on your knowledge of biology.

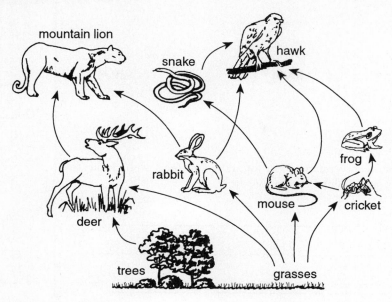

50 If the population of mice is reduced by disease, which change will most likely occur in the food web?

(1) The cricket population will increase.

(2) The snake population will increase.

(3) The grasses will decrease.

(4) The deer population will decrease.

50 ☐

51 What is the original source of energy for this food web?

(1) chemical bonds in sugar molecules

(2) enzymatic reactions

(3) the Sun

(4) chemical reactions of bacteria

51 ☐

52 Which organisms are *not* shown in this diagram but are essential to a balanced eco-system?

    (1) heterotrophs

    (2) autotrophs

    (3) producers

    (4) decomposers

52 ☐

53 State *one* example of a predator-prey relationship found in the food web. Indicate which organism is the predator and which is the prey.　[1]

_____

_____

_____

53 ☐

　　　　　　[15]　　　　　　[OVER]

Base your answers to questions 54 through 58 on the information, diagram, and data table below and on your knowledge of biology.

A student conducted an investigation to determine the effect of various environmental factors on the rate of transpiration (water loss through the leaves) in plants. The student prepared 4 groups of plants. Each group contained 10 plants of the same species and leaf area. Each group was exposed to different environmental factors. The apparatus shown in the diagram was constructed to measure water loss by the plants over time in 10-minute intervals for 30 minutes. The results are shown in the data table.

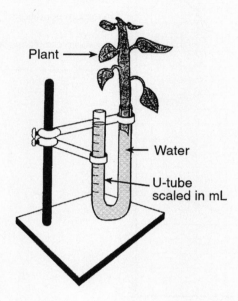

	Average Total Water Loss in mL Over Time			
Environmental Factors	**0 min**	**10 min**	**20 min**	**30 min**
Classroom Conditions	0.0	2.2	4.6	6.6
Classroom Conditions + Floodlight	0.0	4.2	7.6	11.7
Classroom Conditions + Fan	0.0	4.5	7.6	11.0
Classroom Conditions + Mist	0.0	1.3	2.4	3.7

Directions (54–56): Using the information in the data table, construct a line graph on the grid, following the directions below. The data for fan and mist conditions have been plotted for you.

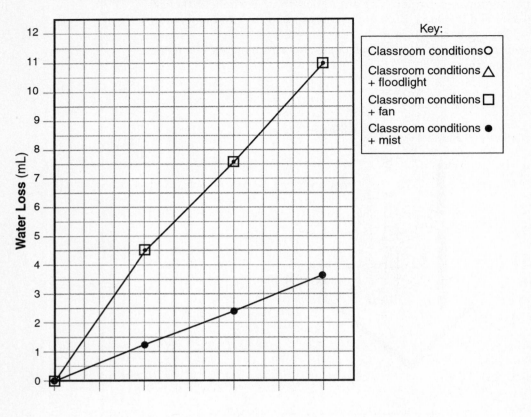

Average Total Water Loss in mL Over Time

Key:
Classroom conditions O
Classroom conditions △ + floodlight
Classroom conditions □ + fan
Classroom conditions ● + mist

Water Loss (mL)

Time (min)

54 Mark an appropriate scale on the axis labeled "Time (min)."   [1]

55 Plot the data for the classroom conditions from the data table. Surround each point with a small circle and connect the points.   [1]

Example:

56 Plot the data for classroom conditions + floodlight from the data table. Surround each point with a small triangle and connect the points. [1]

Example:

57 Identify the environmental factor that resulted in the lowest rate of transpiration. [1]

_____

58 Identify the control group of plants in this experiment. [1]

_____

_____

Base your answers to questions 59 through 61 on the passage below and on your knowledge of biology.

The number in the parenthesis ( ) at the end of a sentence is used to identify that sentence.

They Sure Do Look Like Dinosaurs

When making movies about dinosaurs, film producers often use ordinary lizards and enlarge their images thousands of times (**1**). We all know, however, that while they look like dinosaurs and are related to dinosaurs, lizards are not actually dinosaurs (**2**).

Recently, some scientists have developed a hypothesis that challenges this view (**3**). These scientists believe that some dinosaurs were actually the same species as some modern lizards that had grown to unbelievable sizes (**4**). They think that such growth might be due to a special type of DNA called repetitive DNA, often referred to as "junk" DNA because scientists do not understand its functions (**5**). These scientists studied pumpkins that can reach sizes of nearly 1,000 pounds and found them to contain large amounts of repetitive DNA (**6**). Other pumpkins that grow to only a few ounces in weight have very little of this kind of DNA (**7**). In addition, cells that reproduce uncontrollably have almost always been found to contain large amounts of this type of DNA (**8**).

59 State *one* reason why scientists formerly thought of repetitive DNA as "junk." [1]

_____

_____

_____

60 Which kind of cells would most likely contain large amounts of repetitive DNA?

(1) red blood cells

(2) cancer cells

(3) nerve cells

(4) cells that are unable to reproduce

For Teacher Use Only

60 ☐

61 Write the number of a sentence that provides evidence that supports the hypothesis that increasing amounts of repetitive DNA are responsible for increased sizes of organisms. [1]

____

61 ☐

62 An enzyme and four different molecules are shown in the diagram below.

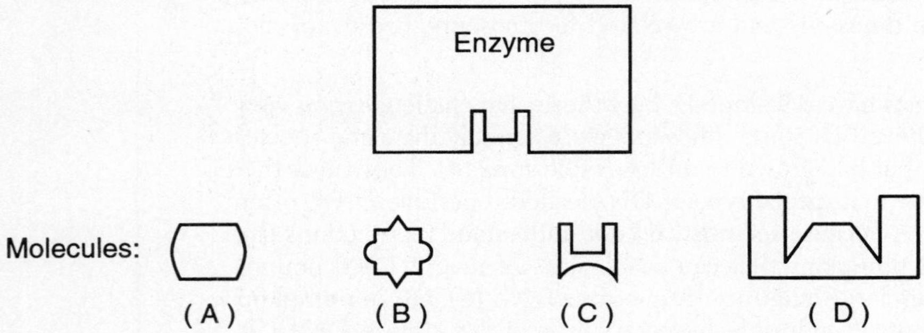

The enzyme would most likely affect reactions involving

(1) molecule *A*, only

(2) molecule *C*, only

(3) molecules *B* and *D*

(4) molecules *A* and *C*

62 ☐

63 The temperature of the environment in which alligator embryos develop influences the sex of the embryos. At higher temperatures, more embryos develop into males while at lower temperatures, more develop into females. What effect might global warming have on the ability of these alligators to survive as a species?   [1]

_____

_____

_____

64 The diagram below shows changes that might occur over time after a fire in a forest area.

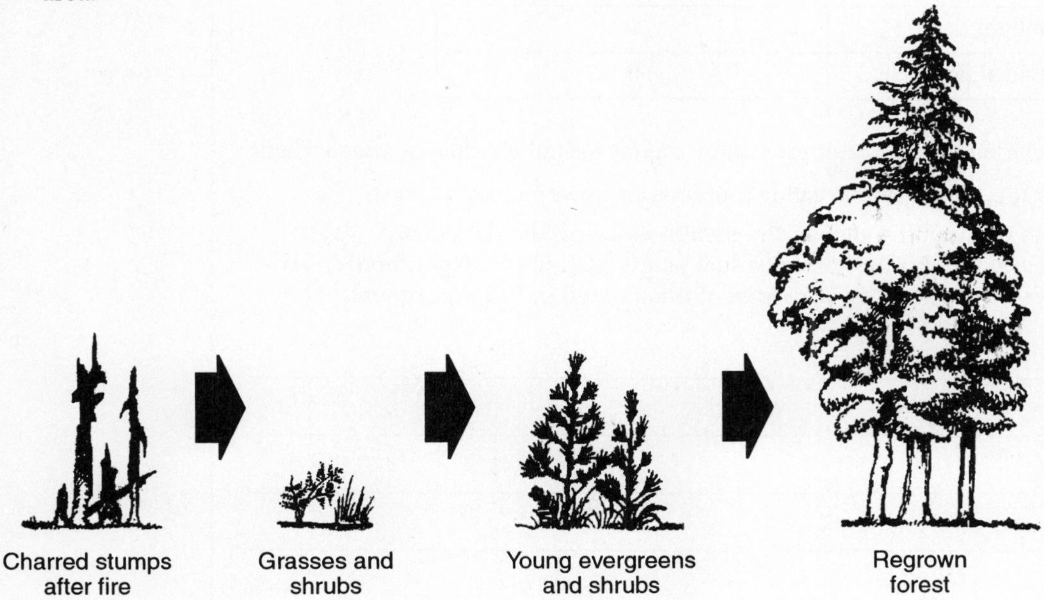

Charred stumps after fire   →   Grasses and shrubs   →   Young evergreens and shrubs   →   Regrown forest

Which statement is most closely related to the events shown in the diagram?

(1) The lack of animals in an altered ecosystem speeds natural succession.

(2) Abrupt changes in an ecosystem only result from human activities.

(3) Stable ecosystems never become established after a natural disaster.

(4) An abrupt environmental change can cause a long-term gradual change in an ecosystem.

64 ☐

Part C

Answer all questions in this part. [20]

Directions (65–73): Record your answers in the spaces provided in this examination booklet.

65 In an experiment to test the effect of light on plant growth, a student used two marigold plants of the same age. The plants were grown in separate pots. One pot was exposed to sunlight, the other to artificial light. All other conditions were kept the same. The height of each plant was measured at the start and at the end of the experiment. The student's data are shown in the table below.

Data Table

Plant Grown In	Increase in Plant Height (cm)
Sunlight	9
Artificial light	8

The student concluded that all plants grow more rapidly in sunlight than in artificial light.

Discuss whether this conclusion is valid. Your answer must include at least:

- the significance of the difference in the results shown in the data table [1]
- the significance of the number of individual plants used in the experiment [1]
- the significance of the number of species of plants used in the experiment [1]

_____

_____

_____

_____

_____

_____

_____

_____

65

66 Select *one* human body system from the list below.

Body Systems

Digestive
Circulatory
Respiratory
Excretory
Nervous

Describe a malfunction that can occur in the system chosen. Your answer must include at least:

- the name of the system and a malfunction that can occur in this system   [1]
- a description of a possible cause of the malfunction identified   [1]
- an effect this malfunction may have on any other body system   [1]

_____

_____

_____

_____

_____

_____

_____

_____

66 ☐

67 Biological research has generated knowledge used to diagnose genetic disorders in humans. Explain how a specific genetic disorder can be diagnosed. Your answer must include at least:

- the name of a genetic disorder that can be diagnosed   [1]
- the name or description of a technique used to diagnose the disorder   [1]
- a description of *one* characteristic of the disorder   [1]

_____

_____

_____

_____

_____

_____

_____

_____

67 ☐

68 State *two* safety procedures that should be followed when conducting an experiment that involves heating protein in a test tube containing water, an acid, and a digestive enzyme.   [2]

(1) _____

_____

_____

(2) _____

_____

_____

68 ☐

Base your answers to questions 69 and 70 on the information below and on your knowledge of biology.

Over the last 30 years, a part of the Hudson River known as Foundry Cove has been the site for many factories that have dumped toxic chemicals into the river. Some of these pollutants have accumulated in the mud at the bottom of the river. The polluted cove water contains many single-celled organisms and simple multicellular animals. Curiously, when the same species from nearby regions with non-polluted sediments are moved to the polluted cove water, they die.

Scientists hypothesized that the organisms living in the cove have evolved so that they are able to survive in polluted water. To test this hypothesis, biologists tried to duplicate the history of the cove in the laboratory. They took a large number of one species of simple animal from a cove with unpolluted mud and placed them in a flask that contained polluted mud from Foundry Cove (diagram 1). Most of the animals died, but a few survived (diagram 2). The scientists then bred the survivors with each other for several generations producing offspring that were descendants of the survivors. When placed in Foundry Cove, most of these descendants survived. The diagrams below represent the steps in this investigation.

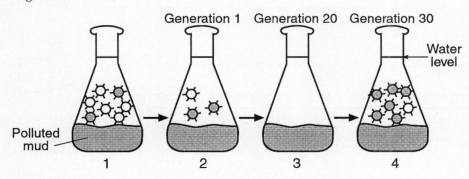

Generation 1 Generation 20 Generation 30

Water level

Polluted mud

1   2   3   4

☼ = Pollution-sensitive individuals   ⬡ = Pollution-resistant individuals

69 On the diagram of the flask below, sketch the animals that would be present in flask 3 after several generations of breeding in the laboratory.   [1]

3

69 ☐

70 Explain how the simple animals of Foundry Cove adapted to the polluted water. Your answer must include an explanation of the role of *three* of the following in this process. [3]

- environment
- genetic variation
- selection
- reproduction
- survival of the fittest

_____

_____

_____

_____

_____

_____

_____

_____

_____

70 ☐

Base your answers to questions 71 through 73 on the information and diagram below and on your knowledge of biology.

The diagram represents a system in a space station that includes a tank containing algae. An astronaut from a spaceship boards the space station.

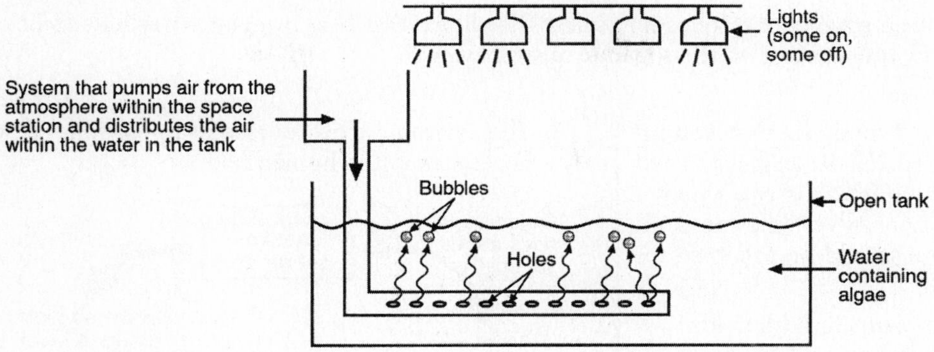

71 Identify *one* process being controlled in the setup shown in the diagram. [1]

____

72 State *two* changes in the chemical composition of the space station atmosphere as a result of the astronaut coming on board the space station. [2]

____

____

____

____

____

____

73 State *two* changes in the chemical composition of the space station atmosphere that would result from turning on more lights. [2]

____

____

____

____

____

____

For Teacher Use Only

71 ☐

72 ☐

73 ☐

Part A

Answer all questions in this part.

Directions (1–35): For *each* statement or question, select the choice that best completes the statement or answers the question. Record your answer on the separate answer paper.

1 A student formulated a hypothesis that cotton will grow larger bolls (pods) if magnesium is added to the soil. The student has two experimental fields of cotton, one with magnesium and one without. Which data should be collected to support this hypothesis?

(1) height of the cotton plants in both fields
(2) diameter of the cotton bolls in both fields
(3) length of the growing season in both fields
(4) color of the cotton bolls in both fields

2 To separate leaf pigments, a biologist should use

(1) chromatography
(2) dissection
(3) an electronic balance
(4) a dichotomous key

3 A food web is more stable than a food chain because a food web

(1) transfers all of the producer energy to herbivores
(2) reduces the number of niches in the ecosystem
(3) includes alternative pathways for energy flow
(4) includes more consumers than producers

4 Which sequence of terms is in the correct order from simplest to most complex?

(1) cells → tissues → organs → organ systems
(2) tissues → organisms → cells → organ systems
(3) cells → tissues → organ systems → organs
(4) organs → organisms → organ systems → cells

5 For which organic compounds must information be encoded in DNA for green plants to synthesize the other three compounds?

(1) sugars   (3) fats
(2) starches   (4) proteins

6 The diagram below represents the actions of two hormones in the human body.

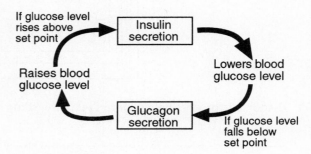

This diagram best illustrates

(1) recombination   (3) insertion
(2) feedback   (4) deletion

7 The pancreas is an organ connected to the digestive tract of humans by a duct (tube) through which digestive enzymes flow. These enzymes are important to the digestive system because they

(1) form proteins needed in the stomach
(2) form the acids that break down food
(3) change food substances into molecules that can pass into the bloodstream and cells
(4) change food materials into wastes that can be passed out of the body

8 While viewing a slide of rapidly moving sperm cells, a student concludes that these cells require a large amount of energy to maintain their activity. The organelles that most directly provide this energy are known as

(1) vacuoles   (3) chloroplasts
(2) ribosomes   (4) mitochondria

9 Meiosis and fertilization are important processes because they may most immediately result in

(1) many body cells   (3) genetic variation
(2) immune responses   (4) natural selection

10 In the diagram below, strands I and II represent portions of a DNA molecule.

Strand I

Strand II

Strand II would normally include

(1) AGC
(2) TCG

(3) TAC
(4) GAT

11 In Siamese cats, the fur on the ears, paws, tail, and face is usually black or brown, while the rest of the body fur is almost white. If a Siamese cat is kept indoors where it is warm, it may grow fur that is almost white on the ears, paws, tail, and face, while a Siamese cat that stays outside where it is cold, will grow fur that is quite dark on these areas. The best explanation for these changes in fur color is that

(1) an environmental factor influences the expression of this inherited trait
(2) the location of pigment-producing cells determines the DNA code of the genes
(3) skin cells that produce pigments have a higher mutation rate than other cells
(4) the gene for fur color is modified by interactions with the environment

12 After a series of cell divisions, an embryo develops different types of body cells such as muscle cells, nerve cells, and blood cells. This development occurs because

(1) the genetic code changes as the cells divide
(2) different segments of the genetic instructions are used to produce different types of cells
(3) different genetic instructions are synthesized to meet the needs of new types of cells
(4) some parts of the genetic materials are lost as a result of fertilization

13 The letters in the diagram below represent genes on a particular chromosome.

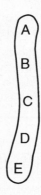

Gene *B* contains the code for an enzyme that cannot be synthesized unless gene *A* is also active. Which statement best explains why this can occur?

(1) A hereditary trait can be determined by more than one gene.
(2) Genes are made up of double-stranded segments of DNA.
(3) All the genes on a chromosome act to produce a single trait.
(4) The first gene on each chromosome controls all the other genes on the chromosome.

14 Information related to the organisms found on Earth during various geological time periods is represented in the chart below.

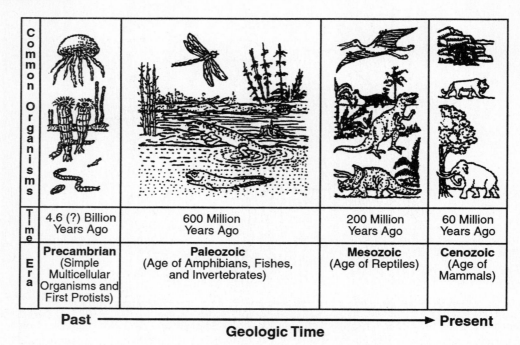

Which statement concerning the first appearance of the organisms over the time period represented in this chart is most likely correct?

(1) Life on Earth has remained the same.
(2) Life on Earth has changed from primitive organisms to more complex organisms.
(3) Life on Earth began with complex organisms and changed to more complex organisms.
(4) Life on Earth has changed rapidly.

15 In an area in Africa, temporary pools form where rivers flow during the rainy months. Some fish have developed the ability to use their ventral fins as "feet" to travel on land from one of these temporary pools to another. Other fish in these pools die when the pools dry up. What can be expected to happen in this area after many years?

(1) The fish using ventral fins as "feet" will be present in increasing numbers.
(2) "Feet" in the form of ventral fins will develop on all fish.
(3) The fish using ventral fins as "feet" will develop real feet.
(4) All of the varieties of fish will survive and produce many offspring.

16 Some stages in the development of an individual are listed below.

(A) differentiation of cells into tissues
(B) fertilization of egg by sperm
(C) organ development
(D) mitotic cell division of zygote

Which sequence represents the correct order of these stages?

(1) A–B–C–D   (3) D–B–C–A
(2) B–C–A–D   (4) B–D–A–C

17 The diagram below represents a cell process.

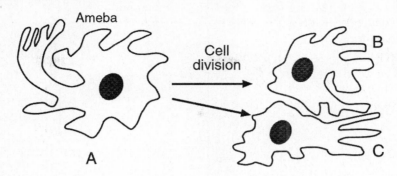

Ameba

Cell division

A

B

C

Which statement regarding this process is correct?

(1) Cell *B* contains the same genetic information that cells *A* and *C* contain.
(2) Cell *C* has DNA that is only 50% identical to cell *B*.
(3) Cell *A* has DNA that is only 75% identical to cell *B*.
(4) Cells *A*, *B*, and *C* contain completely different genetic information.

18 The diagram below shows the bones in the fore-limbs of two different vertebrate species.

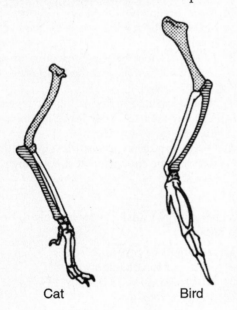

Cat   Bird

The position and structure of these bones could best be used to make inferences about the

(1) food preferences of these vertebrate species
(2) intelligence of these vertebrate species
(3) history of these vertebrate species
(4) reproductive behavior of these vertebrate species

19 Which statement does *not* correctly describe an adaptation of the human female reproductive system?

(1) It produces gametes in ovaries.
(2) It provides for external fertilization of an egg.
(3) It provides for internal development of the embryo.
(4) It removes excretions produced by the fetus.

20 Testes are adapted to produce

(1) body cells involved in embryo formation
(2) immature gametes that undergo mitosis
(3) sperm cells that may be involved in fertilization
(4) gametes with large food supplies that nourish a developing embryo

21 In nature, during a 24-hour period, green plants *continuously* use

(1) carbon dioxide, only
(2) both carbon dioxide and oxygen
(3) oxygen, only
(4) neither carbon dioxide nor oxygen

22 To remain healthy, organisms must be able to obtain materials, change the materials, move the materials around, and get rid of waste. These activities directly require

(1) energy from ATP
(2) the replication of DNA
(3) nutrients from inorganic sources
(4) manipulation of altered genes

23 Which statement describes all enzymes?

(1) They control the transport of materials.
(2) They provide energy for chemical reactions.
(3) They affect the rate of chemical reactions.
(4) They absorb oxygen from the environment.

24 Organisms undergo constant chemical changes as they maintain an internal balance known as

(1) interdependence   (3) synthesis
(2) homeostasis   (4) recombination

25 Which condition would most likely result in a human body being unable to defend itself against pathogens and cancerous cells?

(1) a genetic tendency toward a disorder such as diabetes
(2) a parasitic infestation of ringworm on the body
(3) the production of antibodies in response to an infection in the body
(4) the presence in the body of the virus that causes AIDS

26 Scientific studies have indicated that there is a higher percentage of allergies in babies fed formula containing cow's milk than in breast-fed babies. Which statement represents a valid inference made from these studies?

(1) Milk from cows causes allergic reactions in all infants.
(2) Breast feeding prevents all allergies from occurring.
(3) There is no relationship between drinking cow's milk and having allergies.
(4) Breast milk most likely contains fewer substances that trigger allergies.

27 The diagram below represents a model of a food pyramid.

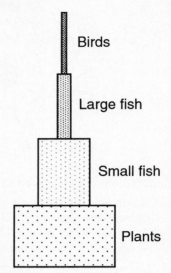

Which statement best describes what happens in this food pyramid?

(1) More organisms die at higher levels than at lower levels, resulting in less mass at higher levels.
(2) Energy is lost to the environment at each level, so less mass can be supported at each higher level.
(3) When organisms die at higher levels, their remains sink to lower levels, increasing the mass of lower levels.
(4) Organisms decay at each level, and thus less mass can be supported at succeedingly higher levels.

28 Which energy transfer is *least* likely to be found in nature?

(1) consumer to consumer
(2) producer to consumer
(3) host to parasite
(4) predator to prey

29 Which ecosystem has a better chance of surviving when environmental conditions change over a long period of time?

(1) one with a great deal of genetic diversity
(2) one with plants and animals but no bacteria
(3) one with animals and bacteria but no plants
(4) one with little or no genetic diversity

30 The diagrams below show some changes in an environment over time.

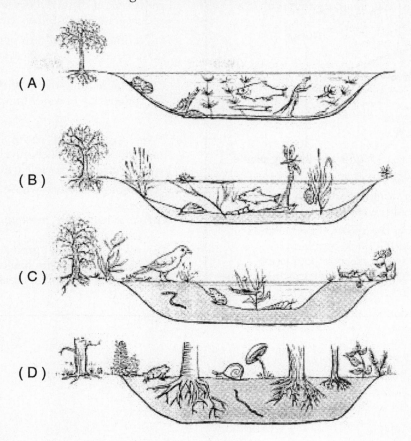

(A)

(B)

(C)

(D)

Which phrase best describes this sequence of diagrams?

(1) the path of energy through a food web in a natural community
(2) the altering of an ecosystem by a natural disaster
(3) natural communities replacing each other in an orderly sequence
(4) similarities between an aquatic ecosystem and a terrestrial ecosystem

31 Which factor is often responsible for the other three?

(1) increase in levels of toxins in both water and air
(2) increase in human population
(3) increased poverty and malnutrition
(4) increased depletion of finite resources

32 By causing atmospheric changes through activities such as polluting and careless harvesting, humans have

(1) caused the destruction of habitats
(2) affected global stability in a positive way
(3) established equilibrium in ecosystems
(4) replaced nonrenewable resources

33 The diagram below illustrates the relationships between organisms in an ecosystem.

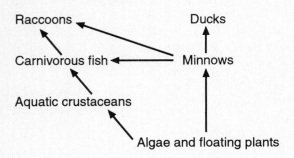

Which change would most likely reduce the population size of the carnivorous fish?

(1) an increase in the autotroph populations
(2) a decrease in the duck population
(3) an increase in the raccoon population
(4) a decrease in pathogens of carnivorous fish

34 Dumping raw sewage into a river will lead to a reduction in dissolved oxygen in the water. This reduction will most likely cause

(1) an increase in all fish populations
(2) a decrease in most aquatic animal populations
(3) an increase in depth of the water
(4) a decrease in water temperature

35 Which method of controlling populations of mosquitoes most likely involves the *least* risk of causing damage to the environment?

(1) draining swamps where mosquitoes deposit eggs
(2) spraying adult mosquitoes with pesticides from airplanes
(3) releasing more predators of mosquitoes native to mosquito habitats
(4) spraying oil on wet areas where mosquitoes breed

Part B

Answer all questions in this part.

Directions (36–63): For those questions that are followed by four choices, circle the number of the choice that best completes the statement or answers the question. For all other questions in this part, follow the directions given in the question and record your answers in the spaces provided.

36 A researcher needs information on antigen–antibody reactions. Searching for which phrase would best lead the researcher to information about these reactions?

(1) protein synthesis

(2) energy sources in nature

(3) white blood cell activity

(4) DNA replication

Base your answers to questions 37 and 38 on the table below and on your knowledge of biology.

Volunteer	Injected with Dead Chicken Pox Virus	Injected with Dead Mumps Virus	Injected with Distilled Water
A	X		
B		X	
C			X
D	X	X	

37 None of these volunteers ever had chicken pox. After the injection, there would most likely be antibodies to chicken pox in the bloodstream of

(1) volunteers *A* and *D*, only

(2) volunteers *A*, *B*, and *D*

(3) volunteer *C*

(4) volunteer *D*, only

38 Volunteers *A*, *B*, and *D* underwent a procedure known as

(1) cloning

(2) vaccination

(3) electrophoresis

(4) chromatography

39 The photograph below shows a microscopic view of the lower surface of a leaf.

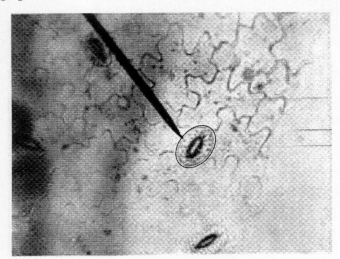

What is the main function of the cells indicated by the black pointer?

(1) regulate the rate of gas exchange

(2) store food for winter dormancy

(3) undergo mitotic cell division

(4) give support to the veins in the leaf

39

Base your answers to questions 40 and 41 on the diagram below and on your knowledge of biology.

40 Which organism carries out autotrophic nutrition?

(1) frog

(2) snake

(3) plant

(4) grasshopper

40 ☐

41 The base of an energy pyramid for this ecosystem would include a

(1) frog

(2) snake

(3) plant

(4) grasshopper

41 ☐

Base your answers to questions 42 through 46 on the information and data table below and on your knowledge of biology.

A biology student performed an experiment to determine which of two species of single-celled organisms would survive best when cultured together in a certain environment. The student placed 10 organisms of each species into a large test tube. Throughout the experiment, the test tube was maintained at 30°C. After the test tube was set up, the population of each species was determined each day for 5 days. The data collected are shown in the table below.

Data Table

Day	Population	
	Species A	Species B
1	10	10
2	16	16
3	32	32
4	48	12
5	60	4

Directions (42–44): Using the information in the data table, construct a line graph on the grid on the next page, following the directions below.

42 Mark an appropriate scale on each labeled axis. [1]

43 Plot the data for species *A* on the grid. Surround each point with a small circle and connect the points. [1]

Example:

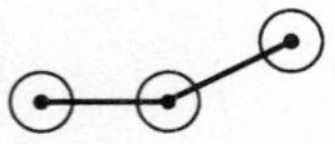

44 Plot the data for species *B* on the grid. Surround each point with a small triangle and connect the points. [1]

Example:

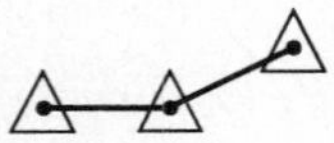

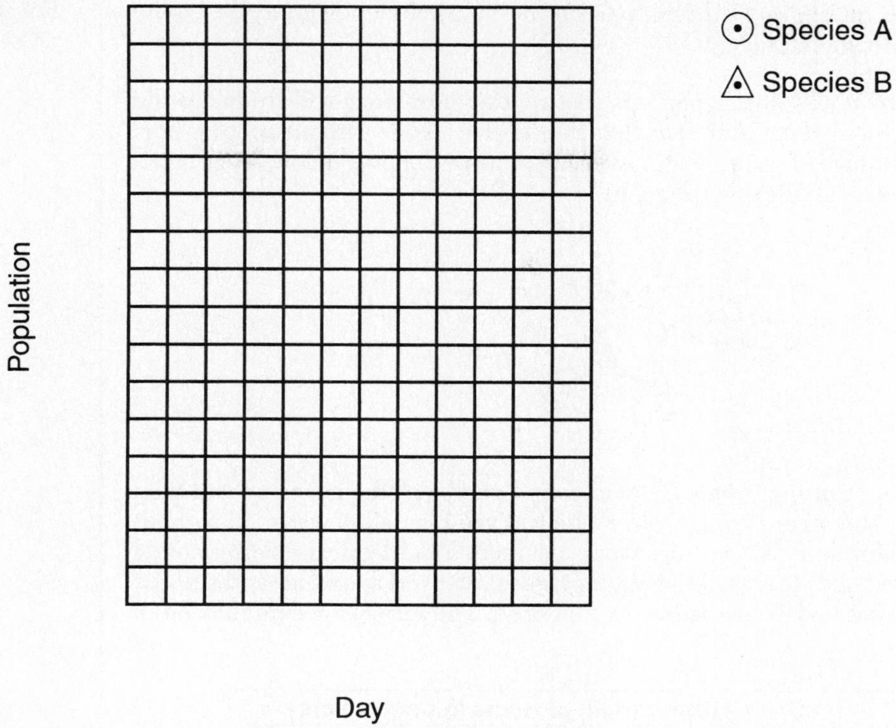

⊙ Species A

△ Species B

Population

Day

42

43

44

45 Based on the daily counts, on which day did it first become evident that one species was better adapted than the other species for survival in the environment provided? [1]

_____

45

46 The difference in the population sizes on the fifth day most likely resulted from

(1) temperature changes

(2) variations in light intensity

(3) competition between species

(4) the buildup of nitrogen gas

46

Base your answers to questions 47 through 49 on the information, diagram, and table below and on your knowledge of biology.

A student wanted to test the hypothesis that rooting hormones will stimulate the production of new roots at a faster rate than would take place without rooting hormones. Two stem cuttings of equal length, similar to the one shown below, were taken from a rose, a begonia, and a geranium plant.

The cut end of one cutting from each plant was dipped into the hormone and then planted in wet sand. The other cutting from each plant was planted in wet sand without dipping it into the hormone. All cuttings were maintained in identical environmental conditions. At the end of 4 weeks, all the cuttings were removed from the sand and the lengths of the roots that had developed were measured. The results are summarized in the data table below.

Plant Cutting	Total Length of Roots in Centimeters	
	Treated with Hormone	Untreated
Begonia	1.50	1.00
Geranium	0.75	0.50
Rose	0.00	0.00

47 The effect of the rooting hormone on the production of new roots was most likely due to the influence of the hormone on the process of

(1) photosynthesis

(2) meiosis

(3) mitosis

(4) excretion

47 ☐

48 Describe *one* way the student could make the experiment more valid.   [1]

_____

_____

_____

48 ☐

49 What purpose did the untreated cuttings serve in this experiment? [1]

For Teacher Use Only

49

Base your answers to questions 50 and 51 on the diagram below of sugar in a beaker of water and on your knowledge of biology.

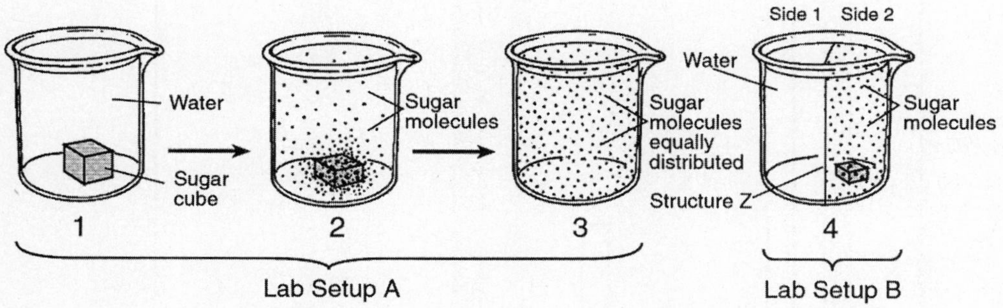

50 What process accounts for the change shown in lab setup *A*? [1]

50

51 In lab setup *B*, structure *Z* prevents the movement of sugar molecules into side 1. Which part of a living cell serves the same purpose as structure *Z*? [1]

51

Base your answers to questions 52 and 53 on the graph below and on your knowledge of biology. The graph shows the relative concentrations of different ions inside and outside of an animal cell.

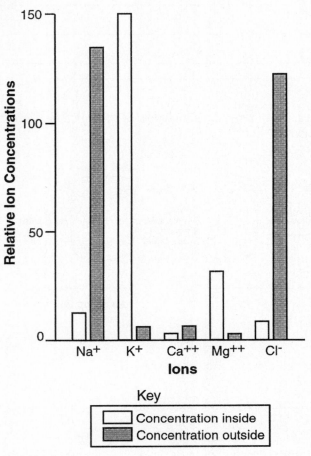

Key

| Concentration inside |
| Concentration outside |

52 Write the symbol of the ion that is closest to equilibrium inside and outside of the cell. [1]

_____

52 ☐

53 Name the process responsible for maintaining high concentrations of K^+ ions inside the cell.   [1]

_____

_____

53 ☐

54 The diagram below shows a biological process.

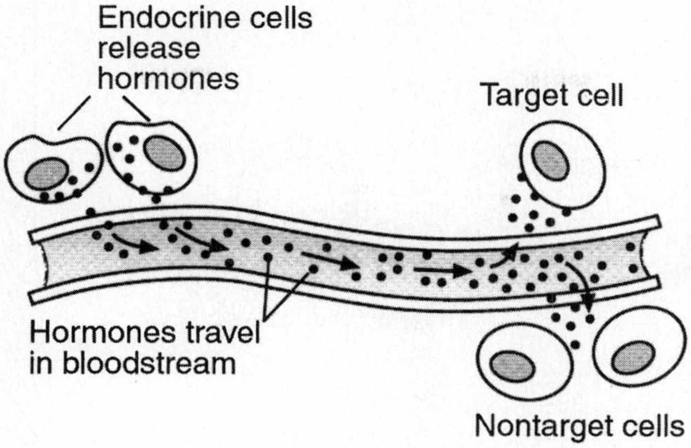

Explain why the hormones attach to the target cell and *not* to other cells in the diagram. [1]

_____

_____

_____

54 ☐

55 The diagram below represents a technique used in biotechnology.

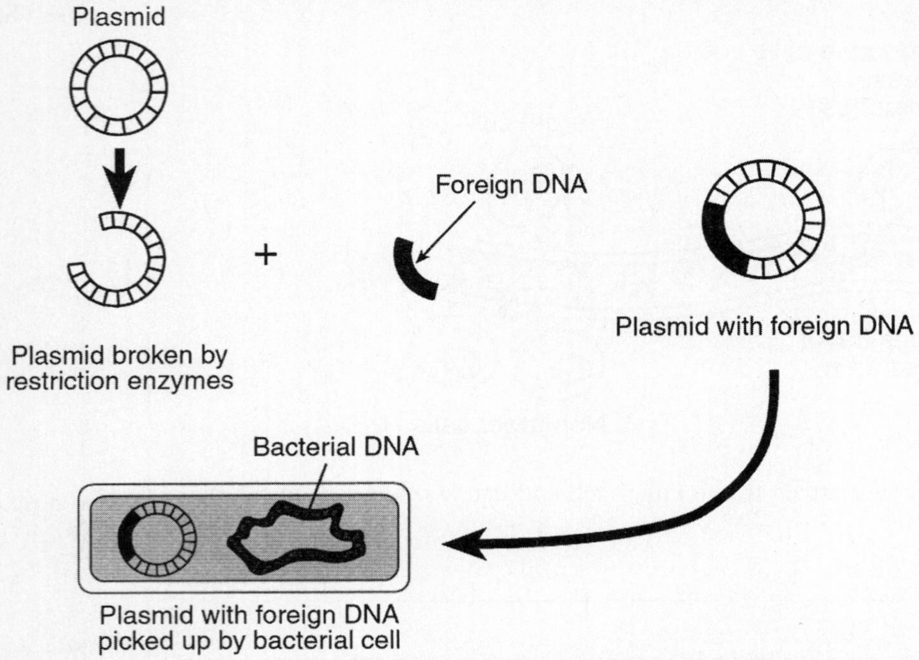

Plasmid

Plasmid broken by
restriction enzymes

Foreign DNA

+

Plasmid with foreign DNA

Bacterial DNA

Plasmid with foreign DNA
picked up by bacterial cell

Name a specific substance that can be produced by this technique and state how
humans have benefited from the production of this substance.   [2]

_____

_____

_____

_____

_____

_____

55 ☐

Base your answers to questions 56 and 57 on the passage below and on your knowledge of biology.

The Human Genome Project

For a number of years, scientists at Cold Spring Harbor Laboratory have been attempting to map every known human gene. By mapping, scientists mean that they are trying to find out on which of the 46 chromosomes each gene is located and exactly where on the chromosome the gene is located. By locating the exact positions of defective genes, scientists hope to cure diseases by replacing defective genes with normal ones, a technique known as gene therapy. Scientists can use specific enzymes to cut out the defective genes and insert the normal genes. They must be careful to use the enzyme that will splice out only the target gene, since different enzymes will cut DNA at different locations.

While the human genome project should eventually improve the health of humans, many people are skeptical and apprehensive, believing that gene therapy would be working against nature and would have religious, moral, legal, and ethical implications.

56 Using *one* specific example, explain why the human genome project is considered important. [1]

_____

_____

_____

57 Explain why scientists must use only certain enzymes when inserting or removing a defective gene from a cell. [1]

_____

_____

_____

58 Explain why, in a mammal, a mutation in a gamete may contribute to evolution while a mutation in a body cell will not. [1]

_____

_____

_____

59 A certain chemical destroys bacteria that have thin cell walls. Bacteria with thick cell walls are not affected. Describe how the introduction of this chemical into a culture containing both types of bacteria could be used to illustrate the theory of natural selection. [1]

For Teacher Use Only

59

60 The diagram below represents a woolly mammoth, a relative of the modern elephant. Woolly mammoths lived during the Ice Age and eventually became extinct.

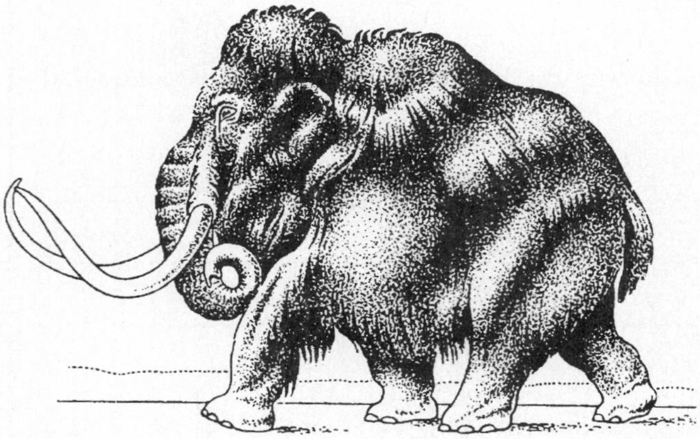

State *one* possible reason this species died out. [1]

60

61 An incomplete diagram of meiosis in the ovary of an animal is shown below.

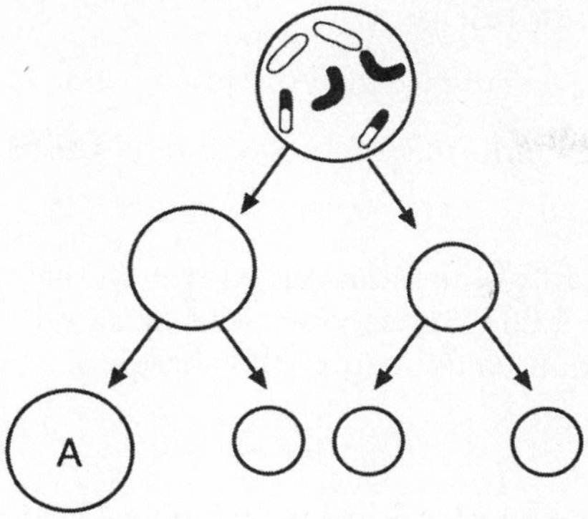

On the diagram below, draw in the chromosomes of cell *A*. Your drawing should show the usual result of the process of meiosis. [1]

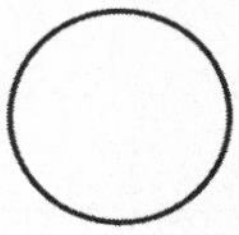

62 The loss of ozone in the upper atmosphere results in an increased amount of ultraviolet light reaching Earth from the Sun. Explain how this increase may be harmful, other than contributing in a small way to global warming, to life on Earth. [1]

63 Recycling can extend the use of nonrenewable resources but can *not* restore them. Humans can restore renewable resources to reduce some negative effects of increased human consumption. Identify *one* resource that is renewable, and describe *one* specific way humans can restore this resource if it is being depleted. [2]

For Teacher Use Only

61

62

63

Part C

Answer all questions in this part.

Directions (64–78): Record your answers in the spaces provided in this examination booklet.

Base your answers to questions 64 and 65 on the information below and on your knowledge of biology.

Mountain lions and big horn sheep are part of the natural food web in the Sierra Nevada mountains. The Fish and Wildlife Service recently declared these sheep an endangered species. This action could lead to the shooting of mountain lions.

64 State *one* reason placing these sheep on an endangered species list could lead to the shooting of mountain lions where the sheep live. [1]

_____

_____

_____

64 ☐

65 State *two* reasons some people would oppose the shooting of the mountain lions. [2]

(1) _____

_____

_____

(2) _____

_____

_____

65 ☐

Base your answers to questions 66 through 68 on the diagram below that represents a human enzyme and four types of molecules present in a solution in a flask.

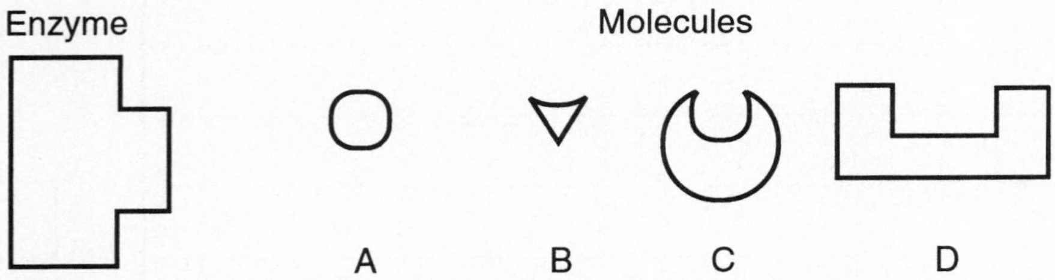

Enzyme   Molecules

A   B   C   D

66 Which molecule would most likely react with the enzyme? [1]

_____

66 ☐

67 Explain your answer to question 66.　[1]

_____

_____

_____

68 State what would most likely happen to the rate of reaction if the temperature of the solution in the flask were increased gradually from 10°C to 30°C.　[1]

_____

_____

_____

69 A diagram of the human female reproductive system is shown below.

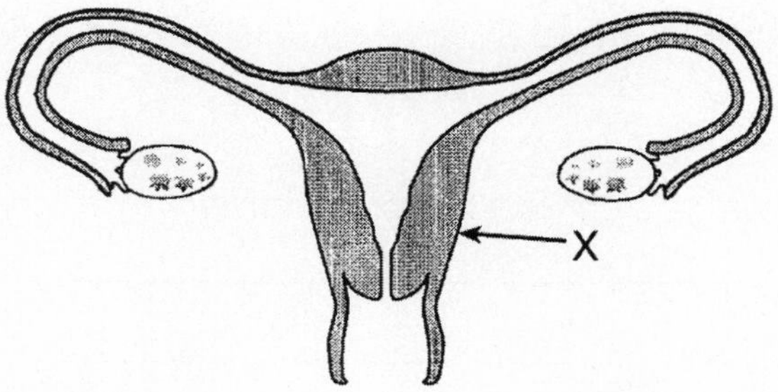

Identify the structure labeled X and explain how it helps to provide nutrition for a developing fetus.　[2]

_____

_____

_____

_____

_____

_____

For Teacher
Use Only

67 ☐

68 ☐

69 ☐

Base your answers to questions 70 through 72 on the food web shown below and on your knowledge of biology.

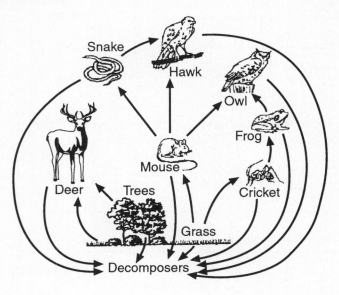

70 A pesticide is sprayed to kill the crickets. State *one* effect this spraying might have on the food web.   [1]

_____

_____

_____

71 What is the significance of the arrow between the trees and the deer in the food web? [1]

_____

_____

_____

72 State the role of the decomposers in the food web.   [1]

_____

_____

_____

[24]

Base your answers to questions 73 through 76 on the information below.

Acid rain can have a pH between 1.5 and 5.0. The effect of acid rain on the environment depends on the pH of the rain and the characteristics of the environment. It appears that acid rain has a negative effect on plants. The scale below shows the pH of normal rain.

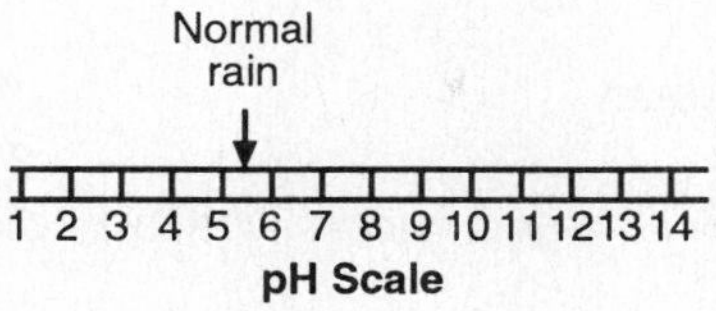

Normal
rain

1 2 3 4 5 6 7 8 9 10 11 12 13 14
pH Scale

Provide the information requested below that should be included in a research plan to test the effect of pH on the early growth of bean plants in the laboratory.

73 State a hypothesis.   [1]

_____

_____

73 ☐

74 Identify the independent variable.   [1]

_____

74 ☐

75 State *two* factors that should be kept constant.   [2]

(1) _____

(2) _____

75 ☐

76 Construct a data table to organize the results.   [1]

76 ☐

Base your answers to questions 77 and 78 on the summary equations of two processes below and on your knowledge of biology.

Photosynthesis

water + carbon dioxide $\xrightarrow{\text{enzymes}}$ glucose + oxygen + water

Respiration

glucose + oxygen $\xrightarrow{\text{enzymes}}$ water + carbon dioxide

77a Choose *one* of the processes.

_____

b Identify the source of the energy in the process you chose.   [1]

_____

c Identify where the energy ends up at the completion of that process.   [1]

_____

77 ☐

78 State *one* reason *each* of the two processes is important for living things.   [2]

Photosynthesis: _____

_____

_____

Respiration: _____

_____

_____

78 ☐

_____

The Living Environment June, 2002

Part A

Answer all questions in this part. [35]

Directions (1–35): For *each* statement or question, write on the separate answer sheet the number of the word or expression that, of those given, best completes the statement or answers the question.

1 The current knowledge concerning cells is the result of the investigations and observations of many scientists. The work of these scientists forms a well-accepted body of knowledge about cells. This body of knowledge is an example of a

(1) hypothesis
(2) controlled experiment
(3) theory
(4) research plan

2 An experimental design included references from prior experiments, materials and equipment, and step-by-step procedures. What else should be included before the experiment can be started?

(1) a set of data
(2) a conclusion based on data
(3) safety precautions to be used
(4) an inference based on results

3 In his theory, Lamarck suggested that organisms will develop and pass on to offspring variations that they need in order to survive in a particular environment. In a later theory, Darwin proposed that changing environmental conditions favor certain variations that promote the survival of organisms. Which statement is best illustrated by this information?

(1) Scientific theories that have been changed are the only ones supported by scientists.
(2) All scientific theories are subject to change and improvement.
(3) Most scientific theories are the outcome of a single hypothesis.
(4) Scientific theories are not subject to change.

4 The dense needles of Douglas fir trees can prevent most light from reaching the forest floor. This situation would have the most immediate effect on

(1) producers   (3) herbivores
(2) carnivores   (4) decomposers

5 Which statement best describes a characteristic of an ecosystem?

(1) It must have producers and consumers but not decomposers.
(2) It is stable because it has consumers to recycle energy.
(3) It always has two or more different autotrophs filling the same niche.
(4) It must have organisms that carry out autotrophic nutrition.

6 In a cell, all organelles work together to carry out

(1) diffusion
(2) active transport
(3) information storage
(4) metabolic processes

7 The ability of certain hormones to attach to a cell is primarily determined by the

(1) receptor molecules in the cell membrane
(2) proteins in the cytoplasm of the cell
(3) amount of DNA in the cell
(4) concentration of salts outside the cell

8 The diagram below represents the organization of genetic information within a cell nucleus.

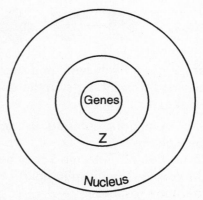

The circle labeled Z most likely represents

(1) amino acids   (3) vacuoles
(2) chromosomes   (4) molecular bases

9 The diagram below represents the change in a sprouting onion bulb when sunlight is present and when sunlight is no longer available.

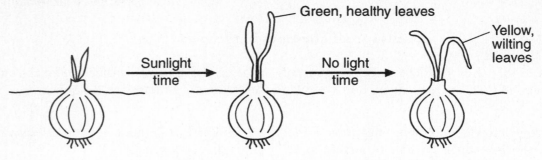

Which statement best explains this change?

(1) Plants need oxygen to survive.
(2) Environmental conditions do not alter characteristics.
(3) Plants produce hormones.
(4) The environment can influence the expression of certain genetic traits.

10 A human zygote is produced from gametes that are usually identical in

(1) the expression of encoded information
(2) the number of altered genes present
(3) chromosome number
(4) cell size

11 Molecule 1 represents a segment of hereditary information, and molecule 2 represents the portion of a molecule that is determined by information from molecule 1.

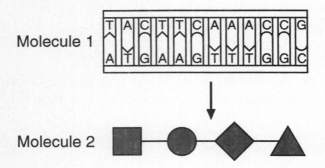

What will most likely happen if there is a change in the first three subunits on the upper strand of molecule 1?

(1) The remaining subunits in molecule 1 will also change.
(2) A portion of molecule 2 may be different.
(3) Molecule 1 will split apart, triggering an immune response.
(4) Molecule 2 may form two strands rather than one.

12 The diagram below shows two different structures, 1 and 2, that are present in many single-celled organisms. Structure 1 contains protein A, but not protein B, and structure 2 contains protein B, but not protein A.

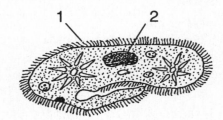

Which statement is correct concerning protein A and protein B?

(1) Proteins A and B have different functions and different amino acid chains.
(2) Proteins A and B have different functions but the same amino acid chains.
(3) Proteins A and B have the same function but a different sequence of bases (A, C, T, and G).
(4) Proteins A and B have the same function and the same sequence of bases (A, C, T, and G).

13 Which process is a common practice that has been used by farmers for hundreds of years to develop new plant and animal varieties?

(1) cloning
(2) genetic engineering
(3) cutting DNA and removing segments
(4) selective breeding for desirable traits

14 Which statement represents the major concept of the biological theory of evolution?

(1) A new species moves into a habitat when another species becomes extinct.
(2) Every period of time in Earth's history has its own group of organisms.
(3) Present-day organisms on Earth developed from earlier, distinctly different organisms.
(4) Every location on Earth's surface has its own unique group of organisms.

15 The diagrams below show the bones in the fore-limbs of three different organisms.

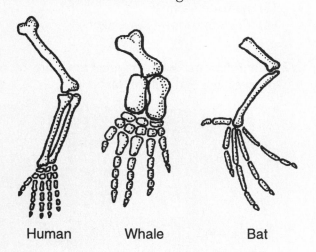

Human   Whale   Bat

Differences in the bone arrangements support the hypothesis that these organisms

(1) are members of the same species
(2) may have descended from the same ancestor
(3) have adaptations to survive in different environments
(4) all contain the same genetic information

16 Which situation would most likely result in the highest rate of natural selection?

(1) reproduction of organisms by an asexual method in an unchanging environment
(2) reproduction of a species having a very low mutation rate in a changing environment
(3) reproduction of organisms in an unchanging environment with little competition and few predators
(4) reproduction of organisms exhibiting genetic differences due to mutations and genetic recombinations in a changing environment

17 Some behaviors such as mating and caring for young are genetically determined in certain species of birds. The presence of these behaviors is most likely due to the fact that

(1) birds do not have the ability to learn
(2) individual birds need to learn to survive and reproduce
(3) these behaviors helped birds to survive in the past
(4) within their lifetimes, birds developed these behaviors

18 "Dolly" is a sheep developed from an egg cell of her mother that had its nucleus replaced by a nucleus from a body cell of her mother. As a result of this technique, Dolly is

(1) no longer able to reproduce
(2) genetically identical to her mother
(3) able to have a longer lifespan
(4) unable to mate

19 Which diagram best represents part of the process of sperm formation in an organism that has a normal chromosome number of eight?

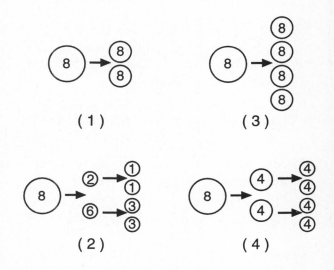

20 ATP is a compound that is synthesized when

(1) chemical bonds between carbon atoms are formed during photosynthesis
(2) energy stored in chemical bonds is released during cellular respiration
(3) energy stored in nitrogen is released, forming amino acids
(4) digestive enzymes break amino acids into smaller parts

21 Allergic reactions are most closely associated with

(1) the action of circulating hormones
(2) a low blood sugar level
(3) immune responses to usually harmless substances
(4) the shape of red blood cells

22 The diagram below represents the human male reproductive system.

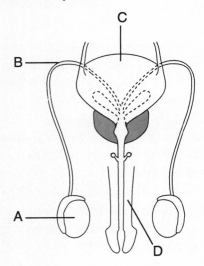

Which pair of letters indicates a structure that produces gametes and a structure that makes possible the delivery of gametes for internal fertilization, respectively?

(1) A and D   (3) C and A
(2) B and D   (4) D and C

23 Microbes that enter the body, causing disease, are known as

(1) pathogens   (3) enzymes
(2) antibodies   (4) hosts

24 The blood of newborn babies is tested to determine the presence of a certain substance. This substance indicates the genetic disorder PKU, which may result in mental retardation. Babies born with this disorder are put on a special diet so that mental retardation will not develop. In this situation, modification of the baby's diet is an example of how biological research can be used to

(1) change faulty genes
(2) cure a disorder
(3) stimulate immunity
(4) control a disorder

25 Which statement illustrates a biotic resource interacting with an abiotic resource?

(1) A rock moves during an earthquake.
(2) A sea turtle transports a pilot fish to food.
(3) A plant absorbs sunlight, which is used for photosynthesis.
(4) A wind causes waves to form on a lake.

26 Which relationship best describes the interactions between lettuce and a rabbit?

(1) predator — prey
(2) producer — consumer
(3) parasite — host
(4) decomposer — scavenger

27 The diagram below represents part of a life process in a leaf chloroplast.

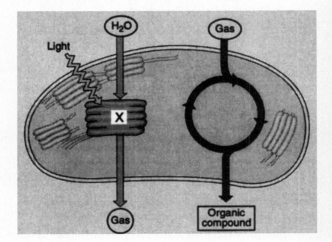

If the process illustrated in the diagram is interrupted by a chemical at point X, there would be an immediate effect on the release of

(1) chlorophyll   (3) carbon dioxide
(2) nitrogen   (4) oxygen

28 The widest variety of genetic material that can be used by humans for future agricultural or medical research would most likely be found in

(1) a large field of a genetically engineered crop
(2) an ecosystem having significant biodiversity
(3) a forest that is planted and maintained by a forest service
(4) areas that contain only one or two species

29 The diagram below shows the interaction between blood sugar levels and pancreatic activity.

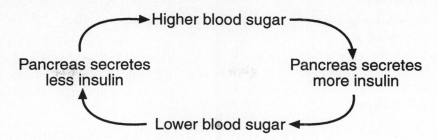

This process is an example of

(1) a feedback mechanism maintaining homeostasis
(2) an immune system responding to prevent disease
(3) the digestion of sugar by insulin
(4) the hormonal regulation of gamete production

30 The diagram below represents an energy pyramid.

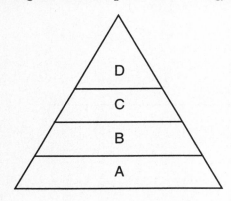

Which organisms would most likely be found at level *A*?

(1) birds   (3) mammals
(2) worms   (4) algae

31 Which human activity would have the most direct impact on the oxygen-carbon dioxide cycle?

(1) reducing the rate of ecological succession
(2) decreasing the use of water
(3) destroying large forest areas
(4) enforcing laws that prevent the use of leaded gasoline

32 The dotted line on the graph below represents the potential size of a population based on its reproductive capacity. The solid line on this graph represents the actual size of the population.

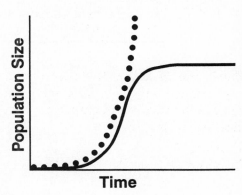

Which statement best explains why the actual population growth is *less* than the potential population growth?

(1) Resources in the environment are limited.
(2) More organisms migrated into the population than out of the population.
(3) The birthrate gradually became greater than the death rate.
(4) The final population size is greater than the carrying capacity.

33 Which concept does the cartoon shown below illustrate?

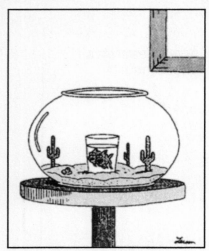

"I love the desert."

(1) Fish require certain environmental conditions for survival.
(2) Fish can adapt to any environment.
(3) Fish alter the ecosystems to improve their ability to survive.
(4) Fish can survive abrupt climate changes.

34 Fertilizers used to improve lawns and gardens may interfere with the equilibrium of an ecosystem because they

(1) cause mutations in all plants
(2) cannot be absorbed by roots
(3) can be carried into local water supplies
(4) cause atmospheric pollution

35 The tall wetland plant, purple loosestrife, was brought from Europe to the United States in the early 1800s as a garden plant. The plant's growth is now so widespread across the United States that it is crowding out a number of native plants. This situation is an example of

(1) the results of the use of pesticides
(2) the recycling of nutrients
(3) the flow of energy present in all ecosystems
(4) an unintended effect of adding a species to an ecosystem

Part B

Answer all questions in this part. [30]

Directions (36–65): For those questions that are followed by four choices, circle the number of the choice that best completes the statement or answers the question. For all other questions in this part, follow the directions given in the question and record your answers in the spaces provided.

36 The list below includes three ways of controlling viral diseases in humans.

- Administering a vaccine containing a dead or weakened virus that stimulates the body to form antibodies against the virus
- Using chemotherapy (chemical agents) to kill viruses similar to the way in which sulfa drugs or antibiotics act against bacteria
- Relying on the action of interferon, which is produced in cells and protects the body against pathogenic viruses

Based on this information, which activity would contribute to the greatest protection against viruses?

(1) producing a vaccine that is effective against interferon

(2) developing a method to stimulate the production of interferon in cells

(3) using interferon to treat a number of diseases caused by bacteria

(4) synthesizing a sulfa drug that prevents the destruction of bacteria by viruses

For Teacher Use Only

36 ☐

37 The effect of pH on a certain enzyme is shown in the graph below.

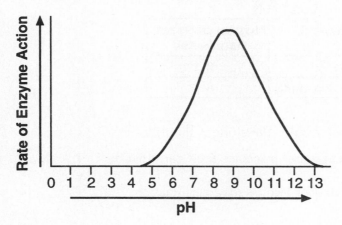

At what pH would the enzyme be most effective?

(1) above 10

(2) between 8 and 10

(3) between 5 and 7

(4) below 5

37 ☐

38 Which graph of blood sugar level over a 12-hour period best illustrates the concept of dynamic equilibrium in the body?

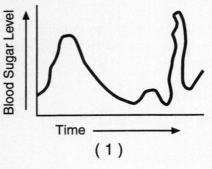

(1)

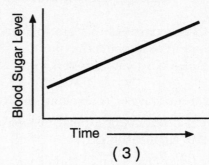

(3)

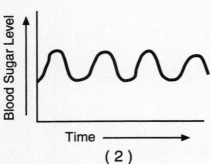

(2)

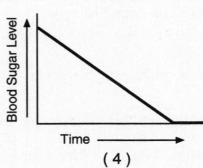

(4)

38 ☐

39 A student hypothesized that lettuce seeds would not germinate (begin to grow) unless they were covered with soil. The student planted 10 lettuce seeds under a layer of soil and scattered 10 lettuce seeds on top of the soil. The data collected are shown in the table below.

Data Table

Seed Treatment	Number of Seeds Germinated
Planted under soil	9
Scattered on top of soil	8

To improve the reliability of these results, the student should

(1) conclude that darkness is necessary for lettuce seed germination

(2) conclude that light is necessary for lettuce seed germination

(3) revise the hypothesis

(4) repeat the experiment using a larger sample size

39 ☐

Base your answers to questions 40 through 43 on the diagram below, which represents the relationships between animals in a possible canine family tree, and on your knowledge of biology.

Canine Family Tree

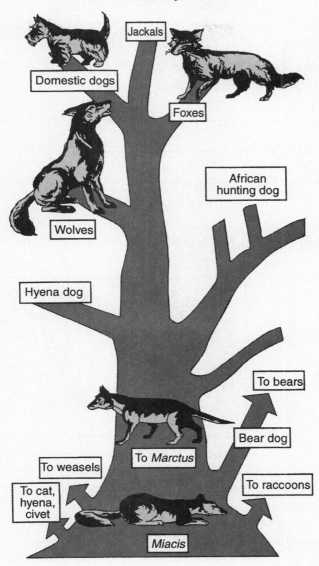

40 According to the diagram, which group of organisms has the most closely related members?

(1) cats, weasels, and wolves

(2) bears, raccoons, and hyena dogs

(3) jackals, foxes, and domestic dogs

(4) African hunting dogs, hyena dogs, and domestic dogs

40 ☐

41 According to the canine family tree, weasels, foxes, and domestic dogs all most likely originated from the

(1) wolf

(3) *Marctus*

(2) bear dog

(4) *Miacis*

41

42 State *one* valid inference regarding the relationship of bears to other animals in the canine family tree. [1]

_____

_____

_____

42

43 The ranges of the African hunting dog and Arctic wolf are represented in the maps shown below.

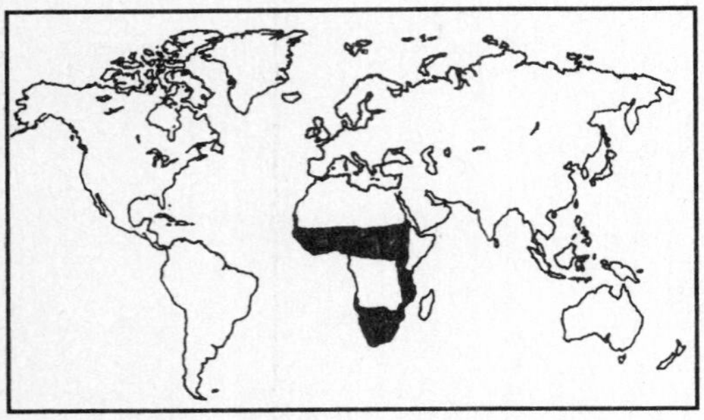

■ Range of the African hunting dog

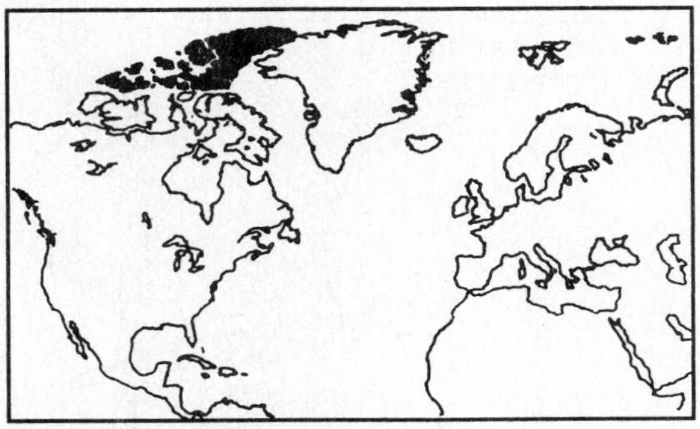

■ Range of the Arctic wolf

State a possible hypothesis that might explain why these two related animals successfully inhabit different areas of Earth. [1]

_____

_____

_____

43

Base your answers to questions 44 through 47 on the data table and information below and on your knowledge of biology. The data table shows water temperatures at various depths in an ocean.

Water Temperatures at Various Depths

Water Depth (meters)	Temperature (°C)
50	18
75	15
100	12
150	5
200	4

Directions (44–45): Using the information in the data table, construct a line graph on the grid following the directions below.

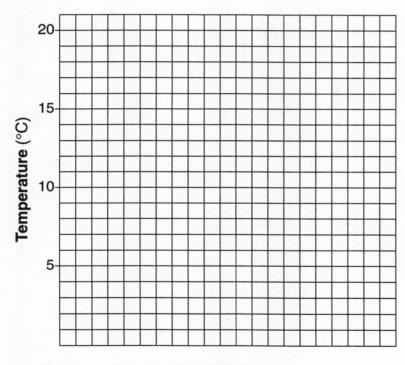

Water Depth (m)

44 Mark an appropriate scale on the axis labeled "Water Depth (m)."   [1]

44 ☐

45 Plot the data on the grid. Surround each point with a small circle and connect the points.   [1]

Example: ⊙—⊙—⊙

45 ☐

46 State the general relationship between temperature and water depth.   [1]

_____

_____

47 The approximate water temperature at a depth of 125 meters would be closest to

(1) 15°C   (3) 8°C

(2) 13°C   (4) 3°C

48 What is the dependent variable in the experiment summarized in the graph below? [1]

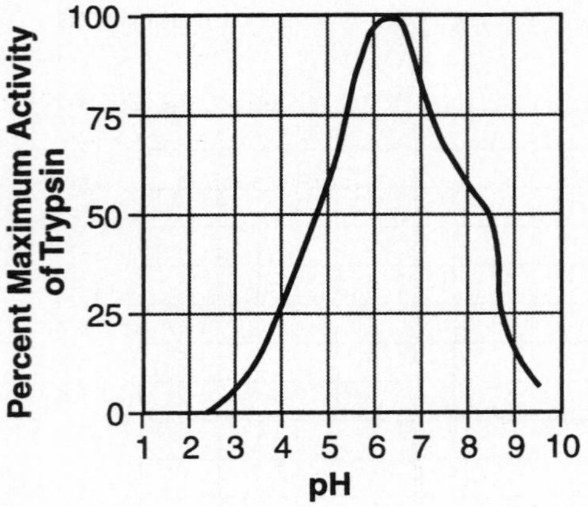

_____

49 Why are offspring of organisms that reproduce sexually *not* genetically identical to their parents?   [1]

_____

_____

50 How can the introduction of a foreign species lead to the extinction of species that are native to an area?   [1]

_____

_____

_____

Base your answers to questions 51 through 54 on the information below and on your knowledge of biology.

Stem Cells

If skin is cut, the wound closes within days. If a leg is broken, the fracture will usually mend if the bone is set correctly. Almost all human tissue can repair itself to some extent. Much of this repair is due to the activity of stem cells. These cells resemble those of a developing embryo in their ability to reproduce repeatedly, forming exact copies of themselves. They may also form many other different kinds of cells. Stem cells in bone marrow offer a dramatic example. They can give rise to all of the structures in the blood: red blood cells, platelets, and various types of white blood cells. Other stem cells may produce the various components of the skin, liver, or intestinal lining.

The brain of an adult human can sometimes compensate for damage by making new connections among surviving nerve cells (neurons). For many years, most biologists believed that the brain could not repair itself because it lacked stem cells that would produce new neurons.

A recent discovery, however, indicates that a mature human brain does produce neurons routinely at one site, the hippocampus, an area important to memory and learning. This discovery raises the prospect that stem cells that make new neurons in one part of the brain might be found in other areas. If investigators can learn how to cause existing stem cells to produce useful numbers of functional nerve cells, it might be possible to correct a number of disorders involving damage to neurons such as Alzheimer's disease, Parkinson's disease, stroke, and brain injuries.

51 What is the process by which stem cells produce exact copies of themselves?

(1) cell division by mitosis

(2) cell division by meiosis

(3) sexual reproduction

(4) glucose synthesis

51 ☐

52 Stem cells may be similar to the cells of a developing embryo because both cell types can

(1) produce only one type of cell

(2) help the brain to learn and remember things

(3) divide and differentiate

(4) cause Alzheimer's and Parkinson's diseases

52 ☐

For Teacher Use Only

53 Until recently, many biologists thought that the brain could *not* repair itself because they thought it

(1) could not make new connections between neurons

(2) had DNA different from DNA in reproductive cells

(3) could form new cells only in certain areas of the brain

(4) lacked stem cells needed to produce new neurons

53 ☐

54 Describe how this new discovery concerning stem cells might help to treat diseases such as Alzheimer's disease or Parkinson's disease. [1]

____

____

____

____

54 ☐

55 The graph below shows the relationship between kidney function and arterial pressure in humans.

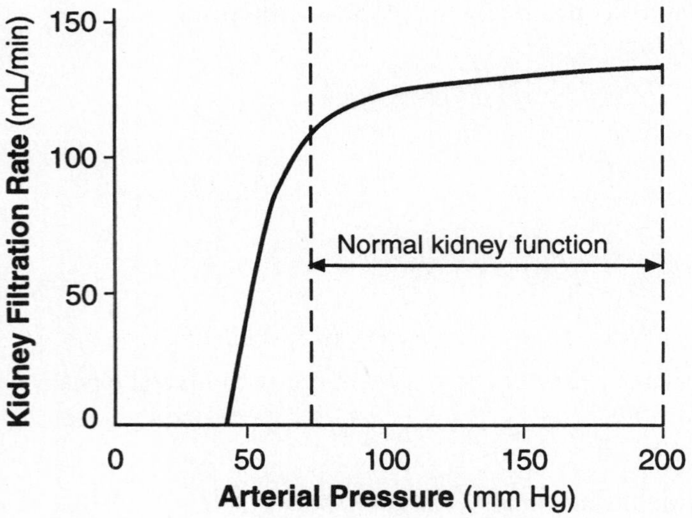

State how a steady decrease in arterial pressure will affect homeostasis in the human body. [1]

____

____

____

55 ☐

Base your answers to questions 56 through 58 on the diagram below illustrating one type of cellular communication and on your knowledge of biology.

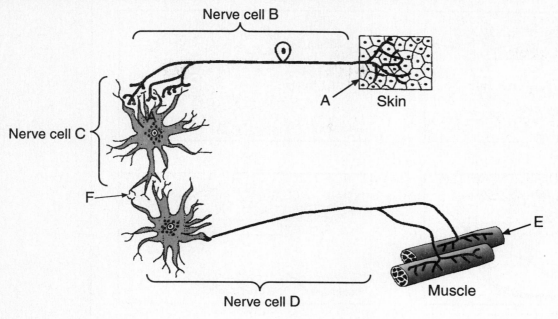

Nerve cell B

Nerve cell C

F

A   Skin

E

Nerve cell D

Muscle

56 In region *F*, there is a space between nerve cells *C* and *D*. Cell *D* is usually stimulated to respond by

(1) a chemical produced by cell *C* moving to cell *D*

(2) the movement of a virus from cell *C* to cell *D*

(3) the flow of blood out of cell *C* to cell *D*

(4) the movement of material through a blood vessel that forms between cell *C* and cell *D*

56 ☐

57 If a stimulus is received by the cells at *A*, the cells at *E* will most likely use energy obtained from a reaction between

(1) fats and enzymes   (3) glucose and oxygen

(2) ATP and pathogens   (4) water and carbon dioxide

57 ☐

58 State *one* possible cause for the failure of muscle *E* to respond to a stimulus at *A*. [1]

_____

_____

_____

_____

58 ☐

Base your answers to questions 59 through 62 on the diagrams of stages of succession below and on your knowledge of biology.

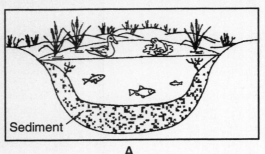

A

C

Sediment

B

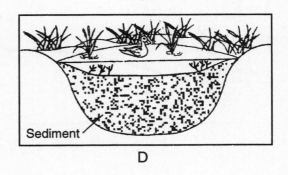

D

59 What is the correct sequence of these stages?

(1) $B \rightarrow A \rightarrow D \rightarrow C$

(3) $C \rightarrow B \rightarrow A \rightarrow D$

(2) $A \rightarrow D \rightarrow C \rightarrow B$

(4) $D \rightarrow A \rightarrow C \rightarrow B$

59 ☐

60 Which statement helps to explain this type of succession?

(1) Species will replace species until an unstable ecosystem is established.

(2) Species are replaced until a stable ecosystem is established.

(3) Humans replace all species and fill all niches.

(4) Changes in plant species are controlled only by the types of animals in an area.

60 ☐

61 Which organisms would most likely be harmed the most by the changes that occurred between these stages?

(1) trees

(3) fish

(2) raccoons

(4) rabbits

61 ☐

62 Identify *one* factor that could disrupt the final stage of this ecosystem. [1]

62 ☐

63 The diagram below represents a food web.

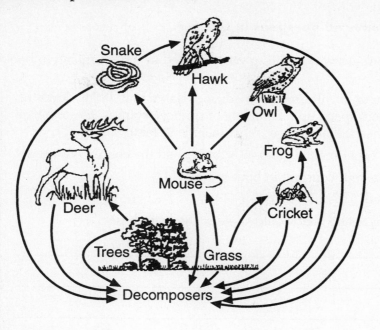

Select and record the name of *one* species in the food web, and explain how its removal could affect *one* of the other species in the food web.   [1]

_____

_____   63 [ ]

64 Identify *one* process that a producer can accomplish that a carnivore can *not* accomplish.   [1]

_____   64 [ ]

65 How do guard cells of a leaf help to maintain homeostasis in a plant? [1]

_____

_____

_____   65 [ ]

Part C

Answer all questions in this part. [20]

Directions (66–72): Record your answers in the spaces provided in this examination booklet.

66 Many people who are in favor of alternative medicine claim that large doses of vitamin C introduced into a vein speed up the healing of surgical wounds. Describe an experiment to test this hypothesis. Your answer must include at least:

- the difference between the experimental group of subjects and the control group [1]
- *two* conditions that must be kept constant in both groups [2]
- data that should be collected [1]
- an example of experimental results that would support the hypothesis [1]

66 ☐

67 Choose *one* ecological problem from the list below.

Ecological Problems

Global warming
Destruction of the ozone shield
Loss of biodiversity

Discuss the ecological problem you chose. In your answer be sure to state:

- the problem you selected and *one* human action that may have caused the problem [1]
- *one* way in which the problem may negatively affect humans [1]
- *one* positive action that could be taken to reduce the problem [1]

_____

_____

_____

_____

_____

_____

_____

_____

_____

_____

67 ☐

68 There are a number of possible methods to control an invasion of gypsy moths in a city park. Several alternatives are listed below.

A A band of material can be placed around each tree trunk, preventing the larvae from crawling up the trunk. The larvae can be picked off by hand each day and destroyed.

B A chemical insecticide can be sprayed from an airplane. The chemical is effective and disappears rapidly, although some may run off into ponds and lakes.

C The trees can be sprayed with a liquid containing naturally occurring bacteria that feed on gypsy moths. These bacteria are believed to be harmless, but the spray is very expensive.

D No action is taken. This allows nature to take its course, which results in major changes in the area concerned. The damage can then be repaired.

Write the letter of the method you would use and give an ecologically sound reason for your choice. [1]

_____

_____

_____

68 ☐

Base your answer to question 69 on one of the cartoons below, which refer to certain concepts of natural selection, and on your knowledge of biology.

Cartoon 1

"Of course, long before you mature, most of you will be eaten."

Cartoon 2

"Listen... I'm fed up with this 'weeding out the sick and the old' business... I want something in its prime."

69 Choose *one* cartoon and write its number in the space below. Identify *one* concept represented in that cartoon, and explain how this concept supports the theory of natural selection. Your answer must:

- identify *one* concept represented in the cartoon you choose   [1]

- briefly explain the concept you identified   [1]

- explain the relationship between this concept and the process of natural selection   [1]

Cartoon Number: _____

_____

_____

_____

_____

_____

_____

_____

_____

_____

_____

69

Base your answers to questions 70 and 71 on the passage below and on your knowledge of biology.

Plastics Produced by Plants

Plastics are generally thought of as materials made exclusively by human technology. However, some plants and bacteria naturally make small amounts of plastics. Furthermore, unlike synthetic plastics, plastics produced by plants and bacteria break down easily in the environment. Synthetic plastics, which are produced from petroleum, are the fastest growing type of waste in the United States. Researchers are learning how to greatly increase the amount of plastic made by plants. One day farmers may grow crops of plastic-producing plants in addition to wheat and corn crops.

A researcher at the Carnegie Institution of Washington was one of the first to attempt to use plants to make plastics. He knew that a common bacterium, known as *Alcaligenes eutrophus*, naturally produced a plastic called polyhydroxybutyrate (PHB), which resembles the type of plastic used to make garbage bags.

However, growing bacteria to produce plastic can be expensive. In order to determine if genetically engineered plants could make plastic, genes were isolated from *A. eutrophus* and inserted into plants. After a few tries, the researchers were able to produce healthy plastic-producing plants.

70 By what process were the plastic-producing plants developed? [1]

_____

_____   70 ☐

71 Explain why the use of the plastic produced by these plants is better for the environment than plastic produced by human technology, and explain why this plastic would be a benefit to future generations.   [2]

_____

_____

_____

_____

_____   71 ☐

_____

72 Systems in the human body interact to maintain homeostasis. Four of these systems are listed below.

Body Systems

circulatory

digestive

respiratory

excretory

a Select *two* of the systems listed. Identify each system selected and state its function in helping to maintain homeostasis in the body. [2]

_____

_____

_____

_____

72a ☐

b Explain how a malfunction of *one* of the four systems listed disrupts homeostasis and how that malfunction could be prevented or treated. In your answer be sure to:

• name the system and state *one* possible malfunction of that system [1]

• explain how the malfunction disrupts homeostasis [1]

• describe *one* way the malfunction could be prevented or treated [1]

_____

_____

_____

_____

_____

_____

72b ☐

The Living Environment January, 2002

Part A

Answer all questions in this part. [35]

Directions (1–35): For *each* statement or question, write on the separate answer sheet the number of the word or expression that, of those given, best completes the statement or answers the question.

1 Which statement accurately compares cells in the human circulatory system to cells in the human nervous system?

(1) Cells in the circulatory system carry out the same life function for the organism as cells in the nervous system.

(2) Cells in the circulatory system are identical in structure to cells in the nervous system.

(3) Cells in the nervous system are different in structure from cells in the circulatory system, and they carry out different specialized functions.

(4) Cells in the nervous system act independently, but cells in the circulatory system function together.

2 An iodine test of a tomato plant leaf revealed that starch was present at 5:00 p.m. on a sunny afternoon in July. When a similar leaf from the same tomato plant was tested with iodine at 6:00 a.m. the next morning, the test indicated that less starch was present. This reduction in starch content most likely occurred because starch was

(1) changed directly into proteins

(2) transported out of the leaves through the guard cells

(3) transported downward toward the roots through tubes

(4) changed into simple sugars

3 Luciferin is a molecule that, when broken down in fireflies, produces heat and light. The rate at which luciferin is broken down in cells is controlled by

(1) a carbohydrate   (3) an enzyme

(2) a simple sugar   (4) a complex fat

4 Communication between cells is affected if there is decreased ability to produce

(1) digestive enzymes and gametes

(2) antibodies and chloroplasts

(3) hormones and nerve impulses

(4) antibiotics and guard cells

5 Tomato plants in a garden are not growing well. The gardener hypothesizes that the soil is too acidic. To test this hypothesis accurately, the gardener could

(1) plant seeds of a different kind of plant

(2) move the tomato plants to an area with less sunlight

(3) change the pH of the soil

(4) reduce the amount of water available to the plant

6 A glucose-tolerance test was conducted to observe the effect of time on glucose concentration in the blood. An animal was fed 10 milliliters of glucose solution. At five different times after the ingestion of the solution, the blood glucose concentration was determined, and the results were recorded in the data table below.

Data Table

Time After Glucose Ingestion (minutes)	Glucose Concentration in Blood (mg/100 dL)
0	75
30	125
60	110
90	90
120	80
180	70

The change in glucose concentration in the blood between 0 and 30 minutes was probably due to

(1) the liver releasing glucose into the small intestine

(2) glucose being absorbed from the digestive system

(3) the synthesis of glucose from starch

(4) glucose being used for cellular respiration

7 The diagram below represents movement of a large molecule across a membrane.

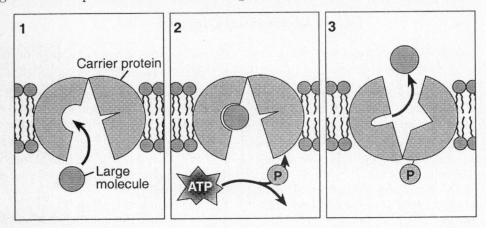

Which process is best represented in this diagram?

(1) active transport   (3) protein building
(2) diffusion   (4) gene manipulation

8 How does the type of reproduction shown in method *A* in the diagram below differ from the type of reproduction shown in method *B*?

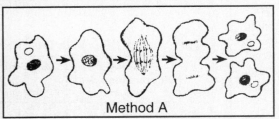

(1) Method *A* illustrates sexual reproduction, and method *B* illustrates asexual reproduction.
(2) Offspring produced by method *B* will be genetically alike, but offspring produced by method *A* will be genetically different.
(3) The two cells shown in the last step of method *A* are genetically alike, but the two cells shown in the last step of method *B* are genetically different.
(4) Offspring produced by method *A* will be genetically like the parent, but offspring produced by method *B* will be genetically different from the parents.

9 When humans first domesticated dogs, there was relatively little diversity in the species. Today, there are many variations such as the German shepherd and the dalmation. This increase in diversity is most closely associated with

(1) cloning of selected body cells
(2) selective breeding
(3) mitotic cell division
(4) environmental influences on inherited traits

10 As a result of sexual reproduction, an organism can pass a gene mutation to its offspring if the mutation occurs in

(1) a body cell   (3) liver tissue
(2) a gamete   (4) white blood cells

11 The diversity within the wild bird species in the diagram below can best be explained by which process?

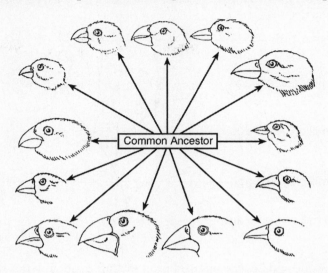

(1) natural selection
(2) asexual reproduction
(3) ecological succession
(4) mitotic cell division

12 What is the most probable reason for the increase in the percentage of variety A in the population of the species shown in the graph below?

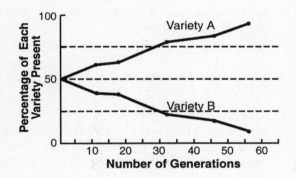

Number of Generations

(1) There is no chance for variety A to mate with variety B.
(2) There is no genetic difference between variety A and variety B.
(3) Variety A is less fit to survive than variety B is.
(4) Variety A has some adaptive advantage that variety B does not have.

13 The type of molecule represented below is found in organisms.

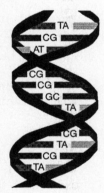

Which statement correctly describes the sequence of bases found in this type of molecule?

(1) It changes every time it replicates.
(2) It determines the characteristics that will be inherited.
(3) It is exactly the same in all organisms.
(4) It directly controls the synthesis of starch within a cell.

14 The diagram below illustrates a proposed evolutionary path of certain organisms, based on the theory of evolution.

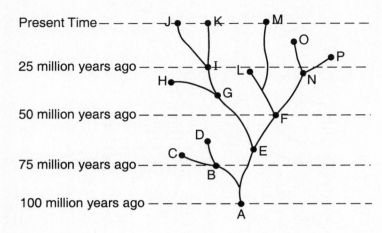

Which statement could best be inferred from the information in this diagram?

(1) Evolution does not involve gradual change.
(2) Evolutionary changes can result in extinction.
(3) Evolution begins with plants.
(4) Evolution produces organisms that all fill the same niche.

15 Which statement best describes the result of some of the processes involved in genetic engineering?

(1) They alter the arrangement of hereditary material.
(2) They provide energy for mitosis and meiosis.
(3) They are necessary for normal gamete formation.
(4) They reduce variation in organisms that reproduce asexually.

16 A characteristic of mutations is that they usually

(1) are caused only by the events of mitosis
(2) do not occur at random
(3) result in different genetic sequences
(4) occur to meet the needs of a species

17 Regulation of sexual reproductive cycles of human males is related most directly to the presence of the hormone

(1) estrogen   (3) testosterone
(2) progesterone   (4) insulin

18 The nucleus is removed from a body cell of one organism and is placed in an egg cell that has had its nucleus removed. This process, which results in the production of organisms that are genetically alike, is known as

(1) cloning
(2) fertilization
(3) biological adaptation
(4) DNA production

19 Most cells in the body of a fruit fly contain eight chromosomes. In some cells, only four chromosomes are present, a condition which is a direct result of

(1) mitotic cell division
(2) meiotic cell division
(3) embryonic differentiation
(4) internal fertilization

20 People with AIDS are unable to fight multiple infections because the virus that causes AIDS

(1) weakens their immune systems
(2) produces antibodies in their blood
(3) attacks muscle tissue
(4) kills pathogens

21 Feedback mechanisms are best described as processes that help

(1) reduce hormone levels to below normal in the blood
(2) destroy hormones in the blood
(3) directly control muscle contraction in the leg
(4) keep body conditions near a normal, steady state

22 A pond ecosystem is represented in the diagram below.

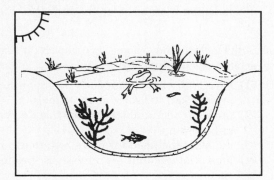

Energy for this ecosystem originally comes from

(1) water   (3) sunlight
(2) consumers   (4) plants

23 Which type of model provides the most complete representation of the feeding relationships within a community?

(1) a material cycle
(2) a predator-prey association
(3) a food chain
(4) a food web

24 An ecosystem will most likely remain stable if

(1) it has more predators than prey
(2) it has a high level of biodiversity
(3) biotic factors decrease
(4) finite resources decrease

25 Heavy cigarette smoking and the use of alcohol throughout pregnancy usually increase the likelihood of

(1) the birth of twins
(2) the birth of a male baby
(3) a baby being born with a viral infection
(4) a baby being born with medical problems

26 The mass of some corn plants at the end of their growth period was 6 tons per acre. Most of this mass was produced from

(1) water and organic compounds absorbed from the soil
(2) minerals from the soil and oxygen from the air
(3) minerals and organic materials absorbed from the soil
(4) water from the soil and carbon dioxide from the air

27 The gene for the production of human insulin is inserted into certain bacterial cells. The offspring of these bacterial cells will most likely be able to

(1) destroy pathogens
(2) reproduce sexually
(3) synthesize this hormone
(4) form human tissue

28 A characteristic of hormones and enzymes that allows them to work effectively with other organic molecules is their

(1) specific shape
(2) small size
(3) concentration of carbon and hydrogen atoms
(4) high-energy bonds

29 Both a deer and a tree react to changes in their external surroundings, helping them to maintain a constant internal environment. This statement describes

(1) predation
(2) homeostasis
(3) antibiotic resistance
(4) autotrophic nutrition

30 Which sequence best represents the flow of energy in the cartoon below?

"Hey, wait a minute! This is grass! We've been eating grass!"

(1) prey → predator
(2) host → parasite
(3) producer → herbivore
(4) autotroph → carnivore

31 What would most likely occur after an ecosystem is disrupted by fire?

(1) The ecosystem would eventually return to its original state.
(2) The ecosystem would return to its previous state immediately.
(3) The ecosystem would evolve into a new ecosystem that is totally different from the original.
(4) The ecosystem would become an ever-changing environment with no stability.

32 Car exhaust has been blamed for increasing the amount of carbon dioxide in the air. Some scientists believe this additional carbon dioxide in the air may cause

(1) global warming
(2) increased biodiversity
(3) habitat preservation
(4) ozone destruction

33 Which statement illustrates how human activities can most directly change the dynamic equilibrium of an ecosystem?

(1) A hurricane causes a stream to overflow its banks.
(2) Increased wind increases water evaporation from a plant.
(3) Water pollution causes a decrease in fish populations in a river.
(4) The ozone shield helps prevent harmful radiation from reaching the surface of Earth.

34 Some factories have a negative impact on Earth's ecosystems because they

(1) have high energy demands that require the use of fossil fuels and nuclear fuels
(2) utilize agricultural technology that decreases soil erosion
(3) decrease the need for finite resources
(4) limit the amount of emissions produced each year

35 For a natural ecosystem to be self-sustaining, many essential chemical elements must be

(1) converted to energy
(2) changed into fossil fuels such as oil and coal
(3) permanently removed from the environment
(4) cycled between organisms and the environment

Part B

Answer all questions in this part.   [30]

Directions (36–63): For those questions that are followed by four choices, circle the number of the choice that best completes the statement or answers the question. For all other questions in this part, follow the directions given in the question and record your answers in the spaces provided.

Base your answers to questions 36 through 40 on the information below and on your knowledge of biology.

For Teacher Use Only

An insect known as a sawfly is found in evergreen forests in North America. Sawfly cocoons are the main source of food for shrews (small mammals) and some bird species. Scientists studied 1-acre plots in various parts of a state to determine the average number of sawfly cocoons, shrews, and robins. The data collected are shown in the table below.

Data Table

Average Number of Sawfly Cocoons per Acre (in thousands)	Average Number of Shrews per Acre	Average Number of Robins per Acre
100	5.0	0
300	7.5	0.5
600	19.0	0.8
900	23.5	1.0
1200	23.5	1.3

Directions (36–38): Using the information in the data table, construct a line graph on the grid provided *on the next page,* following the directions below. You may use pen or pencil for your answer.

36 Mark an appropriate scale on each axis.   [1]

37 Plot the data for shrews. Surround each point with a small circle and connect the points.   [1]

Example:

38 Plot the data for robins. Surround each point with a small triangle and connect the points.   [1]

Example: △—△—△

Average Number of Shrews and Robins per Acre

Average Number of Sawfly Cocoons (x1000) per Acre

39 What is the average number of shrews per acre when the average number of sawfly cocoons is 500,000?   [1]

_____

40 State what would most likely happen to the number of sawfly cocoons per acre if the shrews and robins were removed from the area.   [1]

_____

_____

_____

For Teacher
Use Only

36 ☐

37 ☐

38 ☐

39 ☐

40 ☐

Base your answers to questions 41 through 43 on the information and graph below and on your knowledge of biology.

A Closer Look at Cycles in Predator and Prey Populations

Scientists have hypothesized that the populations of both lynx and snowshoe hares should show cyclic changes with increases in the predator population size lagging behind increases in prey population size, if the assumption is made that snowshoe hares are eaten only by lynx.

Does this out-of-phase population cycle of predators and prey actually occur in nature? A classic example of such a cycle was observed by counting all the fur pelts (skins) from northern Canada lynx and snowshoe hares purchased by the Hudson Bay Company between 1845 and 1935. Population cycles of snowshoe hares and their lynx predators, based on the number of pelts received by the Hudson Bay Company, are shown in the graph below.

As with any field investigation, many variables could influence the relationship between hare and lynx. One problem is that hare populations have been shown to fluctuate even without lynx present, possibly because the carrying capacity of their environment had been exceeded.

To test this hypothesis about population cycles more scientifically, investigators turned to controlled laboratory studies on populations of small predators and their prey.

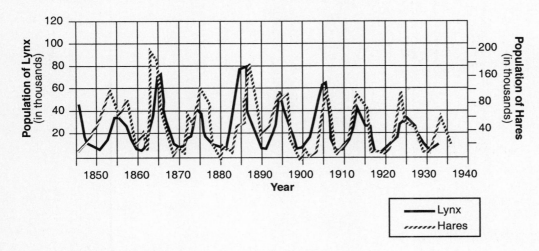

41 Identify *two* variables other than the size of the lynx population that can affect the size of the hare population.   [2]

1. _____

2. _____   41 ☐

42 The phrase "carrying capacity" refers to

  (1) storing extra food for the winter

  (2) the number of organisms a habitat can support

  (3) transporting food to organisms in an area

  (4) the maximum possible weight of an individual organism

  42 ☐

43 Why would scientists want to have a laboratory study on populations of different predators and their prey?   [1]

  _____

  _____

  _____

  43 ☐

Base your answers to questions 44 and 45 on the diagram below, which provides information related to heredity, and on your knowledge of biology.

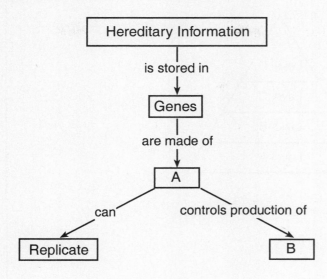

44 The type of molecule in box *A* serves as a template. Explain what this means.   [1]

_____

_____

45 Which molecules are represented by box *B*?

(1) bases

(2) proteins

(3) amino acids

(4) simple sugars

Base your answers to questions 46 through 49 on the energy pyramid below and on your knowledge of biology.

46 Energy from nutrients is transferred to ATP in

  (1) level *A*, only

  (2) levels *B* and *C*, only

  (3) levels *B*, *C*, and *D*, only

  (4) levels *A*, *B*, *C*, and *D*

46 ☐

47 The greatest amount of available energy is transferred from level

  (1) *A* to level *B*

  (2) *A* to level *C*

  (3) *B* to level *A*

  (4) *D* to level *A*

47 ☐

48 Which energy levels could contain carnivores?

  (1) *A* and *B*

  (2) *B* and *C*

  (3) *C* and *D*

  (4) *D* and *A*

48 ☐

49 In a community where grass, cats, insects, and mice are found, which of these organisms would fill level *A*?   [1]

_____

_____

49 ☐

50 A student designed an investigation to determine the effect of temperature on the rate of seed germination. The student placed moist filter paper in each of four culture dishes. Ten bean seeds were placed on the filter paper in each dish. The four dishes were numbered and placed in the dark at different temperatures as follows: Dish 1: 10°C, Dish 2: 15°C, Dish 3: 20°C, Dish 4: 25°C. The total number of germinated seeds in each culture dish was counted each day for two weeks.

Which data table is best for recording the results of this investigation?

Petri Dish	Day	Temperature	Amount of Light
1			
2			
3			
4			

(1)

Day	Temperature			
	Dish 1	Dish 2	Dish 3	Dish 4

(3)

Petri Dish	Amount of Water	Number of Germinated Seeds	Amount of Light
1			
2			
3			
4			

(2)

Day	Number of Germinated Seeds			
	10°C	15°C	20°C	25°C

(4)

50 ☐

51 The Pine Barrens is a government-protected environment located on the eastern end of Long Island. A proposal has been made to allow a shopping mall to be built in the middle of the Pine Barrens. Although the developer has promised jobs for people in the surrounding communities, some community members oppose the building of the mall due to the negative effects it would have on this fragile ecosystem.

Identify *two* negative effects this mall would most likely have on the Pine Barrens.   [2]

1. _____

2. _____

51 ☐

52 In an investigation to determine the change in heart rate with increased activity, a biology teacher asked students to take their pulses immediately before and immediately after exercising for 2 minutes. The data showed an average heart rate of 72 beats per minute before exercising and 90 beats per minute after exercising. If a valid conclusion is to be made from the results of this investigation, which assumption must be made?

(1) In most students, the average heart rate is not affected by exercise.

(2) Exercise causes the heart rate to slow down.

(3) Each student exercised with the same intensity.

(4) The heart rate of each student goes up 18 beats after jogging for 2 minutes.

52 ☐

Base your answers to questions 53 and 54 on the word equation below and on your knowledge of biology.

$$\text{glucose} + \text{oxygen} \xrightarrow[\text{energy}]{\text{enzymes}} \text{carbon dioxide} + \text{water} + X$$

53 Name the process represented by the equation.   [1]

_____

53 ☐

54 Name the molecule represented by letter X.   [1]

_____

54 ☐

_____

Base your answers to questions 55 and 56 on the data table below and on your knowledge of biology. The data table shows the amount of oxygen that will dissolve in freshwater and seawater at different temperatures. The amount of oxygen is expressed in parts per million (ppm).

Data Table

Temperature (°C)	Freshwater Oxygen Content (ppm)	Seawater Oxygen Content (ppm)
1	14.24	11.15
10	11.29	9.00
15	10.10	8.09
20	9.11	7.36
25	8.27	6.75
30	7.56	6.19

55 Write a statement comparing the oxygen-holding ability of freshwater with the oxygen-holding ability of seawater in the temperature range shown.   [1]

_____

_____

_____

55 ☐

56 State how the oxygen-holding ability of freshwater varies with changes in temperature. [1]

_____

_____

_____

56 ☐

Base your answers to questions 57 and 58 on the information below and on your knowledge of biology.

A student completed a series of experiments and found that a protein-digesting enzyme (intestinal protease) functions best when the pH is 8.0 and the temperature is 37°C. During an experiment, the student used some of the procedures listed below.

Procedures

(A) Adding more protease
(B) Adding more protein
(C) Decreasing the pH to 6.0
(D) Increasing the temperature to 45°C
(E) Decreasing the amount of light

57 Which procedure would have the *least* effect on the rate of protein digestion?

(1) A

(2) E

(3) C

(4) D

58 Which two procedures would most likely cause a *decrease* in the rate of protein digestion?

(1) A and D

(2) B and C

(3) C and D

(4) A and E

Base your answers to questions 59 through 61 on the information below and on your knowledge of biology.

An investigation was performed to determine the resistance of two species of *Anopheles* mosquito to the insecticides malathion and dieldrin. In May, two groups of 10,000 insects of each species were sprayed with insecticide. One group was sprayed with malathion, the second group with dieldrin. The number of surviving insects was recorded after the first spraying. The surviving insects were then allowed to reproduce. Several generations of new offspring were produced over the following three months. On the first day of each month they were sprayed, and the number of survivors was recorded in the table below.

Species	Insecticide	Number Before First Spraying	Number of Survivors			
			May	June	July	Aug
Anopheles culifacies	malathion	10,000	31	129	1,654	4,055
	dieldrin	10,000	78	339	1,982	3,106
Anopheles strephensi	malathion	10,000	28	56	1,207	1,744
	dieldrin	10,000	30	71	1,321	2,388

59 State *one* valid conclusion that can be drawn from these data.   [1]

_____

_____

_____

59 [ ]

60 State *one* negative impact that the use of these two insecticides might have on the environment.   [1]

_____

_____

60 [ ]

61 Which graph best represents the number of survivors after spraying in the *Anopheles culifacies* population from May to August?

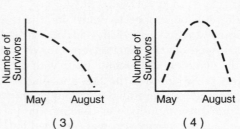

(1)   (2)   (3)   (4)

61 ☐

62 To test the effect of hormones on plant growth, six potted plant seedlings of the same species were measured and then sprayed with auxin (a growth hormone). After four weeks of growth under ideal conditions, the plants were measured again. To set up a proper control for this experiment, the investigator should

(1) spray the same plants with different amounts of auxin

(2) spray auxin on six plant seedlings of the same species and grow them in the dark for four weeks

(3) wash the auxin off three of the plants after two weeks

(4) grow another six plant seedlings of the same species under the same conditions, spraying them with distilled water only

62 ☐

63 A student wanted to determine if slugs preferred green leaf lettuce leaves over purple cabbage leaves for food. Pieces of both leaves were cut. One piece of each type of leaf and one slug were placed in each of ten containers. After three days, the surface area of each leaf section was measured and the results were recorded in a data table. State *one* reason that the results of this experiment might be considered invalid.   [1]

_____

_____

_____

63 ☐

Answer all questions in this part.   [20]

Directions (64–71): Record your answers in the spaces provided in this examination booklet.

Base your answers to questions 64 through 66 on the information below and on your knowledge of biology.

Telomere Tales

The number of times a human body cell reproduces is dependent on the length of its special chromosome tips. These tips, which are known as telomeres, act as cell division clocks. With each division, the length of the telomere shortens until a critical length is reached, signaling cell reproduction to stop. Knowledge of telomeres could be used in cancer diagnosis, in understanding diseases of aging, and in providing information that would lead to the survival of transplanted organs.

As most body cells divide, their telomeres shorten and, in turn, the overall chromosome length is reduced. However, tissues such as bone marrow and most cancer cells lengthen their shrinking chromosome tips with the help of an enzyme, telomerase. As a result, the chromosomes of these rapidly dividing cells never reach critical length, and the cells continue to reproduce.

Transplantation speeds up the aging process in donor cells. The telomeres of transplanted cells are shorter than those in normal bone marrow cells. If telomerase is inserted into donor cells, the donor tissues may live longer. This procedure would greatly benefit organ transplants and the treatment of patients who have HIV (the virus that causes AIDS). For example, blood-forming cells could be removed from these patients early in the disease, cultured with telomerase to extend their telomeres, and then returned to the bodies of the patients as their blood cell counts fall.

64 State the relationship between the presence of telomerase, telomere length, and the number of cell divisions.   [2]

_____

_____

_____

64 ☐

65 Explain how the knowledge of telomerase may lead to an effective treatment for cancer.   [1]

_____

_____

_____

65 ☐

66 State *one* way telomerase could be used to treat patients who have HIV. [1]

For Teacher Use Only

66

67 Vaccinations play a major role in medicine today. Explain the role of vaccines in the prevention of disease. Your answer must include at least:

- a description of the contents of a vaccine [1]
- a description of how a vaccine protects the body from disease [1]
- *one* specific reason certain vaccinations are required for students to attend public schools [1]

67

68 In the past, a specific antibiotic was effective in killing a certain species of bacteria. Now, most members of this bacterial species are resistant to this antibiotic. Explain how this species of bacteria has become resistant. Your answer must include at least the concepts of:

- overproduction   [1]
- variation   [1]
- natural selection   [1]
- adaptation to the environment   [1]

_____

_____

_____

_____

_____

_____

_____

_____

_____

_____

_____

_____

68

Base your answers to questions 69 and 70 on the information and data table below and on your knowledge of biology.

You are the head of the research division of the Leafy Lettuce Company. Your company is experimenting with hydroponic technology. Hydroponic technology involves growing plants in containers of growth solution in a greenhouse. No soil is used. Your first experiment used five groups of five plants of the same size and species. Each group was grown in a different growth solution for the same period of time. The results of the experiment are shown in the table below.

Group	Growth Solution	Average Growth in Height (cm)	Average Surface Area of Leaves (cm^2)	Key
1	H_2O	4.4	7.6	N = Nitrogen
2	H_2O + N	5.1	10.0	P = Phosphorus
3	H_2O + N + P	11.5	37.5	Mg = Magnesium
4	H_2O + N + P + Mg	13.0	125.0	K = Potassium
5	H_2O + N + P + Mg + K	20.3	306.5	

69 Prepare a brief report to the president of the Leafy Lettuce Company summarizing the results of your experiment and identifying another possible variable that could be investigated to improve the growth of the lettuce. In your report, be sure to include:

- a recommendation of the best growth solution to use for hydroponic lettuce [Support your recommendation.]   [2]
- another possible variable (besides the growth solution) that might be investigated to improve the growth of the hydroponic lettuce   [1]
- a recommendation for an extension of this investigation to make it more valid   [1]

_____

_____

_____

_____

_____

_____

_____

_____

_____

_____

69 ☐

70 Could the results of this investigation be used to select the best growth solution for other species of plants? Justify your answer.   [1]

_____

_____

_____

_____

70 [ ]

71 Just like complex organisms, cells are able to survive by coordinating various activities. Complex organisms have a variety of systems, and cells have a variety of organelles that work together for survival. Describe the roles of *two* organelles. In your answer be sure to include:

- the names of *two* organelles and the function of each   [2]
- an explanation of how these two organelles work together   [1]
- the name of an organelle and the name of a system in the human body that have similar functions   [1]

_____

_____

_____

_____

_____

_____

_____

_____

_____

_____

_____

71 [ ]

Part A

Answer all 35 questions in this part.   [35]

Directions (1–35): For *each* statement or question, write on the separate answer sheet the *number* of the word or expression, that, of those given, best completes the statement or answers the question.

1 Which statement describes the best procedure to determine if a vaccine for a disease in a certain bird species is effective?

(1) Vaccinate 100 birds and expose all 100 to the disease.
(2) Vaccinate 100 birds and expose only 50 of them to the disease.
(3) Vaccinate 50 birds, do not vaccinate 50 other birds, and expose all 100 to the disease.
(4) Vaccinate 50 birds, do not vaccinate 50 other birds, and expose only the vaccinated birds to the disease.

2 Scientists have cloned sheep but have not yet cloned a human. The best explanation for this situation is that

(1) the technology to clone humans has not been explored
(2) human reproduction is very different from that of other mammals
(3) there are many ethical problems involved in cloning humans
(4) cloning humans would take too long

3 In an ecosystem, what happens to the atoms of certain chemical elements such as carbon, oxygen, and nitrogen?

(1) They move into and out of living systems.
(2) They are never found in living systems.
(3) They move out of living systems and never return.
(4) They move into living systems and remain there.

4 The main function of the human digestive system is to

(1) rid the body of cellular waste materials
(2) process organic molecules so they can enter cells
(3) break down glucose in order to release energy
(4) change amino acids into proteins and carbohydrates

5 The normal sodium level in human blood is 135 mEq/L. If a blood test taken immediately after a meal reveals a sodium level of 150 mEq/L, what will most likely result?

(1) Antibody production will increase.
(2) The person will move to an ecosystem with a lower sodium level.
(3) The nutritional relationships between humans and other organisms will change.
(4) An adjustment within the human body will be made to restore homeostasis.

6 The diagram below represents a process that occurs within a cell in the human pancreas.

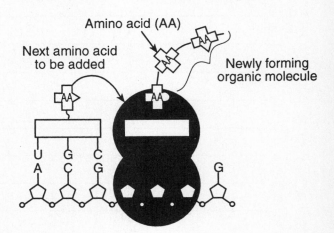

This process is known as

(1) digestion by enzymes
(2) protein synthesis
(3) energy production
(4) replication of DNA

7 When a person's teeth are being x rayed, other body parts of this person are covered with a protective lead blanket to prevent

(1) loss of hair
(2) increase in cell size
(3) changes in DNA molecules
(4) changes in glucose structure

8 The diagrams below represent portions of the genes that code for wing structure in two organisms of the same species. Gene 1 was taken from the cells of a female with normal wings, and gene 2 was taken from the cells of a female with abnormal wings.

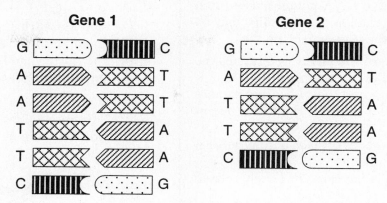

Gene 1   **Gene 2**

The abnormal wing structure was most likely due to

(1) an insertion
(2) a substitution

(3) a deletion
(4) normal replication

---

9 The diagram below represents a cell in water. Formulas of molecules that can move freely across the cell membrane are shown. Some molecules are located inside the cell and others are in the water outside the cell.

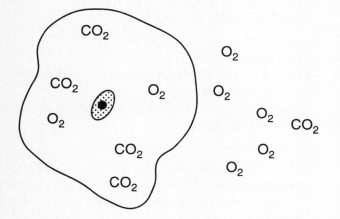

Based on the distribution of these molecules, what would most likely happen after a period of time?

(1) The concentration of O_2 will increase inside the cell.
(2) The concentration of CO_2 will remain the same inside the cell.
(3) The concentration of O_2 will remain the same outside the cell.
(4) The concentration of CO_2 will decrease outside the cell.

10 During the warm temperatures of summer, the arctic fox produces enzymes that cause its fur to become reddish brown. During the cold temperatures of winter, these enzymes do not function. As a result, the fox has a white coat that blends into the snowy background. This change in fur color shows that

(1) the genes of a fox are made of unstable DNA
(2) mutations can be caused by temperature extremes
(3) random alteration of DNA can occur on certain chromosomes
(4) the expression of certain genes is affected by temperature

11 Which phrases best identify characteristics of asexual reproduction?

(1) one parent, union of gametes, offspring similar to but not genetically identical to the parent
(2) one parent, no union of gametes, offspring genetically identical to parents
(3) two parents, union of gametes, offspring similar to but not genetically identical to parents
(4) two parents, no union of gametes, offspring genetically identical to parents

12 To determine the identity of their biological parents, adopted children sometimes request DNA tests. These tests involve comparing DNA samples from the child to DNA samples taken from the likely parents. Possible relationships may be determined from these tests because the

(1) base sequence of the father determines the base sequence of the offspring
(2) DNA of parents and their offspring is more similar than the DNA of nonfamily members
(3) position of the genes on each chromosome is unique to each family
(4) mutation rate is the same in closely related individuals

13 Although all the body cells in an animal contain the same hereditary information, they do not all look and function the same way. The cause of this difference is that during differentiation

(1) embryonic cells use different portions of their genetic information
(2) the number of genes increases as embryonic cells move to new locations
(3) embryonic cells delete portions of chromosomes
(4) genes in embryonic body cells mutate rapidly

14 According to the theory of natural selection, why are some individuals more likely than others to survive and reproduce?

(1) Some individuals pass on to their offspring new characteristics they have acquired during their lifetimes.
(2) Some individuals are better adapted to exist in their environment than others are.
(3) Some individuals do not pass on to their offspring new characteristics they have acquired during their lifetimes.
(4) Some individuals tend to produce fewer offspring than others in the same environment.

15 The energy an organism requires to transport materials and eliminate wastes is obtained directly from

(1) DNA   (3) hormones
(2) starch   (4) ATP

16 New inheritable characteristics would be *least* likely to result from

(1) mutations which occur in muscle cells and skin cells
(2) mutations which occur in male gametes
(3) mutations which occur in female gametes
(4) the sorting and recombination of existing genes during meiosis and fertilization

17 The diagram below shows the human female reproductive system.

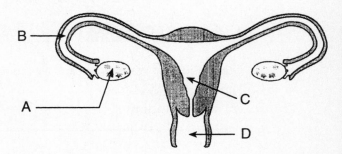

The fetus normally develops within structure

(1) A   (3) C
(2) B   (4) D

18 One way to produce large numbers of genetically identical offspring is by

(1) cloning
(2) fertilization
(3) changing genes by agents such as radiation or chemicals
(4) inserting a DNA segment into a different DNA molecule

19 Most cells in the body of a fruit fly contain eight chromosomes. How many of these chromosomes were contributed by each parent of the fruit fly?

(1) 8   (3) 16
(2) 2   (4) 4

20 Which disease damages the human immune system, leaving the body open to certain infectious agents?

(1) flu   (3) chicken pox
(2) AIDS   (4) pneumonia

21 According to the interpretation of the fossil record by many scientists, during which time interval shown on the time line below did increasingly complex multicellular organisms appear on Earth?

Time Line

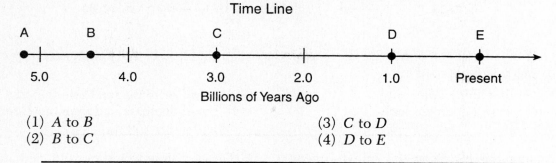

Billions of Years Ago

(1) A to B
(2) B to C
(3) C to D
(4) D to E

---

22 Which characteristic of sexual reproduction has specifically favored the survival of animals that live on land?

(1) fusion of gametes in the outside environment
(2) male gametes that may be carried by the wind
(3) fertilization within the body of the female
(4) female gametes that develop within ovaries

23 What usually results when an organism fails to maintain homeostasis?

(1) Growth rates within organs become equal.
(2) The organism becomes ill or may die.
(3) A constant sugar supply for the cells is produced.
(4) The water balance in the tissues of the organism stabilizes.

24 Which activity is *not* a response of human white blood cells to pathogens?

(1) engulfing and destroying bacteria
(2) producing antibodies
(3) identifying invaders for destruction
(4) removing carbon dioxide

25 In some individuals, the immune system attacks substances such as grass pollen that are usually harmless, resulting in

(1) an allergic reaction
(2) a form of cancer
(3) an insulin imbalance
(4) a mutation

26 A characteristic shared by all enzymes, hormones, and antibodies is that their function is determined by the

(1) shape of their molecules
(2) DNA they contain
(3) inorganic molecules they contain
(4) organelles present in their structure

27 The diagram below shows the relationships between the organisms in and around a pond.

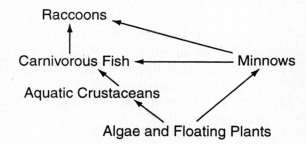

One additional biotic factor needed to make this a stable ecosystem is the presence of

(1) producers
(2) herbivores
(3) decomposers
(4) consumers

28 What is the major environmental factor limiting the numbers of autotrophs at great depths in the ocean?

(1) type of seafloor
(2) amount of light
(3) availability of minerals
(4) absence of biotic factors

29 The diagram below shows a food chain.

Grasses $\longrightarrow$ Rabbits $\longrightarrow$ Bobcats

If the population of bobcats decreases, what will most likely be the long-term effect on the rabbit population?

(1) It will increase, only.
(2) It will decrease, only.
(3) It will increase and then decrease.
(4) It will decrease and then increase.

30 An owl cannot entirely digest the animals upon which it preys. Therefore, each day it expels from its mouth a pellet composed of materials such as fur, bones, and cartilage. By examining owl pellets, ecologists are able to determine the

(1) autotrophs that owls prefer
(2) organisms that feed on owls
(3) pathogens that affect owls
(4) consumers that owls prefer

31 In some areas, foresters plant one tree for every tree they cut. This activity is an example of

(1) lack of management of nonrenewable natural resources
(2) a good conservation practice for renewable natural resources
(3) a good conservation practice for nonrenewable natural resources
(4) lack of concern for renewable natural resources

32 To minimize negative environmental impact, a community should

(1) approve the weekly spraying of pesticides on the plants in a local park
(2) grant a permit to a chemical manufacturing company to build a factory by one of its lakes, with no restrictions on waste disposal
(3) make a decision about building a new road in a hiking area based only on the economic advantages
(4) set policy after considering both the risks and benefits involved in building a toxic waste site within its boundaries

33 Deforestation would most immediately result in

(1) the disappearance of native species
(2) industrialization of an area
(3) the depletion of the ozone shield
(4) global warming

34 El Niño is a short-term climatic change that causes ocean waters to remain warm when they should normally be cool. The warmer temperatures disrupt food webs and alter weather patterns. Which occurrence would most likely result from these changes?

(1) Some species would become extinct, and other species would evolve to take their place.
(2) Some populations in affected areas would be reduced, while other populations would increase temporarily.
(3) The flow of energy through the ecosystem would remain unchanged.
(4) The genes of individual organisms would mutate to adapt to the new environmental conditions.

35 Toxic chemicals called PCBs, produced as a result of manufacturing processes, were dumped into the Hudson River. What was most likely a result of this action on fish in the Hudson River?

(1) Some fish became unfit to eat.
(2) The fish populations increased.
(3) Thermal pollution of the river increased, decreasing the fish population.
(4) The carrying capacity for fish increased in the river.

Part B

Answer all questions in this part

Directions (36–63): For those questions that are followed by four choices, circle the number of the choice that best completes the statement or answers the question. For all other questions in this part, follow the directions given in the question and record your answers in the spaces provided. [30].

Base your answers to questions 36 through 38 on the diagram below, which shows some of the specialized organelles in a single-celled organism, and on your knowledge of biology.

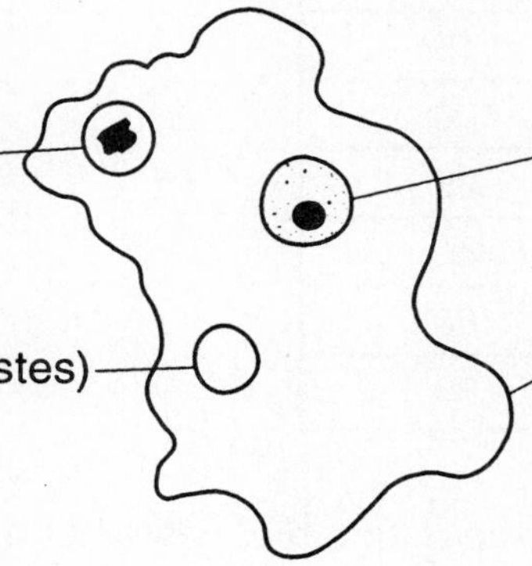

A (contains food)

B (contains liquid wastes)

C (contains DNA)

D (contains receptors)

36 Write the letter of *one* of the labeled organelles and state the name of that organelle. [1]

_____

36 ☐

37 Explain how the function of the organelle you selected in question 36 assists in the maintenance of homeostasis. [1]

_____

_____

_____

37 ☐

38 Identify a system in the human body that performs a function similar to that of the organelle you selected in question 36. [1]

_____

_____

38 ☐

Base your answers to questions 39 through 42 on the information and data table below and on your knowledge of biology.

A student counted the total number of leaves in a group of duckweed plants (*Lemna gibba*) over a 5-day period. The data collected are shown in the table below.

Growth of Duckweed Leaves

Time in Days	Number of Leaves
0	15
1	20
2	25
3	40
4	60
5	80

Directions (39–40): Using the information in the data table, construct a line graph on the grid provided on the next page following the directions below.

39 Mark an appropriate scale on each labeled axis.   [1]

40 Plot the data from the data table. Surround each point with a small circle and connect the points.   [1]

Example:

Growth of Duckweed Leaves

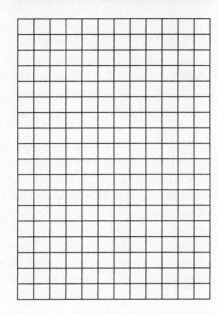

Time in Days

39 ☐

40 ☐

41 The time it takes for the number of leaves to increase from 15 to 30 is approximately

(1) 2.0 days

(2) 2.3 days

(3) 2.9 days

(4) 3.2 days

41 ☐

42 State what would most likely happen to the production of oxygen by duckweed plants if the intensity and duration of exposure to light were increased.   [1]

_____

_____

_____

_____

42 ☐

Base your answers to questions 43 through 47 on the passage below and on your knowledge of biology.

Help Wanted — Bacteria for Environmental Cleanup

The location of a former fuel storage depot and packaging operation in the industrial port of Toronto, Canada, is the proposed site of a sports arena and entertainment complex. The problem is that the soil in this area was contaminated with gasoline, diesel fuel, home heating oil, and grease from the operation of the previous facility. Unless these substances are removed, the project cannot proceed.

The traditional method of cleaning up such sites is the "dig and dump" method, in which the contaminated soil is removed, deposited in landfills, and replaced with clean soil. This "dig and dump" method is messy and costly and adds to landfills that are already overloaded. A technique known as bio-remediation, which was used to help in the cleanup of the *Exxon Valdez* oil spill in Alaska, offered a relatively inexpensive way of dealing with this pollution problem. This cleanup process cost $1.4 million, one-third of the cost of the "dig and dump" method, and involved encasing 85,000 tons of soil in a plastic "biocell" the size of a football field. This plastic-encased soil contained naturally occurring bacteria that would eventually have cleaned up the area after 50 years or more with the amounts of oxygen and nutrients naturally found in the soil. Air, water, and fertilizer were piped into the biocell, stimulating the bacteria to reproduce rapidly and speed up the process. The cleanup by this technique was begun in August and completed in November of the same year. The bacteria attack parts of the contaminating molecules by breaking the carbon-to-carbon bonds that hold them together. This helps to change these molecules in the soil into carbon dioxide and water.

Although this method is effective for cleaning up some forms of pollution, bio-remediation is not effective for inorganic materials such as lead or other heavy metals since these wastes are already in a base state that cannot be degraded any further.

43 The use of bio-remediation by humans is an example of

(1) interfering with nature so that natural processes cannot take place

(2) using a completely unnatural method to solve a problem

(3) solving a problem by speeding up natural processes

(4) being unaware of and not using natural processes

43 ☐

44 The bacteria convert the contaminants into

(1) carbon dioxide and water

(2) toxic substances

(3) proteins and fats

(4) diesel fuel and grease

44 ☐

45 State an ecological drawback to the use of the "dig and dump" method.   [1]

_____

_____

_____

45 □

46 Explain why the cleanup took only 3 months.   [1]

_____

_____

_____

46 □

47 Bio-remediation is *not* an effective method for breaking down

(1) grease

(2) gasoline

(3) fuel for diesel engines and furnaces

(4) heavy metals such as lead

47 □

Base your answer to question 48 on the information and data table below and on your knowledge of biology.

Two species of fish were subjected to a series of treatments. The number of red blood cells flowing per minute through one capillary in the tail of each fish was counted and the average calculated. The data table below shows the treatments given to each species of fish and the results of the various treatments.

Data Table

Treatment	Species of Fish	Number of Fish Used	Average Number of Red Blood Cells
Adrenaline added (1:10,000 solution)	Trout	10	35
Adrenaline added (1:1,000 solution)	Trout	10	50
50% alcohol solution added	Trout	5	78
Temperature reduced (25°C to 4°C)	Trout	6	30
Lactic acid added (1:5,000 solution)	Sunfish	6	90
25% alcohol solution added	Sunfish	6	89
Adrenaline added (1:10,000 solution)	Sunfish	6	17
Temperature reduced (25°C to 4°C)	Sunfish	6	14
Temperature increased (15°C to 25°C)	Sunfish	6	22

48 State *two* errors in this investigation.   [2]

_____

_____

_____

_____

_____

48 ☐

49 Meiosis occurs in the development of sex cells. Mitosis occurs in most other cells. Identify *two* additional differences between these processes.   [2]

_____

_____

_____

_____

49 ☐

50 The chart below shows information about the relationship between the age of the mother and the occurrence of Down syndrome in the child.

Age of Mother	Occurrence of Down Syndrome per 1000 Births
25	0.8
30	1.0
35	3.0
40	10.0
45	30.0
50	80.0

State *one* conclusion that can be drawn from the chart concerning the relationship between the age of the mother and the chance of her having a child with Down syndrome. [1]

_____

_____

_____

50 ☐

51 Using *one* specific example, identify *one* action taken by a mother that could have a negative effect on the embryonic development of her baby. [1]

_____

_____

_____

51 ☐

52 In desert environments, organisms that cannot maintain a constant internal body temperature, such as snakes and lizards, rarely go out during the hot, sunny daylight hours. They stay in the shade, under rocks, or in burrows during the day. Explain how this behavior helps maintain homeostasis in these organisms. [1]

_____

_____

_____

52 ☐

53 In the early 1980s, scientists discovered holes in the ozone shield surrounding Earth. State *one* negative effect this environmental change could have on humans.   [1]

_____

_____

_____

54 In an investigation, students determined the average rate of movement of gill covers of a species of freshwater fish at different temperatures. The results are shown in the data table below.

Data Table

Group	Number of Fish	Temperature (°C)	Average Rate of Movement of Gill Covers per Minute
1	5	10	15
2	6	15	25
3	4	18	30
4	7	20	38
5	6	23	60
6	4	25	57
7	4	27	25

Which labeled axes should be used to graph the relationship between the two variables?

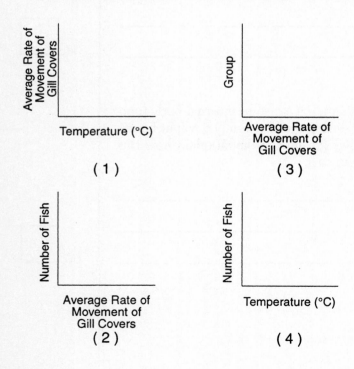

(1)

(3)

(2)

(4)

Base your answers to questions 55 through 57 on the diagram below and on your knowledge of biology. The diagram shows an interpretation of relationships based on evolutionary theory. The letters represent different species.

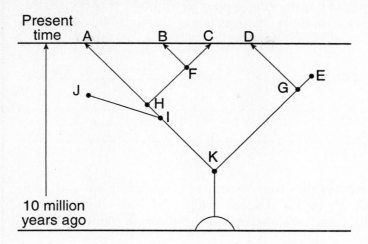

55 Explain why species *B* and *C* are more closely related than species *A* and *C* are. [1]

_____

_____

_____

55 [   ]

56 The diagram indicates that a common ancestor for species *C* and *E* is species

(1) *F*

(2) *G*

(3) *H*

(4) *K*

56 [   ]

57 Which species are *least* likely to be vital parts of a present-day ecosystem?

(1) *A* and *E*

(2) *C* and *D*

(3) *E* and *J*

(4) *B* and *F*

57 [   ]

58 Hemoglobin is a complex protein molecule found in red blood cells. Hemoglobin with the normal sequence of amino acids is able to carry oxygen to body cells effectively. In the disorder known as sickle-cell anemia, one amino acid is substituted for another in the hemoglobin. One characteristic of this disorder is poor distribution of oxygen to the body cells. Explain how the change in amino acid sequence of this protein could cause the results described.   [1]

_____

_____

_____

59 Recently, scientists have been sent to rain forest areas by pharmaceutical and agricultural corporations to bring back samples of seeds, fruits, and leaves before these densely vegetated areas are destroyed. State *one* reason these corporations are interested in obtaining these samples.   [1]

_____

_____

_____

60 Two species of microorganisms were placed in the same culture dish, which included basic materials necessary for life. The size of each population increased during the first three days. After one week, the population size of one species began to decline each day. State *one* possible reason for this decline.   [1]

_____

_____

_____

61 State what could happen to a species in a changing environment if the members of that species do not express any genetic variations.   [1]

_____

_____

_____

62 In certain areas of the United States, the populations of wolves and other predators have decreased. As a result, deer populations in these areas have increased. Describe *one* way that an increase in the deer population can be harmful to humans.   [1]

_____

_____

_____

62 ☐

63 State *one* environmental impact of reduced funding for public transportation (trains, city buses, school buses, etc.) on future generations. Explain your answer.   [1]

_____

_____

_____

63 ☐

☐

Total Score for Part B

Part C

Answer all questions in Part C.

Directions (64–71): Record your answers in the spaces provided in this examination booklet.

Base your answers to questions 64 through 66 on the information below and on your knowledge of biology.

An investigation was performed to determine the effects of enzyme X on three different disaccharides (double sugars) at 37°C. Three test tubes were set up as shown in the diagram below.

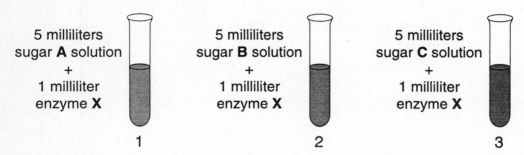

At the end of 5 minutes, the solution in each test tube was tested for the presence of disaccharides (double sugars) and monosaccharides (simple sugars). The results of these tests are shown in the table below.

	Test Tube 1	Test Tube 2	Test Tube 3
Monosaccharide	not present	not present	present
Disaccharide	present	present	not present

64 What can be concluded about the activity of enzyme X from the data table?   [1]

_____

_____

_____

64 [ ]

65 With only the materials list supplied below and common laboratory equipment, design an investigation that would show how a change in pH would affect the activity of enzyme *X*. Your design need only include detailed procedure and a data table. [3]

Materials

Enzyme *X*
Sugar *C* solution
Indicators
Substances of various pH values —
  vinegar (acidic)
  water (neutral)
  baking soda (basic)

Procedure:

_____

_____

_____

_____

_____

_____

Data Table:

65

66 State *one* safety precaution that should be used during the investigation.   [1]

_____

_____

_____

_____

66 ☐

67 For many years, humans have used a variety of techniques that have influenced the genetic makeup of organisms. These techniques have led to the production of new varieties of organisms that possess characteristics that are useful to humans. Identify *one* technique presently being used to alter the genetic makeup of an organism, and explain how humans can benefit from this change. Your answer must include at least:

- the name of the technique used to alter the genetic makeup   [1]
- a brief description of what is involved in this technique   [1]
- *one* specific example of how this technique has been used   [1]
- a statement of how humans have benefited from the production of this new variety of organism   [1]

_____

_____

_____

_____

_____

_____

_____

_____

_____

_____

_____

67 ☐

68 All living organisms are dependent on a stable environment.

   a Describe how humans have made the environment less stable by:
- changing the chemical composition of air, soil, and water   [1]
- reducing the biodiversity of an area   [1]
- introducing technologies   [1]

_____

_____

_____

_____

_____

_____

_____

   b Describe *two* specific ways recently used by humans to reduce the amount of chemicals being added to the environment.   [2]

_____

_____

_____

_____

_____

68 ☐

69 A European species of rabbit was released on a ranch in Victoria, Australia. The species thrived and reproduced rapidly. The rabbits overgrazed the land, reducing the food supply for the sheep. The *Myxoma sp.* virus was used to kill the rabbits. The first time this virus was applied, it killed 99.8% of the rabbits. When the rabbits became a problem again, the virus was applied a second time. This time, only 90% of the rabbits were killed. When the rabbits became a problem a third time, the virus was applied once again, and only 50% of the rabbits were killed. Today, this virus has little or no effect on this species of rabbit.

Explain what happened to the species of rabbit as a result of the use of this virus. You must *include* and *circle* the following terms in your answer.   [4]

- gene
- adaptive value *or* adaptation *or* adapted
- variation
- survival of the fittest

_____

_____

_____

_____

_____

_____

_____

_____

_____

_____

69 ☐

Base your answers to questions 70 and 71 on the information in the newspaper article below and on your knowledge of biology.

Patients to test tumor fighter

Boston—Endostatin, the highly publicized experimental cancer drug that wiped out tumors in mice and raised the hopes of cancer patients, will be tested on patients this year.

"I think it's exciting, but ... you always have the risk that something will fail in testing," said Dr. Judah Folkman, the Harvard University researcher whose assistant, Michael O'Reilly, discovered endostatin.

Endostatin and a sister protein, angiostatin, destroy the tumors' ability to sprout new blood vessels. This makes cancer fall dormant in lab animals, but no one knows if that will happen in humans.

The Associated Press

70 Explain why it is necessary to test these experimental drugs on human volunteers as well as on test animals.   [1]

_____

_____

_____

70 [ ]

71 State *one* reason that mice are often used by scientists for testing experimental drugs that may be used by humans.   [1]

_____

_____

_____

71 [ ]

[ ]

Total Score for Part C

Glossary

abiotic nonliving parts of the environment

acid a compound that releases hydrogen ions when dissolved in water; a substance, such as vinegar, with a sour taste

acid rain rain that is more acidic than normal

active transport the process by which cells use energy to transport molecules through the cell membrane from areas of low concentration to areas of high concentration

adaptive value any trait that helps an organism survive and reproduce under a given set of environmental conditions

agarose a gel-like substance used in bacterial cultures

AIDS (acquired immunodeficiency syndrome) the disease that results when the HIV virus attacks the human immune system

allergy a condition in which a person's immune system is overly sensitive to environmental substances that are normally harmless

amino acid any one of several building blocks of protein

animal a complex, multicellular organism with specialized tissues and organs, but no cell walls; a heterotroph that obtains energy by consuming other organisms

antibody a protein, produced by the immune system, that either attacks invading pathogens or marks them for killing

antigen a molecule found on the outer surfaces of cells that the immune system recognizes as either part of the body or an outside invader

antihistamine a substance that reduces the effects of histamines and the symptoms they cause

artificial selection the process of breeding two organisms with desirable characteristics to produce offspring that have the advantages of both parents

asexual reproduction a method of reproduction in which all the genes passed on to the offspring come from a single individual or parent

assumption something accepted as true that may or may not actually be true

ATP (adenine triphosphate) a compound that stores energy in cells

autotroph an organism that produces its own food; the source of energy for all other living things on Earth

bacterium any one of many single-celled organisms without a distinct nucleus

balance a tool that measures mass by comparing the unknown mass of an object with an object of known mass

base a compound that produces hydroxide ions when dissolved in water

bias a tendency to favor something; prejudice

biochemical process a chemical process that occurs in a living thing

biodiversity the variety of species in an area

biome large groups of ecosystems with similar climates and organisms; examples include the tundra, taiga, temperate forest, chaparral, tropical rain forest, desert, temperate grassland, tropical savanna grassland, and polar and high-mountain ice

biosphere all of Earth's ecosystems, collectively; the biologically inhabited portions of Earth, including all of the water, land, and air in which organisms survive

biotechnology the combination of technology and biological sciences

biotic the living parts of the environment

bond the chemical link between atoms that hold molecules together

calibrate to adjust the scale of a measurement tool

carnivore an organism that survives by eating animals

carrying capacity the largest population of any single species that an area can support

catalyst a substance that can speed up the rate of a chemical reaction without being changed or used up during the reaction

cell the basic unit of structure and function that makes up all organisms

cell membrane the thin boundary between the cell and its environment

cellular respiration the process in which nutrients are broken apart, releasing the chemical energy stored in them

Celsius a temperature scale based on 100 equal units, with 0 as the freezing point of water and 100 as the boiling point of water

chloroplast the green organelle that contains chlorophyll; where photosynthesis takes place

chromatography a laboratory technique used to separate mixtures of molecules

chromosome a thick, threadlike structure that contains genetic information in the form of DNA

circulation the flow of materials within a cell as well as between parts of a multicellular organism

classify to group things based upon their similarities

climax community a relatively diverse and stable ecosystem that is the end result of succession

clone an organism that is genetically identical to the organism from which it was produced

cloning a technique used to make identical organisms

community a combination of all the different populations that live and interact in the same environment

competition the struggle between organisms for the same limited resources in a particular area

compound light microscope a tool that uses more than one lens and a light source to magnify an object

conclusion the decision made about the outcome of an experiment; usually based on how well the actual result matches the predicted result

consumer an organism that obtains its energy from producers

control that group in an experiment in which everything—except the variable to be tested—is identical; the standard of comparison in an experiment

controlled experiment an experiment in which all variables—except for the one being tested—are exactly the same

coverslip a thin slice of glass that covers the specimen on a slide

cytoplasm the jellylike substance that is between the cell membrane and the nucleus and that contains specialized structures

data the results of specific trials or tests completed during experiments

decomposer an organism, generally a bacterium or fungus, that consumes dead organisms and organic waste

decomposition the process whereby dead organisms, as well as the wastes produced by living organisms, are broken down into their raw materials and returned to the ecosystem

deforestation forest destruction that results from human activity

dependent variable the part of an experiment that is changed to test a hypothesis

depletion a serious decline or reduction

detrimental damaging; harmful

deviation a change from normal circumstances

dichotomous key a guide that compares pairs of observable traits to help the user identify an organism

differentiation the process that transforms developing cells into specialized cells with different structures and functions

diffusion the movement of molecules from areas of high concentration to areas of low concentration

digestion the process that breaks down large food molecules into simpler molecules that the organism can use

direct harvesting the destruction of an organism, or the removal of an organism from its habitat

disease a condition, other than injury, that prevents the body from working as it should

dissection the act of cutting apart a dead organism to examine its internal structure

DNA (deoxyribonucleic acid) the material found in all cells that contains genetic information about that organism

dynamic equilibrium the constant small corrections that normally occur to keep an organism's internal environment within the limits needed for survival

ecological niche the specific role played by an organism or a population of organisms in the ecosystem

ecological succession the process by which an existing community is replaced by another community

ecology the study of how living things interact with one another and with their environment

ecosystem all the living and nonliving things that interact in a specific area; a subdivision of the environment

egg a sex cell produced by a female

electronic balance a balance that measures mass automatically

electrophoresis a tool that allows scientists to separate mixtures of molecules according to size

element a substance consisting of only one kind of atom

embryo an organism in the early stages of development (prior to birth)

endocrine glands various hormone-producing glands that secrete substances directly into the blood or lymph

endoplasmic reticulum an organelle that transports proteins and other materials from one part of the cell to another

energy flow the movement of energy through an ecosystem

energy pyramid a diagram showing how food energy moves through the ecosystem

environment every living and nonliving thing that surrounds an organism

environmental impact statement a statement that includes an analysis of how a new project or technology might affect the environment

enzymes proteins that speed up the rate of chemical reactions in living things

equilibrium a state of balance and stability

estrogen a hormone (produced by the ovaries) that controls female sexual development and the reproductive process

evidence support for the idea that something is true

evolution the process by which species have changed over time

excretion the removal of all the wastes produced by the cells of the body

experiment a series of trials or tests that are done to support or refute a hypothesis

expressed the way that an unseen gene is seen in an organism as an actual physical trait

extinction the disappearance of all members of a species from Earth

Fallopian tubes that part of the female reproductive system where the egg cell is fertilized by the sperm cell

feedback mechanism a cycle in which the output of a system either modifies or reinforces the first action taken by the system

fertilization the process that combines a sperm cell and an egg cell

fetus the unborn, developing young of an animal during the later stages of development

finite limited

flow of energy the movement of energy through an ecosystem

food chain a representation that identifies the specific feeding relationships among organisms

food web a representation of many interconnected food chains that shows the feeding relationships among producers, consumers, and decomposers

forceps a tool used mainly during dissection to lift out small parts, to move structures, and to pry parts open

fossil the preserved remains of ancient organisms

fossil fuel a fuel, such as coal and gas, that comes from the remains of organisms that lived millions of years ago

fossil record a collection of fossils used to represent Earth's history

fungus the kingdom of organisms that are mostly multicellular, have cell walls made of chitin, and are heterotrophic

gamete an egg or sperm cell; a sex cell

gas exchange the process of obtaining oxygen from the environment and releasing carbon dioxide

gene a segment of DNA (on a chromosome) that contains the code for a specific trait

gene expression see *expressed;* the result of activated genes

genetic engineering a set of technologies that humans use to alter the genetic instructions of an organism by substituting DNA molecules

genetic recombination the formation of a new combination of genes during sexual reproduction

genetic variation the normal differences found among offspring

geologic time Earth's history as revealed by layers of rock

global warming a increase in Earth's average surface temperature caused by an increase in greenhouse gases

glucose a sugar that is a major source of energy for cells

graduated cylinder a tool used to measure the volume of a liquid

greenhouse effect the trapping of heat by gases in the atmosphere

greenhouse gas an atmospheric gas that traps heat

growth an increase in the size or number of cells

guard cells specialized cells that control the opening and closing of the pores on the surface of a leaf

habitat the place where an animal or plant lives

herbivore an organism that eats only plants

heredity the passing of traits from parent to offspring

heterotroph organism that cannot make its own food; a consumers

histamine a chemical that is released as the immune system's reaction to an allergy

homeostasis the ability of an organism to maintain a stable internal environment even when the external environment changes

hormone a chemical produced in the endocrine glands

host the organism in a parasitic relationship that provides a home and/or food for the parasite

hot water bath in the science laboratory, usually a large beaker of water heated on a hot plate; used to heat test tubes that contain a flammable liquid, such as alcohol

humerus the long bone in the upper part of the arm

hypothesis a statement that predicts a relationship between cause and effect in a way that can be tested

immune system the body's primary defense against disease-causing pathogens

immunity the body's ability to destroy pathogens before they cause disease

independent variable a factor that might influence the dependent variable in an experiment

indicator a substance that changes color when it encounters certain chemical conditions

industrialization the process of converting an economy into one in which large-scale manufacturing is the primary economic base

inference a conclusion or deduction based on observations

infinite without limits or bounds

inorganic a type of molecule that does not contain both carbon and hydrogen but can contain any other combination of elements

insulin a hormone that prompts glucose to move from the blood into body cells, resulting in a lower glucose level in the blood

limiting factor any factor in the environment that limits the size of a population

lipid any one of a group of organic compounds that includes oils, fats, and waxes

magnification the ability of a microscope to make an object appear larger

mass a measure of the quantity of matter in an object

meiosis the process that results in the production of sex cells (sperm and egg)

meniscus the curved surface at the top of a column of liquid

metabolism all the chemical reactions that occur within the cells of an organism

metric ruler a tool used to measure the length of an object

microbe any microscopic organism

micrometer a unit of length equal to one millionth of a meter

microscope a tool that uses a lens or a combination of lenses to magnify an object

mitochondria pod-shaped organelles that contain enzymes used to extract energy from nutrients

mitosis the process that divides the cell's nucleus into two, each with a complete set of genetic material from the parent cell

model a representation used to explain or demonstrate a process or structure; also used to predict what might occur in a new situation

molecule a particle in which two or more atoms combine to form a single unit; the smallest unit of a compound

muscular system a body system comprised of tissue that contracts when it is stimulated; the combination of muscles that enables the body to move

mutation any alteration in the sequence of DNA

natural selection the process by which the organisms that are best adapted to a specific environment survive and produce more offspring than organisms that are not as well adapted

niche the specific role played by an organism in its ecosystem

nitrogen cycle the movement of nitrogen from the atmosphere to the soil and organisms and then back to the atmosphere

nitrogen fixation the process by which nitrogen forms compounds that can be used by living things

nonrenewable resource any resource, such as fossil fuels and minerals, that cannot be replaced

nuclear fuel an energy source that results from splitting atoms

nucleus a large structure within a cell that controls the cell's metabolism and stores genetic information, including chromosomes and DNA

nucleic acids large, complex organic molecules that contain the instructions cells need to carry out their life processes

nutrient a substance that provides the body with the materials and energy needed to carry out the basic life of cells

objective one of the lenses of a microscope

observation any information that is collected with any of the senses

ocular the eyepiece lens of a microscope

opinion ideas people have that may or may not be based in fact

optimum the most favorable condition

organ a body structure made of different kinds of tissues combined to perform a specific function

organ system several organs that work together to perform a major function in the body

organelle a structure within the cell that carries out a specific function

organic term used to describe molecules that contain both hydrogen and carbon

organic compound a compound that contains both hydrogen and carbon

ovary the organ of the human female reproductive system that produces an egg cell, the female gamete

overproduction the potential for a species to increase its numbers beyond the area's carrying capacity

oviduct the part of the female reproductive system where the egg cell is fertilized by the sperm

oxygen-carbon dioxide cycle the movement of oxygen and carbon dioxide between living things and the environment

ozone shield the layer of ozone gas in the upper atmosphere that protects Earth from some of the sun's radiation

pancreas an endocrine organ that secretes insulin

parasite an organism that survives by living and feeding on other organisms

parasitic relationship an arrangement in which one organism lives in or on a host organism, deriving some or all of its nourishment from the host, to the host's detriment

pathogen an organism that invades the body, causing disease

peer review the process by which scientists carefully examine the work of other scientists to look for possible flaws in their experimental design or their interpretation of results

pH a measure of whether a substance is acidic, neutral, or basic

photosynthesis the process by which some organisms are able to capture light energy and use it to make food from carbon dioxide and water

pioneer species the first organisms to become established in a new habitat

pipette a laboratory tool that looks like a slender tube but works something like an eyedropper

placenta the organ that enables nutrients and oxygen to pass from the mother's blood to the fetus, and waste products to pass from the fetus to the mother's blood

plant any complex, multicellular organism that obtains energy through photosynthesis and consists of cell walls and specialized tissues and organs

poaching illegally capturing or killing an organism

pollution a harmful change in the chemical makeup of the soil, water, or air

population all the individuals of a single species that live in a specific area

predator an animal that hunts and kills other animals for food

predator-prey relationship the connection between predators and prey that limits the growth of both populations

prey an animal that is hunted and killed by predators

primary succession the first group of communities that moves into a previously lifeless habitat

producer an organism that makes its own food from light energy and inorganic materials

progesterone a hormone associated with sexual development and the reproductive system

proportion the relationship of one thing to another in terms of size, number, amount, or degree

protist a single-celled organism with both its genetic materials and its organelles enclosed in membranes

quarantine confined isolation

radius one of the two long bones of the lower forearm

receptor molecule certain protein molecules in the cell membrane that can receive chemical messages from other cells

recombination the additional mixing of genetic material from a sperm and egg which results in a unique combination of genes

refute to disprove

replicate to copy

renewable resource Earth's resources, such as our food supply and solar energy, which, given time, can be replaced

research plan the initial stage of an experiment that involves finding background information, developing a hypothesis, and devising an experimental method for testing the hypothesis

respiration the process by which the chemical bond energy stored in nutrients is released for use in cells

reproduction the process by which organisms produce new organisms of the same type

ribosome one of the tiny structures in the cell that is the site of protein production

rider one of the devices that is moved along the beam of a balance

scavenger a carnivore that feeds on the bodies of dead organisms

science a way of learning about the natural world and the knowledge gained through that process

scientific literacy a basic knowledge of the natural world combined with an understanding of the diverse ways that scientists gain knowledge

scientific theory a concept, which has been tested and confirmed in many different ways, that explains a wide variety of observations

secondary succession a type of change that occurs when a disturbance empties an existing habitat without destroying the soil

selective breeding the process of choosing a few organisms with desirable traits to serve as the parents of the next generation

sensor a structure that reacts to stimuli by sending a nerve impulse to the brain

sex cell an egg (female) or a sperm (male)

sexual reproduction a method of reproduction that involves two parents to produce offspring that are genetically different from either parent

sibling a brother or sister

simple sugar the result of digested starches

skeletal system the body system that contains the bones, provides shape and support, and protects internal organs

smog a kind of air pollution that results when certain pollutants react with sunlight

species a group of organisms that share certain characteristics and can mate with one another, producing fertile offspring

sperm the male sex cell

splice to join two things together

stain a chemical used to make cell structures more visible when viewed under a microscope

steady state the condition in which something remains relatively constant in spite of minor fluctuations

stereoscope a microscope that uses two eyepieces; often used for dissections

stimulus any change in the environment that causes an organism to react

stomata a tiny pore found on the underside of most leaves

subunit the section of a DNA molecule that contains a sugar, a phosphate, and a base

symbiotic a kind of long-term association between members of different species in which at least one species benefits and neither species is harmed

synthesis a life process that involves combining simple substances into more complex substances

tare button a function on an electronic balance that returns the mass reading to zero

technology all of the practical scientific knowledge that has been used to meet human needs

template the pattern for a new molecule

testes the male reproductive organ that produces sperm and the hormone testosterone

testosterone a hormone associated with male sexual development and reproduction

theory an explanation, supported by many observations and/or experiments, that can be used to accurately explain related occurrences

thermal pollution a kind of water pollution in which the temperature of the water increases

tissue a group of specialized cells that perform a specific function

toxic poisonous

trait a characteristic that is passed from parent to offspring through the genes

trade-off an exchange or agreement made to reach a compromise

transpiration the process whereby plants absorb water through their roots and eliminate it through tiny pores on the undersides of their leaves

triple-beam balance a tool, with a single pan and three bars calibrated in grams, used to measure mass

tumor a clump of cells that develops when cancerous cells divide uncontrollably

ulna one of the two long bones in the lower forearm

uterus the organ, in female animals, where the embryo develops into a fetus

vaccine a substance made of weakened, killed, or partial pathogens and designed to protect the body from future invasions of that pathogen

vacuole storage sacs within the cytoplasm of a cell that may contain either wastes or useful materials, such as water or food

vertebrate an animal with a backbone

virus a nonliving particle of protein and genetic material that reproduces by invading the cell of a living organism

volume the space occupied by something

water cycle the process by which water continuously moves from Earth's surface to the atmosphere and back

zygote the cell that results from the joining of the egg and sperm

Index

resources 109-110, 112
    nonrenewable 109, 110
    renewable 109-110
respiration 9, 20. *See also* cell respiration
respiratory system 9
results, experimental 139-141
ribosomes 4
safety
    equipment 160
    laboratory 147-165
    with microscopes 152
scavengers 93
science
    definition of 131
    inquiry 132-141
    skills 132-146
scientific literacy 134
selective breeding 47-48, 73
sex cells 54, 55, 56-57
    and evolution 76
sexual reproduction 10, 12, 40, 53, 54
skeletal system 10
skills
    laboratory 147-165
    microscope 150-152
    in science 132-146
slide preparation 152-153
smog 119
soil formation 110
species 53, 74, 79
    endangered 63, 78, 154
    extinction 80
    imported 115
    loss 121-122
    nonnative 115
    roles in ecosystems 91, 121-122
sperm cell 54, 57, 61, 68, 77
staining slides 152, 155
starch 19, 20

statistics 140
stereoscope 150
stimulus-response 25, 26-27
succession, ecological 101-102
synthesis 2, 6, 18
    as life process 2
    of proteins 43
systems, body
    defined 3
    human 8-12
technology 116-117, 121
temperature
    body 26, 27
    effect on enzymes 22-23
testosterone 61, 62
thermal pollution 118
tissues 3
toxic wastes 118
traits, genetic 39-40, 43
transplants, organ 31
ultrasound 63
ultraviolet radiation 120
uterus 61
vaccines 30-31
vacuoles 4, 11, 153
variables
    dependent 135
    independent 136
variation, genetic 57, 59
    and evolution 74, 76-78, 80
    sources of 76-77
viruses 2, 29, 30
water
    pollution 117
    as resource 117
water cycle 110-111
wet mount slides 152
white blood cells 30, 31
zygotes 59